Appropriating
Hemingway

ALSO BY RON MCFARLAND

The Long Life of Evangeline: *A History of the Longfellow Poem in Print, in Adaptation and in Popular Culture* (McFarland, 2010)

The Rockies in First Person: A Critical Study of Recent American Memoirs from the Region (McFarland, 2008)

Appropriating Hemingway

Using Him as a Fictional Character

Ron McFarland

McFarland & Company, Inc., Publishers
Jefferson, North Carolina

LIBRARY OF CONGRESS CATALOGUING-IN-PUBLICATION DATA

McFarland, Ronald E.
   Appropriating Hemingway : using him as a fictional character / Ron McFarland.
      p.   cm.
   Includes bibliographical references and index.

   ISBN 978-0-7864-7977-1 (softcover : acid free paper) ♾
   ISBN 978-1-4766-1826-5 (ebook)

   1. Hemingway, Ernest, 1899–1961—In literature.
   2. Hemingway, Ernest, 1899–1961—Characters.   I. Title.
   PS3515.E37Z741746 2015
   813'.52—dc23   2014040118

BRITISH LIBRARY CATALOGUING DATA ARE AVAILABLE

© 2015 Ron McFarland. All rights reserved

No part of this book may be reproduced or transmitted in any form or by any means, electronic or mechanical, including photocopying or recording, or by any information storage and retrieval system, without permission in writing from the publisher.

On the cover: lobby card from *The Old Man and the Sea*, 1958 (Warner Bros. Pictures/Photofest)

Printed in the United States of America

McFarland & Company, Inc., Publishers
  Box 611, Jefferson, North Carolina 28640
    www.mcfarlandpub.com

For my father,
Earl A. McFarland,
who taught me, among countless other things,
to love fishing, the outdoors, and language,
and imparted to me his wit and playfulness.

Contents

Acknowledgments	ix
Preface	1
One—Appropriating Ernest Hemingway	7
Two—Young Hemingstein	30
Three—Hemingway Makes the Twenties Roar	49
Four—Hemingway and the Threatening Thirties	76
Five—Ernest Hemingway: Our Man in Havana	104
Six—Sci-fi Papa; or, Hemingway in Speculative Fiction	127
Seven—With Hem Obsessed	149
Eight—Hemingway on Stage, Screen and Television	168
Nine—Hem Among the Poets	198
Conclusion	227
Chapter Notes	235
Works Consulted	246
Index	255

Acknowledgments

I am particularly grateful to the University of Idaho and to the chair of the English department, Professor J. Gary Williams, for providing me with a sabbatical and for funds that enabled me to travel to the Hemingway Collection at the John F. Kennedy Library in Boston, to the Hemingway home in Key West, and to the American Literature Association's annual conferences in Boston, on a couple of occasions, where I have presented papers drawing on this research. Susan Beegel, longtime editor of the *Hemingway Review,* has been kind and extraordinarily helpful all along the way. My first foray into these literary bypaths was a poem entitled "Altercation" that appeared in the *Review* in its spring 1997 issue. Four years later the *Review* published my essay "Hemingway and the Poets," and several of my reviews of novels that are the subject of this book have also appeared therein.

I've also drawn on three of my essays which were published in earlier forms, and I am grateful to the editors for having offered the following works an initial airing: "Three Novels on Hemingway in Cuba," *North Dakota Quarterly* 76.1/2 (Winter/Spring 2009), 151–160; "Recent Takes on the Missing Hemingway Manuscripts," *Journal of Popular Culture* 44.2 (April 2011), 314–332; and "The World's Most Interesting Man," *Midwest Quarterly* 54.4 (Summer 2013), 414–430. The latter essay received the Victor J. Emmett ,Jr. Memorial Award for 2013, which provided me with the opportunity to offer at lecture at Pittsburg State University in southeastern Kansas ("Was Ernest Hemingway a Narcissist?"). Professor Stephen Meats and his wife and colleagues, including Professor Emmett's daughter, treated me and my wife most hospitably during our visit.

My enthusiasm for fictional takes on Hemingway was fueled early on when the late H. Palmer Hall, publisher of Pecan Grove Press at St. Mary's

University in San Antonio, named my chapbook, *The Hemingway Poems,* its summer 2000 award winner.

I have been most fortunate in the cooperation of several poets and publishers who have permitted me to quote, at times copiously: Kelsey Ford for "An Elegy for Ernest Hemingway" by Thomas Merton from *The Collected Poems of Thomas Merton* (© 1963 by the Abbey of Gethsemani, reprinted by permission of New Directions Publishing Corp.); Susan Beegel and the *Hemingway Review* for Paul Ramsey's "Elegy for Ernest Hemingway" (copyright by The Ernest Hemingway Foundation); Julia Kardon for Philip Schultz's "The Hemingway House in Key West" from *Deep within the Ravine* (Viking, 1984); John Koethe for "E.H." in *Poem a Day* published through the Academy of American Poets (September 20, 2013); Frederick T. Courtright of BOA Editions and the John Logan Literary Estate, Inc., for John Logan's "Papa's House, Son's Room," from *John Logan: The Collected Poems* (1989); William Goldstein and Red Hen Press for Gaylord Brewer's "A Brief Hemingway Encounter" in *Devilfish* (1999) and "The Hemingway Look-alike Society Meets Bimini Bay Developers" in *Barbaric Mercies* (2003). I've imposed particularly on Gerald Locklin's poems from *The Hemingway Colloquium* (Event Horizon Press, 1999), David Ray's poems from *Hemingway: A Desperate Life* (Whirlybird Press, 2011), and David P. Reiter's poems from *Hemingway in Spain: Words and Images*, 2nd ed. (Interactive Press, 2007). Thank you all!

My wife, Georgia Tiffany Toppe, who is a gifted poet and talented research assistant and editor, has enabled me and propped me up throughout the years I've devoted to this book. Any oversights or errors in the text are mine, and despite her efforts.

Preface

Exactly how I got into the business of reading and thinking about the biographical fiction concerning Ernest Hemingway I cannot say for certain, but I think it began with Vincent Cosgrove's *The Hemingway Papers,* which was published in classic pulp fiction form as a Bantam Book in 1983. I stumbled across it at a used-book store shelved with books by and about Hemingway. "What happened to Ernest Hemingway one Paris night is an unsolved mystery," it says on the front cover. I was also intrigued by that "mystery." As a Hemingway scholar in a very small way, my immediate recourse had been to the conventional biographies and critical commentaries, and of course I was aware of his own account of the affair in *A Moveable Feast.* Before long, though, I encountered other fictional takes on the lost manuscripts and found myself fascinated by that extra-scholarly approach to Hemingway. Several of the novels have been reviewed in *Hemingway Review,* and Kirk Curnutt makes passing reference to a few of the titles in *Literary Topics: Ernest Hemingway and the Expatriate Modernist Movement,* volume two (2000).[1] I've come to think of these texts as not so much overlooked as they are intentionally ignored or outright spurned. These writings generally fall into the netherworld of "popular fiction" and are at least akin to what is now being called "fan fiction." Writers of fan fiction are mightily enticed by unsolved mysteries and curious gaps in the life of their fannish fixation. I think it's appropriate that my essay on the lost manuscripts appeared in the *Journal of Popular Culture.*

Even before I wrote that essay, though, and before I read Cosgrove's little thriller, I had been writing poems in which Hemingway was turning up as a character; and I was having some small success getting them into print here and there. When I investigated, I found there were quite a few poems dealing with Hemingway, sometimes as elegies, eulogies, or tributes, and other times refashioning him as a character, as I had been doing, often much more seriously than I've been inclined to do. My essay on that subject appeared in *Hemingway Review* about a dozen years ago. As I encountered more and more fiction in which Hemingway appeared as an important character, I began to think of how he and his writing—and the legends and myths surrounding him—had in effect been "appropriated" in various ways, by a wide variety of writers who had an almost equally wide variety of aims in mind. Some of the appropriators clearly intend to celebrate Hemingway as man and writer, even while recognizing his many flaws; others clearly intend to denigrate the man and sometimes his writing as well.

One might challenge the premise that these texts have made important contributions to Hemingway studies other than the most obvious one, which is to keep the name alive in the public consciousness and at least indirectly to promote the writing. That sort of thesis does strike me as vulnerable, even after having worked my way through the stories, novels, plays, and poems that are the subject of this book. One might argue that while the life and legend are sustained by such texts, if not exaggerated and distorted, the work is largely disregarded. I remain haunted by a scene near the end of Milan Kundera's novel *Immortality* (1990), in which a character declares that he doesn't read novels and finds memoirs "much more amusing and instructive."[2] In particular, he claims to have enjoyed "a marvelous biography of Hemingway" that unmasks him as a fraud, a liar, a sadist, a misogynist, and a megalomaniac. The man finds that "reading *about* Hemingway is a thousand times more amusing and instructive than reading Hemingway" (336). I address this passage later, but it still nags at me. I do not for a minute suspect that the same could be said about the biography of many other writers—Faulkner, Steinbeck, Flannery O'Connor, Philip Roth, Flaubert, Tolstoy, Dickens, Achebe, Alice Munro. About whom, other than Ernest Hemingway, might Kundera have written such passages with as much credibility? Given his novel, as we shall see hereafter, Kundera might answer, "Goethe."

It may be worth noting here that Kundera offers the perspective of a European novelist who has himself been nominated for the Nobel Prize on various occasions. For better or worse, Hemingway has become the signature U.S. writer. Certainly the last thing any admirer of Hemingway's writing would want to see is a scenario like the one to which I just alluded, in *Immortality*. But whether the biographical fictions and the related plays and poems offer incentives for the continued reading of Hemingway's fiction may be debatable. Even the writers who make some overt effort to connect their narratives with Hemingway's stories and novels do not really aim primarily to advocate for the writing. They have their own stories to tell and usually their own characters, other than Hemingway, to advance. Consequently, this book makes no bold assertions along these lines. I would love to be able to say confidently that encountering Paula McLain's *The Paris Wife* or Dan Simmons' *The Crook Factory* or Michael Palin's *Hemingway's Chair* will drive readers back to the Nick Adams stories or *A Farewell to Arms*, but I remain more skeptical than hopeful.

What I'm doing here is investigating what I see as a curious phenomenon, most of the conceptual underpinnings of which I have attempted to spell out in the opening chapter. *Appropriating Hemingway* comes down largely to a study in popular fiction, particularly the subset I've identified as fan fiction. The readers of these texts are, as a rule, Hemingway fans by definition. They have already read some, if not all, of Hemingway's writing, at least the best of his novels and stories, and they are well aware of at least the basic biography along with the unsavory details. Indeed, it may be that the "unsavory details" account for much of Hemingway's attraction, for both the appropriators and their readers. The more the fans are aware of Hemingway's life and work, the more they will bring to the text of the biographical fiction and the more pleasure they will acquire from seeing how the writers solve mysteries such as the dissolution of Ernest's marriage with Hadley, or the broken friendship with fellow writer John Dos Passos, or what went on with Hemingway's espionage operations in Cuba during World War II, or what drove him to his suicide in Ketchum.

Throughout the book I have supplied biographical and historical contexts for the various appropriations, even though I am aware that many readers may already be familiar with what I have offered and a lot more. I have constructed Chapters Two through Five chronologically, beginning with a novel entitled *Hemingsteen* that offers up a portrait of Ernest as a young man, a boy, really, about to graduate from high school and leave his home for a job as a cub reporter with the *Kansas City Star*. That novel ends before seventeen-year-old Ernest gets to Kansas City. Without going into great detail in any chapter so far as context is concerned, I've made an effort to reflect on what we know, thanks to the many biographies and memoirs, or what we think we know, about what Hemingway was doing at the time, and particularly what he was writing. The sixth chapter concerns mostly speculative treatments of Hemingway and his writing, science fiction and fantasy, even a little of the supernatural, so the context is not important for those fictions. The same applies to the seventh chapter, which deals with what I call Hemingway-obsessed characters. While some avatar or emanation of Hemingway often appears in the other chapters of this book, he does not appear as a character in Chapter Seven, "With Hem Obsessed."

My intention has been to characterize the biographical fiction rather than to carry out rigorous analysis. My approach has often, though not exclusively, been descriptive and explanatory, an effort to give the various texts their day in court. I want readers to have a fairly good sense of what transpires in this or that novel, story, script, or poem. I have attempted to hold plot summary to a minimum, but a certain amount of it seems necessary. Was I going to be selective in this endeavor, perhaps highly so, or not? Certainly I could have opted to focus attention on just the ten or twelve best novels, perhaps a couple of the plays or recent movies, and a handful of relevant poems. I decided instead to be inclusionary, even as I knew from the outset I would surely overlook this or that novel, story, poem, play or film. The inclusion reaches well beyond what I think of as a few really good texts in the various genres—"good" in the sense of showing some sophistication of writing quality and style, some complexity and insight, especially with respect to how Hemingway is portrayed as a character. I have also included observations on a few self-published novels which themselves vary considerably in quality. I have winced at times, rather like poet Wallace Stevens' high-toned old Christian woman. Some of the writing I've dealt with in these pages is distant indeed from "novelties of the sublime":

> This will make widows wince. But fictive things
> Wink as they will. Wink most when widows wince.[3]

As I've moved through the chapters, I've provided brief comments by way of identifying the writers, only a few of whom are likely to be familiar to most of the readers I imagine looking into this book. It surprised me to see how many of these writers of what would generally be regarded as distinctively nonliterary fiction—a category that covers an immense expanse from what might be sniffed at as potboilers or pulp fiction to really quite accomplished best sellers—possess sometimes impressive academic credentials. Many writers of these appropriations either teach or have taught creative writing at the university level. I have offered some reflections on popular fiction and on the writers thereof along with a broad and rather loose array of other topics that might be considered corollary or ancillary to the central concerns of this book. Given the nature of the texts under consideration, I have indulged my tendency when it comes to dealing with recent or contemporary writing to make use of book reviews, treating them with some deference as serious critical inquiry. But in this case I have gone beyond that to include at times the comments of bloggers and other online commentators, and in one chapter I indulged my whimsical impulses by delving into the blurbs.

While teaching a class or writing a book I like to place myself "in conversation" with some text or texts of relevant literary criticism or biographical or cultural context. For example, while teaching a Shakespeare course not long ago, I conversed with Harold Bloom's plump volume *Shakespeare: The Invention of the Human* (1998). While completing this book, I have been conversing with Paul Hendrickson's remarkable (and also plump) volume *Hemingway's Boat* (2011), subtitled *Everything He Loved in Life, and Lost*. Hendrickson's exhaustive and meticulous research would put most literary scholars, even of the old school, to shame. Reading Hendrickson's book, I found myself at times thinking of how moved he must have been and of how much fun he must have been having. This particular undertaking has not drawn me to exotic locales like Oak Park or Key West or Bimini in the Bahamas, nor has it required that I prowl the precincts of the Hemingway collections at the John F. Kennedy Library in Boston or at Princeton University. Typically, scholars rely on primary and secondary sources. It could be said that in mixing it up with these biographical fictions, I am often plunging into tertiary sources. In effect, setting aside Hemingway's writing, my primary sources are also, paradoxically, tertiary. In the process, I've found myself traveling along some odd literary byways and have encountered an assortment of Hemingwayans whose observations on the Old Brute might qualify as exotic. Hemingway's writing as examined by critics and scholars has drawn a host of biographers to his life. Now his life as appropriated by writers of biographical fiction may return us to his writing.

One

Appropriating Ernest Hemingway

> *The man was a bearish celebrity when literature still bred celebrities; his work remains a touchstone of artistic ardor and luminously clean prose.—*
> John Updike, "Foreword," *Coffee with Hemingway* (2007)

One is inclined to agree with Nathan Heller that "Ernest Hemingway would be aghast to see what has become of Ernest Hemingway."[1] One doubts, for example, that Hemingway would have yearned to be a character in popular pulp fiction, pursued by Hermann Goering in Vincent Cosgrove's *The Hemingway Papers* (1983), or incorporated into a trilogy of crime novels written by Craig McDonald between 2008 and 2011, or joining Jesus in a graphic novel in pursuit of Hitler. But he did want to "endure," Carlos Baker notes in citing Hemingway's "watchword"—"*Il faut (d'abord) durer*."[2] And as the bountiful record of biographies, photo books, and, especially, the fiction featuring him demonstrates, Hemingway's endurance both embraces and transcends his writing. Scores of biographies, memoirs, and studies of aspects of Hemingway's life (his cats, his booze, his boat) have been published, at least forty in the last dozen or so years. These, and the several books of photographs focused on him, may be taken simply as homage to a great writer. But what do we make of the thirty-odd novels and a number of short stories, along with poems and pieces written for stage, screen, or television, that fictionalize Hemingway, that in effect "appropriate" him as a character?

The appropriations of Hemingway in fiction have much to tell us about the nature of authorship, celebrity, and American culture in the late twentieth and early twenty-first centuries, especially the way the lines between author, character, and reader are blurring. In *Reading Desire: In Pursuit of Ernest Hem-*

ingway (1999), Debra A. Moddelmog writes "the recognition that the public Hemingway was a creation that masked as much as it revealed," thus prompting a "search for the private man behind the public mask."[3] But she concludes that the search will inevitably be frustrated, for, like his writing, Hemingway is constantly being rediscovered and reinvented. Moddelmog adds what some might read as a postmodern sort of caveat: "all critics reveal themselves in the act of interpretation, be it the interpretation of a text or an author" (41–42). While my purposes diverge considerably from hers, I am in agreement with her contention that "the author is constantly reconstructed by social and ideological factors" that encourage us "to see the historical author as a subject moving through history, a shifting, fragmented figure rather than a stable, arrested absolute" (39).

My working premise is that, in the final analysis, the appropriations of Hemingway in popular fiction offer not just complication, but also enrichment to what Moddelmog calls the "textual nature" of the "historical author" that proves to be "simultaneously stable and unstable, tentative and determined, illusory and graspable" (40). This flurry of paradox, contradiction, and oxymoron might well be said to define the United States, particularly during the modern period, in particular the first half of the twentieth century. Hemingway has emerged as modern America's eidolon in all applications of that term, from false idol to admired ideal; and the biographical fictions that feature him as a character run the gamut from clumsy, womanizing drunk and bully to handsome, charismatic sportsman and man of action—and sometimes, almost as an afterthought, writer. In his first published book, *Three Stories and Ten Poems* (1923), Hemingway concluded a poem on his boyhood idol and role model, Theodore Roosevelt, with these lines: "And all the legends that he started in his life / Live on and prosper / Unhampered now by his existence."[4] These words ring ironically prophetic. My book is essentially a commentary on how the legends Hemingway created for himself have lived on and prospered—and have been interestingly altered—via a variety of authors who have appropriated him for their stories and novels "unhampered," particularly now, "by his existence."

The Scope of the Project

On the first page of his study *Fame Became of Him: Hemingway as Public Writer* (1984) John Raeburn writes, "Hemingway's literary achievement is tangential to understanding [his] public fame."[5] Moreover, "Hemingway was the architect of his public reputation" (7) in an age of celebrities celebrated, if not at times created, by an emergent mass media scarcely imaginable to the previous century, the one in which Hemingway was born, on July 21, 1899. For all practical purposes, commercial radio did not begin in the U.S. until late in 1920, and the motion picture industry was in its infancy when Hemingway was growing up. Ernest would have been sixteen when Charlie Chaplin appeared in *The Tramp*. Letters sent home from Kansas City, notably to his sister Marcelline, portray the star-struck eighteen-year-old cub reporter mooning after the silent film actress Mae Marsh (the talkies were another nine years down the road). In his hometown of Oak Park, Illinois, and in Kansas City young Hemingway would encounter early Pathé newsreels dealing with World War I. Whatever else Ernest Hemingway was, he was a man of the media, earning his income at least sporadically as a reporter and war correspondent between 1918 and 1945; and during the Spanish Civil War he would participate as cowriter and narrator in the filming of the propaganda cinema *The Spanish Earth* (1937). In short, he understood mass media and appreciated its reach and its power. As Robert Paul Lamb observes in his study of Hemingway's short fiction, "Hemingway's literary career coincided with, and fed off of, the rise to dominance of the mass media in the United States. During this period ... the United States was transformed from a culture of character into a culture of personality in which how one was seen became a more important indicator of the self than what one actually did" (8). Hemingway, with the aid of his editor, Maxwell Perkins, and his publisher, Scribner, "rushed headfirst into the public limelight." The results have been phenomenal.

Counting informal memoirs like Milt Machlin's *The Private Hell of Hemingway* (1962) and family memoirs like Madelaine "Sunny" Hemingway Miller's *Ernie* (1975) and Mary Welsh Hemingway's *How It Was* (1976) and the more academic run of biographies, extending from Charles Fenton's *The Apprenticeship of Ernest Hemingway: The Early Years* (1954) through the five-volume tour de force of Michael Reynolds and beyond, Ernest Miller Hemingway's existence has by now been variously helped or hampered by well over a hundred such volumes, and the end is not in sight. A hasty survey of such books uncovers titles that range from at least three on Hemingway and Michigan and another three on Hemingway and Cuba to Paul Hendrickson's best-selling *Hemingway's Boat* (2011) and Craig Boreth's *The Hemingway Cookbook* (2012). Some of the biographical texts play it straight and close to the vest, like Carlos Baker's *Ernest Hemingway: A Life Story* (1969), which many regard as the standard single-volume biography. Other ambitious undertakings, like Kenneth S. Lynn's *Hemingway* (1987), have proved controversial. True aficionados can stalk their prey with the aid of Noel Riley Fitch's *Walks in Hemingway's Paris* (1989) and Stuart McIver's *Hemingway's Key West* (1993). These and many other such books, though surely not all of them, make worthwhile reading, depending on one's interests, which may or may not have all that much to do with enthusiasm for, or curiosity about, Hemingway's writing. Literary scholars, for instance, might prefer Kirk Curnutt and Gail D. Sinclair's *Key West Hemingway: A Reassessment* (2009) to McIver's slim text, which might serve better as a tourist guide.

The foregoing is not to suggest that Ernest Hemingway was reluctant to hamper his own existence with nonfiction in support of his stories and novels. The legends and myths are drawn not just from the apocrypha of Gertrude Stein's 27 rue de Fleurus, and Sloppy Joe's bars in Havana and Key West, and the Floridita in Havana. We have the contributions of *Death in the Afternoon* (1932), *Green Hills of Africa* (1935), *The Dangerous Summer* (1960, 1985), *A Moveable Feast* (1964, restored edition 2009), and *True at First Light* (1999) or *Under Kilimanjaro* (2005), the former volume being subtitled with intriguing ambiguity *A Fictional Memoir*. And presently, building on the foundation laid by Carlos Baker in his *Ernest Hemingway: Selected Letters, 1917–1961* collection of 1981, we have the first two volumes of what will surely prove to be Hemingway's definitive contributions to his self-contrived legend: *The Letters of Ernest Hemingway* (edited by Sandra Spanier and Robert W. Trogdon and published by the Cambridge University Press). Albert J. DeFazio III has joined in editing the second volume. In a lecture at the University of Idaho's Hemingway Festival on September 5, 2012, Professor Spanier observed that the initially projected twelve volumes will more likely extend to no fewer than sixteen. These letters may, or may not, bring about a significant reconsideration of the writer's life and fiction. Will the letters, the first volume having appeared to some fanfare in the fall of 2011, confirm our predispositions concerning Ernest Hemingway or prompt us to interrogate them? The response may (or should) be a function of those predispositions, but if we are inclined either (a) to idolize or (b) to vilify the man behind the fiction and behind the public images, many, but not all, of which he created himself, then yes, reading the letters will likely alter in some way how we think about him. And perhaps even the way we respond to his fiction.

But it's as if all these accessories after the fact—and setting aside the plethora of published books and essays on his writing (the Modem Language Association bibliography currently lists more than 4,400 such items, including theses and dissertations)—were not enough, as if all of the above were insufficient to account adequately for the writer most of the literary world (beyond the United States, perhaps, more eagerly than in them) regard as the nation's leading literary light, presumably eclipsing even the writer Hemingway himself would have nominated, Mark Twain. Many writers have gone on to write fictional biographies and just plain fictions about Hemingway as well, and about characters obsessed with Hemingway's writing or with his myth or legend. These fictions extend from stories and novels into such genres as play and film scripts and poems. Celebrities, after all, attract fans, and, in effect, virtually all of the writers I will deal with hereafter may be described as "fans." And fans, after all, are fanatics pretty much by definition.

The concept of fandom requires at least some preliminary observations. Joli Jenson opens her essay addressing the problems inherent in addressing "fandom" as pathology with the assertion that "the literature on fandom is haunted by images of deviance."[6] The fan typically has been characterized as "an obsessed loner, suffering from a disease of isolation, or a frenzied crowd member, suffering from a disease of contagion. In either case, the fan is seen as being irrational, out of control, and prey to a number of external forces" (13). Jenson's view is that too much analysis and commentary on fandom proceeds from a presumption of a "savannah of smug superiority" (25), and she appeals for a broader base of inquiry that explores "what it means to desire, cherish, seek, long, admire, envy, celebrate, protect, ally with others. Fandom is an aspect of how we make sense of the world, in relation to mass media, and in relation to our historical, social, cultural location" (27). In effect, Jenson is requesting a more respectful treatment of fans. Essentially I am pursuing a more respectful regard for fan fiction of a rather particular sort.

If you look up "biographical fiction" on your library's WorldCat site, you will find thousands of items listed (nearly 20,000 in fact), including such titles as William Styron's *Confessions of Nat Turner*, Thomas Pynchon's *Mason & Dixon*, Irving Stone's *The Agony and the Ecstasy*, Joe Haldeman's *The Hemingway Hoax*, Clancy Carlile's *The Paris Pilgrims*, Dan Simmons' *The Crook Factory*, Paula McLain's *The Paris Wife*, and William McCranor Henderson's *I Killed Hemingway*. If you look up "fictional biography" you will discover nearly 27,000 items, mostly biographies of fiction writers, including Michael Reynolds' five-volume biography of Hemingway and numerous critical studies— for example, Linda Wagner-Martin's *Hemingway: Eight Decades of Criticism*. The contents of these listings are a bit of a hodgepodge, a pair of very fuzzy sets, but the entries on biographical fiction include dozens of novels in which Ernest Hemingway appears as a major (sometimes central) or minor (sometimes very peripheral) character. It could be argued, however, that certain novels, like Christopher Cook Gilmore's *Hemingway* (1988), Michael Murphy's

Hemingsteen (1978), and in some ways Naomi Wood's *Mrs. Hemingway* (2014), at least come close to being "fictional biographies."

Among the many questions almost every student of Hemingway's writing confronts sooner or later (or is confronted by) is whether the work can be, or should be, separated from its creator. Is it necessary, or even at all useful, to know something of the life of the writer? Does what we know of any writer's life help us appreciate or understand the work, or does it distract us from it? Presumably, most readers would agree that it depends on the writer. Knowing a lot more than we do about William Shakespeare or John Donne or Cormac McCarthy might prove quite valuable when it comes to acquiring a thorough understanding and appreciation of their writing—or it might not. To what extent was Hemingway fictionalizing his own life, just as later writers have done? Did he egregiously plunder his life story in ways that no other writer has ever done, or did he merely draw on personal experiences as most fiction writers do? To what extent did he reconfigure his life experiences in order to draw on them in his fiction? And in that process, one might ask, did he not make a public spectacle of himself? It is certainly true that as a man of the media Hemingway knew how to present himself in the media, knew how to fashion himself as a celebrity at a particular moment in history when the celebrity and the concomitant cult of personality were being fashioned, from Babe Ruth to "Lucky Lindy." Raeburn observes that most writers "accept their social obscurity and content themselves" with it, but Hemingway "wanted immediate public recognition and approbation and he labored to get them" (9). "He created a public persona to match his prose," his most complete biographer, Michael Reynolds, wrote, "becoming the person he wanted to be."[7] Reynolds also notes that Hemingway wore his mask of an "invented self" with increasingly less ease as he aged. David M. Earle concludes "the man was tortured by his own fame in the 1950s, even though he was complicit in its construction."[8]

The recent publication of the first two volumes of his complete correspondence will verify that young Ernest (or Ernie, as he often signs himself in his personal letters) clearly promotes himself in his letters to family and friends. Perhaps we all do that in such letters, more or less. Young Hemingway's letters are filled with boasting of his attainments as fisherman, boxer and fledgling writer: "Got 100 percent on an ancient hist. test. Cicero is a pipe [that is, lead-pipe cinch]. I could write better stuff than he could with both hands tied behind me."[9] Thus speaks the boyish enthusiasm of the sixteen-year-old, we might note. But more than thirty years later, in an often cited letter to his publisher, Charles Scribner, he elaborated on his competitive view of writing as sport (in this case, boxing match) in which he emerged, usually, victorious: "I started out trying to beat dead writers that I knew how good they were. (Excuse vernacular) I tried for Mr. Turgenieff first and it wasn't too hard. Tried for Mr. Maupassant (won't concede him the de) and it took four of the best stories to beat him.... Mr. Henry James I would just thumb him once the first time he grabbed and then hit him once where he had no balls and ask the referee to stop it" (*Selected Letters*, 673). He concedes that he wouldn't want to take on Tolstoy in a twenty-round bout, "but I would take him on for six and he would never hit me and [I] would knock the shit out of him and maybe knock him out." In what he calls "the big book," the epic of land, sea, and air of which *The Old Man and the Sea* was to be a small part, perhaps a sort of coda, he tells Scribner he intends to take on Melville and Dostoyevsky. Needless to say, this is playful bragging, Hemingway as comical *miles gloriosus*, and if we take him too seriously here, as perhaps all too many do, we may well find him insufferable.

Biographical Fiction and Pop Fiction

A subset of historical fiction, novels listed as "biographical fiction" are often, but not always, cross-referenced to the character involved (for example, Michelangelo or Ernest Hemingway), but of course they are not shelved accordingly. Librarians probably don't give the matter a second thought. If readers want what Hemingway liked to call the "true gen," the reliable intelligence or facts, on the life and times of Nat Turner, Michelangelo, or Hemingway, they do not turn to historical or biographical fiction but to history and biography. Literary critics and scholars spend their efforts largely on examining the profound complexities of Hemingway's fiction and the enigmatic contradictions of his life, usually (but not always, or at least not exclusively) as details of the life elucidate or in some way bear on the fiction. In a quite different context, Toni Morrison cautions "it would be irresponsible and unjustified to invest Hemingway with the thoughts of his characters."[10] She refers here to some racist remarks made by Harry Morgan in *To Have and Have Not* (1937). But perhaps one might argue it is both responsible and justified to suppose that his characters are invested with *some* of Hemingway's thoughts, as Morrison notes: "An author is not personally accountable for the acts of his fictive creatures, although he is responsible for them" (86). She then goes on to deny that "Hemingway shared Harry's [racist] views." The fictive Hemingways who appear in the appropriations that are the subject of this book result from a blending of what the writers decide to use and exaggerate—or knowingly distort—of his life and what they choose to borrow from his characters.

Historical and biographical fiction often, but not always, falls into the realm of popular reading, that "*lasciate ogni speranza*" world of escapist and formulaic fiction, of detective and spy novels, horror novels, thrillers, and pulp fiction. And, of course, "best sellers." Any reader of Hemingway's fiction, both today and when it first appeared in the 1920s, would be aware it comfortably bestrides the literary and nonliterary worlds, to the extent such worlds are separable. And visitors to almost any bookstore will encounter that ostensible gulf, even as the distinctions may appear to be fading somewhat: Fiction here, Literary Fiction or Literature there. These are fuzzy sets indeed. One imagines Stephen King trying to sneak into Literary Fiction, but alas. Are the novels of T. Coraghessan Boyle Literary? And if not, might they someday be so regarded? What about Don DeLillo's or E.L. Doctorow's or Barbara Kingsolver's fiction? Toni Morrison won a Nobel Prize, so she is "in." Danielle Steele and Tom Clancy? Not likely. Those writers must weep their way to the bank. And why are the works of Charles Dickens and Mark Twain, not to mention Ernest Hemingway, regarded as Literature? Conventional responses include such phrasing as "withstanding the test of time" and "holding up under serious scrutiny" (to look backward at L.C. Knights and F.R. Leavis's literary review founded in 1932). And how much "time" does that test involve? Presumably, it pertains at least to the next generation after the author's demise; traditionally, the hundred-year mark is mentioned. And as to the "scrutiny," who is it that says this or that book is "good"? Who makes it Literature?

Critical theorist Roland Barthes is said to have described literature as "what gets taught." Terry Eagleton deserves whatever credit is due for having brought that observation to light.[11] It is at least provocative as such premises go. It "must be *difficult*," T.S. Eliot wrote when commenting on "the poets in our civilization" in 1921 (italics in original),[12] and literary modernists like James Joyce and William Faulkner may be said to have extended that premise to fiction: the criterion of complexity. Must all serious readers read Proust and Mann? Public-school teachers may struggle to force their often unwilling students to the "next level" at the same time they strain simply to get them to read something, anything at all. This "next level" may refer not to more sophisticated, complex, or more "literary" texts, but simply to adult as opposed to adolescent fiction, a level often complicated by strictures of local school boards, principals, or parents who are troubled for quite different reasons by titles as various as *The Scarlet Letter*, *Huckleberry Finn*, and *The Grapes of Wrath*. Are high school seniors ready for *The Great Gatsby* and *The Sun Also Rises*? Most of them are, but anyone who has taught in the public schools will concede that not all of them are. Is Fitzgerald's novel a better fit than Hemingway's? Which novel of the "Great War" works better in the classroom, *All Quiet on the Western Front* or *A Farewell to Arms*? Both novels are accessible, but Remarque's has the advantage, perhaps, of involving no illicit sexual liaison. Accordingly, Remarque's novel may "get taught" in public schools more often than Hemingway's.

These issues pertain quite directly to Hemingway's firm grasp on the ever-mutable (perhaps increasingly mutable) literary canon, and indirectly to the plethora of biographical fictions that have accumulated over the past thirty-odd years. To repeat, at least thirty novels and a number of short stories, not to mention numerous stage and film productions and poems, fictionalize Hemingway—in effect, "appropriate" him as a character. Commentary on such texts brings us into the world of popular fiction, in fact, into the world of popular culture. Some of these books may be said to have literary claim in their own right. How many of them transcend such categories as pulp fiction or potboilers? Paula McLain's novel on Hemingway's first wife, Hadley, *The Paris Wife* (2011), was within its first year translated into French, German, Spanish, Italian, Portuguese, Russian, Chinese, Dutch, Polish, Hebrew, Korean, and Serbian. McLain is by no means a familiar author, but her biographical fiction has become something of a *cause célèbre*, eagerly taken on by book clubs and reading groups (a Bookclub-in-a-Box reading guide was available by January of 2012).

The Hemingway Image/s

In his prologue to a "brief biography" written for Linda Wagner-Martin's *A Historical Guide to Ernest Hemingway* (2000), Michael Reynolds describes Hemingway as "a child of the twentieth century," asserting "his life seemed to embody the promise of America: with good fortune, hard work, talent, ambition, and a little ruthlessness a man can create himself in the image of his choosing" (15). One can be, in effect, a self-made man. Most students of Hemingway's life and writing and legend (or myth)—and surely the order might be argued—would agree that his wounding in combat on July 8, 1918, shortly after his arrival in northern Italy, amounts to a sort of crux. He was a couple of weeks shy of nineteen years old. His boyish enthusiasm about warfare is implicit in a note he wrote to an unidentified friend at the *Kansas City Star* a month before his wounding:

> Having a wonderful time!!! Had my baptism of fire my first day here, when an entire munition plant exploded. We carried them in like at the General Hospital, Kansas City. I go to the front tomorrow. Oh, Boy!!! I'm glad I'm in it. They love us down here in the mountains.[13]

The contrast is striking between this casual observation on the munitions plant near Milan and the version we encounter in the short story "A Natural History of the Dead," which he wrote about a dozen years later (it first appeared in the 1932 publication of *Death in the Afternoon*). How universal such boyish enthusiasm has been over the centuries of war may be debated, but consider that of young George B. McClellan, about to graduate second in his class at West Point and destined to serve as an engineer in the Mexican War, as he expresses it in a letter to his sister dated May 13, 1846: "Hip! Hip! Haarrah! War sure enough! Ain't it glorious!"[14]

In *The Young Hemingway*, Michael Reynolds writes, "He had experienced the quintessential modern experience—the violence of war."[15] Whether that sentiment is valid or not, his wounding would bring about Hemingway's initial public offering, his first of many opportunities to commoditize himself, when an eager reporter for the *New York Sun* met his boat at the pier in early January 1919. Consequently, the event warrants some further attention. The first significant information Ernest's family received about his wounding was sent on July 14, 1918, within a week of the event, in a letter from his friend and fellow ambulance driver Theodore (Ted) Brumback, who had worked with him at the *Kansas City Star* and who had seen service on the Western Front. News accounts celebrating Hemingway as the first American casualty on the Italian front (he was not) and announcing his citation with the Silver Medal for Valor ("a very high medal indeed," Brumback informed the proud but anxious parents) did not include an important sentence that appears in that letter: "A third Italian was badly wounded and this one Ernest, after he had regained consciousness, picked up on his back and carried to the first-aid dugout" (*Letters*, 115). Scholars and biographers have varied over the decades as to whether to credit this statement. Ernest's letter to his family dated July 21 (his nineteenth birthday) features his crude sketch of himself "drawn from life" and labeled "227 wounds" (*Selected Letters*, 13; *Letters*, 119). Brumback's letter informed the family that although "some two hundred pieces of shell were lodged in him," only a few bits of shrapnel were "large enough to cut deep" (two in the knee and two in the right foot), but he may have understated the severity of the wounds in order to deflect their concern (115).

Significantly, perhaps, Ernest's letter of July 21 indicates that a bullet, presumably not a fragment from the Austrian mortar shell, had entered both his knee and his foot, and he writes of "all the other bullets and pieces of shell" that have been removed (12, 118). In fact, he writes of bullets striking both his left and right knees. In short, Hemingway's account supports his later statements to the effect that he was struck by machine gun bullets as well as shrapnel from a trench mortar. He makes no reference, however, to having carried a wounded Italian soldier to an aid station, badly wounded as he was, apparently in both legs. Brumback tells the parents that Ernest "says he does not remember how he got there [to the hospital] nor that he had carried a man until the next day when an Italian officer told him about it and said it had been voted upon to give him a valor medal for the act" (115–116). One question that has plagued scholars and biographers is whether the badly wounded young Red Cross officer did in fact lug the injured soldier out of harm's way. Did he say as much to "Brummy," and if he did, was it an exaggeration or an outright distortion?

In an essay attempting to come to terms with this momentous event, Robert W. Lewis writes, "Hemingway apparently delighted in putting people on, sometimes apparently for no other reason than devilment."[16] But also sometimes, as various commentators have noted, it was for sheer self-aggrandizement. He could not resist. He was only eighteen and then became nineteen, and he was being heralded as a hero. Clad in his fashionable, tailor-made uniform, he addressed students at his alma mater, Oak Park High School, "vividly" picturing the "gruesome sights" of battle and focusing some of his comments on the Arditi, shock troops of the Italian army.[17] He claimed to have been decorated by the king himself. At times he would imply, perhaps assert outright, that he served with that elite unit (Reynolds, *Young Hemingway*, 18, 32, 56). Lewis provides a translation of the citation for the silver medal to the effect that Hemingway "rendered generous assistance to the Italian soldiers more seriously wounded by the same explosion and did not allow himself to be carried elsewhere until after they had been evacuated" (224), but nowhere is he explicitly credited with having assisted a wounded soldier to safety. Only in his frequently cited letter to the family dated August 18 does Ernest suggest that he "got up" after he was injured and "got my wounded into the dug out" before he "collapsed" (*Selected Letters*, 14; *Letters*, 131). Lewis concludes from his research that "the silver medal was awarded to all soldiers who were wounded, and that the war cross [the second decoration Hemingway received] was awarded to all who were engaged in action in the war" (224). He also concludes that Ernest's "youthful accounts" in his correspondence and later—for example, while speaking at his old high school in Oak Park, Illinois—were exaggerations that derived "not from his desire to deceive so much as from sportiveness" (217).

Lewis is not alone among commentators who have connected Hemingway with Harold Krebs, the Marine veteran of the story "Soldier's Home" who returns the summer after the war has ended and finds that "to be listened to at all he had to lie."[18] The title appears to be quite intentionally ambiguous, suggesting both the possessive, along with the implicit question as to whether Krebs's parents' home is still in any real sense his own, and the contraction, which asserts that the soldier "is home." Significantly, Krebs decides his lies are "quite unimportant" and that they consist "in attributing to himself things other men had seen, done or heard of, and stating as facts certain apocryphal incidents familiar to all soldiers" (111–112). Paul Smith summarizes the critical commentary on this story as of the late 1980s, noting its date of composition in the spring of 1924 and emphasizing the biographical implications.[19] One might deduce that Harold Krebs, who resents his pious mother and does not wish to "settle down to work" (*Complete Short Stories*, 115), might aspire to the writer's life. But there appears to be no evidence of that in the story, though there is considerable evidence of such a vocation in the stories involving Nick Adams as a protagonist, particularly in the famously deleted third part of "Big Two-Hearted River," which would be the concluding, anchor story of *In Our Time* (1925). Students of Hemingway's short stories not uncommonly speculate as to why "Soldier's Home" is not a Nick Adams story. Perhaps, anticipating correctly enough that readers would come to connect him autobiographically with Nick Adams, Hemingway made a point of distancing himself from Krebs, locating the story in Oklahoma instead of the familiar Nick Adams world of upstate Michigan, summer home of the Hemingway family.

By the time he was writing "Soldier's Home" Ernest Hemingway had been married for about two-and-a-half years to the first of his four wives, and the first of his three sons, John Hadley, was six or seven months old. He and his wife Hadley, about eight years his senior, had been living in Paris since the end of 1921, and three of his stories along with ten poems had been published in a limited edition (300 copies) in the summer of 1923. The family was living mostly on Hadley's trust fund, supplemented by Ernest's freelance journalism for the *Toronto Star*. Ernest Hemingway was well along in the process of becoming "the center," as his biographer Carlos Baker puts it, and "the originator of his own universe" (vii). No commentator on Hemingway's complex and often contradictory character has improved on Baker's observations in the opening four pages of his foreword, in which he reflects on the "carefully cultivated stoical fortitude" of a man he also describes as an "ethical hedonist."

Excerpts from Baker's portrait of Hemingway include the following: an "immensely ambitious young man, unfailingly competitive, driven by an urge to excel"; possessed a sustained "hatred of politicians, poseurs, intellectuals, cowards, and apron strings"; "shy and diffident" but an "incredible braggart"; a "sentimentalist quick to tears" but also a "bully who used his anger like a club"; a "warm and generous friend" who could become a "ruthless and overbearing enemy"; a "non-hero longing for heroic status and sometimes achieving it"; "perpetual student," "omnivorous reader," "brilliant naturalist," "curious questioner"; a "romantic liar for whom the line between fact and fiction was thinner than a hair," but also, like any good journalist, deeply committed to what he liked to call "the true gen" (the hard facts known only to insiders); a "man driven by pride" who yet regarded it as a deadly sin, but was proud of his "manhood, his literary and athletic skills ... his reputation, his capacity for drink, his prowess as fisherman and wing shot ... his self-reliance, his wit ... his medical and military knowledge" (vii–viii).

Baker's list goes on. It is fascinating, and it goes a long way to accounting for why Ernest Hemingway has become an apt "character" for literally dozens of writers, male and female, of all literary genres, from Keith Abbott, whose fiction connects him with "underground" or countercultural authors like Richard Brautigan, to Milton Wolff, the last commander of the Lincoln Battalion, during the Spanish Civil War, who met Hemingway in Spain and portrays him briefly in his autobiographical novel *Another Hill* (1994). Among the better-known authors whose work includes tributes to Hemingway by re-creating him as a character are poets Archibald MacLeish and Yevgeny Yevtushenko, playwright Tennessee Williams, and fiction writers Ray Bradbury, Philip Roth, Joyce Carol Oates, Milan Kundera, and, more recently, William Kennedy, in his novel *Changó's Beads and Two-Tone Shoes* (2011).

Iconic Hemingway

Various biographers have commented on Hemingway's powerful "physical presence, which over the decades has proven to be iconic. He was a big man, a six-footer usually weighing around 210 pounds and he wore size eleven shoes. He was handsome: his complexion was "ruddy," his eyes brown, his hair at first "brownish black and straight." He had dimples in both cheeks. Whether sporting the mustache he wore as a young man or the full beard he grew in his forties and is featured in the famous black-and-white photograph by Yousuf Karsh taken in 1954, which Frederick Voss describes as "nothing short of leonine," Hemingway "took" well.[20] The Karsh photograph features him in a pricey Christian Dior turtleneck sweater that his wife Mary bought in Paris.

Iconic as the Karsh photograph may be, however, Voss elected to use for his cover a photo by an unidentified photographer, taken around 1927: "Ruggedly handsome" and "emphatically virile," declares the inside cover flap. Whether he is depicted with mustache in his mid-thirties posing with a huge marlin or horns of kudu and oryx, or with full white beard in his mid-fifties posing with a leopard, Hemingway has become (for better or worse) an "American icon." In his introductory essay to Voss's book, *Picturing Hemingway: A Writer in His Time* (1999), Michael Reynolds reflects on his "frenetic public and private life" (2) and concludes he "became who he wanted to be" (8). "Pictorially speaking," Frederick Voss confidently asserts, "Hemingway is the best-documented writer in all of American letters" (13).

Among such volumes, Voss's is the one most focused on the artistic qualities of the images. A quick survey of the "coffee-table" books devoted to the iconography of Ernest Hemingway might begin with some sort of disclaimer as to the possibly derogatory implications of that subgenre, inasmuch as the books do make significant contributions to the Hemingway story. The visual contexts may not be all, but they play an important part. Their history might be said to begin with the half dozen portraits that appeared in Charles Fenton's *The Apprenticeship of Ernest Hemingway: The Early Years*, published in 1954, much to Hemingway's consternation. By the time what may be regarded as the authorized biography, Carlos Baker's *Ernest Hemingway: A Life Story*, appeared a dozen years later in 1966, the gallery had expanded to a hundred, including a photograph of the author aged seven weeks, photos of various family members, and several images that would become more or less definitive over the decades: Ernest trout fishing at age five, as a grinning hospital patient in Milan (July 1918), in his "Spagnolini uniform" (displaying his two decorations), in Paris with his hands jammed into the pockets of his tweed sports coat (1924), posed with African trophy horns in 1934, boxing at Bimini in 1935, typing *For Whom the Bell Tolls* in 1939, and receiving the Bronze Star in 1947. The cover of Baker's biography features the Karsh photograph mentioned above.

The iconography of Ernest Hemingway is as impressive as that which exists for the more prominent saints. Lloyd Arnold's *Hemingway High on the Wild* (1968), concentrating on the Idaho experience, is among the earliest such volumes. The substantial text, written from a warmly familiar perspective, opens in the summer of 1939 when Hemingway and Martha Gellhorn visited Sun Valley, where he wrote much of *For Whom the Bell Tolls*. Arnold portrays the sociable and personable Hemingway that people liked to be with. The Idaho-based documentary film *Hemingway in the Autumn* (1997) similarly offers a portrait of his convivial and friendly personality. Arnold's pictures show a companionable man hunting, not exotic African big game but familiar birds (ducks, pheasant) and big game of the American West. Hemingway's three sons show up frequently in the first half of the book along with Martha Gellhorn, and Gary Cooper shows up fairly often. About halfway among the eighty-odd photographs, Mary Welsh, Hemingway's fourth wife, enters the scene.

Among the less familiar writings of renowned British novelist Anthony Burgess is his photo-biography, *Ernest Hemingway and His World* (1978), which is echoed in the title of A.E. Hotchner's more ambitious photo study that appeared ten years later. More than a hundred images figure in Burgess's small book (7" × 9") published by Scribner, but it stands apart from some of the coffee-table books partly because of the author's often probing, sometimes edgy commentary. Burgess cuts Papa Hemingway very little slack. Hotchner, however, a journalist who made much of his reputation from being Hemingway's friend and writing about it, notably in the memoir *Papa Hemingway* (1966), comes across as considerably more circumspect. Whether that wording suggests "more objective" or "less judgmental" may best be left to the reader to decide. Hotchner's *Hemingway and His World* (1989), probably the most successful of the picture books, runs to nearly twice the length of Burgess's volume and at 9.5" × 11.5" fits more obviously the common notion of the coffee-table book.

Hemingway was nearly fifty when he met Ed Hotchner ("Hotch," as he often called him), who was born in St. Louis in 1920, graduated from Washington University Law School in 1941, and served as a military journalist in the Air Force during World War II. Hotchner adapted several of Hemingway's works for the stage and television, and he later developed a close friendship with the actor Paul Newman. In his foreword, Hotchner celebrates Hemingway's "courageous exploits" but draws attention to his "shy and gentle" side and to his boundless generosity, "charismatic personality," and "genius for friendship."[21] But he does observe that "Ernest's standards of friendship were very high and difficult to define" and that he demanded those friends to "measure up," that they be "straight and unphony and formed in their own image" (10). Of course such commentary might ring as somewhat self-serving, but it does address what some of Hemingway's detractors have described as Papa's inclination to turn on his "sons and daughters" when he thought they misbehaved. Hotchner's book comprises about 450 images in addition to ample text detailing Hemingway's life and career, including color photos of pertinent sites, works of art, and book covers.

While some might argue that Hotchner's *Hemingway and His World* would need no successor, or perhaps would not even admit one, there have been several candidates, including Frederick Voss's *Picturing Hemingway*, mentioned above, published on the centennial of Hemingway's birth by the Smithsonian National Portrait Gallery in concert with Yale University Press; James Plath's *Historic Photos of Ernest Hemingway* (2009), which offers only minimal commentary by way of captions; and Boris Vejdovsky and Mariel Hemingway's *Hemingway: A Life in Pictures* (2011), containing well over 300 images, more than 200 of which feature Hemingway himself, apart from relatives, fellow writers and friends, and related locales. It seems not enough that Hemingway's words should survive him, but his physical likeness lives on as well. Most of the nearly eighty images in Voss's book, some of them in color, portray Hemingway himself, although a few are devoted to such friends and associates as F. Scott Fitzgerald, Maxwell Perkins, and Charles Scribner. Color reproductions of both of Henry Strater's portraits, dating from 1922 and 1923, appear in Voss's collection, along with such items as Man Ray's 1923 gelatin silver print, Waldo Peirce's oil "Death in the Gulf Stream" (1932), along with his 1937 portrait for the cover of *Time* magazine, and the "Tarzanlike Lampoon" of Miguel Covarrubias in gouache from 1933 that went unpublished. The triggering event for the Covarrubias caricature was Hemingway's irate response to critic Max Eastman's perceived assault on his virility in his review of *Death in the Afternoon*. As Voss suggests, "Humor at his own expense was never Hemingway's long suit" (31), and in this case it came to a physical confrontation in Maxwell Perkins' office four years later. In a recent item appearing on slate.com, Nathan Heller aptly asserts that Hemingway, thanks partly to these icons, has become "the literary equivalent of the Nike swoosh or [McDonald's] golden arches."

At least in passing, one might also take note of the dozens of films that have been shaped or torqued out of Hemingway's fiction, including recent efforts like *Hemingway's Garden of Eden* (2010), alongside classics such as the Gary Cooper and Helen Hayes version of *A Farewell to Arms* (1932) and the 1946 version of "The Killers," which starred Burt Lancaster and Ava Gardner (and which Hemingway apparently preferred to other cinematic efforts). Two full-length books have been devoted to the study of films based on Hemingway texts. More than a dozen documentary films are also extant and generally available, ranging from the five-part TV miniseries *Hemingway* (2001), featuring Stacey Keach in the title role, to such items as *Hemingway: Wrestling with Life* (*Biography*, 1998) and the PBS American Masters film *Ernest Hemingway: Rivers to the Sea* (2005). Some of the documentaries are quite modest, running just an hour and presenting mostly stills or brief interviews with scholars or those who knew Hemingway in various contexts, an example being *Hemingway in Autumn* (1997), which focuses on his years in Sun Valley and Ketchum. Idaho. A full-length documentary, *Cooper and Hemingway: The True Gen*, premiered in October 2013.

I propose that the documentaries resemble conventional biographies, while the more elaborate, costly Hollywood productions, e.g., *In Love and War* (1996), starring Sandra Bullock and Chris O'Donnell, and *Hemingway and Gellhorn* (2011), starring Nicole Kidman and Clive Owen, qualify as appropriations. These are commented on briefly in Chapter Eight, "Hemingway on Stage, Screen, and Television," along with a number of films that depict Hemingway in cameo roles: *The Moderns* (1988), with Kevin O'Connor as Hemingway, and Woody Allen's *Midnight in Paris* (2011), with Corey Stoll in the Hemingway role.

"To become such an icon is a mixed blessing," Michael Reynolds has written, "for the ravenous public quickly sucks the real man dry." What Hemingway wanted does not differ from what nearly all serious writers want: "to be the best writer of his generation; he wanted his writing to last forever." But unlike many other writers, male or female, "he also wanted to live the strenuous life as preached by his childhood idol, Teddy Roosevelt." Hemingway "took the risks we could not afford; played the game for which we lacked the skills; sustained the hurts that we avoided; and wrote the stories that moved us." The greatest risk might be, as Reynolds observes, that the writer could be reduced almost to an "afterthought" (*Picturing Hemingway*, 8) as the author became "an authentic artifact" (9). Those who read the various "appropriations," or "remakes," or, to use a term from pop music, "covers," of Hemingway as a character will often perceive a reluctance to portray him as a writer. After all, the process of writing is altogether consuming, but it is not very entertaining. When Hemingway attempted to portray the writer's life in his fiction, as in the fortunately deleted third part of "Big Two-Hearted River," he most often failed. Jake Barnes appears to be one of the few actively employed characters in *The Sun Also Rises*, but we are only faintly aware of his work as a journalist. Would-be writers like Robert Cohn in that novel, or Hubert, the self-subsidized poet in "Mr. and Mrs. Elliot," are dealt with rather harshly. David Bourne, in the posthumously published (and heavily cut and edited) *The Garden of Eden* (1987), must be Hemingway's best fictional portrait of the writer at work, grasping for the "one true sentence" that became one of Hem's mantras and struggling with his hyper-complicated personal life. In his nonfiction, from *Death in the Afternoon* (1932) to *A Moveable Feast* (posthumously published in 1964), and occasionally in the posthumous Africa memoirs published in two versions as *True at First Light* (1999) and *Under Kilimanjaro* (2005), he also portrays, with considerable effect, the writer's life and its challenges. "A man who writes a novel or a short story is a liar ipso facto," Hemingway declares in the latter "autobiographical novel" (per the dust jacket flap). "His only excuse is that he makes the truth as he invents it truer than it would be."[22]

Hemingway's World

Geographically, Hemingway "did" upstate Michigan, Key West, Ketchum and several other American sites in between, but perhaps what is more important, in a way, he did France, Austria, Switzerland, Spain, Italy, Kenya, the Bahamas, and Cuba, along with other international places. Too often his cosmopolitanism has been overlooked. Part of Hemingway's universality owes to his life as a world traveler—or, perhaps more accurately, "dweller," as he did not merely visit most of those places but resided in them for varying lengths of time—and to the exotic settings of his fiction. No American writer of any consequence before or since, including Henry James, whose investigation and appraisal of the expatriated American anticipated Hemingway's, has so passionately embraced the world and so variously demonstrated geographical latitude. The four episodes of the 1999 BBC documentary *Michael Palin's Hemingway Adventure* attest to the continuing fascination with Hemingway's footprints. Searching for the briefcase full of manuscripts that Hadley lost when boarding a train in Paris in 1922, German novelist Gerhard Köpf's bibliophilic protagonist, who likes to call himself "Hemingstein" (one of Ernest's favorite boyhood nicknames for himself), visits Ketchum (Idaho), Pamplona, Key West, Oak Park and Chicago, Toronto, Cody (Wyoming), Cuba, Venice, Kenya, Berlin, Paris, Ezra Pound's retreat in Brunnenburg, the Hemingways' ski resort in Schruns (Austria), and even Hong Kong.

Historically, picking up with his wounding in World War I and his move to Paris with Hadley at the end of 1921, Hemingway lived and wrote, in fiction and nonfiction (including his journalism), the events that defined the first half of the twentieth century: the Jazz Age, or Roaring Twenties, and the expatriate world of the Lost Generation, followed by the Great Depression and World War II. Most of Michael Reynolds' second paragraph from his "Brief Biography" mentioned above summarizes Hemingway's life and times with a terse eloquence that Hemingway himself might have appreciated:

Before he turned twenty-five Ernest Hemingway was already friends with James Joyce, Ezra Pound, and Gertrude Stein, and he had written most of the stories that were published as *In Our Time* (1925). Before he was thirty Hemingway had buried his father (a suicide) and written two of the best novels to come from his generation: *The Sun Also Rises* (1926) and *A Farewell to Arms* (1929). At thirty-six he reported the Spanish Civil War to neutral Americans [and wrote an epic novel drawn from that experience, *For Whom the Bell Tolls* (1940)]. At forty-four he reported on the Normandy invasion from a landing craft off Omaha Beach. At forty-six he married his fourth wife. At fifty-three he won the Pulitzer Prize for fiction [for *The Old Man and the Sea* (1952)] and survived two plane crashes in Africa. At fifty-four the Nobel Prize was his. On the morning of July 2, 1961, Ernest Hemingway slipped two shells into his favorite shotgun and quite deliberately blew the top of his head away [15–16].

Significantly, perhaps, the concluding sentence, which I temporarily cut from Reynolds' paragraph, rings as passive and anticlimactic: "He was survived by three wives, three sons, numerous rumors, five unpublished books [since published in one shape or another], and a distinguished if frequently misunderstood body of work" (16). The phrase "frequently misunderstood" might be said to apply as well to Hemingway's life story.

Literary critics and scholars have pursued Hemingway's work and life with nearly equal gusto for something approaching ninety years now, if one starts the record with reviews of his first published writing. Writers of biographical fiction featuring Hemingway have drawn on their work and in the process joined in their interpretations and speculations. "I'm going to be praised by the highbrows and read by the lowbrows!" the twenty-five-year-old Ernest exclaims to his wife Hadley in Christopher Cook Gilmore's *Hemingway* (1988), which opens with Hem's wounding in Italy and ends with his suicide in Idaho.[23] This fictitious prediction, supposedly uttered on the eve of Boni and Liveright's publication of the stories of *In Our Time*, would become a cliché, as is a sentiment that echoes throughout Craig McDonald's recent trilogy of crime novels, in which his protagonist, a private eye named Hector Lassiter, a longtime Hemingway intimate and fellow writer, "lives what he writes and writes what he lives."[24]

How Hemingway is treated as a fictional character varies wildly. In novels featuring a character obsessed with the man, the writing, and the legend— Michael Palin's *Hemingway's Chair* (1995) and Gerhard Köpf's *Papa's Suitcase* (1994)—Hemingway is idolized, at least by the protagonist, who may himself be treated at times as a bit of a buffoon. In novels like Karl Alexander's *Papa and Fidel* (1989) and Dan Simmons' *The Crook Factory* (2000), Hemingway comes off as an action-hero. For reasons that invite some speculation, writers of mysteries and crime novels appear to have been especially drawn to Hemingway, sometimes to assist their protagonist and other times to behave as a sort of foil. The fictional Hemingway we encounter in Keith Abbott's *Rhino Ritz* (1979), a speculative novella in which Hemingway teams up with F. Scott Fitzgerald to operate a detective agency employed to rescue the kidnapped Sherwood Anderson, is clearly depicted as a comic sleuth. He's much more effectual, though not without some tomfoolery, in Michael Atkinson's *Hemingway Deadlights* (2009), which offers up Hemingway in 1956 Key West and Cuba solving the case of a friend's murder and turning up other improbable criminal activities as well. Cuban mystery writer Leonardo Padura Fuentes provides one of the more sympathetic portraits in *Adiós Hemingway* (2005), which features Hemingway in Cuba in 1958 struggling to complete *A Moveable Feast* as a present-day former police officer attempts to solve an old murder case that dates back to Hemingway's last days at the Finca Vigía. Hemingway does not fare nearly as well in Patrick Kendrick's intrigue, *Papa's Problem* (2008), which takes place in 1939 Key West; but in Atkinson's 2010 thriller, *Hemingway Cutthroat*, he proves to be an adept investigator in 1937 Spain torn by the civil war.

This leads to the crux of the problem when it comes to the biographical fictions that feature Ernest Hemingway in one shape or another: What do these appropriations amount to? What, if anything, do they provide for serious readers and students or scholars of Hemingway's life and writing? Might not even the most carefully researched and presumably well-intended of these, e.g., Roland L Bessette's *Sunrise at Ketchum: A Biographical Novel of Ernest Hemingway* (2009), get in the way or obfuscate matters? Do they add, or detract, from the luster? Do they—can they, given the nature of the subgenre—add anything to the biographical facts, or to the interpretation thereof, or to the way we read the work? Taken individually or as a whole, as a rather diverse set, do they enhance the reputation of the man and his work, or do they—obviously, some people might object—simply add to the confusion, contributing primarily to the already dense layers of myth and legend?

Or are such questions as these beside the point? Presumably these writers of popular fiction, akin (at least) to what has been called "fan-fiction," set out to write good, entertaining novels, not to contribute to the critical inquiry into Hemingway's life and work. Much of the interest of these appropriations owes to their subject, and he would not be of much abiding interest if not for his writing. Yet, again presumably, none of these writers undertook what generally appears to have been considerable research simply in order to write about Hemingway and his times and what may or may not have been his exploits.

From Ray Bradbury to Naomi Wood, whose 2014 novel, *Mrs. Hemingway*, depicts the marriages with his four wives, the apparent intent of these authors has been to write good fiction for what may be described as a rather specific audience. The issue as to whether "good" fiction has resulted from their efforts is of course debatable, and I suppose it is not likely that any of the titles will ever attain the status of "literature," or that any of the writers necessarily yearned to be thought of as "literary." These texts—stories and novels, poems and plays—were devised for readers familiar with Hemingway. That simple premise may be as far as one should go when it comes to feigning a hypothesis. Most of the authors clearly expected at least minimal familiarity with Hemingway's writing. Gilmore's *Hemingway* presents the most obvious case for the expectation of a broad, if not deep, acquaintance with the fiction, and a novel such as McLain's *The Paris Wife* surely loses much of its resonance in the latter third for those who are unfamiliar with *The Sun Also Rises*.

Were most of these biographical fictions conceived with Hemingway scholars in mind? Surely they were not, although just as surely we may assume most of the writers proceeded with the awareness that their efforts would be scrutinized and judged by Hemingway enthusiasts or aficionados of every sort, scholars included. Any egregious mistakes would come to light and would potentially open their efforts to ridicule. The life and work of Hemingway have been as open to interpretation and assessment to these writers of popular fiction as they have been, and will continue to be, for literary scholars and commentators. Some of these writers, as will be apparent, have judged Hemingway quite harshly, to the extent, in fact, that we might be inclined to question their motives. But this examination of their efforts does not proceed from the assumption that only positive perspectives on Hemingway's life and work are acceptable, nor does it proceed from the assumption that such perspectives ought to be objective, balanced, fair, or even judicious. The world of these Hemingway appropriations is the world of popular fiction, not the world of literary scholarship, except perhaps as they might be connected with the relatively recent phenomenon of "fan fiction."

As Karen Hellekson and Kristina Busse approach the issues of "fandom" and "fanon" (as opposed to "canon") in *Fan Fiction and Fan Communities in the Age of the Internet* (2006), the applications tend toward popular media like the *Star Trek* and the *X-Files* movies, and many of the texts live on the internet or in cyberspace. But Deborah Kaplan's essay in that collection, "Construction of Fan Fiction Character Through Narrative," addresses some concepts particularly relevant to my study. Virtually all of the writers whose texts are dealt with in this book may be described either as "fans" or as "anti-fans" of Ernest Hemingway's life and writing, both of which phenomena serve as what Kaplan describes as "source texts."[25] "Rewriting characters for a work of fan fiction is an interpretive act," Kaplan proposes, "in which the text offers one possible understanding of character." Two points must be emphasized here: First, Hemingway-as-appropriated is an amalgam of his life story, both as he wrote it in such books as *A Moveable Feast* and as his dozens of biographers have represented it, and of his often highly autobiographical fiction, as read and interpreted by critics and scholars and by those who have written the appropriations. Second, the biographical fictions or appropriations are not limited to the perspectives of fans, but also comprise the views of anti-fans, whose aim appears either to correct or to debunk the public image and the legends that have accumulated around Hemingway over the past ninety years.

Hemingway is the "character" and in many ways the "source text" as well. These fans and anti-fans constitute an "interpretive community," and "the roots of fan fiction's characterization lie both in this interpretive community and in an individual interpretation of the source text's characters" (Kaplan 136). Significantly, the Hemingway appropriations conform to the basic nature of fan fiction, which proceeds from the premise that the reader is well aware of the appropriated character:

> The reader, before ever beginning a specific work of fan fiction, already knows the physical appearance of the primary characters, as well as their back-stories, their reactions to certain life events, their voices, their base characterizations, and fanon [as in canon] construction of character [136].

In most of the Hemingway appropriations, unlike most fan fiction, readers will encounter other important characters, frequently the protagonist, in fact, who will not be familiar, but what draws readers into membership (perhaps only temporary) in the "interpretive community of fandom" is the source text that is Hemingway himself.

One might or might not regard the representation of Ernest Hemingway in pulp fiction, notably in the men's magazines of the 1950s, as a subset of fan fiction. David M. Earle's well illustrated book, *All Man! Hemingway, 1950s Men's Magazines, and the Masculine Persona* (2009), probes the subject thoroughly, proceeding from the observation that "it would be difficult to overemphasize the popularity of Hemingway in the 1950s, and this celebrity is at its most extreme and sensational in these magazines" (4). Earle also observes that the "popular representation of Hemingway as both serious author and public figure, sensitive artist and masculine ideal, has often been overlooked in both biographies and critical studies." Earle asserts the error in the "elitist" notion that Hemingway was "antagonistic to the popular marketplace": "In truth, Hemingway not only sought out a popular audience but was himself heavily influenced by popular literature" (19).

There is much of manifest America and of Ernest Hemingway in Carl Sandburg's familiar ode to Chicago, a city that perhaps has as much claim to be Hem's hometown as Key West or Havana, or Paris or Venice or Ketchum. (Hemingway mentions having met Sandburg through a mutual friend in early 1921—see Chapter Nine.) Metonymically, Hemingway, like Chicago, comes across as "husky" and "broad-shouldered," "stormy" and "brutal," "proud to be alive and coarse and strong and cunning," a "tall bold slugger," a "laughing" young braggart, "an ignorant fighter who has never lost a battle."[26] Perhaps not so "ignorant," after all, but certainly "fierce" and, without a doubt, "proud."

Two

Young Hemingstein

Editors of Hemingway's letters are aware that his domineering and overbearing, but also doting, mother, Grace, saved nearly every scrap of his writing she came across, beginning with a note addressed to his father (Papa) when the boy was just eight years old.[1] In her introduction to the first volume of what is projected to be a nearly complete edition of the letters, Sandra Spanier indicates that more than 6,000 letters survive. More than forty of those, many of them just notes running two or three lines of printed text, were written before he turned eighteen. Of Ernest's five siblings, four sisters and a brother who was nearly sixteen years his junior, three wrote memoirs and two of those include reflections on his boyhood. The photographic record of Ernest's boyhood and adolescence is nearly as extensive as that which was spawned by his fame as a writer: we know how he looked at virtually every stage of his life. In fact, we have multiple images of Ernest Hemingway doing everything from roasting marshmallows to posing with a fishing rod and a squirrel rifle, possibly an air rifle, all by the age of five or six. We also have multiple sources, for example, of Ernest as a little boy telling his mother he was "fraid of nothin."[2]

In *At the Hemingways* (1961), Marcelline ("Marsh," "Ivory") Hemingway Sanford, a year and a half older than Ernest, describes her mother's musical education of the children, noting that she and Ernest frequented the opera in Chicago and that Ernest took piano lessons from age five and struggled with the cello until his senior year in high school. She also lists the nicknames he devised for the siblings and for himself, notably Old Brute, Eoinbones (or Oinbones) and Hemingstein (or Stein)—later, he added Wemedge to his monikers.[3] Swimming, boating (rowing or canoe paddling), hiking, fishing and hunting were activities mostly reserved for the family trips to northern Michigan at Walloon Lake near Petoskey, Michigan. Marcelline notes that both she and Ernest read the Horatio Alger novels when they were in third and fourth grade, "and Ernest took them seriously" (134).

Horatio Alger Jr. (1832–1899) specialized in juvenile fiction that featured rags-to-riches stories of success gained through honesty and hard work. The son of a Unitarian minister of modest means, Horatio Alger attended Harvard when Henry Wadsworth Longfellow was a professor of modern languages and the renowned Swiss paleontologist and zoologist Louis Agassiz taught "natural history" courses that could include everything from geology to comparative anatomy. Alger graduated eighth in his class of 88 in 1852 and served a couple of years as a Unitarian minister. His first major success in books for boys was *Ragged Dick; or, Street Life in New York with the Bootblacks* (1868). His novel *Rough and Ready; or, Life Among the New York Newsboys* (1869) might have had special appeal to Ernest, who had a weekly newspaper route. Nearly a hundred such titles poured from Alger's pen between the mid–1860s and the time of his death at the end of the century. Marcelline also takes note of her brother's reading of *Dracula* in 1913 and of such classics as the novels of Sir Walter Scott, Charles Dickens, and Robert Louis Stevenson, including *The Suicide Club* (1878). The bulky "green cloth volume" of Thackery's *Vanity Fair*, she asserts, "we read from cover to cover." Their reading also included Shakespeare's plays and "every word of the King James version of the Bible," on which they passed a "detailed test." It might well be that Horatio Alger ranked equally with Dickens, Shakespeare, and the Bible as an early literary and personal influence on Hemingway.

Marcelline also details Ernest's membership in the high school rifle club, the debating society, and the swimming team, along with his largely unsuccessful efforts to see playing time on the varsity football squad. Both she and Ernest excelled in their English classes, and she remembers he wrote short stories in the style of Poe, O. Henry, and Ring Lardner (he sometimes signed his articles for the high school newspaper as "Ring Lardner Jr."). So thorough is the record on Ernest Hemingway's evolution as a writer that a collection of his high school "writings," mostly journalism for the school weekly newspaper *Trapeze*, was published in 1993 as *Hemingway at Oak Park High*. He sometimes signed himself "Hemingstein." Then "suddenly," Marcelline writes, during his junior year, "Ernie became interested in girls" (144). This is the Ernest Hemingway that would emerge in the first of the biographical fictions or appropriations, though not under his own name: John Dos Passos' *Chosen Country* (1951). Although Ernest plays a fairly small role in Dos Passos' novel, which has been described as something of a tribute to his late wife, Kate Smith Dos Passos, Hemingway was not at all amused. I shall return to that novel later.

Of more immediate interest is the first novel to feature Ernest Hemingway as the protagonist, Michael Murphy's *Hemingsteen*, which was published to very little fanfare in 1978 by Autolycus Press in St. Louis.[4] The variant spelling (-steen for -stein) may or may not have been intentional on Murphy's part. In a one-page introduction to *Hemingsteen* dated June 1977, Murphy explains that the "idea for this book originated with Hemingway in his statement about the Oak Park novel," which would have been explicitly autobiographical and, perhaps ironically, for that reason was never written. In a letter to Charles Fenton in 1952, Hemingway said he had tried but failed to write such a novel: "I had a wonderful novel to write about Oak Park and would never do it because I did not want to hurt living people" (13; *Selected Letters*, 764). Michael Reynolds, in his foreword to a reissue of Marcelline Hemingway Sanford's *At the Hemingways*, proposes that in not writing about Oak Park, "no other important American author has been so kind to his home town" (xiv). On similar grounds, not wanting to "hurt living people," Hemingway stalled the release of his memoir, *A Moveable Feast*. Murphy's novel seeks to do what much fan fiction does: fill in the gaps. Where hints or innuendos are suggested or where unresolved conundrums or mysteries linger, the writer of fan fiction steps in.

Michael Murphy's short novel begins in the summer of 1917 as eighteen-year-old Ernest makes his decision not to go off to college, as his parents wish, but to head for Kansas City, where he will find employment as a cub reporter for about half a year before joining the ambulance service in order to see action in World War I on the Italian front. Although he was an excellent shot (and a fine wing-shot), Hemingway's eyes, like his mother's, were weak, so he was not permitted to enlist in military service. In the second chapter, Murphy turns the clock back to 1914, when the fourteen- or fifteen-year-old Ernest encounters a couple of yeggs at a lunch counter in a scene reminiscent of the two hit men he will have young Nick Adams meet in "The Killers."

Hemingway's Al and Max, "dressed like twins" in derby hats and overcoats too tight for them, complain about the food and make sarcastic comments on the town and the "bright boys" in it before tying up Nick and the cook and brandishing a sawed-off shotgun (*Complete Short Stories*, 216). Murphy's characters, one named Jack and the other unnamed, are both "dressed in moleskin pants and checked shirts" (8). One of them has "a triangular shaped pock-scarred face" and the other is described simply as "fat." Despite the fact that they do not appear to be twin-like otherwise, they do somewhat resemble a sort of "vaudeville team," as Hemingway puts it in his story (219). When the counter man in Murphy's novel asks the "gentlemen" whether that will be all, the tone of their response is reminiscent of the voices we hear in "The Killers":

The fat one looked up at him and over at the thin one. He said out of the corner of his mouth, "He called you a gentleman, Jack."

"Well, ain't that pretty," Jack said. He slurped his coffee through his tight straight mouth with a noise you could have heard a block away. "That makes three of us, I guess" [11].

The fat one then empties his coffee on the counter and calls it slop. Hemingway would likely have eschewed the cliché "heard a block away," but Murphy's Ernest borrows a word from Hemingway's "The Battler" (and elsewhere) when he declares sympathetically, "'A couple of *cruts*, that's what they are'" (12, italics added).

Not coincidentally, young Ernest and his pals, like Nick Adams, find themselves in the town of Summit, located about fourteen miles southwest of Chicago, or ten miles south of Oak Park. Presumably, readers are to suppose that a more mature Hemingway would think back on this sort of episode from his boyhood and refabricate it as serious fiction. Murphy supplies here an implicit backstory for "The Killers." Christopher Cook Gilmore's novel *Hemingway* (1988) provides the most numerous examples of this practice among the biographical fictions, but practically none of the appropriators can resist the urge to hint at how this or that story or episode from a novel might have been born. Readers of biographical fiction, and particularly of fan fiction, thrive on such moments, presumably gratified at the confirmation of their insider status.

Many appropriators find occasion to imitate various features of Hemingway's style, particularly that of the early fiction on through *A Farewell to Arms* (1929), and nearly all of them show signs of having been influenced by it, especially when it comes to the prominent role of dialogue, which turns out to be not so amenable to successful imitation as one might predict. Murphy states his "intention" was "not to be unremittingly imitative of Hemingway's style, but rather to suggest the form and posture he might have adopted toward the events in this book." He adds he has "used necessarily some techniques and devices that are identified with his work" (vii). Murphy and others imitate the style partly out of admiration, perhaps, but also because it imports into their texts a sort of verisimilitude. The reader seems to be hearing the voice of Hemingway. Murphy's narrative does not move chronologically but freely back and forth between the years 1911 and 1917, when Ernest was between eleven and eighteen years old. We encounter frequent conflicts with his mother, the domineering Grace, that would likely have been attractive to Kenneth S. Lynn in concocting his 1987 biography, *Hemingway*, which proceeds from the premise of Ernest's "veritable obsession with his mother."[5]

In 1911 the eleven- or twelve-year-old Ernest talks with his father about shooting crows, "one of the crookedest birds there is," according to his father, and also "a menace" (28). At the end of this brief chapter (the average chapter runs only about eight pages), Ernest's father, who "knew everything," warns his son that "the most cunning and dangerous critters around" are human, "but you will learn about the meanness and cunning of your fellow man in time" (32). As for the crows, Ernest's father advises they may be shot "any time and everywhere," but he must never hunt in an "unsportsmanlike" manner. Carlos Baker notes that from the age of four Ernest was a member of the Agassiz Club, devoted to nature studies, a local branch of which his father was leader.[6] As Susan Beegel observes in "Eye and Heart: Hemingway's Education as a Naturalist," the Agassiz method involved very close observation of natural phenomena and "object-oriented science education."[7] The Swiss naturalist Louis Agassiz (1807–1873) had a distinguished career at Harvard, where he was professor of both zoology and geology from 1847 until his death.

One of the most bizarre episodes in this collage-like novel depicts a fevered dream wherein the thirteen- or fourteen-year-old Ernest undergoes a torturous inquisition at the hands of his father as His Eminence the Bishop, and his mother, mostly concerning details of the Hemingway family history and of Oak Park's founding. He dreams he is in the woods with his hands bound behind him, and his father beats him frequently with a razor strap throughout the interrogation, which ends only when he confusedly confesses to mostly unspecified wrongdoing and pleads for forgiveness.[8] The mother, masked and wearing a black dress, appears at times to be "on his side," but not consistently so. The impression one gets is that young Ernest's unempathic parents sent him confused messages as to who he was and what was important. For example, when Ernest agrees to confess, his father is about to send him to his room, but his mother insists the flogging be resumed. At the end of the episode Ernest is alone and at ease in the silent forest: "The silence would be there with you alone and knowing of yourself" (80).

The longest chapters run no more than a dozen pages, and that, along with abrupt chronological shifts from chapter to chapter, contributes to the episodic effect; in short, there is no clear narrative arc in the novel. The next chapter after the nightmare inquisition, which occurs in 1913, is set in 1916 (the chapter after that one kicks back to 1915) and concerns the sensational murder trial of Marion Lambert, a high school girl from Lake Forest who was apparently poisoned by her boyfriend, William Orpet, a student at the University of Wisconsin. Orpet was acquitted. Comically commingled with the conversation about the trial between Ernest and his sisters Marcelline, Madelaine (Sunny), Carol, and Ursula is a rundown of family nicknames, Ernest's in this case being "Old Brute." As the episodes ricochet between the covers, we see Ernest at a football game stewing on the bench, and later at a speakeasy with some friends as they chat with a stripper and drink rye whiskey. At age sixteen Ernest stumbles and stammers through the reading of one of his stories, the best in the class that term: "After that he did not care for public readings" (43). In his book on Hemingway's experiences in Spain during the civil war, Stephen Koch portrays him stumbling miserably through a speech at Carnegie Hall in June of 1937 on the film *The Spanish Earth:* "He was strangling on his tie. He'd try to yank it loose. Then he'd return to his almost whiny monotone."[9] His discomfort with speaking in public would carry over to his refusal to attend the Nobel Prize ceremonies in Stockholm in 1954.

When he runs a mock initiation for new members of the Rifle Club, Ernest shows himself to be something of a bully, but more characteristic of the episodes in *Hemingsteen* are those that focus on his awkward relationships with girls. At age sixteen he obtains a classmate's telescope in exchange for writing the boy's papers. He uses it to spy on a girl named Betty Smyth, and in the passage that follows, we see further evidence of Murphy's imitation of the Hemingway style:

> He saw the Smyth girl taking off her clothes one night. Betty Smyth, who liked to use the name Elizabeth, was standing at the window in the bedroom on the second floor. He saw much more than he had ever seen before of any girl. It made him quite uneasy. Then when it was over and he felt quite strange about it he lay back in bed and felt his heart beat fiercely in his chest [137].

In this brief sample, what we hear are doubled repetitions: the Smyth girl/Betty Smyth, he saw the Smyth girl/he saw much more, quite uneasy/quite strange. This is followed by the very short, flat, declarative sentence that comes across as something of an understatement: "It made him quite uneasy." But it's the last sentence in that paragraph, broken by no commas, that most clearly echoes the Hemingway voice.

Despite feeling guilty, Ernest watches her again, and in the following sentences we again hear Hemingway's voice, notably in the ambiguous use of the neuter pronoun "it":

> It was his own possession in a way, he did not want to share it. He did not want to talk about the girl. It was a fragile thing to share with anyone, since they would talk and he would be exposed, and if he talked the whole thing could go wrong. All the same he watched her on those nights and felt guilty afterwards and never got the courage up to ask her out. No. he would never touch it. He wanted it but would never touch it [138–139].

Adolescent Ernest's squeamishness about sexual matters and his objectification of sexuality appear frequently in his fiction. One thinks, perhaps, of Liz Coates in the early story "Up in Michigan": "She was frightened but she wanted it. She had to have it but it frightened her now" (*Complete Short Stories*, 62). The supposedly neuter or gender neutral pronoun, obviously heavy with sexual innuendo here, appears seven times in six lines of text in the Finca Vigía edition of the story. In "The Snows of Kilimanjaro" some form of the pronoun "it" appears no fewer than 22 times in one 17-line passage, this time referring to death (54). Perhaps no writer of note has ever derived so much connotation out of that simple, denotative word.

By the time *Hemingsteen* ends, young Ernest (age seventeen, perhaps) experiences his sexual initiation, thanks to an experienced twenty-year-old young woman named Dorothy. He reasserts his decision not to head off to college, and he shows himself, on the verge of heading for Kansas City, to be petulant and peevish with a girl named Rebecca, who is a college-bound friend of his sister. His childish and jealous treatment of her, however, ironically leads him to write through his confusion, and in the process he experiences a sort of epiphany as he begins to discover himself as a writer:

> And writing it he heard the muffled rhythm of the rain on the roof and then he listened to the voices of the people he had known, their voices and some laughter and there was a meaning to the laughter that he suddenly discovered, a meaning and a beauty to their lives that he had never known before, and listened, hearing knowing them and, for the first time, writing them: writing then as he had never written, he felt a stirring of a kind inside him, of a kind he'd never known before. Not in the way he knew it now [196].

Students of the evolution of Hemingway's prose style might note that the rambling sentence above (93 words) linked with conjunctions (the rhetorical device of polysyndeton) suggests the much later influence of Gertrude Stein's syntax, so it amounts to a stylistic anachronism here. The closing sentence totals just eight words.

Michael Murphy's novel, portions of which were published in a now apparently defunct "magazine of the Middle west" called *Inland*, opens and closes in the summer of 1917, by which time Ernest has made his momentous "decision" to go to Kansas City, feeling that "nothing, or almost nothing, that had been any good was any longer any good" (6).

A similar sentiment is reflected in *Hemingway's Boat* (2011) when Paul Hendrickson quotes Ernest's brother Leicester: "*He loved everything up to a certain point, and then nothing was any good any more*" (262). In the closing sentences of *Hemingsteen* Ernest thinks, "Well he had to tell them. There wasn't any getting there without the telling them" (204). As Marcelline tells the story, however, the decision was not quite so momentous. "College educations for all of us were a hopeful part of my parents' plans," she writes, and Ernest had talked of going to Cornell or the University of Illinois (149). But Ernest "put off deciding" and tried to line up something at the *Kansas City Star* through their uncle, "and Dad hoped he could help Ernest get a summer job on that fine paper" (150).

As it happened, he had to wait until October, so he spent the summer of 1917 doing farm work in Michigan. Ernest's letters home in September are full of digging potatoes and picking apples broken up with comments on his fishing exploits: (August 6) "The other night I caught three rainbow trout that weighed 6 lb. 5½ lb and 3½ lb respectively also a two lb. brook trout in Horton Bay. That is the largest catch of trout that has ever been made there" (*Letters*, 41). Significantly, Ernest adds in this letter from Walloon Lake to his Grandfather Anson Hemingway that he plans not to attend the University of Illinois "this fall" and that he might seek a job with the *Chicago Tribune* in order to be "fixed" so he can go to college the next year. In his September 6 letter to his family, Ernest recounts fighting a six-pound musky on his fly rod, for which he received "18¢ per pound" against his room and board (43).

Curiously absent, for the most part, both in his letters and in Murphy's novel, is much in the way of interest in, or even awareness of, the war raging in Europe. That would change after Hemingway got himself established in Kansas City. Ernest's first letter home from there is dated October 17, 1917. Just a week later he wrote to his father about the arrival of a troop train headed to Fort Doniphan, and in a letter to his siblings dated November 5, he boasts of being "a beautiful soldier," having joined the Missouri Home Guard (*Letters*, 57). On October 21 of that year U.S. troops would experience their first combat action. In a letter to his parents dated November 15 Ernest describes his Missouri Home Guard uniform in some detail, but in an earlier letter to Marcelline ("old Ivory") he asserts, "I intend to enlist in the Canadian Army soon.... Honest kid I cant [*sic*] stay out much longer.... If you enlist in the Canadian forces you are given as much time as you specify and then go to either Toronto or Halifax and the[n] to London and in three months you are in France. They are the greatest fighters in the world and our troops are not to be spoken of in the same breath.... I couldnt [*sic*] face any body after the war and not have been in it" (59). As it happened, Hemingway's future literary rival William Faulkner would in fact enlist in the Canadian forces, signing up as a cadet pilot for the RAF on July 10, 1918, but the war would end before he shipped out.[10] Ernest's letter from New York City to his family dated May 14, 1918, proudly lays out his officer's Red Cross uniform, "cocky field service cap" and all, guaranteed to make him "look like a million dollars" (97).

Hemingway's boyish enthusiasm about the military and the war would not have to last him for long, as he would arrive in Italy on the fourth of June and be seriously injured by a trench mortar shell at the Piave River northeast of Venice on the night of July 8, about the time twenty-year-old Faulkner was taking the train for Toronto. But the fact is, as anyone familiar with his biography knows, Hemingway's boyish enthusiasm for war ("the best subject of all," he would write in a 1925 letter to F. Scott Fitzgerald) and for things military would last him the rest of his life (*Selected Letters*, 176).

Unlike Michael Murphy's biographical fiction, John Dos Passos' *Chosen Country* takes Hemingway, renamed George Warner, through World War I and into postwar Chicago, but he first appears as an adolescent about the same age as he is in various chapters of *Hemingsteen*. Also, unlike the case of Michael Murphy, John Dos Passos is quite well known, and the backstory behind the publication of his appropriation differs considerably from that of the former biographical fiction. Although some biographers believe Hemingway and Dos Passos met in Italy in 1918, considerable evidence to the contrary exists. They most likely met in Paris early in 1924, and Dos Passos joined Hemingway and Hadley, whom he admired, at the festival of San Fermin in Pamplona on June 25. Dos Passos' biographer Townsend Ludington indicates that Dos Passos and Crystal Ross, his fiancée to be, and Ernest and Hadley "saw each other almost daily" that spring.[11] Ernest's first extant letter to Dos, as he called him (spelled phonetically as "Daws" at times), is dated April 22, 1925, thanking him for assisting Sherwood Anderson in shepherding, or "jamming" through, the publication of the stories of *In Our Time* at Liveright. Most likely Dos was spared an appearance in the roman à clef *The Sun Also Rises* (1926) because he did not accompany Hemingway and his crew to Pamplona in the summer of 1925. But it may also be that Ernest so valued his friendship at the time that he decided not to cast him in a role.

Certainly that was not the case a dozen years later when Hemingway's widely unadmired novel, *To Have and Have Not*, appeared in October 1937. By that time Ernest and Hadley had divorced, and he had married the wealthy heiress Pauline Pfeiffer and moved to Key West. The move occurred in April 1928, at Dos Passos' urging (he had hiked into the Keys in the spring of 1924). In 1926 Crystal Ross broke off with Dos, and in the spring of 1929 he met and fell in love with Kate (Katy) Smith, who had been one of Ernest's boyhood friends and possibly a girlfriend, or more likely a would-be girlfriend, during a couple of summers at Walloon Lake. In his biography of Hadley, Gioia Diliberto insists "Kate confessed to Hadley that she was in love with him [Ernest]" when they first met at her brother Y.K.'s apartment in Chicago.[12] In her biographical fiction, *The Paris Wife* (2011), Paula McLain has Hadley confront Ernest about the matter, to which he responds rather evasively that he "didn't encourage her."[13] The nature of the relationship between Hem and Katy (nicknamed "Stut" or "Butstein") is a bit complicated for biographers and scholars by the text of a somewhat fragmented story entitled "Summer People," written in 1924 but not published until 1972 in Philip Young's *Ernest Hemingway: The Nick Adams Stories*. The story is also included in the *Complete Short Stories* (496–503). In this story Nick goes by one of Hemingway's boyhood nicknames, "Wemedge," and Kate goes by her actual name or by "Stut." They consummate their passion in one of Hemingway's most erotic scenes, once again dominated by the neuter pronoun "it": "'I love it, I love it, I love it. Oh, come Wemedge. Please come. Come, come. Please, Wemedge. Please, please, Wemedge.' 'There it is,' Nick said." As if that terse statement were not anticlimactic enough, Nick concludes the story with smug self-satisfaction and banal prayer, followed by the sentence, "Still there wasn't anything you could do, not a thing" (503).

Whether Hemingway retained some sort of boyhood longing for Kate Smith remains speculative at best. His letter of congratulations to Dos on his marriage to her, sent from Madrid and dated September 4, 1929, seems genuine in its sentiments, and the couple became fairly frequent visitors to Ernest and Pauline in Key West. As will be seen hereafter, they show up in several of the appropriations, at least in passing. By the time Ernest and Dos met, Dos Passos, three years his senior, was fairly well known for his controversial antiwar novel, *Three Soldiers* (1921), and he would rapidly define himself as a voice of the literary left through such novels as *Manhattan Transfer* (1925), *The 42nd Parallel* (1930), and *1919* (1932). Hemingway called the latter work "bloody splendid" in a letter of March 26, 1932, even as he advised his friend not to let any "noble communist" into his third book of the portended *USA Trilogy*, which would be completed in 1936 with the publication of *Big Money* (*Selected Letters* 354). Hemingway's disinclination to involve himself wholeheartedly in political and social issues had drawn some adverse criticism during the depression-torn 1930s, and the publication of nonfiction books like his celebration of bullfighting, *Death in the Afternoon* (1932), and his discourse on big game hunting, *Green Hills of Africa* (1934), along with his game fishing articles in the newly founded *Esquire* magazine simply fed the fires.

Nevertheless, Hemingway was hard at work, or perhaps more aptly struggling, with a novel that would voice his contempt for the idle, luxury-driven rich and promote himself as a champion of the everyday working stiff. That *To Have and Have Not* was lacerated by the likes of Bernard DeVoto and Sinclair Lewis may not have mattered so much as the fact that reviewers like Alfred Kazin and Malcolm Cowley saw in it some suggestion of a new alignment.[14] Lewis observed in his review of the "thin, screaming little book" for *Newsweek* that "perhaps" Hemingway could still be "the greatest novelist in America" if he would "stop trying to save Spain and start saving Ernest Hemingway" (*Critical Reception*, 178). In fact, Hemingway was by that date, the middle of October 1937, reporting on the Spanish Civil War for the North America Newspaper Alliance (NANA) in Madrid. In the process, his long friendship with Dos Passos would come to a painful end (see Chapter Four).

Following the breakup of their friendship in 1938, we have little in Hemingway's published letters to suggest any making of amends, despite the statement of his son John ("Jack," "Bumby") in a much later interview that Dos and Katy "came through [Havana] after World War II and Papa was so pleased to see him; they were as happy as bedbugs."[15] In her memoir Mary Welsh Hemingway mentions a brief visit from Dos in August of 1948, noting that "little wit crackled," but "at least Ernest managed to repair some rifts in their friendship from long before."[16] In September 1947 Katy was killed in an automobile accident, with Dos Passos at the wheel. Although Hemingway sent a consolatory telegram as soon as he heard about it, some commentators agree with Bernice Kert in *The Hemingway Women* that "Ernest never forgave Dos for Katy's death."[17] On the other hand, writing from the Finca Vigía on September 17, 1949, Hemingway professed himself "delighted" with the news of Dos Passos' recent marriage to Elizabeth Hamlin, writing "all good luck kid," inviting them to visit, and signing himself "Tu amigo, Ernesto" (*Selected Letters*, 677). In short, it seems unlikely that Dos Passos intended his appropriation of Hemingway to be in any sense vindictive.

The foregoing amounts, perhaps, to all too much backstory for the fairly brief appearances of Ernest Hemingway under the cover name of George Elbert Warner in Dos Passos' novel *Chosen Country* (1951). In Chapter Four of this book I have proposed that Dos quite possibly never recognized himself in *To Have and Have Not*, in what later scholars have perceived as an obvious "caricature," in Richard Gordon, the "tanned-faced, sandy-haired, well-built man" who writes novels on social issues.[18] Dos Passos was by no means either "sandy-haired" (he was bald) or "well-built." Hemingway, however, certainly did see himself as portrayed in George Elbert Warner, as he indicates in a letter from the Finca dated July 29, 1952, to Charles Fenton, who would be his first biographer with *The Apprenticeship of Ernest Hemingway* (1954). Hemingway begins his lengthy letter with the assertion that Fenton's article "contains many inaccuracies." As an "example of the true gen" that Fenton did not "get," Hemingway lashes out sarcastically at "Honest John Dos Passos," who marries his friend Katy Smith and "kills her dead finally when he drives into the back of a truck" (*Selected Letters*, 774, 775). Writing in a state of what seems white-hot fury, Hemingway offers up what he calls the "true gen" on "a novel called *Chosen Country*": "A big part of it is about Michigan and I am one of the more loathsome characters in it. He takes badly remembered anecdotes he heard at *our* table when he was a *guest* [italics added in both cases] and fouls them up a little more.... Dos makes the loathsome character who is supposed to be me in the book then betray Kate, Y.K. [her brother] et al by publishing a photograph and writing a feature story in some Chicago newspaper accusing them of weird sex cult rites" (775–776). Not a fan of either book reviewers or literary scholars, Hemingway urges Fenton to "drop the entire project."

In *Chosen Country*, as in the posthumously published *Century's Ebb* (see Chapter Four), Dos Passos represents himself as the lawyer Jay Pignatelli, like himself the illegitimate son of an amorous liaison. He is apparently eighteen or nineteen when he meets the flirtatious Lulie Harrington (Kate Smith) at a lakeside hotel party, and it is there that we get our first impressions of Doctor Warner's son "Georgie," as Lulie calls him. He is toting a double-barrel shotgun in order to shoot birds in the orchard, despite the law. Lulie/Katy obviously dislikes Doctor Warner, who speaks in "squeaky complaining tones" and whose "two red lips curled cruelly above a scraggly gray beard."[19] When she first sees Georgie she recognizes that his voice has changed, one of several indications that she is older by several years, though she seems quite girlish as Dos Passos portrays her. (Like her friend Hadley Richardson, Kate Smith was nearly eight years older than Hemingway and five years older than Dos Passos.) Lulie/Katy sees Georgie as "a lout," but a "sweet lout," with his hair tousled and a "line of grime round the open neck of his blue shirt" (59). In short, he is hardly more than a boy, and she sees him as wearing a "stagy expression ... when he felt he was being big about something" (60). She even goes so far as to tease him about the infamous porcupine episode that occurred in 1913, according to Marcelline's account, when Ernest would have turned fourteen. "Father had the greatest contempt for so-called sportsmen who killed ruthlessly for the fun of killing or to boast about the size of the bag," she recalls, so Ernest and his pal were compelled to eat their victim (*At the Hemingways*, 81–82).

Georgie talks of wanting to go into the woods and live like the Indians, who, he claims, "are dirty and no account just like me." By the time we are told his parents cannot afford to send him to college and his grades are low, we are perhaps surprised to realize he is as old as seventeen or eighteen. When Lulie invites Georgie, who resents the diminutive version of his name, to go out on the lake with her in her red canoe, we are probably not surprised to find him clumsily tipping them over when, despite her warning, he tries to cast. Georgie's grumbling complaint that "it's no fun going fishing with a girl" accentuates his lack of maturity. Unlike Murphy's adolescent version of Ernest, or of Ernest's characterization of himself in "Summer People," for that matter, Dos Passos' stand-in is by no means ready for his sexual coming-of-age. "We don't count you as a girl," Georgie explains, "You're one of the Tribe" (67). This, we are told, is because she passed the "initiation," which included biting off the head of a live perch (a very small one, she says).

Lulie's date for the dance that evening is Joe Newcomer (probably standing in for Carl Edgar, who had a crush on Katy Smith), a college sophomore she teasingly calls "Decent Respectable." Joe's shy roommate, Jay Pignatelli, comes with him. Jay/John is nervous, wears glasses, sports a prominent Adam's apple, and speaks English with an accent; also like Dos Passos, he is lanky and dances badly (78). As Jay and Lulie dance awkwardly past a window, Lulie notices Georgie and her younger brother Ben (Bill Smith) "jeering" at them; a short time later she sees their "skulking figures disappearing around the corner of the post office" and glimpses Georgie's "scowling face" (80, 81). Georgie's childish behavior reaches something of a climax when he and some pals show up with bandannas tied across their faces as if they were outlaws and he informs Lulie that the "Tribe" does not "allow its women to consort with foreigners." When he points his shotgun at Jay's feet and orders him to "dance," Lulie snatches off the bandanna and scolds him as if he were a child, at which point Georgie shoots out a pole light.

Two summers later Jay is in Harvard Law School, World War I is underway, and Georgie, who spends most of his time talking and fishing, shows no particular signs of maturity. In fact, he once more gets spilled from a boat, this one a sloop with Joe Newcomer at the helm, and he gets his fishing lure hung up on the seat of his pants to boot. Later, Doctor Warner shows up complaining that Georgie has been arrested for shooting out some streetlights in a nearby town. Lulie resists Joe's proposed engagement, and as that chapter ends, about a third of the way through the novel, Georgie and a friend from Montana announce, in terms rather similar to those Ernest used in his letter home (see above), that they are going to enlist in the Canadian army. Georgie then proposes that she marry whichever one of them survives, declaring straight from the pages of a romance novel, "You're the only girl I'd ever want to marry" (143). At that point Jay Pignatelli's story pretty much takes over as he enlists in the ambulance service out of Harvard and sees action on the Western Front, as did Dos Passos. At that point, as well, we might predict Ernest's fury, whether the premise of the biographical fiction were accurate or not. If he had harbored such feelings for Katy Smith in the past, as appears likely, he would have felt betrayed and exposed in Dos Passos' novel.

George Elbert Warner resurfaces in the sixth chapter, about halfway through the novel, as a Marine Corps lieutenant, home from the war, mustache and all. He meets Lulie, still unmarried, on an elevator in the Chicago building where she works (245). His friend Jasper, from Montana, also has survived the war as a Marine captain, and the two men share vague, boyish plans about ranching in the West, but nothing comes of that. Dos Passos may have decided on that branch of the service for his version of Ernest based on Harold Krebs in "Soldier's Home." Confronted with Prohibition and Lulie's brother Zeke's (Y.K. or Kenley Smith) unfortunate marriage to the "snubnosed Mugsie" (Y.K.'s wife Genevieve went by the name "Doodles"), George finds himself wishing he had stayed in the Marines. Lulie tells her aunt that Georgie, now a cub reporter, has "grown up to be the handsomest young man you ever saw" (255). Nevertheless, Lulie sees him too often break into "one of his horrible black scowls" (279), so we recognize that although she does not intend to marry "Decent Respectable," George Elbert Warner will not prove the right man either. Following a picnic that reminds Lulie of happier times, she discovers Mugsie has accidentally shot a man with Zeke's war souvenir Luger. The scene constitutes a fictionalized version of Y.K. Smith's mistress's effort to shoot Doodles in 1924. Y.K.'s mistress missed Doodles, then shot and killed the janitor, after which she poisoned herself (Diliberto, 45, 175). Apparently neither Ernest nor Hadley was at all fond of Doodles. Georgie takes advantage of the juicy news item passed on to him and informs Lulie that he's playing in "a highly competitive game" (304), phrasing that accurately reflects Hemingway's view of writing, whether journalism or fiction.

In the scandal that ensues, Mugsie does her best to smear Zeke, and the newspapers fuel the fire. Georgie, Lulie soon realizes, has "turned out to be a snake" (311). Lulie needs a lawyer, so Joe Newcomer, aka "Decent Respectable," suggests his former roommate, Jay Pignatelli, and the last third of the novel concerns Jay's successful courtship of Lulie. Whether Hemingway was accurate in describing his portrayal by Dos Passos as "loathsome" might be disputed. Georgie is immature and "disagreeable," even ludicrous at times, but perhaps what hurt more was the fact that in this biographical fiction the Hemingway hero, and indeed Ernest himself, or at least his counterpart in the character of George Elbert Warner, is made light of and does not get the girl.

While Michael Murphy's *Hemingsteen* apparently passed by without a review, the publishers managed to acquire blurbs from the likes of Hemingway's "authorized biographer" Carlos Baker, apparently by selective editing, to the effect that it is an "engaging novel" that "comes forward with a subtle and generally believable blend of fact and fiction." Murphy, the Baker blurb declares, is "a renowned journalist." The inside cover flap describes Murphy as an "author-scholar" who has published thirteen other items on Hemingway, but in fact I could track down only the single brief item described above. According to one Helen Scott, not otherwise identified, Murphy's research involved interviewing "more than 200 of Hemingway's contemporaries over a 20-year period" (back inside cover flap). A back-cover blurb was also provided by Nils Hardin, a cofounder of Pulpcon, which dates back to 1972 and which met in Columbus, Ohio, in July of 2013 to celebrate "the history of the pulps."[20] Hardin writes, "Every lyrical paragraph blends facts and invention in a way that vies with Hemingway himself as a master of modern narration, subtle symbolization and economy of style."

Predictably, given that John Dos Passos would likely make almost any list of the top dozen or so writers of fiction in the U.S. between 1920 and 1950, the reviews of *Chosen Country* were fairly numerous, though uneven. An anonymous reviewer for *Time* found little to recommend it, but Arthur Mizener, writing in the *New York Times Book Review*, declared it "might well be John Dos Passos' best novel," asserting that "all the gifts which produced *Manhattan Transfer* and *U.S.A.* are as alive as they ever were."[21] In his generous review, Mizener claims to detect "new power and integrity" in the novel because Dos Passos "sees what he knows with a new and more human understanding." Charles J. Rolo, however, reviewing the book for *Atlantic*, found it "a greater success" than the other three novels since Dos Passos' shift to the right politically, but he was "continually reminded of the far greater power of *U.S.A.*" Rolo suggests that in his "maturity" Dos Passos "lacks the passion of his earlier revolt."[22]

The extent to which Hemingway may be said to have "appropriated" himself in his fiction, most notably in such characters as Nick Adams and Thomas Hudson in the posthumously published *Islands in the Stream* (1970), is related to my study at least tangentially. Some biographers and memoirists, and many writers of biographical fiction, have committed themselves to the quest for connections between his biography and his fiction. Did young Ernest, perhaps no older than ten, actually witness a primitive caesarean on an Indian woman as we encounter the event in "Indian Camp," the lead story of *In Our Time* (1925)? Marcelline writes: "Daddy let Ernie help him when he treated the Ottawa Indians up the lake. Once I remember it was a gunshot wound that Ernie watched being cleaned out.... Later, Ernie watched an operation" (134). Perhaps one should go no further than to hypothesize that such experiences most likely influenced that story, just as his would-be romance with the nurse Agnes von Kurowsky influenced "A Very Short Story" and *A Farewell to Arms*. Observing how congenial her brother could be and how, like their father, "he had a rare talent for friendship," Marcelline adds that he "soaked up other people's experiences like a blotter, and later he sometimes gave them out as his own." This was true specifically of the Nick Adams stories, she adds, many of which were based "on the experiences of a fellow reporter on the *Kansas City Star*" (156).

Certainly, Michael Murphy's novel is the product of a devoted fan, and that would be obvious irrespective of Helen Scott's information on the extensive research he invested in the project. Just as certainly, John Dos Passos' novel is not the product of a fan, but neither should it be described as the work of an anti-fan. (One feels inclined to coin a neologism like "fanemy," as in the response to the guard who challenges, "Who goes there? Fan or fanemy?") In his "informal memoir," published in 1966 as *The Best Times*, Dos Passos reflects warmly on the 1920s and early 1930s, concluding before the painful events of the Spanish Civil War in 1937 and 1938. In some of his comments one can detect some features of George Elbert Warner: "Certainly in his younger days, for all his moods and changing fancies, he had an invigorating effect on every one he went around with.... He was a moody kind of fellow even then. Sorry for himself."[23] George's inclination to be self-pitying may have been what rankled Hemingway most of all. On the other hand, reflecting on how he helped Hemingway scrape together the funds to purchase Joan Miró's painting *The Farm* (1922), Dos writes, "Whether it was politics or literary work or painting he would take the guff out of a situation with a wellplaced [sic] fourletter [sic] word" (144). In his observations on the publication of *Torrents of Spring*, which Dos found "really funny" in places but needlessly offensive to Sherwood Anderson, Dos Passos wonders whether the book was "just a heartless boy's prank" (158), and here he comes close to describing his version of young Ernest Hemingway under the assigned name of Georgie Warner. One might argue that Dos Passos is more or less exculpating his former friend, five years dead by the time the memoir was published, or else that he was being rather cleverly condescending.

Some of the "best times," Dos Passos writes in his memoir, were those spent in Key West with Ernest and Pauline. In that context he describes his first meeting with his wife-to-be Kate Smith, and he briefly defines how her character in *Chosen Country*, Lulie Harrington, thinks of Georgie: "She called Hem Wemmage and treated him affectionately-condescendingly as a girl does her younger brother" (200). Looking back at events from a perspective of some thirty years, Dos Passos concludes "things got rocky between Ernest and me more often than they used to," but he offers that this "may have been as much my fault as his." This pertains to their relationship prior to the civil war in Spain (see Chapter Four). Together with Katy it could be said that Dos thought it important to keep Hemingway from becoming too much a fan of himself: "The famous author, the great sportsfisherman, the mighty African hunter: we tried to keep him kidded down to size" (219). They would fail in that endeavor.

Joli Jenson concludes her essay on the problems connected with viewing fandom as deviant behavior with a statement obviously relevant to this study: "Thinking well [instead of derisively] about fans and fandom can help us think more fully and respectfully about what it means today to be alive and human."[24] But what happens, we might ask ourselves, if the "other" one is obsessed with is in fact oneself? Such an impulse might be described as a form of egotism, a character or personality trait ascribed to Hemingway often enough. In fact, one might readily list a hundred such "character traits" or "personal characteristics" from those indexed in the many biographies of Ernest Hemingway. Denis Brian indexes more than fifty drawn from his interviews with Hem's relatives and acquaintances in *The True Gen* (1988), including "egotism" and "emotional honesty (genuineness)," "insecurity," "kindness and generosity," "modesty," "shyness" and "aggressiveness" (353). Take your pick, one is tempted to say. At the head of such lists should always be "complexity," but the traits would certainly include competitiveness, charisma or magnetism or personal charm, and masculinity or machismo or chauvinism. Moreover, for nearly every trait, one might propose an equal but opposite counter-trait.

Was Hemingway more than typically narcissistic? This question assumes that some degree of narcissism is universal in the human personality. Burness E. Moore, among others who have investigated the subject in recent years, has cautioned against the tendency to use the term "narcissism" too casually for "narcissistic disorder," which pertains to pathological as opposed to normal, if not universal, narcissistic impulses.[25] Until he was almost sixteen Ernest was the only boy in a family of four sisters, and both of his parents doted on him. Outgoing (particularly with his male friends), good-looking, athletic, witty, a talented writer even in his high school days (albeit not noticeably "gifted" at that time), Ernest was popular as a teenager, and he returned from the Great War as something of a hero, even if that heroism was somewhat of his own making. Hemingway was perhaps not a particularly good athlete, but he was "athletic." According to biographer Peter Griffin, Ernest barely managed to qualify for a varsity football letter, and his "token event" on the varsity swimming team was "plunging: diving from poolside and floating along as far as possible without coming up for air."[26] He was probably more adept with his cello in the school orchestra than he was with a football on the gridiron.

Hemingway's letters show him to have been extraordinarily self-absorbed, and he was all his life given to exaggerating his achievements. But he was an avid reader and was blessed (or cursed) with a writer's vivid imagination and propensity to fantasize. He was hypersensitive to insults and to criticism of both his writing and his behavior. He elicited always a great need to be admired; indeed, he demanded admiration. Yet he could discard friends quite abruptly at times and on apparently slight provocation. He tended always to be the center of attention and to dominate conversation. These traits, carried to an extreme, typify those often associated with narcissistic disorder or pathological narcissism.

Without delving at all deeply into the psychology of narcissism, one might at least hypothesize that at issue is whether what Reuben Fine and other psychologists describe as "healthy" or "pathological" narcissism pertains here.[27] One might propose in Hemingway's case that while his youthful narcissism was healthy enough, it evolved or deteriorated toward pathology, or toward the self-loathing that culminated in his suicide. To oversimplify the matter, if the narcissistic manifestations or symptoms become so severe that the individual's capacity to deal with reality is compromised, then the narcissism may tend toward psychotic or schizophrenic behavior, and therefore threaten the self. Burness Moore believes narcissism "should be considered pathological only when, in a qualitative or quantitative way, it seriously interferes with affective stability, reality testing, adaptation, and harmonious relations between the self and objects in particular" (248). Typically, the diagnostic features of narcissism begin with megalomania or a "grandiose sense of self-importance," which is particularly problematic if that sense is not supported by commensurate talent and achievements[28] (*Diagnostic and Statistical Manual*). So where's the problem, one might be inclined to ask, given Hemingway's considerable talent and achievement? The answer might be that what was a healthy enough narcissism when Hem was twenty or forty might have become pathological by the time he was in his fifties and his achievements had declined.

The etiology of narcissism is apparently not well understood at present, but most analysts connect it with parental problems, either unempathic parents or overindulgent or doting parents. Significantly, perhaps, with particular relevance to Hemingway, Fine observes, "healthy narcissism is an outgrowth of a loving relationship with the mother" (79). Ernest Hemingway's detestation of his mother is little short of legendary, and John Dos Passos says it about as succinctly as anyone: "Hem was the only man I ever knew who really hated his mother" (*Best Times*, 210). But then one might counter that, after all, the matter of narcissism is not so much individual as it is social or cultural. James Joyce's Gabriel Conroy in "The Dead" (1914) perceptively describes his times as a "thought-tormented age." Perhaps ours is more likely to be viewed as a "personality-tormented" or even a "fame-tormented" age, an age fit enough then for fanatics, or fans. It has been said that the mythical figure of Odysseus has been replaced by that of Narcissus in the contemporary United States.[29]

And what if one does become a fan of oneself? Well, then, as some reviewers and critics would observe in 1950, the fan of his own achievement, if he happens to be a writer, risks self-parody in the form of a novel like *Across the River and into the Trees*. Numerous book reviewers responded in terms similar to those of Philip Rahv: "This novel reads like a parody by the author of his own manner—a parody so biting that it virtually destroys the mixed social and literary legend of Hemingway that has now endured for nearly three decades" (*Critical Reception*, 319). Fortunately for that legend, *The Old Man and the Sea* appeared two years later. On the positive side with respect to *Across the River and into the Trees*, E.B. White would find in that much maligned novel the inspiration for a delightful parody entitled "Across the Street and into the Grill," published in the *New Yorker* on October 14, 1950. A single sentence should illustrate White's achievement here: "'Schrafft's is a good place and we're having fun and I love you,' Pirnie said."[30] From a certain perspective, of course, this sort of send-up also amounts to a kind of appropriation, for if Hemingway's protagonist Colonel Richard Cantwell is a self-appropriation of sorts, then White's Mr. Pirnie is an appropriation at one remove: he is Pirnie-as-Cantwell-as Hemingway. And E.B. White's name may be added to the list of the writers of fan fiction, or, perhaps one might argue, of fanemy fiction.

Three

Hemingway Makes the Twenties Roar

How fine it must have been, how energizing, how downright inspirational for a young writer and his bride to be in Paris in the early 1920s. Ernest and Hadley arrived in Paris on December 20, 1921. James Joyce's controversial epic *Ulysses*, which had been serialized between March of 1918 and December of 1920 in *Little Review*, would be published in February of 1922. D.H. Lawrence's novella *The Fox* would appear later that year in *Dial*. E.M. Forster's *A Passage to India* would appear in 1924. F. Scott Fitzgerald's *The Great Gatsby*, Theodore Dreiser's *An American Tragedy*, and John Dos Passos' *Manhattan Transfer* would constitute a sort of triumvirate of American literary masterpieces in 1925. And that would bring them only to the middle of the decade, by which time Ernest's first full-length book of short stories, *In Our Time*, was attracting reviews any established author would have been glad to receive. In all likelihood, given the epistolary record and indefatigable reader that he was, Hemingway read all of these titles. In a note to Scott Fitzgerald dated January 5, 1930, Ernest writes that he hopes reading Robert Graves makes him "glad you missed the war!"—Graves' autobiographical novel *Goodbye to All That* had appeared in 1929. Hemingway notes dismissively, "Have read Lady Chatt—It didn't hold me" (*Selected Letters*, 320).

Regarded from the perspective of nearly ninety years, the reviews of *In Our Time* read as almost startlingly perceptive, initiating a critical dialogue or discourse that remains pertinent today. "Ernest Hemingway has a lean, pleasant, tough resilience," began the anonymous reviewer for the *New York Times Book Review*. "His language is fibrous and athletic, colloquial and fresh, hard and clean; his very prose seems to have an organic being of its own" (*Critical*

Reception, 7). "Mr. Hemingway packs a whole character into a phrase," the reviewer continues, "an entire situation into a sentence or two. He makes each word count three or four ways." Paul Rosenfeld, writing for *New Republic*, began with the following: "Hemingway's short stories belong with cubist painting, Le Sacre du Printemps, and other recent work bringing a feeling of positive forces through primitive modern idiom. [...] Emphatic, short, declarative sentences follow staunchly one upon the other, never precipitously or congestedly or mechanically, and never relenting" (*Critical Reception* 9). "The short sentences bite like acid," declared Schuyler Ashley for the *Kansas City Star*, where Ernest had written as a cub reporter just seven years earlier. "The infrequent expletives snarl and rumble like loaded trucks under a viaduct" (*Critical Reception*, 10).

It is important that we revisit these early reactions to Hemingway's prose, because we are possibly in danger of forgetting how momentous it was, how great his stylistic impact, how much he was perceived as a pioneer, an innovator in prose in his day. No wonder, we might reflect, he attracted the attention of such writers as Fitzgerald and Dos Passos. And when he capped this achievement the very next year with *The Sun Also Rises*, which some still regard as a major contender for the mythical title of The Great American Novel, he immediately became a star. And he had always wanted to be a star. Coincidentally, William Carlos Williams, already a well-known poet, had in 1923 published a novella by that very title, *The Great American Novel*, a satire overshadowed by the volume of his poems which also appeared that year, *Spring and All*. In October of 1926, when *The Sun Also Rises* was published to great acclaim, not including that of his mother, who described it as "one of the filthiest books of the year" (Baker, 180), Ernest was 27 years old, the father of a three-year-old son, and a man on the brink of ending his five-year marriage to Hadley. In addition to *Torrents of Spring*, the satiric novella that also appeared in 1926, and a half dozen stories appearing in magazines after the publication of *In Our Time*, he would turn out the stories of *Men Without Women* in 1927. Hemingway would wrap up the decade with one of his other most significant novels, *A Farewell to Arms*, in 1929, but that would be written from another country, in Key West, Florida, and under the influence of his new muse, Pauline Pfeiffer Hemingway.

All of this literary history represents only a portion of Hemingway's "work," as he calls it persistently throughout the pages of his memoir of the early years in Paris, *A Moveable Feast*, published posthumously in 1964 with a "restored edition" in 2009.[1] In 1924 Ernest also wrote the story "Summer People" mentioned in Chapter Two and by then had written other stories and a portion of a novel lost by Hadley in December of 1922. These manuscripts that Hadley took with her on a visit to Ernest, who was in Lausanne, Switzerland, covering a peace conference, were stolen from her compartment on the train and have generated more biographical fiction of a wider variety than any other single event in Hemingway's life. If that episode does not involve the most important mystery-gap available to appropriators and followers of fan fiction, it does at least constitute what one might describe as the most intriguing one. I shall return to this in considerably more detail hereafter. So far as the 1920s are concerned, Hemingway's perspective on the decade includes not only the fiction and memoir mentioned above, and several poems and numerous journalistic pieces, most of them collected in *Dateline: Toronto* (1985), but also *The Garden of Eden*, written in the late 1940s and published posthumously in 1986 in a heavily cut and edited and therefore very controversial form. Events in that novel apparently occur mostly in 1923. One might even go so far as to include the 1936 short story "The Snows of Kilimanjaro" because of its flashbacks to the decade of the Twenties.

A bit of backstory is necessary to fill in the spaces between the fictional appropriations of Ernest the adolescent as represented in the previous chapter and Ernest the young man of the 1920s. Following his return to Oak Park in 1919, more than two months after the armistice ended the First World War, Hemingway lingered a while—"loitered," his mother might have said. He posed as war hero, embellishing his stories in the manner of Harold Krebs, the troubled veteran of "Soldier's Home," in public talks. In March of 1919 Agnes von Kurowsky, the nurse with whom he had become infatuated, wrote him the letter that crushed him: "I know that I am still very fond of you, but, it is more as a mother than a sweetheart."[2] This "Dear John" missive followed at least fifty letters from Agnes to Ernest that are included in *Hemingway in Love and War: The Lost Diary of Agnes von Kurowsky* (1996). Unfortunately, Ernest's letters to Agnes were destroyed by one of her subsequent lovers. While many of her letters to him open with the salutation "Dear Kid," a number also begin with such greetings as "Ernie dearest" or "Best beloved," and as Henry S. Villard observes in his introductory note, "the letters pour out a veritable torrent of loving solicitude" (91). The, at least momentarily, heartbroken veteran spent the summer of 1919 at Walloon Lake writing, or trying to write. Between January and April of 1920 he was doing some freelance writing for the *Toronto Star*.

Ernest summered again at Walloon Lake, turning twenty-one on July 21, 1920, and in that context he received a letter from his mother that Kenneth Lynn describes as "a rejection slip with a vengeance" (117). The immediate occasion of the letter was a secret midnight rendezvous at the lake that included Ernest and his friend Ted Brumback, four years his senior and a fellow veteran ambulance driver on the Italian front, Ernest's sisters Ursula and Sunny, and four neighbors, who appear to have been the instigators of the incident. Biographers generally have observed that the event provided the spark to light Grace Hemingway's already smoldering fuse. The letter runs more than eight hundred words and begins as follows: "For three years, since you decided, at the age of eighteen years, that you did not need any further advice or guidance from your parents, I have tried to keep silence and let you work out your own salvation." Quoted in full in Lynn's biography and elsewhere, the letter is dated July 24 and was hand-delivered by Grace three days after that. The second paragraph begins with an analogy that was to become the controlling metaphor or conceit for the entire screed: "A mother's love seems to me like a bank. Each child that is born to her, enters the world with a large and prosperous bank account, seemingly inexhaustible." As Ernest would soon realize, the key word here would be "seemingly." "Up to adolescence," Grace writes, that account is "heavily drawn upon," and there are only a few "deposits of pennies, in the way of services willingly done, some thoughtfulness and 'thank yous.'" With the account "perilously low" as adolescence passes, the mother-bank finds itself still paying out, and the account "needs some deposits, by this time, some good sized ones in the way of gratitude and appreciation" (Lynn, 117). Many mothers she knows of are receiving such recompense, but not she, so, "unless you, my son, Ernest, come to yourself, cease your lazy loafing, and pleasure seeking—borrowing with no thought of returning—stop trying to graft a living off anybody and everybody—spending all your earnings lavishly and wastefully on luxuries for yourself—stop trading on your handsome face, to fool little gullible girls, and neglecting your duties to God and your Saviour Jesus Christ—unless, in other words, you come into your manhood—there is nothing before you but bankruptcy: *You have over drawn*" (118). The letter goes on for another three of four paragraphs.

Ernest promptly moved to a boardinghouse about seven miles away in Boyne City and embarked on a therapeutic fishing and camping trip with three buddies and his pal Ted (Brummy), who had also been exiled from the family lake cottage "Windemere" (Hem's mother spelled it without the usual medial r). In a letter dated August 8 to his friend Grace Quinlan, seven years his junior (so she would then have been about fourteen), Ernest explains that he and Ted "were dragged along [to the infamous midnight party at the lake] and really acted as chaperones!" He complains that he and Ted were given no chance to explain themselves and insists "Mother was glad of an excuse to oust me as she has more or less hated me ever since I opposed her throwing two or three thousand seeds [dollars] away to build a new cottage for herself when the Jack [cash] should have sent the kids to college" (*Letters*, 238). Certainly, Ernest does not appear at all contrite: "Am so damned disgusted I dont [*sic*] care to have anything more to do with them for a year at least" (239). His next extant letter to his mother, however, is dated just two months later (October 8, 1920), mentions having seen his father a couple of times, and expresses no ill feelings over the affair. Later that month he would be living in Chicago, writing for a Midwest farm journal, and being introduced to his wife-to-be Hadley Richardson. They would marry the next year, September 3, 1921, at Horton Bay, Michigan, not far from Walloon Lake. They would spend their two-week honeymoon at Windemere. The most frequently reproduced wedding photograph shows Grace smiling approvingly on the couple to her right and looking "motherly and overheated in a long flowered dress with a tasseled cord at the waist" (Baker, 81).

At this point, or slightly before it, the appropriations by what Lisa A. Lewis calls "The Adoring Audience," the fans, might be said to take over the narrative. In effect, the writers of biographical fiction are attempting to pre-empt, or perhaps simply to supplement, the territory of the biographers, who speak for what John Fiske in his essay "The Cultural Economy of Fandom" refers to as "official culture."[3] "Fandom," Fiske writes, "is typically associated with cultural forms that the dominant value system denigrates.... It is thus associated with the cultural tastes of subordinated formations of the people, particularly with those disempowered by any combination of gender, age, class and race" (30). Like the economic system, the "cultural system promotes and privileges certain cultural tastes and competences, particularly through the educational system, but also through other institutions such as art galleries, concert halls, museums, and state subsidies to the arts, which taken together constitute a 'high' culture." This "socially and institutionally legitimated" culture Fiske calls "official," as distinct from "popular culture which receives no social legitimation or institutional support.... Cultural capital thus works hand in hand with economic capital to produce social privilege and distinction" (31). "Fandom," Fiske suggests, "is a peculiar mix of cultural determinations. On the one hand it is an intensification of popular culture which is formed outside and often against official culture, on the other it expropriates and reworks certain values and characteristics of that official culture to which it is opposed" (34). Fiske describes the relationship between fan and official cultural capital as complex and "often contradictory": "at times fans wish to distance themselves from the official culture, at other times, to align themselves with it" (42).

This sometimes awkward relationship between official and popular culture, or what some would call highbrow and lowbrow, might be said almost to define the nature of biographical fiction in general. In writing a novel that incorporates Hemingway as a character (or Beethoven or Michelangelo or Dante), the author connects himself, for various reasons or motives, to official or highbrow culture, even though he must be aware that the resulting text will not likely be welcomed into the canon of the official culture. It could be argued, I think, that biographical fiction tends by its nature to mediate (albeit not inevitably) between highbrow and lowbrow, between official culture and popular culture. In this respect, Hemingway's fiction, and his professed attitude toward official culture, is particularly apposite. On numerous occasions he assumed a pugnacious stance toward canonical writers, playfully offering to punch them out, even though he insisted upon the necessity of reading them (including the novels of Henry James), as he informs Arnold Morse Samuelson, the young man he calls the Maestro ("Mice" for short) in an essay published in *Esquire* for October 1935.[4] Hemingway's message, delivered with playful pontification that perhaps too many have taken too seriously, is that "otherwise [the writer] doesn't know what he has to beat."[5] Obviously, Hemingway had every intention of joining the canonical ranks of the authors he bested, but his style here, and in his fiction, and in the way he lived just as obviously courted a popular readership.

In a frequently cited letter to Charles Scribner dated September 7, 1949, mentioned in Chapter One, Hemingway declares himself "a man without any ambition, except to be champion of the world" (*Selected Letters*, 673). To Faulkner in a letter dated July 23, 1947, and cited less often he wrote, "You are better than Fielding or any of those guys and you should just know it and keep on writing. [...] Why do you want to fight Dostoevsky in your first fight? Beat Turgenieff—which we both did soundly [...] Then nail yourself DeMaupassant," and so on with reference to Stendhal and Flaubert (*Selected Letters*, 624). In phrasing that sounds very 21st century, Hem adds near the end, "Anyway I am your Bro. if you want one that writes and I'd like to keep in touch" (625). Part of the appeal here comes in Hemingway's use of the vernacular, the speech of popular culture and fiction, one might say. Throughout his life, although he was obviously attracted to the lifestyles of the rich and famous, Hemingway championed the working classes. The novel *To Have and Have Not* offers only the most obvious example of his disesteem for the wealthy and the intellectual elite and his respect for the blue collar world. Nick Adams will not grow up to be a doctor, a lawyer, or a Babbitt. "My sympathies are always for exploited working people against absentee landlords," he wrote to the novelist Harry

Sylvester from Key West on February 5, 1937, "even if I drink with the landlords and shoot pigeons with them. I would as soon shoot them as the pigeons" (*Selected Letters*, 456). The marriage that connected him with Pauline's patrician family and her wealthy Uncle Gus Pfeiffer may have put him in the company of the landlords, but Ernest never felt fully at ease in the world of the wealthy or of the culturally elite. From a certain critical perspective it is not so surprising that Hemingway developed a popular following from the outset. What is surprising is how much he acquired and sustained in the way of "cultural capital" with the "official culture."

At least six novels of varying stature have featured Ernest Hemingway prominently, even if not as the protagonist, as he was in Paris during the 1920s: Vincent Cosgrove's *The Hemingway Papers* (1983), Howard Engel's *Murder in Montparnasse* (1992), Tony Hays' *Murder in the Latin Quarter* (1993), Clancy Carlile's *The Paris Pilgrims* (1999), Craig McDonald's *One True Sentence* (2011), and Paula McLain's *The Paris Wife* (2011). Hemingway also makes an important cameo appearance in Walter Satterthwait's *Masquerade* (1998). The account of Ernest in Paris also dominates the first third of Christopher Cook Gilmore's novel *Hemingway* (1988), which appeared as a TV miniseries that year starring Stacy Keach as Ernest. Reviewing the film for the *New York Times*, John J. O'Connor described it as "a lavish, six-hour film biography ... a thoroughly serious and generally intelligent effort to capture the essence of the man and the writer."[6] Gilmore's novel is essentially a version of German writer and director Bernhard Sinkel's film script. Although he concedes the film "fails as often as it succeeds," O'Connor commends its "wonderful sense of place and time," Wolfgang Treu's photography for being "dazzlingly on the mark," and Keach's capacity to sculpt a Hemingway that lays bare "the considerable flaws while retaining an edge of sympathy." O'Connor allows as how "in this age of women's liberation, and men's enlightenment, Hemingway does not, indeed cannot, emerge as the most likely of role models." One can only wonder how Hem might have responded to such a premise: Ernest Hemingway as "role model."

Hemingway left his own versions of Paris embedded in his stories and novels, and most directly in his memoir *A Moveable Feast*, which like most books in that genre play it loose with the facts, adhering more to the emotional than to the literal truth. Presumably, that is what endears them to us. If writers of their own life narrative opt for greater objectivity, they tend toward autobiography. The memoir has just enough of that supposedly reliable nonfiction to convince us that we aren't reading a novel: these events really happened. But we are not expected to suppose the events and dialogue happened exactly as stated. Hemingway's posthumously published memoir of the 1953–54 African safari, *True at First Light* (1999), was subtitled "A Fictional Memoir." Some students of the subgenre might regard that subtitle as redundant: if "memoir," then of *course* "fictional."

Paula McLain's *The Paris Wife* is written from Hadley's point of view, and from the first pages it reads rather convincingly as if it were a memoir. So perhaps one is not surprised to learn she has also written a memoir, *Like Family: Growing Up in Other People's Houses* (2003). McLain, who is also the author of two books of poetry, went on to receive her MFA from the University of Michigan in 1996. Her other credits include the 2008 novel *A Ticket to Ride*.

The "credentials," so to speak, of the authors of biographical fiction vary as widely as do those of any set of novelists and short story writers. McLain's might be said to suggest those of writers whose work represents what John Fiske labels "official culture." More commonly the writers of these appropriations have been, or are, journalists, and a good number of them have made some reputation as writers of so-called genre fiction like crime or detective novels. All of these writers have based their fiction on research, some of it quite extensive, but in writing of Hemingway's Paris, or more accurately "the Hemingways' Paris" or "Hadley's Paris," Paula McLain had access to an exceptional body of materials because biographers have been particularly curious about Hadley Richardson Hemingway. In addition to her appearance in *A Moveable Feast*, which is widely regarded as Hemingway's tribute to Hadley, she is featured prominently in the interviews conducted by Denis Brian for *The True Gen* (1988) and in Bernice Kert's *The Hemingway Women* (1983), and she is the subject of two biographies, Alice Hunt Sokoloff's *Hadley: The First Mrs. Hemingway* (1971) and Gioia Diliberto's *Paris Without End: The True Story of Hemingway's First Wife* (1992, 2011). Hadley, who remarried in 1933, died in 1979 at the age of 87. McLain lists an impressive array of sources at the end of her novel, including the Hemingway Collection archived at the John F. Kennedy Library in Boston.

"Though I often looked for one, I finally had to admit that there could be no cure for Paris." So begins Paula McLain's best-selling novel, perhaps playing off Hemingway's observation near the end of *A Moveable Feast*: "There is never any ending to Paris."[7] McLain's novel has been translated into at least a dozen languages (including Serbian and Hebrew) and widely adopted by book clubs, and has made its author the subject of more than half a dozen interviews, including one featured in *Hemingway Review*. The latter point brings up a curious issue: Does this novel have something that might make it other than the fan-fare of popular culture? Academe tends to marginalize a great deal when it comes to contemporary writing—that's more or less the role of English professors as critics and scholars. Traditionally, English professors have rallied to the canon (see Chapter One), but one significant feature of the postmodern era has been an assault on the canon for various reasons (too male, too white, too deceased) and a concomitant opening up thereof. Axiomatically, what the academy does not choose to marginalize, or cannot, it "contains."

Does inclusion of an interview with Paula McLain in *Hemingway Review* constitute some sort of elevation into the official culture by at least some forces representing the academy? Perhaps not, if we are to accept the comments of reviewers for the *New York Times*. Janet Maslin finds McLain's Hadley to lack subtlety: "She's thick, and not just in physique. She's slow on the uptake, and she can be a stodgy bore."[8] The first third of the novel, Maslin complains, "moves ploddingly." Maslin also objects to "clumsy foreshadowing." While she concedes that "what it lacks in style is made up for in staying power," she condemns the book as "a work of literary tourism that expertly flatters its readers." But, after all, few readers are entirely immune to flattery. Brenda Wineapple writing a few weeks later for the *New York Times Book Review* finds "the reconstruction of Hadley's youth" in the first thirty or so pages to be "livelier and fresher" than most of the novel, but she objects to what she sees as Hadley's "cloying naiveté" early on and to her "passive aggression" later.[9] Wineapple finds Hadley reduced to the status of "a Hemingway character manqué," in fact, to Jake Barnes's "female counterpart ... symbolically impotent and resolutely unmodern." Hadley, she concludes, "rarely emerges from her wistful cocoon" and "is hardly more than a stereotype, alas, caught in a world of her own making." Writing for the *Los Angeles Times*, Susan Salter Reynolds treats the novel even more rudely: "The problem with this book-length swoon is that writer and reader overlook cliché after cliché, pedestrian writing and overpowering sentiment. [...] Hadley, who was by all accounts, her own woman, ends up as spineless and simpering as a character can be outside an out-and-out bodice-ripper."[10] Reynolds regards the novel as "a Hallmark version" of the Paris years.

Predictably, Paula McLain's responses in interviews offer a very different impression of what she intended and believes she achieved with *The Paris Wife*. In her interview with McLain in *Hemingway Review*, Hemingway scholar Gail Sinclair indicates that the novel spent thirty weeks on the *New York Times Best Sellers* list.[11] Noting the fortuitous synchronicity of her novel with Woody Allen's film *Midnight in Paris*, featuring Corey Stoll as a clownish Hemingway who speaks in the same terse sentence patterns in which he writes, McLain proposes two reasons for its popularity: "we are all nostalgists" and "people like historical fiction because there are teaching moments, and they get a little history lesson along the way" (120). She doubtless speaks for many writers of biographical fiction when she observes, "The places I wanted to go no biographer would ever presume to go, and I wanted to have the freedom to imaginatively access their [Hadley's and Ernest's] interior worlds." Sinclair suggests McLain has taken considerable "artistic license" in the process, to which McLain responds by drawing attention to the scene in which Hadley reflects on how things will change when she tells Ernest they are going to have a baby (*The Paris Wife*, 145–147), indicating what is clear to any Hemingway aficionado, that she took that "moment" or "frame" from the story "The Cat in the Rain" (*Complete Short Stories*, 129–131). In an online interview with Fifi Flowers, McLain describes her writing style as "poetic," reflecting her lifelong love of language, of "beautiful words, a well-made sentence, and a particularly memorable image."[12]

Of course the book reviews of *The Paris Wife* were by no means uniformly negative. Reflecting on the reviews published in the *New York Times* and in the *Los Angeles Times*, Donna Rifkind, writing for the *Washington Post*, asks, "So who's right: enthusiastic book-buying audiences or unsympathetic critics?"[13] She concludes, "score one for the consumers," finding the novel "a richer and more provocative book than many reviewers have acknowledged." Admirers of popular culture and fan fiction would agree. As of this writing (November 2014) there are 1,921 Amazon.com reader reviews of the novel, 949 of which award it five of a possible five stars, an overall 4.2 rating. "For what that's worth," some academicians might sniff. Stephanie Deutsch, writing for the *Washington Times*, considers one of the "strengths" of the novel to be "its willingness to grapple with emotional complexity."[14] She regards it as "a tribute to the writer's ability that the reader's sympathies shift back and forth between the two parties. Both contribute to the mounting tension between them, though by the end of the marriage most readers are likely to have taken sides (and not with him)."

In the interview with Gail Sinclair, McLain responds to Janet Maslin's criticism of her portrayal of Hadley, insisting she "liked her [Hadley's] point of view, passive though it might be. [...] I like that she wrestled with how she was failing herself, too" (121). In effect, McLain is defending her decision not to manipulate or torque the historical person she takes Hadley to have been, and in that respect she reveals her choice not to "take liberties," as Sinclair puts it. Such "liberties," as will become apparent hereafter, might be described as the heart and soul of most of the appropriations of Ernest Hemingway.

Commenting on a Canadian reviewer who took her to task for not exploiting the lost manuscripts episode in order to present Hadley as a "saboteur" or a bitter feminist consciously attempting to undermine the career of her neglectful husband, as Clancy Carlile had done in *The Paris Pilgrims* (1999), McLain asserts that she thinks such "liberties" would be "obnoxious" and "opportunistic" (121). (We shall hear much more of the lost manuscripts shortly.) "The real Hadley," she points out in a discussion with Brian A. Klems of *Writers Digest*, "didn't have edge, and certainly not at this point in her life."[15] McLain also responds to her treatment of Ernest Hemingway, which, in an interview conducted by her publishers at Random House, she describes as showing a side of him "we've never seen before—tender, vulnerable, and very human."[16] Sinclair particularly asks about the five italicized chapters (of a total 47 in addition to the prologue and epilogue) in which McLain attempts to "channel" Hemingway by shifting the narrative viewpoint to third person and by imitating his prose style to some extent. Those sections, McLain confesses, "were terrifying to write" (125). And yet, judging by the practice of several appropriators, the impulse to imitate the distinctive Hemingway style proves all but irresistible. How successfully McLain pulls it off relative to others who have tried it, notably MacDonald Harris in *Hemingway's Suitcase* (1990), may be a decision best left to their readers.

Like most writers of the biographical fictions concerning Hemingway, McLain introduces scenes and creates dialogue that anticipates what knowing readers will have encountered in the fiction. Part of the pleasure of fan fiction for the aficionado, after all, is the fan's insider status. When Hadley and Ernest make love for the first time at the end of the eighth chapter, Hadley says, "I'd love to look like you. [...] I'd love to be you," adding, "I'd never said anything truer. I would gladly have climbed out of my skin and into his that night, because I believed that was what love meant" (59)—in effect, the submergence or acquiescence of the self in or to the other. Those familiar with Hemingway's writings will recall such moments as Catherine Barkley's declaration about a third of the way through *A Farewell to Arms*: "There isn't any me. I'm you. Don't make up a separate me."[17] Irrespective of the context, which is of course quite important, this moment in Hemingway's novel—which might be regarded as not merely un- or non- but outright anti-feminist—proves to be a hard sell for many contemporary readers, of both genders. The desire to be one and even to blur gender distinctions also becomes a major motif in the posthumous novel, *The Garden of Eden*, where, from the outset, Catherine Bourne assumes an androgynous stance as both wife and "brother" to her husband, David.

This passage and others like it in *The Paris Wife* might be read variously, perhaps depending on who does the reading. Does McLain's imaginative representation of Hadley's thinking at this point strike us as the trite or cliché sentiment of a Harlequin romance, or does it approach something of the idealized love we encounter in John Donne's poems? The lover's sentiment at the end of "Lovers Infiniteness" is repeated fairly often throughout Donne's "Songs and Sonnets": "But wee will have a way more liberall, / Than changing hearts, to joyne them, so wee shall / Be one, and one anothers All."[18] In "The Extasie," the male speaker, through what he calls an "interinanimation" of the souls in the process of the sexual union, claims a new and "abler" soul will be produced (40). This particular poem has remained something of a crux in the body of Donne's secular poems: is it a clever, highly intellectualized poem of seduction, or is it a celebration of the ideal union in human love, which involves both the body and the soul? One might argue that McLain has nothing quite so abstruse in mind. She merely wishes to speculate on how Hadley might have perceived their relationship, and in the process, she implies that Hadley's view of it might have profoundly affected Ernest's thinking and writing on the subject. Hadley, as McLain defines her, is a thoughtful protagonist. "It would be the hardest lesson of my marriage," Hadley reflects from the perspective of many years (the epilogue jumps to the time of Ernest's suicide in 1961), "discovering the flaw in this thinking" (59).

The Paris Wife, after all, is a love story. In the last of the italicized sections, in which we witness Hemingway trying to come to grips with the dissolution of his marriage and his new life with Pauline, he tries to rationalize his conflicted vision: "He still loved Hadley afterward. He couldn't and wouldn't stop loving her, maybe ever, but she'd killed something in him, too. He'd once felt so anchored and solid and safe with her, but now he wondered if he could ever trust anyone. [...] Pauline was his future. He'd made his promises and was committed to giving her all he had. But if he was honest with himself, he knew he didn't trust her either. That part of love might be lost to him forever" (303). The context of this passage concerns Hadley's loss of his manuscripts in 1922, which Ernest describes here as "the most terrible thing he'd ever lived through," worse even than the near-death experience of his wounding: "his work, that was him. When it was gone he felt entirely empty, like he might simply recede and become air—a hurt place and a feeling around nothingness."

How destructive the lost manuscripts were—how deeply Hemingway felt estranged from Hadley as a result, how much he might have blamed her— remains a bone of contention among readers and scholars. In *A Moveable Feast*, he makes light of the matter and shows considerable empathy for the distraught Hadley, hardly more than a year into their marriage. Given the passage of thirty or so years, perhaps it was easy enough for Ernest to present himself as magnanimous, telling the *Best Short Stories* editor, Edward O'Brien, that "it was probably good for me to lose early work," and more or less diffidently referring to "the things being gone" as he consoled his "suffering" wife (74). At the same time, however, he writes that his statement about the loss of early work being "probably good" was just "all that stuff you fed the troops," and he rather provocatively writes of taking the train for Paris and remembering "what I did in the night after I let myself into the flat and found it was true." What *did* he do, writers of biographical fiction have wondered? What must that lone and anxious train ride to Paris have been like for him? And whatever *did* become of those lost manuscripts? Such gaps call out to the writers of biographical fiction. Appropriators of quite variant inclinations have found this episode too tempting to resist.

In a letter to his mentor and friend Ezra Pound, written less than two months after the fiasco, Hemingway refers to "the loss of my Juvenilia," as if it were not a matter of great moment. But he adds that he "went up to Paris last week and found that Hadley had made the job complete." The phrasing clearly connotes at least a dash of conjugal accusation. He tells Ezra not to advise him that the loss is all to the "good," because "I ain't yet reached that mood. 3 years on the damn stuff" (*Selected Letters*, 77). As I have suggested elsewhere, if his dating of the trip to Paris in this letter were correct, more than a month would have elapsed between the painful announcement of the pages lost on December 2 and his return to Paris in mid–January. Biographer Kenneth Lynn speculates, "Perhaps he got drunk and sought out a whore, or thought about killing himself" (188). J. Gerald Kennedy asserts "Ernest never forgot or entirely forgave" the loss and it "helped doom a relationship soon thereafter complicated by Hadley's pregnancy."[19] Artist Henry (Mike) Strater, in an interview published in *The True Gen* (1988), declares, "He was very upset because it showed how little she valued what he was doing" (41). Reading that statement, one finds oneself wanting to amend—not "valued" but perhaps "understood."

Michael Reynolds opens his book *Hemingway: The Paris Years* (1989) with a dramatic scenario in which Hem takes the express train to Paris, where he has "twelve hours to feel sorry for himself, to find someone to blame for his losses," and he notes that Ernest's passport was stamped December 3, indicating he had immediately returned to Paris via the fast train.[20] Presumably, then, Ernest was assuming an air of nonchalance in his letter to Pound that belied the facts of the matter. That he could not quite put the episode to rest is attested by the often overlooked or disregarded four-chapter fragment of a novel entitled "The Strange Country," included in the *Complete Short Stories*. The editors indicate Hemingway wrote on the piece intermittently between 1946 and 1951 as preliminary work for what would become the posthumously published *Islands in the Stream* (1970). The "strange country" in this case is the Everglades, and the time is the mid–1930s, just before the civil war broke out in Spain in 1936. Roger, the protagonist, is a writer who at one point recalls that his first wife, mother of his son Andrew, "a lovely girl and very beautiful and kind," met him at the Lausanne Conference and lost his manuscripts in transit (646).

The fragment as published ends with that episode as Roger tells Helena (aka "daughter" and "the girl") that when he entered the apartment to find all of his writing was in fact gone, he "felt almost as though [he] could not breathe" (647). He then went into the bedroom, where he lay down and "put a pillow between my legs and my arms around another pillow and lay there very quietly. I had never put a pillow between my legs before and I had never lain with my arms around a pillow but now I needed them very badly" (648). He tells Helena the contents amounted to eleven stories, a novel, and some poems: "I knew that everything I had ever written and everything that I had great confidence in was gone." He was left "in despair" (648). The concierge herself broke into tears when Roger told her of his loss, he tells Helena. Roger decides then to be "practical," and to write "a better novel," though he laments the loss of the stories (650). Various readers have also suggested some connection between the lost valise and Catherine's quite intentional and vindictive burning of David's stories in *The Garden of Eden*.

The novels pertaining to the lost manuscripts range from Vincent Cosgrove's *The Hemingway Papers* (1983) and Clancy Carlile's *The Paris Pilgrims* (1999), in which Hemingway appears as the main or an important character, to such novels as Macdonald Harris's *Hemingway's Suitcase* and Joe Haldeman's science fiction novella *The Hemingway Hoax*, both published in 1990, and Gerhard Köpf's *Papa's Suitcase* (1994) and Diane Gilbert Madsen's *Hunting for Hemingway* (2010). The latter novels will be among those taken up hereafter, as they involve Hemingway-obsessed characters in various ways. Christopher Cook Gilmore's movie novelization, *Hemingway* (1988), may be unique among the biographical fictions dealing with Paris in the Twenties in that it makes no mention of the lost manuscripts.

While *The Paris Wife* comes across as meticulously researched and memoir-like, as mentioned above, Vincent Cosgrove's *The Hemingway Papers* lives up to William White's description of it in his review for *The Hemingway Review* as a "wildly implausible tale."[21] Cosgrove, a retired reporter and editor for the

New York Daily News, now lives in California and runs a blog called "My Hyperbaric Film Festival." His only other book credit is *Tin for Sale: A Crooked Cop's Journey from the NYPD to the Mob*, cowritten with John Manca, who worked as a detective for the New York Police Department in the 1950s and 1960s before he got involved with the mob and lost his badge. Manca served as technical advisor on the Martin Scorsese films *Goodfellas* (1990) and *Casino* (1995). Cosgrove cites a passage from Carlos Baker as one of his epigraphs for the short, fast-paced novel: "Whatever it was he did that December night remained his secret for the rest of his life" (103). Presumably, Ernest did more than hug his pillow.

Unlike such novels as *The Paris Wife* or *The Paris Pilgrims*, *The Hemingway Papers* trades directly on the writer's name and implicitly makes an appeal to the Hemingway buff or aficionado.[22] McLain's and Carlile's novels offer a zeitgeist and rely considerably on a familiar cast of characters: as with most historical fiction, name-dropping is not a vice (despite what some reviewers might insist), but a virtue. Such books are all about run-ins with Gertrude Stein and Alice B. Toklas here, or with Ezra Pound or Zelda and Scott Fitzgerald there. The true insider will recognize the likes of Mike Strater, Robert McAlmon, or Chink Dorman-Smith at once. In fact, Carlile generally identifies his chapters in such a way that readers may feel they are on a first-name basis: "Sylvia," "Hadley," "Ezra." Vincent Cosgrove opens his novel by contriving a clever foreword to establish an aura of authenticity. Introducing himself as an admirer of *A Moveable Feast* curious about the lost suitcase episode, he tells us he has "read every book, researched every possible source" (xii). Even the use of Roman numerals for the foreword (as with Paula McLain's [Hadley's] "Prologue") contributes subtly to the novel's verisimilitude, and of course the writer signs his name to it. Through a connection at the *Daily News*, he gets in touch with a writer named Sara Morgan Hartunian, then in her eighties, who knew Hemingway in Paris during the Twenties and wrote a book about "what Hemingway did that night in Paris" (xxi). After her death a year or so later, she sends the manuscript of the book to Vince Cosgrove, who creates a *Who's Who* entry for her and even adds a rather elaborate biographical note for her at the end of the novel on the same page as his own brief notice.

"He was one of the handsomest men I ever met," the octogenarian tells the fictional Cosgrove, and she calls him "the most talented American writer of this century" and "a genius": "Oh, I know all about his shortcomings—his temper, his pettiness, his vindictiveness. But those paled against his generosity and warmth and wisdom. He was a very special, very gifted man and I thank God I was lucky enough to know him" (xx–xxi). One feels tempted to say that

Ernest could not have phrased it better himself. This sort of eulogy does recur in the appropriations, predictably, along with quite a bit of contumely. Before the novel gets underway, Cosgrove offers up Sara's brief introduction, in which she tells of her first meeting with Hemingway and reports that their "relationship never went beyond friendship ... we never had an affair" (3). At about the time Hadley is reading and admiring the draft of Ernest's latest story, presumably one of the lost manuscripts, Hermann Goering, renowned German air ace in the First World War and Hitler's second in command in later years, is busily kidnapping the Grand Duchess Anastasia, rumored to be the last surviving child of the last Russian czar, Nicholas II, in order to collect ransom money that will help fund the nascent Nazi party. Stories of Anastasia's supposed escape circulated for decades after the entire family was executed in 1918. Readers in 1983 might well have been familiar with the intrigue via the 1956 movie *Anastasia*, starring Ingrid Bergman and Yul Brynner.

It is not my intention to summarize the plot of this action-packed page-turner, but suffice it to say that a Bolshevik steals the wrong bag, which falls into the hands of the Nazis, who briefly kidnap Ernest after he returns to Paris. But Ernest does manage to rough up Goering a bit, and he enjoys a hasty romance with a woman appropriately named Renata, a moniker obviously intended to resonate with aficionados who will recall the name of the young countess from *Across the River and into the Trees* (1950). A spoiler alert may be required at this point: Renata turns out to be Anastasia herself! But in light of the fact that his manuscripts go up in smoke, Ernest can only tell himself, with respect to the bedding of the Grand Duchess of Russia, "Big deal" (190). At the end of the novel, Sara Morgan asks Ernest why he doesn't plan to use the events as the plot of a novel, to which he replies, "I don't want to write a potboiler" (192). So it is that Cosgrove invites the reader to participate in a moment of playful self-mockery.

Pulp fiction or potboiler—and *The Hemingway Papers* may be described as both—such light fictions serve a variety of purposes, and they do not expect to be taken seriously. They are thrillers really, the stuff of romantic escapism. Efforts like Clancy Carlile's in *The Paris Pilgrims* (1999) are more elaborate in several ways. The novel runs more than twice the length of Cosgrove's, and it is the product of more extensive research and a more ambitious conception. Moreover, Carlile (1930–1998) was a considerably more experienced writer. His credits include the novel *Honkytonk Man* (1980), which led to the Clint Eastwood movie of that title two years later, and *Children of the Dust* (1995), which concerns a bounty hunter of mixed African American and Cherokee blood in 1880s Oklahoma Territory. It was made into a TV miniseries in 1995 starring Sidney Poitier. A two-hour DVD was released in 1999 under the title *A Good Day to Die*. (Carlile's *Children of the Dust* should not be mistaken for Louise Lawrence's postapocalyptic novel by the same title, published in 1985.)

Sylvia Beach, proprietor of the renowned Shakespeare and Company bookstore between 1919 and 1941, is granted the distinction of having both the first and the last words in *The Paris Pilgrims*. Hemingway regarded himself as her "best customer" for most of those half dozen years between 1922 and 1928, and he immediately attempts to buffalo Sylvia on that "blustery January day in 1922" with a cock-and-bull story of having had a fling with the Dutch spy Mata Hari, who was executed in October of 1917, and of fighting with the elite Italian shock troops, the Arditi.[23] Beach describes him as "handsome [...] in a rugged, unshaven, masculine way" (2), but being a lesbian, she does not feel romantically drawn to him. What she detects, though, is his irresistible "enthusiasm" and his capacity to "generate excitement in others [...] an excitement that almost made truth irrelevant" (6). Ernest checks out some "heavy" reading—Turgenev's *Fathers and Sons*, Tolstoy's *War and Peace*, and Lawrence's *Sons and Lovers*—and he takes note of her galley proofs for Joyce's *Ulysses*. Hadley, whose viewpoint dominates no fewer than twenty of the 45 chapters, Sylvia sees as "androgynous" and "masculine in appearance" (12). Carlile portrays Hemingway in the next chapter (Hadley's point of view) as "inordinately" interested in lesbianism and reading Havelock Ellis on the subject as he prepares to visit Gertrude Stein (35).

How does Carlile know about Hemingway taking the besotted James Joyce back to his place in a wheelbarrow and other "titillating things," *New York Times* reviewer Christopher Lehman-Haupt asks? "He doesn't, of course. [...] Mr. Carlile has simply drawn on material from memoirs, biographies and fiction focused on Paris in the 1920s and mixed it with his own teeming, sometimes nasty imagination."[24] He observes, understatedly, "The portrait painted of Hemingway here is not pleasant." As Lehman-Haupt notes, Hemingway is portrayed as "a boastful liar, a sadistic bully, a sore loser [...] an unreliable lover [...] a moody, weepy, self-pitying drunk and a bigot and anti–Semitic and hater of male homosexuals." As he points out, the negative aspects of Hemingway's personality and behavior have long been familiar, but "experiencing them so vividly makes you dislike Hemingway intensely by the novel's end." We see little of Ernest's efforts to make himself into the master of modernist prose, and finally, as Lehman-Haupt words it, he "comes off as a blowhard and a creep." Oddly, the reviewer concludes "it's fun to read about these people in the flesh [...] to see them in the framework of their everyday lives." But one does wonder about Carlile's motives with this anti-fan, or what I've elsewhere called "fanemy," fiction, which invites "ignorant and naïve readers to confuse what is known with what Mr. Carlile has made up."

In effect, the novel comes to a lurid climax in Spain in the spring of 1923 when Hemingway drunkenly sodomizes writer and editor Robert McAlmon (1896–1956), who is known to have been bisexual. "He had no conscious desire to be sodomized by Hemingway," Carlile writes, "but he had no will to resist, either" (410). Michael Reynolds describes McAlmon as "a bitchy man" who "was attractive to both men and women" (*Hemingway: The Paris Years*, 106, 107). McAlmon was married as a matter of mutual convenience to wealthy lesbian novelist Winifred Ellerman Bryher, whose resources allowed him to set up as a publisher; it was through McAlmon's small press that Ernest would have his first book ushered into print, *Three Stories and Ten Poems* (1923). The 58-page text was produced in a limited edition of three hundred copies; an unsigned first edition of the book begins at $40,000 today on the rare book market. Reynolds notes that Hemingway was "a man whom homosexuals found attractive," but "there is no evidence that Hemingway found homosexuals attractive, or that he ever encouraged them, but neither did he necessarily rage in the presence of homosexual men" (129). On the other hand, Scott Donaldson asserts that Hemingway's "virulent scorn" for homosexuals and his "contempt for homosexual writers" like Oscar Wilde and André Gide became so strident that he eventually opened himself "to counterattack by psychologically-oriented critics."[25]

The central and most sympathetic character of Carlile's novel, which covers just the first twenty months of their sojourn in Paris, is clearly Hadley, and one might go so far as to argue that the villain of the piece, unlike McLain's *The Paris Wife*, is Ernest. When it comes to the episode concerning the lost suitcase of manuscripts, Carlile has it that Ernest requests Hadley to bring them in order to impress Lincoln Steffens at the Lausanne Conference (213). When Hadley arrives distraught at the train station in Lausanne, Carlile has Ernest quite gratuitously ask her, "For Christ's sake, have you slept with a nigger?" (217). But he does not depict an outraged Ernest. Rather, Hadley is "amazed" to see him "accept the disaster without a word of reproach" (220), and their ardent lovemaking has predictable consequences, as Hadley has forgotten to bring her diaphragm. Lincoln Steffens (1866–1936), then a journalist and writer of some note, speculates that Hadley has been "careless about her husband's work" and has failed to understand his life as a writer. "It was not inconceivable" to Steffens, according to Carlile, "that Hadley had unconsciously arranged for the valise to be stolen" (219). When Hadley announces her pregnancy to Ezra Pound, he speculates that her loss of the manuscripts was "the result of an attempt—perhaps subconscious, perhaps not—to deprive Hem of a literary livelihood and keep him dependent on her trust fund." With the coming child, Hem would be "hooked for sure" (257). Before long we find that Ernest has begun "to connect her pregnancy with the loss of his manuscripts" (261).

Ultimately, neither Ernest nor Hadley comes off very well in Carlile's novel. The pregnant Hadley, for example, is gently seduced by a woman named Renata (the source of that name has been mentioned earlier), and Ernest gets himself clobbered in a boxing match and lies about the results before the novel draws to a close. In one of the more powerful chapters, Ernest, who has complained off and on since the night of the conception about being too young to be a father (see 221, 334), contacts the noted lesbian author Djuna Barnes about abortions. Not long afterwards, Hadley comments in some detail on the story "Out of Season," which annoys her for reasons obvious to those who have read it. At the end of the chapter she informs Ernest she is not going to have an abortion (396).[26] Later, she worries about Ernest's "mythomania," his "refusal to distinguish memory from imagination and fantasy from fact," and whether that might be "a symptom of mental illness" (425). Ernest's response, as Carlile presents it, amounts to one of his more positive moments in the novel: "Sometimes writers lie unconsciously, then remember their lies with remorse, maybe even shame. But mostly a writer is a liar in full flower. [...] That seems to be my criterion for the truth—not what happened, but what could have happened. [...] That's what we writers are for, to improve on the scheme of things, to do what God should have, to make things happen the way they ought to have happened" (426, 427). Such moments in this novel tend to counter the all too frequent portraits of Hemingway as thoughtless, crude, and mean-spirited, and at the same time this one undercuts his frequently proclaimed adherence to expressing the truth in his writing. The result is that we perceive Hemingway as something of a divided self, a person burdened with contradictions, and at that point we may be at odds with ourselves whether to read him as confused or as complex. Significantly, although Carlile assigns Hemingway not a single chapter in this novel, he remains firmly lodged at its core as something of a centripetal force.

No such issue presents itself in two crime novels set in 1920s Paris in which Hemingway plays important roles: Tony Hays's *Murder in the Latin Quarter* (1993) and Craig McDonald's *One True Sentence* (2011). A Tennessee native and world traveler, Hays holds degrees in history, educational psychology, and creative writing from Tennessee Technological University and Texas A&M at Commerce. He is author of ten books, including recent forays into

Arthurian mysteries. *Murder in the Latin Quarter*, billed as a "Who's Who Dunit Mystery," was his second book. Hays's novel covers about one week in the spring of 1922 and opens with the discovery of a body in the back of Sylvia Beach's bookstore. The prime suspect in the murder is none other than James Joyce. The main character is Jack Barnett, a struggling writer and World War I air ace with 21 kills to his credit who suffers from nightmares and other symptoms of what would today be called post-traumatic stress disorder.[27] The similarity of Jack Barnett's name to that of Jake Barnes of *The Sun Also Rises* is not at all coincidental, but his wound is clearly psychological, as he is eventually relieved to discover. Sylvia calls on her writer and artist friends to solve the mystery and exculpate Joyce.

Hemingway's role in the novel is clearly subordinate, limited largely to moments where "a pout" grows on his lips (20), perhaps reminiscent of Dos Passos' characterization in *Chosen Country*, or his mustache twitches (59). Barnett describes him as "likable, annoying sometimes, but likable. Big and friendly" (13). The major difference between them, as Jack sees it, is that he himself writes for money, while Hem writes for love. As in Cosgrove's *The Hemingway Papers*, the recently fledged National Socialists are involved (although the failed "beer hall putsch" did not occur until November of 1923), and we again encounter Hermann Goering. The major villains in this novel, though, are a "splinter group of radical Communists" who plan to assassinate British prime minister David Lloyd George (177). In what might be regarded as a classic "fanfic" moment, Hays replays the scene from *A Moveable Feast* in which Gertrude Stein describes the short story "Up in Michigan" as "inaccrochable," or not appropriate for display (78–79). The title of the story is not mentioned, but the fanfic reader knows what it is, unlike Jack Barnett, one might observe, who tells Stein (and us) he hasn't read any of Hem's stories and "probably won't" (80). One detects a certain irony here, inasmuch as Tony Hays has obviously read and admired Hemingway's fiction, while his protagonist has not. But Barnett eventually does read his old friend's fiction, as in the epilogue we encounter Jack and Hem fishing together, with Jack recognizing himself in the character of Jake Barnes: "It wasn't that I minded him appropriating my life, but he didn't have to let everybody know it was my life" (209).

Craig McDonald's mystery *One True Sentence* (2011) also covers the events of a single week but deals with those occurring two years later, in February 1924. McDonald is an Ohio State University graduate in English and journalism, and his books include more than half a dozen crime novels and three books of nonfiction interviews with other crime writers. *One True Sentence* concludes a trilogy in which Hemingway appears as an important character paired with his good friend Hector (Hec) Lassiter, a crime writer who "lives what he writes and writes what he lives." The first novel in the trilogy, *Toros and Torsos*, appeared in 2008 and spans the decades from 1935 through 1959; the second book, *Print the Legend* (2010), is set in Ketchum, Idaho, mostly in the mid–1960s, and concerns Mary Hemingway and the mystery of Ernest's suicide. *One True Sentence*, then, goes back to where it all started and bears the title of what emerges from the pages of *A Moveable Feast* as one of Hemingway's mantras (12). Although their careers have diverged, both Hec and Hem embrace that maxim. As Lassiter explains it in *Toros and Torsos*, the writers play a sort of writing exercise game: "One of us writes—or really, speaks—a few words. Perhaps the start of a sentence. The other one tries to give it the best finish—make it a clear, true sentence."[28] *One True Sentence* has been translated into French as *Le Phrase qui tue* (2012).

In this novel a group of anarchists called Nada (Spanish for "nothing") led by a sinister man who calls himself, á la William Blake, "Nobodaddy," is killing off the editors of little magazines of the sort that were publishing such pioneers of literary modernism as James Joyce, D.H. Lawrence, Ezra Pound, and, of course, Ernest Hemingway. Alarmed, Gertrude Stein, herself a mystery fan, undertakes to round up the major crime novelists, including Hector Lassiter, in order to solve the mystery. Lassiter, like Hemingway, was wounded while driving ambulances in Italy. Among the crime writers is a woman named Brinke Devlin, who bears more than coincidental similarities with Lady Brett Ashley of *The Sun Also Rises*, even to the point of making her grand entrance surrounded by an escort of homosexuals. Later in the novel she echoes Brett in requesting one of "'you chaps'" to buy her a drink.[29] Knowing that Hem favors Rioja Alta, Hector buys them a bottle, another wow-moment for the readers of fanfic. Brinke describes Hector's stories as "gritty and real and gripping" (28), perhaps in the mode McDonald would regard as his own. Like Lady Brett's, Brinke's hair is fashionably bobbed, but McDonald passes up on the opportunity to appropriate an analogy that Hemingway must surely have taken from the world of hard-boiled detective fiction: "She [Brett] was built with curves like the hull of a racing yacht, and you missed none of it with that wool jersey."[30] Such phrasing may recall that of one of the pioneers of noir, Dashiell Hammett, whose short stories had appeared in print by 1923, although his first novels, *Red Harvest* and *The Dain Curse*, did not come out until 1929.

As in Hays's crime novel, McDonald's Hemingway plays a decidedly subordinate role to the main character, and in both novels, as in all of the Twenties or Paris appropriations, readers are expected to be aware that Ernest is a young writer who has not yet really entered the ring: both the short stories of *In Our Time* and the novel *The Sun Also Rises* are yet to be. We do get some insights into the stories, as indicated above, however—particularly in *The Paris Wife*, which takes us to the publication of *The Sun Also Rises*. In the other novels, the writers drop hints that this or that character or episode might have led Hemingway to his fictional representations. Again, as with the appearance of a canary on a train ride late in *The Paris Wife* (292), suggestive of the story "A Canary for One," which would not appear until *Men Without Women* in 1927, the reader of fan fiction relishes his or her insider status. Brinke Devlin goes so far as to suggest to Hector that Hem might be "the perfect red herring [...] a good likely distraction—in terms of a false suspect" (70). In fact, Hem is later arrested as a murder suspect, a move that Gertrude Stein describes as "absurd" (107).

In a portion of a novel in progress provisionally entitled "Rhapsody in Black," Hector presents what is surely intended to be an imitation of the terse Hemingway style:

> They killed Hale Jones for looking at a white girl. His killers hanged Hale from a light post with a piece of cut-down clothesline.
> The man who tied the knot was Sheriff Billy Davis. The sheriff stood six-three and weighed two hundred and fifty pounds. He was a defrocked Texas Ranger with notches carved into the butt of his Colt [76].

The brief passage concludes: "Hale hadn't yet turned ten." Hector, we are told, "wasn't bowled over" by his own effort here; he thinks it reads like "journalese." But part of the play is that, in his efforts to write "one true sentence," Hector Lassiter is creating the paradigm for the early Hemingway style, perhaps most evident in some of the vignettes or inter-chapters of *In Our Time*: "They hanged Sam Cardinella at six o'clock in the morning in the corridor of the county jail. The corridor was high and narrow with tiers of cells on either side. All the cells were occupied" (*Complete Short Stories*, 171). Like Hector's passage, Hemingway's ends with a flat, understated irony, though the gulf that separates the two prose pieces is wide and deep: "The priest skipped back onto the scaffolding just before the drop fell."

Implicated in the murders are the nihilistic, indeed anarchistic, surrealists under the leadership of the mysterious Nobodaddy. Predictably, neither Ernest nor Hector has any use for their art or ostensible vision. McDonald had already pilloried the surrealists in the earlier written book of the trilogy, *Toros and Torsos*, in which avant-garde photographer Man Ray (1890–1976) is a favorite target. The occultist Aleister Crowley, briefly mentioned in *A Moveable Feast* (88), appears in the novel, as does novelist Ford Madox Ford, whom Hemingway describes memorably as "an ambulatory, well-clothed, up-ended hogshead" with halitosis (*A Moveable Feast*, 83). Even the poet-doctor William Carlos Williams enters the novel when Hector dislocates his ankle and bruises his fist punching out the obnoxious Crowley. In that context Hemingway asks to borrow Hector's typewriter to work on a story about "a pregnant squaw. I think it's damn fine. Maybe my best yet" (143). Fans will recognize "Indian Camp," the opening story of *In Our Time*, another example of the gratification available to the informed reader.

In a commentary for the online blog "The Rap Sheet," Craig McDonald notes that Hemingway appeared as "a kind of off-camera presence" in his first novel, *Head Games* (2007), but with the conclusion of *One True Sentence*, he will no longer appear in the projected eight-book Hector Lassiter cycle.[31] Reflecting on the question, "Why Hemingway?," McDonald offers that he wanted to comment on such "key artistic movements" as modernism, surrealism, and postmodernism, but also, and surely of more significance, because as a young man he was deeply influenced by *The Sun Also Rises* and particularly by *A Moveable Feast*, which he concedes does come across as "contrived or even disingenuous." But he describes himself as "a trust-the-art, not-the-artist kind of guy," and he adds, apropos of my present undertaking, "Hemingway became my master and kind of the literary equivalent of what Elvis represents to rockers—the goal and the cautionary example." In effect, McDonald touches here, in passing, upon two icons of fandom. He describes *One True Sentence* as "a noir turn on *A Moveable Feast* and a kind of post-modern dark comedy about the mystery genre itself."

Curiously, given his role as a minor character, it is the "Maigret-like French inspector" Simon Aristide who comments on the American writers and artists as a "queer lot" who "find it necessary to come here to reinvent yourselves […] to recast yourselves in your own self-images. What is it about Paris that draws you all here to reimagine yourselves in some new persona?" (243). Hemingway was in fact a longtime admirer of Georges Simenon's Maigret mysteries, but these did not begin to appear until 1930. McDonald also has his police inspector offer Hem one of his most oft-quoted lines, to the effect that courage is "grace under pressure," supposedly something Simon Aristide's grandfather used to say.

A similar sort of playful undercutting occurs during a cameo appearance by Hemingway in Walter Satterthwait's *Masquerade* (1998) when Ernest sets upon undercover Pinkerton agent Jane English (Turner) at a soiree in Gertrude Stein's 27 rue de Fleurus. It is Jane who suggests to the flirtatious young writer, after he has "examined" her bosom, "perhaps to satisfy himself that it had not ambled off since his last survey," that Paris is "'a sort of moveable feast.'"[32] The implication here and in McDonald's *One True Sentence* is that Hemingway kept his ears open and was very much an opportunist—as any writer is, one might be tempted to say. Author of more than a dozen mysteries. Satterthwait has been influenced by Dashiell Hammett and Mickey Spillane; in his other novels he appropriates such characters as Lizzie Borden, Harry Houdini, and Oscar Wilde. As Satterthwait presents Ernest through Jane's eyes, he is "quite simply astonishing. [...] He is big and robust and strikingly handsome [...] in a vibrant, vigorous, dimpled, curiously boyish American fashion." In fact, Satterthwait's description of Hemingway might set some record for fanfic adjectives: he is also described as "charming," and as Jane basks "in the full glare of that beaming smile and those beaming eyes," she is nearly swept away by "all that churning male energy" (193).

But all of the foregoing merely sets up the reader for one of the most comical portraits of Ernest Hemingway in fiction, as he comes across as a "slightly rumpled" gamekeeper when it comes to his dress (perhaps one thinks of D.H. Lawrence's Mellors here, appositely enough), and we soon find him dribbling red wine from his lips and sporting "a morsel of coq au vin" between his teeth, which he dislodges with his index finger (199). He lumbers about the crowded room and prattles about bullfighting (to employ Jane's verbs), knocks paintings askew, and eventually stumbles into a table and bumps a bust of the emperor Hadrian onto the floor, where it does not break but does strike Picasso's ankle, causing him to limp to the other side of the room (195). Satterthwait stumbles himself with an anachronism whereby Jane claims to have read and admired the story "Big Two-Hearted River," which was not written until 1924 and not published until 1925, though the novel occurs in 1923. Such a scenario is played in the spirit of good fun, though. It has nothing of the acrimony apparent in what I have elsewhere called "fanemy" fiction, Carlile's crude autoerotic episode involving Robert McAlmon, for example. Would Hemingway have found Satterthwait's scene amusing? Perhaps not. Probably not, in fact, given the general agreement among his biographers that he found it difficult to laugh at himself, which may be a more significant character flaw than some might suppose. Henry (Mike) Strater, in his interview with Denis Brian, asserts that Hemingway had a good enough sense of humor, but "he had no humor about himself" (43).

Under the pseudonym of Jason Miller Waddington ("Wad") in Canadian novelist Howard Engel's *Murder in Montparnasse* (1992), however, we encounter a more serious version of Ernest Miller Hemingway (in addition to the shared middle name, note the parallel rhythm here) in his role as mystery solver and crime fighter along with Canadian journalist Michael Ward. (Engel's renaming of Hemingway is of course reminiscent of Dos Passos' George Elbert Warner.)[33] Howard Engel resides in Toronto and is a founder of Crime Writers of Canada. Author of twenty books, including three works of nonfiction, Engel formerly worked as a writer and reporter for the CBC. The news release on his investiture with the Order of Canada in 2007 indicates "it was his books about a Jewish private investigator [Benny Cooperman] that turned him into a Canadian icon of the mystery genre."[34]

The action is set in the fall of 1925 as a Jack-the-Ripper–like killer prowls the streets murdering young women. In what turns out to be one of the more clever of the Twenties appropriations, Engel blends the consternation over Hemingway's roman-à-clef, *The Sun Also Rises*, to be published the next year, with what is offered up as itself a roman-à-clef, thus necessitating the scatter of pseudonyms which are glossed in what the supposed writer, William Duff Gaspard, claims in an editorial note are his grandfather's papers. As a result, Hemingway comes off as Waddington but is reminiscent at times of Jake Barnes. Meanwhile, the real-life Harold Loeb, model for the pathetic Robert Cohn, is renamed Hal Leopold, doubtless with a wink at the notorious Leopold and Loeb murder case of 1924 in Chicago. In effect, then, Hal Leopold is Harold Loeb is Robert Cohn. The editorial note suggests a gesture toward verisimilitude similar to that undertaken by Vincent Cosgrove in *The Hemingway Papers*. Engel's Hemingway is capable of chastising himself as a "son of a bitch" and a "first-rate bastard" (166), particularly over the way he has treated Priscilla/Hadley, who often goes by Hadley's actual nickname of "Hash," as he is in the process of leaving her for Julia/Pauline. He is also, as the narrator Michael Ward discovers, "a far more complex figure" than he had supposed (27). Sylvia Beach, who appears under her actual name, as do several personages, like Gertrude Stein, tells Ward that Waddington/Hemingway is just "play-acting" when it comes to his pose as a boxer and insists that "underneath" all of that Wad/Hem remains "a shy man" (187).

The Hemingway subplot is well integrated into the pursuit of the killer, partly through his ongoing concern about the lost manuscripts, even though he tells Ward that he behaved stoically about it all: "Survival is the most important match on the card, kid. So, I got back to work and I forgot what was in that suitcase because it was the heart, bone and blood of two years' work" (126). One might note, of course, that Wad's/Hem's choice of phrasing at the end does tend to compromise his supposed capacity to put it all behind him. Lady Biz Leighton, based on Lady Duff Twysden, the model for Lady Brett Ashley, suggests, in fact, that "Wad's" interest in Julia/Pauline and other women dates from the loss of the manuscripts (19). As Hal/Harold/Robert puts it, Wad/Hem "hasn't been able to love Hash since she lost his manuscripts" (69). Howard Engel connects the plotlines by having the murderer, a doctor and amateur writer named Anson Tyler, also be the thief of the missing manuscripts. Ward conjectures that Dr. Tyler—who had been romantically involved with a murdered model who was a peripheral member of the Paris Pilgrims, to appropriate Carlile's term—was motivated by envy over "Wad's" "apparent ease with words": "To him, with your talent for friendship, your sloppy manner around the Quarter—maybe he thought you were unworthy of your genius. A genius has to be humble, he thought—I'm really only guessing—and Wad, you're a lot of things, but humble isn't one of them" (289).

Engel's Hemingway, therefore, is not presented uncritically. Hal/Harold/Robert insists, for example, that Waddington/Hemingway "doesn't know how to forgive people. He just strikes them off his list" (69). Wad/Hem also manages quite literally to strike Leopold/Loeb/Cohn when he flirts audaciously with Biz/Duff/Brett, proving his boast of boxing skill is not empty, and he even clobbers Ward when he thinks his friend has mentioned him to the police as a suspect in the case, though he does promptly apologize. He subsequently tells Ward "the only safe place to be is numbered among the enemy" (169). One woman in the group informs Ward that "'with Waddington it is always the career that comes first. The career demands that he find a richer woman'" (202). That woman will be Julia/Pauline. As the novel ends, Wad/Hem is about to take the train on the fateful trip to Schruns, Austria, where he will ski with Priscilla/Hadley and fall in love with Julia/Pauline.

Engel makes an unusual move when it comes to the lost manuscripts: the police do recover them, but Waddington/Hemingway does not bother to retrieve them, insisting to Ward that their recovery was just a rumor and that the two years of lost labor has now become something of a "legend." Ward agrees "it did make a better story this way" (299). As it turns out, Michael Ward has proven to be quite correct.

Writers of biographical fiction featuring Hemingway tend to ignore the gap between his divorce of Hadley in December 1926 and his marriage to Pauline in May 1927 and their departure from Paris for Key West in the middle of March the next year. Gilmore's novelization, for instance, leaps from Paris in 1926 to the African safari in 1933. Left unattended to are the birth of Ernest and Pauline's sons Patrick, in 1928, and Gregory, three years later, the deeply disturbing suicide of Ernest's father in December 1928, and the writing and great success of *A Farewell to Arms*, published in September of 1929. For the appropriators, the Hemingway 1920s means Hadley and Paris "in the early days when we were very poor and very happy" (*A Moveable Feast*, 211). Hemingway fans know the bittersweet nostalgia of that phrasing would not become manifest for another thirty years. In the envoi to *Hemingway: The Homecoming* (1992) Michael Reynolds depicts Ernest as "a native son in transit [...] unsure if he was merely visiting or returning for another decade" and traveling now "much heavier than ever before."[35]

Four

Hemingway and the Threatening Thirties

> *John Dos Passos was one of the few people at certain times whom Ernest could really talk to. [...] They had a lot to say to each other. There wasn't anyone else around for Ernest like that.*—Hadley (Mowrer) in Denis Brian, *The True Gen* (1988)

The early 1930s would find Ernest and Pauline Hemingway comfortably ensconced in their Key West home, having arrived in April of 1928 on the advice of their mutual friend from Paris days, novelist John Dos Passos. Their first son, Patrick, would be born in Kansas City, Missouri, on June 28, 1928, as would their second son (Ernest's third), Gregory, on November 12, 1931. Just over five months after Patrick's birth, Ernest's father, Dr. Clarence ("Ed") Hemingway, struggling with his finances and suffering from depression, would kill himself with a .32 caliber revolver. Ernest tended to blame his mother and to accuse his father of cowardice, ironically, given his own suicide 33 years later. By the time Ernest's second collection of short stories *Men Without Women* had been published, in mid–October of 1927, he would have been married to Pauline Pfeiffer for about five months, so despite the title, he had not been without a woman at all. The book features such stories as "Hills Like White Elephants," "The Undefeated," "A Canary for One," and "The Killers." Despite the rather dismissive review of Virginia Woolf, castigating the stories for "superfluity of dialogue," for being too "self-consciously virile," and for being "a little dry and sterile" (*Critical Reception*, 54), the book was well received. Dorothy Parker, for instance, declared it "a truly magnificent work" (58), and Edmund Wilson, one of the leading critics of the age, wrote, "He is not a moralist staging a melodrama, but an artist presenting a situation of which the moral values are complex" (62). Seven years later, M.R. Rosene, in listing *Men Without Women* among the five best books published since 1900, would assert that "The Undefeated" was "the best American short story since Crane's 'The Open Boat'" (65).

Ernest wrote *A Farewell to Arms* mostly in Key West, and it was published to considerable fanfare on September 27, 1929, and serialized in *Scribner's* magazine between May and October of that year. John Dos Passos, his fellow novelist and friend from the Paris days, opened his review by declaring it "the best written book that has seen the light in America for many a long day" (*Critical Reception*, 95). Agnes W. Smith, writing for the *New Yorker*, thought it "Hemingway's greatest work" (78), and Bernard DeVoto concluded that Hemingway "for the first time justifies his despair and gives it a dignity of tragic emotion" (86). By the end of 1932, as the Great Depression got into full swing, the movie version of the novel, starring Hemingway's friend Gary Cooper and Helen Hayes, would be lining his bank account with Hollywood dollars. This is not to say that Hemingway would ever allow himself to feel wealthy, or even well off; nor would he allow himself to be gracious about the largesse of Pauline's uncle Gus, whose wealth bankrolled his famous African safari in the winter of 1933-34, as well as other excursions and expenses.

Relative to the great successes of the 1920s, the publications of the 1930s are a mixed bag as most readers, critics, and scholars have assessed them: the bullfighting documentary, *Death in the Afternoon* (1932); the third and last collection of short stories, *Winner Take Nothing* (1933), which includes "A Clean, Well-Lighted Place" and "The Gambler, the Nun, and the Radio"; the big-game hunting piece that would today most likely be classified as "creative nonfiction," *Green Hills of Africa* (1935); the stab at a proletarian novel that comes as close to experimental fiction as anything he would ever write, *To Have and Have Not* (1937); a trio of his most ambitious stories, "The Capital of the World," "The Snows of Kilimanjaro," and "The Short Happy Life of Francis Macomber," the latter two his most critically acclaimed over the decades and all appearing in 1936; half a dozen short stories from the civil war in Spain, including "Old Man at the Bridge," all published in 1938 or 1939; and his one effort at playwriting, the three-act drama on subversive activity in the Spanish Civil War, *The Fifth Column* (1938), which ran 87 performances on Broadway, starring Lee J. Cobb and Franchot Tone, in 1940. Despite all of that, along with numerous journalistic pieces written from Madrid and out of Key West for the newly hatched (1933) *Esquire* magazine, the Thirties tend to be shrugged off as a decade of wheel-spinning or even retrograde motion by the thirty-something author who liked to be called "Papa." His epic novel of the civil war in Spain, *For Whom the Bell Tolls* (1940), would alter that view. One might think of it as either the culmination of the Thirties or as the commencement of the Forties.

Among the numerous portraits and thumbnail sketches of Ernest Hemingway in his thirties, the one Paul Hendrickson offers early in *Hemingway's Boat* (2011) strikes me as being as good as any and better than most:

> He was rugged, handsome, youthful, trim-waisted, owner of a killer grin and an even more killer ego, the reigning monarch of American literature, a sportsman and sensualist glorying in his life, in the external physical world [14].

Ernest purchased the *Pilar* in the spring of 1934, thereby launching his avocation as deep-sea, big-game fisherman, master of the marlin and many other species as well. He was also the father of three sons, two of whom, Patrick (who would turn six that summer) and Gregory (who would turn three that fall), lived at home in what was at the time one of the most remote places in the United States, so remote that the locals, who called themselves "Conchs," liked to toy with the notion of an autonomous Conch Republic. "Home" was the house on Whitehead Street, built in 1851 as the finest house in the Keys, extensively remodeled by Ernest and Pauline, and today maintained as a museum for hordes of Hemingway aficionados and fans whose presence Papa would surely have despised. The Ernest Hemingway House was designated a National Historic Landmark in November 1968.

As with all things Hemingway, there would be a price to be paid, and the costs would be borne by all concerned, perhaps most of all by himself. As always, Ernest amassed a group of cohorts he referred to as "the Mob" to accompany him on drinking bouts at Sloppy Joe's and other spots, including his own home and those of local friends like Charles and Lorine Thompson. He would dress beyond casual in grubby shorts held up by cord or, later (after World War II), by his famous "*Gott Mit Uns*" belt and shabby shirt. An acquaintance describes him as having looked like "an ordinary hippie."[1] His appearance in the opening scenes of the 2012 movie *Hemingway and Gellhorn*, starring Clive Owen and Nicole Kidman, seems to have a firm foundation in fact: disheveled, bewhiskered, hair tousled, shirt dirty and blood-stained. The 28-year-old journalist met the 37-year-old author at Sloppy Joe's Bar in late December 1936, by which time Ernest's marriage to Pauline was already disintegrating. Ernest and Martha Gellhorn connected in Spain in 1937, but his divorce from Pauline was not finalized until November of 1940. He left Key West after Christmas 1939 for the Finca Vigía (Lookout Farm) outside Havana. By that time Hemingway was forty years old and beginning to add a few pounds to his already substantial bulk, though he was by no means flabby (McIver, 87). Both biographers and appropriators seem to take almost perverse delight in the fact that Hemingway put on weight once he became middle-aged.

One of the most notable cameo appropriations of Hemingway occurs early in Philip Roth's *The Great American Novel* (1973), a dozen pages featuring the sportswriter known as Smitty ("Call me Smitty," the prologue begins with a wink at *Moby Dick*) fishing for sailfish with Hem in March of 1936, a few months before Martha showed up in Key West. Critics are fond of quoting the garrulous Smitty's observation: "When he [Papa] was having a good day they didn't make them any more generous and sweet-tempered, but when he was having a bad day, well, he could be the biggest prick in all of literature."[2] The men are accompanied by a vacationing "slit" from Vassar (the stand-in college for Martha's Bryn Mawr in *The Fifth Column*) who proposes a few traditional competitors for the mythic title of The Great American Novel: *Moby Dick, Huckleberry Finn, The Scarlet Letter*. In his most memorable rebuttal, Hem declares, "Vassar, *Moby Dick* is a book about blubber, with a madman thrown in for excitement" (27).

When Papa declares it is he who will write that novel, a "large fierce gull" swoops down and utters, "Nevermore!" (30). The gull escapes before Hem can grab his pistol, but he then threatens to use it on himself before Smitty (Word Smith—Papa calls him "Frederico") calms him down, arguing, "Who would want to kill himself over a novel?" (30, 31). Over what, then, Ernest asks, "A whale? A woman?" To which the Vassar woman responds, "Wouldn't it be pretty to think so?" (32). Smitty interjects sardonically, "A few hours with a man like Hem had changed her forever, as it changed us all. That's what a great writer can do to people." Or possibly, speaking for Philip Roth, Smitty believes that sentiment, or wants to. At the end of the episode Papa holds his pistol on a telegraph operator and, repeatedly using the phrase "bright boy" from his story "The Killers," compels him to agree that Papa's style is all his own, after which he sends a telegram to the other contenders for author of The Great American Novel and to the "Department of Literatoor" at Vassar, declaring, "The Great American Novelist, *c'est moi*. Signed, Papa" (35). After that, Smitty says, Hem would write him from time to time threatening to kill him for using his "style": "But of course in the end the guy Hem killed for using his style was himself" (36). In effect, Roth's brief appropriation here comes off as simultaneously disparaging and in a way eulogistic.

A varied set of appropriations represent the Key West period in fiction, but the most vivid of the 1930s fictions are set not in Florida, but in war-torn Spain. A little more than a third of Christopher Cook Gilmore's *Hemingway*

(1988) occurs during the Thirties, starting with a safari scene in the Serengeti in the winter of 1933 featuring Philip Percival, the white hunter, and Pauline. As in the movie starring Stacy Keach, the scene is composed largely of pieces from *Green Hills of Africa*, "The Short Happy Life of Francis Macomber," and "The Snows of Kilimanjaro." The scene then shifts to Key West and a fishing adventure with John Dos Passos (a marlin is "apple-cored" by sharks, as in *The Old Man and the Sea*), followed by the disastrous Labor Day hurricane of 1935, the meeting between Ernest and Martha Gellhorn at Sloppy Joe's, sixteen pages on the war in Spain, and another sixteen pages, mostly in Key West, on the disintegration of Hemingway's marriage with Pauline. Typical of most novelizations, Gilmore's book comes off as a plot summary, or perhaps more accurately as a storyboard heavy on dialogue.

More narrowly focused is Alfredo José Estrada's *Welcome to Havana, Señor Hemingway* (2004), which is set in 1933 during the revolution to overthrow Gerardo Machado. Erika Robuck's *Hemingway's Girl* (2012) takes place in Key West during the 1935 hurricane and focuses on tensions in Ernest and Pauline's marriage well before Martha Gellhorn entered the scene. Craig McDonald's *Toros and Torsos* (2008) also begins in 1935 before moving to Spain and 1937 about a third of the way through. Michael Atkinson's *Hemingway Cutthroat* (2010) is set in 1937 Madrid, as are some episodes of John Dos Passos' posthumously published novel, *Century's Ebb* (1975), in which Hemingway appears under the pseudonym George Elbert Warner, as in *Chosen Country*. Finally, Patrick Kendrick's *Papa's Problem* (2008) is set, rather implausibly, as it happens, in 1939, the "problem" indicated by the title being both the troubled marriage to Pauline and Papa's being suspected of having murdered a young prostitute.

In addition to having been translated into Polish (but not so far into Spanish), Alfredo José Estrada's *Welcome to Havana, Señor Hemingway* has been published in two very different formats, the 2004 paperback edition, which is constructed in conventional fashion and consists of 47 short chapters, and the 2005 hardcover edition, which is divided into eleven chapters with a prologue and an epilogue and which scrambles events in a sometimes confusing anti-chronological manner that suggests a sort of stream-of-consciousness approach, or perhaps a collage similar in nature to Michael Murphy's *Hemingsteen* (Chapter Two). Both versions open with the same provocative sentence: "My grandfather once knocked down Ernest Hemingway, or so I was told."[3] The title comes off even more provocatively, as it is murmured to Hemingway when he is in bed with a prominent chorus girl named La Chinita, at which he mumbles, "Call me Papa" and then falls asleep (79). It is appropriate that a Cuban-born author would turn out at least one of the appropriations, inasmuch as Hem lived about equally (roughly twenty years each) in the vicinity of Oak Park and Chicago and of Havana and the Finca. Like his protagonist, Javier López Angulo, the narrator's grandfather, Estrada is Harvard educated and has worked as a journalist, including several years in Miami as editor of the Latino magazine *Vista*. One might propose as the other bookend to *Welcome to Havana* Cuban mystery writer Leonardo Padura Fuentes' *Adiós Hemingway*, which looks back to Hem's departure from his beloved home in 1958 (Chapter Five).

Because of his sojourn at Harvard, Javier at first feels distant both from Havana and from the political intrigue, which also figures significantly in Hemingway's *To Have and Have Not* (1937). By the novel's end, however, both Javier and Hemingway get caught up in the action. As Steve Paul observes in his comments for *Hemingway Review*, Estrada offers us "the rum-swilling, skirt-chasing, fist-throwing, fish-battling Americano of legend."[4] As the popular revolution by various groups, including the ABC (known as the abecedarios), in consort with Franklin D. Roosevelt's special envoy, Sumner Welles forces Machado to step down in August 1933, Javier marries and embarks for New York and then Paris. Hemingway reads a news account of the event while on safari. In the closing chapter the narrator returns to find La Chinita now almost ninety. She reflects on Hemingway's infatuation with Jane Mason, noting that it was his grandfather Javier who truly loved her, but as for Hemingway, "he never loved anyone. It was the price he paid, I suppose. I would see him from time to time, sitting alone in the Floridita, drinking himself blind. I've never seen a man so alone" (334).

As Steve Paul suggests, Hemingway tends to take over the novel at times (110), serving at least as a co-protagonist. And although Estrada offers a wide array of characters, from the American banker Walter Huggins and his playboy son Freddy to such historical persons familiar to aficionados as Charles Thompson and Joe Russell, Hemingway is fully integrated into the narrative, whereas in some of the appropriations he seems merely to be spliced in for audience appeal. While Estrada features Hemingway in action, whether drinking, love making, marlin fishing, or pigeon shooting, he does occasionally show him struggling with his writing, in one instance working on the story that will become "Fathers and Sons." One might argue that Havana herself serves as a sort of co-protagonist, the city is it was in the Thirties as a Yankee playground. In his author's note, Estrada explains that the "abortive revolution of 1933" opened the door for the rise to power of Fulgencio Batista, whose "Revolt of the Sergeants" would contribute significantly to Machado's fall. Estrada has also written something of a love song to Havana, *Havana: Autobiography of a City* (2008), which begins, "You can easily find Havana on the map of the imagination."[5] He devotes a chapter of this familiar history to Hemingway.

Readers of Erika Robuck's *Hemingway's Girl*, like those of Estrada's novel or of Vincent Cosgrove's *The Hemingway Papers* (Chapter Three) are almost certainly attracted to the text by the title. On the other hand, one can readily imagine a potential purchaser or reader who would be alienated by the very mention of Hemingway's name. Perhaps that hypothetical reader or purchaser might by attracted by a novel entitled *Steinbeck's Girl* or *The Faulkner Papers*. Presumably, writers like Cosgrove, Estrada, and Robuck have weighed the matter and opted for what they see as an advantage in choosing to appropriate Hemingway's moniker: X number of readers might decide neither to buy nor to read this novel, but Y number of readers may well be attracted by whatever it is they associate with the name. They might have always enjoyed reading Hemingway's fiction, or long been fascinated with Hemingway as a cultural icon or as a near mythic figure or as a man known to have lived on the edge. Such Y-readers will be curious, perhaps suspicious, about the role he will play in this or that novel. What will such hypothetical readers bring to the text? Of course, the answer to that question will vary, as it does with any text. Some of us are far more "ready" to read and enjoy a Shakespeare play or to attend and appreciate a performance than others are.

In certain respects the relativity of fandom when it comes to written texts or "literature" is implicit in the classic essay (in poetic form) of literary criticism, Horace's "Ars Poetica" (ca. 18 BC), which reached many English readers in Sir Philip Sidney's "The Defense of Poesy," first published in 1595. In that treatise he maintained that the "end," or goal, of poetry, which at that time would have meant all of what we now call "literature" or "belles lettres" or "creative writing" (prose included), is "to teach and delight." The concept might be rephrased "to edify and entertain" with some etymological awareness of the Latin origins of the former infinitive suggesting "edification" or "building," a sort of intellectual and even moral edifice. One might argue that the more serious readers, audiences, or fans emphasize edification and are those whose tastes represent "official culture," while the fans, audiences, or readers whose tastes represent "popular culture" lay stress on entertainment, or so-called entertainment value. Obviously, Horace, Sidney, and their successors intend that both edification and entertainment are to be expected of the best writing. Graham Greene is known to have distinguished between his "novels," like *The Power and the Glory* (1940), and his thrillers or "entertainments," like *The Confidential Agent* (1939). Surely many, if not most, readers also make such distinctions, searching for "light reading" for the summer or for a long plane ride and opting at other times for something more conceptually or stylistically complex. We pull a book from the shelves and perhaps glance at the cover and notice the blurbs.

Some readers, though probably far fewer than most publishers would like to believe, are attracted by blurbs. One is inclined to speculate that a science of "blurbology" ought to exist. It would be a new and inexact science, perhaps more loosely an "art," the concept of the blurb on the cover of a book having been hatched apparently by the enterprising author, art critic, and humorist Frank Gellet Burgess in 1907. An 1887 MIT graduate, Burgess was employed as a drawing instructor at the University of California at Berkeley until losing his job over a prank in 1894. After that, he founded a humor magazine called the *Lark*, for which he penned one of the most famous nonsense poems in the English language, "The Purple Cow," the full title of which was "The Purple Cow: Reflections on a Mythic Beast Who's Quite Remarkable, at Least":

> I never saw a purple cow
> I never hope to see one;
> But I can tell you, anyhow,
> I'd rather see than be one![6]

All of this may seem a rather circumlocutory approach to the half dozen blurbs that figure on the cover of *Hemingway's Girl*, Robuck's second novel, her first having been self-published. Her third novel, *Call Me Zelda*, on F. Scott Fitzgerald's notorious and also legendary wife, appeared in May 2013.

Jenna Blum's front-cover blurb assures us we will "love this robust, tender story of love, grief, and survival on Key West in the 1930s" and that the book is "addictive." But who is Jenna Blum that we should trust her word? Thanks to the Internet, it is as easy to answer that question as it is to learn about the origins of the blurb itself. She is a graduate of Kenyon College with a master's degree in creative writing from Boston University, and she is the author of two best-selling novels. The Amazon.com Web site will inform us that she is one of "Oprah's Top Thirty Women Writers." The other five blurbs on the cover, also by women novelists, promise that the book is "dazzlingly written and impossibly moving [...] a supernova" (Caroline Leavitt, author of nine novels and teacher of creative writing for UCLA and Stanford online), and that it "brings to life the captivating and volatile world of a literary legend" (Portland, Oregon, based novelist Kristina McMorris). One feels oneself to be as certainly hooked as one of Hemingway's legendary marlins.

Robuck's novel, already available on audio CD and in Kindle version, comes equipped with a reader's guide that provides a seven-page interview or "conversation" with the author and two and a half pages of discussion questions appropriate for a reading group. The front matter includes a rather murky black and white photograph of Hemingway as he looked when he lived in Key West during the 1930s, apparently on board the *Pilar*, and a letter addressed to the reader informing him or her that the author "fell in love with Hemingway" when she was a girl of nineteen "while reading *A Farewell to Arms*."[7] After the acknowledgments at the end of the novel, including her expression of gratitude to the staff of the John F. Kennedy Library in Boston and the staff of the Hemingway House in Key West, Robuck lists a bibliography of a dozen or so titles, noting from the start that "nothing gave me more insight into animating Hemingway than his own works" (325).

One approaches this novel, then, with the clear sense that it has been hyped as only the finest fanfic can be, and a hasty survey of supportive statistics indicates the hype has been quite successful. The goodreads.com site, as of July 7, 2013, lists 1,062 ratings and 289 reviews, for a composite of 3.94 of a possible five stars. The Amazon.com site lists 134 customer reviews, of which 71 awarded the book a five-star rating for an average of 4.3 stars. We are dealing here with "popular fiction," after all, a romance. Not surprisingly, then, the initial 17 ratings of the novel at goodreads.com (with commentaries, some of them rather detailed) are offered by women readers, after which we find a single male, who awarded it five stars and offered a commentary running nearly seven hundred words. His commentary is followed by that of another 22 women readers before we meet the next male, who rates the novel with just three stars and observes, "I'll tell you what you do: you jazz things up by making Ernest Hemingway one of your characters!" And to that, I can only say A-*men*. That sentiment is at least partially what my book is about, although I would argue there's more to it than that. For the record, which is not likely to last for long, given the nature of such customer or reader reviews, 17 of the next 20 reviews and commentaries were prepared by women readers, most of whom rated it five stars, but one of whom allocated only two.

Such admittedly haphazard findings tend to confirm the consensus that women read more than men do, particularly in the U.S., and that they read considerably more fiction than men do. National Public Radio in 2007 reported on an Associated Press and Ipsos survey conducted in the U.S., Canada, and Britain that found not only a decrease in the number of books being read, but also "among avid readers [...] the typical woman read nine books in a year, compared with only five for men" and "men account for only 20 percent of the fiction market." "By this measure," according to Lakshmi Chaudhry, a contributing editor to *Nation*, "'chick-lit' would have to include Hemingway and nearly every other novel."[8] A study published in *Science* magazine in October 2013 found that reading "literary fiction" promotes "empathy."[9] That premise has long been dear to the hearts of literature professors and teachers all over the world. Whether it applies equally, or at all, to popular fiction might be open to debate.

Surely, however, even Hemingway would have been surprised to discover that more than a dozen years into the 21st century his reputation, and his legend, for that matter, lie to some degree in the hands of women readers and scholars. Perhaps he would relish the irony of it all. From Susan Beegel, longtime editor of *Hemingway Review*, to such notable scholars as Linda Wagner-Martin, Sandra Spanier, Debra Moddelmog, and Rose Marie Burwell, women have revitalized the critical inquiry into Hemingway and his writing. And amidst the numerous writers of biographical fiction—the appropriators—among the most renowned at the present moment are Paula McLain, Erika Robuck and Naomi Wood.

Hemingway's Girl opens with a sort of prologue wherein the Cuban-American protagonist, Mariella, now a mature woman with a grown son, lands a large marlin, then later reacts hysterically to the news of Hemingway's suicide. The first chapter brings us back to January 1935, when at age nineteen Mariella first sees Ernest refereeing a boxing match. Her deceased father thought Hem was "a decent guy," but her mother (like Hem's mother) has read one of his books and "deemed it vulgar" (6). Mariella is "consumed," we are told, with making money to help support her embittered mother and two sisters in the midst of the Depression. Mariella soon becomes the Hemingways' housekeeper, and in that role she becomes familiar with Pauline and the two sons. Predictably, Ernest soon makes a move on her, but Mariella adroitly maneuvers away, though she does feel attracted to the world-famous 36-year-old author who is also Key West's leading, or at least most notorious, citizen. She checks out *The Sun Also Rises* and likes it, admiring Jake Barnes, who has "no patience for phonies" (28), a trait she quickly detects in Hemingway himself and which we are implicitly expected to extend to her.

Soon enough, Mariella finds herself falling for a 33-year-old veteran named Gavin Murray, who is connected with the work camps on Lower Matecumbe Key, which would be devastated by the deadly Labor Day hurricane. Gavin is "intrigued" with the notion that she might be "Hemingway's girl," but she is not, at least not in the romantic sense, although Robuck does tease her readers with that possibility. Mariella is reading *A Farewell to Arms* when she feels what some readers might describe as a Harlequin Romance moment: "She felt something in her belly more and more each time she was around Hemingway, but that couldn't be love, could it?" We feel quite relieved when she quickly suspects "it must be that other thing" (85). Nevertheless, Mariella does think of herself as having some choice to make between Gavin and Ernest. Of significance, when Ernest suggests he might write her into one of his stories, Mariella dissuades him: "When you put people on your pages, you take something away from them" (65). He promptly strikes out a passage in his notebook. Ironically, Robuck herself is doing precisely what her protagonist Mariella and other characters in the biographical fiction resent.

Robuck invests her image of Hemingway with numerous characteristics the biographers have noted over the decades: he feels awkward and somewhat resentful of Pauline's money (73), and he considers his father a coward for having committed suicide (75). Mariella finds him drunk, rude, and angry at a party where he comes on to the attractive Jane Mason (126). On the island of Bimini in the Bahamas, one of Ernest's favorite ports of call, Robuck has him give Mariella a lesson on his male characters, as he insists that his women are not "weak," as she suggests, but are "there to highlight what macho jackasses the men are" (195). At moments like these Robuck, like other appropriators, makes an overt effort at reassessment or even, it might be argued, at promoting a revisionist perspective. This observation about Hemingway's women is by no means original with Robuck, but as is often the case with fan fiction, the writer aligns herself with a particular side in an ongoing critical debate.

Later during the Bimini trip Mariella finds herself feeling "increasing disdain for him" and she resents his flirtation with Pauline's sister Jinny and with herself, for that matter: "He used to seem so authentic, but lately she found him replaced by a sunburned, overfed legend of his own making. She felt strongly that he was in character, forever trying to hold up his image for the men around him" (206). Few appropriators seem capable of presenting this sort of critical view of Hemingway as a man without becoming derogatory, or even downright malicious. Robuck's reflections here, offered via Mariella, come across as thoughtful and motivated by an effort to understand Hemingway even as she concedes his shortcomings. These reflections also help to establish Mariella's credibility as an objective and perceptive protagonist. She has not simply been swept off her feet by the magisterial author. She can be critical without being contemptuous.

Perhaps Robuck's best achievement when it comes to the appropriations is her portrait of Pauline, whom she describes as "open to no one except him" (120). She feels compassion for Pauline, who dyes her hair so that it looks "brassy" in an effort to compete with Jane Mason (148, 150), and she feels sympathy for Pauline as she tries to understand Ernest's cruelty and Jane Mason's infidelities: "Did the rich play by a different set of rules? And did Pauline deserve it?" (for having started her relationship with Ernest when he was married to Hadley [215]). Soon after that, Pauline confesses her guilt over what she did to Hadley, Mariella comforts her, and Pauline apologizes for her jealous suspicions about Mariella and Papa. What Ernest needs, Jane Mason confides to Mariella when she informs her they have not have not been having an affair, is "good, true friends" (236), and that is what Mariella turns out to be. But back in Key West, as the hurricane rages outside, Pauline's jealousy gets the better of her and she turns on Mariella and Ernest, accusing him of being "weak" like his "miserable excuse for a father" (286). Ernest cowers under her rage, which she then directs at Mariella in a vicious peripeteia: she reveals that Mariella's father also committed suicide. But in a protracted epilogue that consists largely of letters from Papa, Pauline redeems herself with a letter of apology dated early in September 1951, a month before her death. In the letter Pauline accepts the "justice" of the sad outcome of her marriage with Ernest and calls herself a "fool" for believing she could be his only true love: "We all know, of course, that Ernest's only true love is his writing" (317).

In Gilmore's *Hemingway*, as in the film and in Robuck's novel, Ernest takes the *Pilar* in search of corpses after the hurricane of 1935 strikes the Keys. In *Hemingway's Boat* Paul Hendrickson describes it as "the first recorded Category 5 event in the country's history" (331). Gavin Murray survives the storm, which serves as the climactic event of Robuck's novel. Requested by the leftist periodical *New Masses* to turn out an article on the tragedy, Hemingway responded with nearly three thousand vitriolic words under the title, "Who Murdered the Vets?" Gilmore records Ernest's editor at Scribner, Max Perkins, as being upset over his willingness to publish in a Marxist magazine, but Ernest does not back down, arguing, as he does in his article, that the government sent the poorly paid veterans down to the Keys "to get rid of them" (98). Both Gilmore and Robuck draw haunting details from the article, but their fictional representation is no more lurid than what we encounter in Hemingway's text.

Robuck, in fact, reprints enough of the article to run a good three pages in her novel, in the process paying tribute both to the hundreds who died and to the considerable dramatic impact of Hemingway's scathing sarcasm aimed at the rich. Hendrickson describes the writing as "scant on hard journalistic fact and documentation" but "long on his passion" (332). The furious article perhaps deserves more attention than it has received over the past eighty years, as it records Hemingway's deep distrust and resentment of the wealthy, whom he holds responsible for abandoning the "bonus-marching variety of veterans," some of whom "had been on the bum since the Argonne." They "are not property," he writes. "They are only human beings; unsuccessful human beings, and all they have to lose is their lives" (9). The wealthy yachtsmen, he maintains, would never risk spending the hurricane months of August through October in harm's way. Hemingway would bring some of this anger to bear in the latter pages of *To Have and Have Not*.

Robuck's decision to reprint most of the article from *New Masses* helps her to establish the image of Hemingway as a compassionate, as well as passionate, voice of the working class and as a writer who did not shun social and political commitments during the Great Depression, an accusation that was leveled against him at the time and that still has some adherents. In his negative review of *Green Hills of Africa* (1935), Granville Hicks, who was then the most prominent Marxist literary critic in the U.S., described Hemingway as "by all odds the clearest and strongest non-revolutionary writer of his generation" (*Critical Reception*, 158). He commended "Who Murdered the Vets?" as a step in the right direction and as evidence that Hemingway might be able to write about "a great theme," as Herman Melville had prescribed for those who would write a "great novel."

For Ernest Hemingway, and for those who have written biographical fiction in which he appears as an important character, the 1930s may be said to have begun in Key West and ended in Havana, or at nearby Finca Vigía. But between 1930 and 1939, as Michael Reynolds' elaborate chronology for *Hemingway: The 1930s* attests, Ernest was all over the place: in and out of Kansas City, Spain, Wyoming, New York City, Bimini, Kenya, and Piggott, Arkansas, a town of about four thousand today in the northeastern corner of the state where a Hemingway-Pfeiffer Museum is maintained at the former home of Pauline's parents. In July of 1937 alone Ernest was in Bimini, New York City, Washington (for a screening of the propaganda documentary *The Spanish Earth* at the White House), Hollywood, and then back to Bimini, where he was fishing and reading proofs of *To Have and Have Not*. But the single time and place that has drawn the most attention of the appropriators is 1937 Madrid, and the two major characters who have accompanied Ernest as the subjects of appropriation, are Martha Gellhorn and John Dos Passos.

Dos Passos makes no appearance in Milton Wolff's autobiographical novel of the Spanish Civil War, *Another Hill* (1994), but Martha Gellhorn shows up with Ernest in a couple of important scenes. Wolff (1915–2008) portrays himself as Mitch Castle in the novel, an officer in the International Brigade who, as Wolff did, comes to command a machine gun unit in the

Abraham Lincoln Battalion. Castle first sees Hemingway at Chicote's Café as "a man who looked too military to be civilian and too civilian to be military, a tall, heavy-set character with dark hair and a black mustache, a handsome broad-faced man whose wide shoulders were in constant motion."[10] Later, at the Hotel Florida, Hemingway insists that Mitch read a draft of the play that will be *The Fifth Column*, and Mitch claims to like it but disputes the part about Loyalists executing prisoners (116). Hemingway does not show up again until near the end of the novel, along with Martha Gellhorn at the Hotel Majestic in Barcelona. Wolff portrays Hemingway as defensive about his political savoir faire and resentful about being lectured on "how to write for the cause" (352). Ernest's rhetoric here comes off quite credibly: "An artist has only one obligation, and that is to be true to his art, to be a craftsman and to tell it truly. When it comes to the fighting, you fight to win ... any damned way you can. Dirty, dishonest, mean. That's fighting the war, and I know as much about that as anyone here. I'm as much of a compañero as anyone here or anywhere else, comrade, and don't you forget it, Comrade Preacher" (353).

Castle submits that he would not be in Spain himself if it were not for writers like Hemingway, but as he sees it, the issue comes to theory and practice, or "application," and when it came to that, "Hemingway didn't know his ass from a hole in the ground." That makes no sense to Castle (Wolff) because he knows Ernest is "savvy," but he concludes that "Hemingway understood but was on Hemingway's side first and the masses' second" (356). Mitch Castle firmly believes Ernest is being too "goddamned subjective about it all" and "everyone who believes in this has to do his job, whatever that may be—writing, talking, or fighting—with that in mind. To stop fascism, to prevent the next war from happening" (360). In his last important passage in the novel, Hemingway refuses any altruistic vision, proclaiming, "It's all a dirty business and we have to do the best with it we can, each man with another." "Never getting any better?" Martha asks. "Not knowing if you are," Ernest responds, and Martha accompanies him out of the room, planting "a light, sweet-smelling kiss on Castle's cheek" and remarking, "What I mean is, you're all so damned wonderful" (362).

Although various biographers of both authors credit the story, it does not appear likely that John Dos Passos (1896–1970), who had served as an ambulance driver on the Western Front, met eighteen-year-old Ernest Hemingway when he was driving ambulances in northern Italy in June 1918 (Chapter Two). Certainly, neither writer could claim any clear recollections along that line. Their long and arduous friendship most likely began in the spring of 1924, when Hemingway's vignettes of *in our time* had just been published in a limited edition (just 170 copies) and when Dos Passos was working on what would become his first important novel, *Manhattan Transfer*. Dos Passos' second novel, the controversial *Three Soldiers*, had made a splash on its publication in 1921, and Hemingway comments on it in passing in a letter to Robert McAlmon dated August 5, 1923. Hemingway was at work polishing the stories that would appear in 1925, with the vignettes interspersed, as *In Our Time* (the capitalized title distinguishes this volume from the 1924 text). In fact, his first letter to Dos Passos, or "Dos," is dated April 22 of that year. Ernest thanks him, along with Sherwood Anderson, for "jamming" through its publication at Liveright. In that letter Hemingway admires Dos Passos for his drinking skills and laments the deletion of "Up in Michigan" because in it "the girl got yenced" (*Selected Letters*, 159; *Letters* II, 322). "Jesus," Hemingway writes, "I wish you were over here so we could get drunk like I am now and have been so often lately" (157, 322).

In his posthumously published *The Paris Pilgrims* (1999), Clancy Carlile (see Chapter Three) allocates a chapter or more to most of the crowd that Hem and Hadley ran with during their first twenty months in Paris, from Sylvia Beach to Picasso. Chapter 31 he reserves for Dos Passos, who feels "wonderful" that April day, pleased with his new friends Gerald and Sara Murphy and in love with Crystal Ross, until he comes upon a besotted Ernest Hemingway, "unshaven, bleary-eyed, rumpled, drunk, and belligerent" (355). The first words out of Hem's mouth are, "What the fuck are you doing here, Dos Passos?" Carlile follows various biographers in describing Hem and Dos as "almost opposites": "Hemingway, a big, loud-talking, take-charge, rough-and-ready kind of fellow; Dos Passos, shy, retiring, soft-spoken, who only now and then allowed his feelings to overflow into whimsy" (356). A self-pitying drunk, as Carlile portrays him, Hemingway rails against the "phony fuckers" of Montparnasse (357). Hadley is away in Italy, and Hem thinks he has seen his beloved nurse Agnes von Kurowsky, from his hospital stay in Milan after his wounding in 1918. He curses Dos for refusing to drink with him: "You goddamn prissy college boys!" (359). Then he adds a quick "fuck you!" and slams the door in his face.

The antagonism that Carlile's Hemingway expresses toward Dos Passos in the early 1920s appears to have no foundation, but by the late 1930s, their friendship would come to a painful end. Biographers of both writers have suggested that Hem was not as comfortable as he claimed to be with the marriage in 1929 of Dos to his boyhood friend, and perhaps would-be girlfriend, Kate (Katy) Smith, about eight years his senior and a summer denizen of Walloon Lake in upstate Michigan as early as 1916. She was also a good friend of Ernest's first wife, Hadley, whom she had known as a girl and with whom she had gone to school in St. Louis. Early in Paula McLain's *The Paris Wife*, Hadley confronts Ernest with her suspicion that Katy is very much in love with him. Ernest, she says, "took it with a strange calmness" (53). Dos opposed Hem's divorce of Hadley, whom he admired well before he met Kate Smith. But he was also friends with Pauline Peiffer, who would become the new Mrs. Ernest Hemingway in 1927, and he would oppose the dissolution of Pauline and Ernest's marriage ten years later, when he found Ernest and Martha Gellhorn romantically connected in war-torn Madrid. As mentioned above, Ernest and Pauline relocated to Key West partly on Dos Passos' recommendation, and it was while visiting them there that he met and fell in love with Katy Smith.

So far as John Dos Passos is concerned, one could argue that the biographical fictions begin with Hemingway himself in the much unloved novel *To Have and Have Not* (1937) with the odious, or perhaps simply pathetic, character of Richard Gordon, the leftish novelist of mediocre talent whose appearance disrupts the Key West world of Harry Morgan and who is often taken to be a harsh caricature of Dos Passos. Gordon's nadir comes when his wife lashes out at him for his "picknose love" (they are childless), for his bitter jealousy, and for "changing your politics to suit the fashion, sucking up to people's faces and talking about them behind their backs" (186). Helen Gordon (standing in for Katy Smith Dos Passos) delivers her finest insult when she venomously refers to her husband as "you writer." Not all readers would agree with James R. Mellow's assertion that Richard Gordon, the "phony-radical" novelist on vacation in Key West, "is obviously based on Dos Passos,"[11] or even with Donald Pizer's more carefully worked out commentary arguing that Gordon "resembles Dos Passos in a number of easily recognizable characteristics," from his writing of proletarian fiction and his childless marriage to his "peripatetic existence."[12] Robert E. Fleming, for example, maintains that in the novel as published Gordon "bears almost no resemblance to John Dos Passos."[13]

When it comes to ascertaining the rationale for Dos Passos' pioneering appropriation of Hemingway as a character in the novel *Chosen Country* (1951), as indicated in Chapter Two, it may well be that Richard Gordon's role in *To Have and Have Not* is altogether irrelevant. Certainly the many reviews, preponderantly negative, make no connection between Richard Gordon and Dos Passos, whose image had recently (August 10, 1936) graced the cover of *Time* magazine. It has been suggested that Ernest, who could not claim a major success since the publication of *A Farewell to Arms* in 1929, was jealous of Dos Passos, whose epic trilogy, *U.S.A.*, had just been triumphantly completed with the publication of *Big Money* and the write-up in *Time*. I have discovered no evidence that Dos Passos saw himself reflected in the character of Richard Gordon in *To Have and Have Not*; but Dos Passos' biographer, Townsend Ludington, observes that Arnold Gingrich, editor of the then newly fledged magazine *Esquire* (beginning publication in 1933 and a major outlet for Hemingway's sometimes rather lightweight sports journalism), thought "the pathetic figure" of Gordon "so much like Dos that he warned Hemingway of the possibility of libel after reading the manuscript of the book" (333).

As I have observed, one might object that a roman à clef does not necessarily qualify as biographical fiction, and that is one reason I prefer the term "appropriation." In any event, I contend that the first such fictional appropriation of Hemingway was not likely prompted by the "caricature" of Dos Passos as Richard Gordon in *To Have and Have Not*. Considerably more momentous were events connected with the Spanish Civil War and the dissolution of their fifteen-year friendship over the José "Pepe" Robles Pazos affair. Briefly, Robles had been a friend of Dos Passos since they met in Spain in 1916. He had been teaching at Johns Hopkins and had translated some of Dos Passos' fiction into Spanish with such success that Hem would claim in a letter of June 26, 1931, that Dos was "the great writer of Spain" and that he was hard put to convince people in Madrid that "we are old pals" (*Selected Letters*, 342). By November of 1936 Robles, who had resigned his position at Johns Hopkins and was a committed Loyalist, was serving as a colonel in the Republican army and as translator for Soviet General Vladimir Gorev. By the end of March the next year, when Hemingway arrived in Madrid to serve as correspondent for the North American Newspaper Alliance (NANA), Robles had been executed, presumably by Soviet agents. Stephen Koch's effort to unravel the mysteries in his carefully researched *The Breaking Point: Hemingway, Dos Passos, and the Murder of José Robles* (2005) reads almost like a Hemingway appropriation in its own right.

According to Koch, a novelist and former director of the graduate writing program at Columbia and current director of the Peter Hujar Archives (photographs), the Soviets recognized that Dos Passos' fervor for communism had waned. Moreover, the Russians deemed Hemingway a considerably more important public figure and believed Hem would be easier to manipulate, given his political naivety. Dos Passos and Hemingway were to work with the committed Dutch communist filmmaker Joris Ivens on the propaganda documentary *The Spanish Earth*, but in that connection as well, Dos was to be shunted aside in favor of the more influential Hemingway. Koch also dwells on Hemingway's evolving romantic relationship with the journalist, and Hem's eventual third wife, Martha Gellhorn (1908–1998), who, Koch writes, was "downright rude" to Dos Passos.[14] Other major players in the unfolding drama were *Pravda* correspondent Mikhail Koltzov, American news reporter and Stalinist Josephine (Josie) Herbst, Spanish foreign minister Julio Alvarez del Vayo, and the head of the secret police, Pepe Quintinilla (sometimes spelled "Quintanilla"), the so-called Executioner of Madrid. As Koch writes it, "Josie and Hem" chose to "blindside Dos" (147) with news of Robles' execution on allegations that he was a fascist spy who was also suspect because he had a brother serving with Franco's forces. Koch represents Hemingway as "glowing with confidence and cruelty" with the news of Robles' death (153): "He had been shot as a proven fascist collaborator, a renegade, a dirty spy, a betrayer of his friends" (154).

Koch's phrasing might be somewhat hyperbolic, but Hemingway's biographers have conceded, as Michael Reynolds observes, that "it was not Hemingway's information that so irritated Dos Passos, but the manner of his imparting it: too knowing, too officious, too ready to accept Robles as a traitor to the Republic" (*Hemingway: The 1930s*, 273–274). Noting that with "sadistic nicety" he made the revelation at a "festive luncheon" honoring a unit of the International Brigade, Kenneth Lynn writes that Hem "offhandedly informed Dos Passos that Robles had been executed" and that he "had got what he deserved" (448–449). As the title of Koch's book indicates, this would prove to be the "breaking point" of their long friendship. The tenor of the fractured relationship is more than adequately captured in the vicious letter Hemingway wrote to Dos Passos from Paris taking issue with a piece antipathetic to the actions of the communists in Spain he had read by Dos in *Common Sense* in December 1937: "A war is still being fought in Spain between the people whose side you used to be on and the fascists" (*Selected Letters*, 463). Koch's book spells out the by now familiar problem of the schism in the Republican ranks that was exploited by Stalin and that contributed significantly to their loss to the fascists under Francisco Franco. Hem's letter, dated about March 26, 1938, slams Dos for not having been in Spain all that long, and for not realizing the Russians weren't all that bad, and for selling out—and while you're at it, Hemingway adds, why not pay me back some of what you "owe"? The letter rings as painfully today as it must have seventy-five years ago: "Good old friends you know," Hemingway writes near the end, "knife you in the back for a quarter. Anybody else charge fifty cents" (464). "Hell," he writes, "Honest Jack Passos'll knife you three times in the back for fifteen cents and sing Giovanezza for free" (464) and so on. The "Giovinezza" was an Italian fascist "hymn" (the lively piece is accessible via YouTube).[15]

In *Hemingway* (1988), Christopher Cook Gilmore depicts a diffident

Ernest as he responds to Dos's news that Robles has been arrested. Turning back to his dinner, Hemingway says callously, "Shouldn't have taken up with the Fascists ... you'll find another interpreter" (113). When Koltzov, the reporter for *Pravda*, tells Hemingway that Robles has been shot, Ernest calls it "political murder" (120). Later, though, at a screening of *The Spanish Earth* in Carnegie Hall, he angrily demands of his old friend Dos, "How much did they pay you to betray Spain and the cause?" (122). Koch, however, points out that Dos Passos was not invited to the standing-room-only event where Hem, always uncomfortable at public speaking, offered up "a pack of Popular Front platitudes rehashed in Hemingwayese" (224).

We meet both Hemingway and Dos Passos in 1935 Key West in Craig McDonald's *Toros and Torsos* (2008), part of a trilogy featuring his crime novelist Hector Lassiter, who famously "lives what he write and writes what he lives" and who shares Ernest's passion for turning out "one true sentence" (the title of McDonald's 2011 novel, which takes place in 1924 Paris—see Chapter Three). In an October 2008 interview McDonald notes that Lassiter is based on detective novelist James Crumley, who died that year in Missoula, Montana. Asked how long he had been interested in Hemingway, McDonald responded, "Since my teens, really. I've read it all ... too much, probably—all the novels and short stories, many times. The posthumous stuff, the letters, the journalism. And I have, literally, a bookcase of stuff on Hem ranging from biographies to memoirs to deep-think scholarly studies. I'm steeped in Hemingway to a level that might well be unhealthy."[16]

Hector Lassiter's torrid romance in Key West is interrupted by the devastating Labor Day hurricane of 1935 (the centerpiece of Erika Robuck's *Hemingway's Girl*), which killed more than four hundred people, and by bizarre homicides that involve what amount to a surrealist cult. The sinister surrealists show up again in war-torn 1937 Madrid, where Lassiter encounters Hemingway and Dos Passos. McDonald's Dos Passos, "slope-shouldered, pot-bellied and bald," suffers some indignities from the "surly" Hemingway.[17] Hec Lassiter, whose combat record far surpasses Ernest's, claims to have come largely to spy on Martha Gellhorn with "her goddamn Bryn Mawr drone" (128). He learns of how Hemingway supposedly informed Dos Passos of Robles' death after Hem informs him that he and Dos are "quits for keeps" (183). "I was trying to spare that fucking Portuguese bastard's delicate sensibilities," Hemingway rants, assuming that Dos Passos would give up his search, "so I finally told him today. Told him the truth. Robles was arrested and put in front of a firing squad for espionage shortly after the arrest. He's dead. End of story." Hector asks if he broke the news to Dos in just those words. Of course he did. Hem then insists that Dos has not really been a friend "for a very long time" (184). When Hector knocks on his door somewhat later, Dos Passos responds, "Friend or Hemingway?" (203). McDonald's appropriation is informed by Koch's book, among other sources, as he notes in his acknowledgments. At the end of the second part of the four-part novel, Hector is being more or less willingly seduced by Pauline in Key West when Hem comes in and punches him in the jaw. The novel ends in 1959 (except for an epilogue on Hemingway's suicide) with Hemingway being accorded the pleasure of gunning down an art critic.

Unlike other versions of the Robles affair, Michael Atkinson's novel *Hemingway Cutthroat* (2010), set entirely in 1937 Spain, offers a thoroughgoing dose of historical revisionism in which Hemingway, the protagonist, "sets out to find who killed José Robles Pazos [...] and who's covering it up" (front flap of dust jacket).[18] Atkinson is also a poet and screenwriter and has taught for the past sixteen years at Long Island University. His debut novel, *Hemingway Deadlights* (2009), is set in 1956 Key West; therefore, *Hemingway Cutthroat* amounts to a sort of prequel. The dust jacket blurbs for *Deadlights*, to be considered hereafter, promise "a hard-boiled mystery drenched in tequila and scorched by the blazing Key West sun" and "hilarious dialogue, irreverent literary shoptalk, and so much excellent sun-soaked atmosphere that you'd best consume it along with a few pitchers of something cool."[19] Such are the delights promised by what one might call nonliterary fiction, despite the offer of some "literary shoptalk."

Like other novelists of biographical fiction, Atkinson takes some pleasure in describing the unhandsome Dos Passos, "who rather resembled a portly, balding supporting character from Blondie, but with watery, slightly crossed eyes" (8). In a sentence that reads like one of the crosscut moments near the end of Hemingway's "The Capital of the World," set in prewar Madrid, Atkinson writes, "José Robles walked as he was pulled on a rope, John Dos Passos drank cognac alone [in Paris], Ernest Hemingway drank sangria with a teenage girl" (8). By the end of the first chapter, Robles is dead, and at the start of the next chapter Dos arrives in Madrid at Hem's hotel room but without bringing provisions. In his interview with Denis Brian, John (Jack) Hemingway retells the story of how angry his father was that Dos Passos didn't bring ample "provision" to the Hotel Florida and says, "Papa thought that was unforgivable" (127). In what must be Atkinson's invention, Hemingway is described as a longtime friend of Robles, whom he met in 1917 in Italy (not plausible, given that Hem did not arrive until the summer of 1918) and who had visited him in Key West. "So Robles was a good egg," Hem reflects, "not cracked or rotten [...] a man of confidence and humor" (18), albeit a bit naïve and ambitious.

Contrary to many, if not most, of the appropriations, particularly as they relate to the Robles affair, Atkinson's Hemingway comes across as thoughtful and perceptive about himself, being aware, for example, that Dos Passos and others think him "an opportunist and an egomaniac" and that his main interest in the civil war is to find a place "where he can drink, screw, eat, and make a public spectacle of himself" and that he is unwilling to "make the sacrifices" for the war against the fascists (19). He is also aware of the "emptiness of acquiring things, the maddening ephemerality of sex and drunkenness, the addictive irritation of fame, the absence of something in his life he could hold and look at and declare meaningful" (18–19). This Hemingway is even willing to admit to Dos Passos that the forthcoming novel *To Have and Have Not* is "spiteful" and "a mess" (24). The Russian authorities, already in command of the war on the Republican side, stonewall the two American authors. But once Hem finds out from American journalist Josie Herbst that Robles has been executed, he promptly and sensitively informs Dos Passos: "The word is, Dos, that Robles is dead" (44). At this point, Hemingway takes over the investigation, speaking with the dangerous head of security, Pepe Quintinilla, seeking out the site of Robles' execution, searching for evidence, even speaking with Márgara, Robles' widow, whose husband, she says, "had all your books" (118).

What ensues is a healthy dose of boozing, sex, and violence, including a scene in which Ernest is tortured at the hands of American communist George Mink, whom Koch describes as "an enforcer [...] a goon, a gangster [...] a hit man for Stalin" (191–192). But Hemingway is too important to torture very severely, so he is warned to leave Spain and then released. He even manages to survive the attack on Guernica. At the end of the novel, none other than Pepe Quintinilla, the "Executioner of Madrid" himself, eagerly informs Hem at a café of how he had the Madrid police chief, Juan Posada, tortured and killed. Then he provides Hemingway with a press pass that will enable Ernest to leave Spain safely. But instead of allowing his mind to linger on that "assassin" or to be "haunted by images of suffering," Hemingway turns to his writing: "He was merely caught by the sentence he'd been writing, which was about killings and bad memories, and he could hear the pulse of it better in his head now, better than before. [...] When it rolled further on by its own steam, he smiled. Where he was in that sentence, it was vicious and dark, but it was better than where he was. It was safe, it had balance, and it was his" (259). And so that novel ends with the implication that even writing of the brutality and violence that would inform the pages of *For Whom the Bell Tolls* buffered Hemingway from the deeper darkness of reality. If Stephen Koch were to read *Hemingway Cutthroat*, he would surely wince at the whitewashing. For an even harsher portrait of Hemingway in his dispute with Dos Passos than the one offered in Koch's book, see my comments on Ben Pleasants' play, *The Hemingway/Dos Passos Wars* (1997), in Chapter Eight.

As it happens, John Dos Passos was to write his own version of the Robles affair in *Century's Ebb* (1975), which was published about five years after his death. In that context he provided what amounts to his second appropriation of Hemingway as a character, following *Chosen Country* (1951) by more than twenty years (see Chapter Three). Dos Passos tells his own story between 1937 and the end of 1968 in a series of chapters entitled, "The Later Life and Deplorable Opinions of Jay Pignatelli," a successful lawyer.[20] As in his other novels, beginning with *Manhattan Transfer* (1925), Dos Passos interpolates chapters of documentary materials, ranging from "1939" and "1948" to "Ike's Flying Conscience" and "The Execution of Malcolm Little." Surely the most poignant moment in the novel must be the death of Lulie/Katy in an automobile accident with Jay/John at the wheel. Dos Passos does not spare himself, even to the point of having Lulie/Katy ask just before the crash if he wouldn't prefer to allow her to drive. The fiery sunlight blinds him, and the next thing he knows, he is aware of his wife lying dead on the seat beside him, "her skull crushed like an eggshell" (221). The concluding chapter of the novel opens on December 24, 1968, and is entitled, "Christmas on the Moon."

In *Century's Ebb*, as in *Chosen Country*, Hemingway appears under the name George Elbert Warner. Dos Passos is the attorney Jay Pignatelli; Robles appears as Ramón Echeverria. Lulie, Jay's wife (Katy Smith Dos Passos), declares she is "so mad at him [George/Ernest] for walking out on Madeline [Pauline]" she "could beat him with a stick" (36). Jay/John discovers George/Ernest before he departs for Spain, "sober" but "in a nasty temper," in his New York hotel room, which is "piled confusedly with books and newspapers, guns, cases of fishingrods, and even half-unpacked dufflebags from the last safari he had taken with Madeline [Pauline]. A stuffed sailfish stuck its bill out from the excelsior of a packingcase beside a number of rolled-up leopard skins" (37). Jay/John also discovers a "hippopotamus foot that served for a wastebasket" stuffed with empty whisky bottles. Jay/John speaks admiringly of the Dutch filmmaker Dirk de Jager (Joris Ivens) as George/Ernest goes into his "shadowboxing routine." Shortly thereafter we meet Hilda Glentower (Martha Gellhorn). Lulie/Katy does not at all care for Hilda/Martha, whom George/Ernest refers to as "Doe."

When Jay/John arrives in Spain at the Hotel Florida, the first thing George/Ernest abruptly asks is how much "grub" he brought, as Jack Hemingway reported to Denis Brian in the late 1980s. Then Hilda/Martha shows up decked out in "an oversize silver fox stole," pointedly ignoring Jay/John (81). Readers familiar with Hemingway's three-act play, *The Fifth Column*, which had a brief run on Broadway in 1940, may recall the parallel with Dorothy Bridges, the correspondent who resembles Martha Gellhorn and who is described in Act 3, Scene 1 "trying on a silver fox cape before a mirror."[21] The scene is also played out in the 2012 film *Hemingway and Gellhorn* when Martha reluctantly buys a fur piece from a needy *madrileña*. George/Ernest speaks quite dismissively of "your professor bloke's disappearance" but then warns him, as Ernest did caution Dos, as to the dangers of the Fifth Column infiltrating Madrid from within, advising him not to "put your damn mouth to this Echeverria [Robles] business. [...] Just suppose your professor took a powder and joined the other side" (*Century's Ebb*, 82). When Jay/John meets Hedda Gelber (Josephine Herbst), she sneers at him, calls him a "social Fascist" (87), and warns him against "raising a fuss about an indiscreet Spanish professor" (88): best for Jay/John just to go back to the states and raise money to finance the film.

In a letter to Lulie/Katy, Jay/John describes a visit to the village that would figure in the documentary film *The Spanish Earth* and laments the "foreigners mixed up in this business," foreigners he finds "detestable" (89). The dispute between Dos Passos and Hemingway, who sided with Ivens on this issue, preferring more attention to battle scenes, is also carried out in *Hemingway and Gellhorn*. Jay/John then tells of how George/Ernest endangered them all with a show of "bravado" when he exposed himself to enemy artillery fire. Curiously, in Dos Passos' version, it is not George/Ernest who informs him of Echeverria's/Robles' death, but Juan (Juanito) Posada, whose brother Alfredo is a concert pianist. The pair are probably intended to suggest the brothers Pepe and Luis Quintanilla, the latter a noted artist. "We are living through terrible times," Juanito says rather disingenuously. "To overcome them we have to be terrible ourselves" (91). Jay/John leaves Spain after acquiring a death certificate for Echeverria's/Robles' widow so that she can collect on an American insurance policy. Feeling "a heartbroken admiration for the ordinary people," he clearly sees "the steel fanaticism of the Communist apparatus," as he explains in a letter to Lulie/Katy (92). In a brief and painful scene at the railroad station in Paris that replays an actual confrontation that occurred on May 11, 1937, George/Ernest confronts Jay/John (Lulie/Katy is also present) about his fading enthusiasm for the communist role in Spain and pulls back his fist "as if to hit him" (99). The event is recounted in Townsend Ludington's biography of Dos Passos (374) and elsewhere.

If Dos Passos was aware of Hemingway's anger over how he was portrayed in *Chosen Country*, the images of him in *Century's Ebb* show nothing in the way of a desire for atonement, posthumous or otherwise. The last we hear of George/Ernest occurs in a scene following the screening of *The Spanish Earth* at the White House, to which event Jay/John was not invited. After that, Jay/John receives angry letters on the subject of his supposed repudiation of the Republican cause, and the head of his law office insists he see a psychiatrist named Dr. Horatio Tybalt, "a roundfaced thickset man with tangled gray hair and protruding blue eyes," who promptly inquires, "When did you last have homosexual relations with this man who was shot?" (181). Jay/John asserts that the question is both "impertinent" and "silly." When Jay/John asks why he is so sure he is "suffering from a delusion," the doctor responds "a lot of people" who are writing of the conditions in Spain are setting forth political opinions that contradict his—George/Ernest, for example. On that subject, the psychiatrist indicates he would very much like to psychoanalyze George/Ernest, pointing out with "a low chuckling laugh" that "he needs it is badly as you do but for different reasons" (182). Like Carlile's sex scene involving Robert McAlmon and Ernest in *The Paris Pilgrims*, the scene at the psychiatrist's office is suggestive of the sub-subgenre of "slash fiction," in which heterosexual men are placed, or displaced, into homosexual relations.

Dos Passos' sly dig at his old friend might be regarded as typical of his understated manner. Despite Hemingway's anger over his portrayal in *Chosen Country* in 1951 (Chapter Three), of which, after all, Dos might never have been made aware, Dos Passos wrote a kind note to him on October 23 of that year in sympathy over the death of Pauline: "I was very fond of her. Lord it seems longer than half a lifetime ago, when I first met the dark-haired Pfeiffer girls with you in Paris. October's a month when everything seems far away and long ago."[22] That last sentence rings wistful indeed. Dos Passos also mentions Hemingway in a letter addressed to Sara Murphy and sent from Spain in August 1961, a month after Hemingway's suicide in Ketchum, Idaho: "Until I read of his poor death I didn't realize how fond I'd grown of the old Monster of Mt. Kisco" (623). Dos might have found some way in *Century's Ebb* to reflect on George's/Ernest's last painful years, culminating in his suicide, but perhaps that he chose not to do so constitutes something of a tribute to his old friend.

Very little has been made of Dos Passos' last novel, partly because it was not completed, but also because it does reflect his rather extreme political shift to the right. Townsend Ludington, in his brief comments on the book, suggests almost apologetically that "*Century's Ebb* is not so much a diatribe from the Right as a final statement in which Dos Passos, who had devoted his career to observing America, hoped to awaken other Americans with his words." Dos Passos was much disturbed with the antiwar demonstrations and riots of the 1960s, and in fact the novel does often paint "a dark, even a savage picture," as Ludington concludes (506), but Dos Passos "had become, as he himself claimed, a disillusioned moralist and as a result a more complete—and even harsher—satirist of the American scene" (507).

Was *Century's Ebb*, as some have conjectured, Dos Passos' attempt to even the score with Hemingway's portrait of him as the "pilot fish" that lured the wealthy sharks to their feeding frenzy on Ernest and Hadley's idyllic marriage in the mid–1920s, as portrayed so memorably near the end of *A Moveable Feast*, published posthumously in 1964 after significant editing by Mary Hemingway and others? Elizabeth "Betty" Dos Passos told Denis Brian in an interview published in *The True Gen* (1988) that her husband "never understood why Hemingway described him as a 'pilot fish' in *A Moveable Feast*. [...] They were all mutual friends. It wasn't a question of any one person attracting other people. [...] In the earlier days Hemingway had a great sense of humor, then as time went on my husband felt he was always playing a part, shadowboxing, and pretending he was somebody else" (75). Townsend Ludington posits that the pilot fish portrait in *A Moveable Feast* was a response to the George Elbert Warner portrayal in *Chosen Country*: "The description of Dos Passos was no fictionalized rendering but the direct statement of Hemingway at his most mean-spirited, the saddest of final words about a friendship that had been important for them both" (457).

Significantly, Ludington does not propose that the unfavorable portrait of George/Ernest in *Century's Ebb* was intended to counter the pilot fish reference in *A Moveable Feast*. One might, after all, reflect that in neither case are actual names mentioned. In his essay "The Hemingway-Dos Passos Relationship," published in the *Journal of Modern Literature* in 1986, Donald Pizer observes the "temptation to think of the four accounts as having a punch-counterpunch sequence: *To Have and Have Not* followed by *Chosen Country* followed by *A Moveable Feast* followed by *Century's Ebb*."[23] He concedes there "probably" is "something of the 'counterpunch' in *A Moveable Feast*," but he finds it "more meaningful and useful" to consider the texts from the standpoint of each writer's "suggestive self-revelation." Hemingway biographer James R. Mellow, pursuing the punch-counterpunch angle, writes that Hem "more than paid back Dos Passos for his treatment of him in *Chosen Country*" (591).

Pizer's intriguing thesis, however, is that these four appropriations constitute "a largely unconscious attempt by each writer to project into the other some of the tormenting anxieties of his own psychic life and thus of his work as a whole" (111). Pizer proposes that these appropriations should not be "considered as efforts to 'talk' to each other. Each writer was rather talking principally to himself. Each one had a powerful ghost in his own psychic closet to exorcise—the one [Hemingway] of guilt at the betrayal of a loved one, the other [Dos Passos] of a desired but later rejected code of masculinity" (128). However one comes to think about these fictions, the personal cost to Hemingway was considerable. Jeffrey Meyers, in his biography of Hemingway, argues that the "break with Dos Passos was an important turning point in Hemingway's life." After having quarreled with a broad array of literary friends, from Sherwood Anderson and Gertrude Stein to F. Scott Fitzgerald (who would die in 1940) and now John Dos Passos, Ernest would, after 1937, "have no close writer-friends. [...] In the 1940s and 1950s he knew soldiers, sportsmen, cronies, millionaires, hangers-on, actors and parasites—but he had no friends who were artists."[24]

In "Old Hem Was a Sport," an article published in the June 29, 1964, issue of *Sports Illustrated*, just three years after Hem's suicide, John Dos Passos began with what Hemingway himself might have agreed was "one true sentence": "Some of the best times I ever had in my life were with Ernest Hemingway in Key West."[25] That was during the early 1930s, and it was not in Spain. Later in the piece Dos Passos writes, "We called Hem the Old Master in those days because nobody could stop him from laying down the law, or sometimes the Mahatma on account of his having appeared in a rowboat with a towel wrapped around his head to keep off the sun. He had his crotchety moments even then, but he was still a barrel of monkeys to be with." It would be pleasant if that article had ended there, or perhaps in the next "true sentence": "This was a period when life seemed enormously comical to all of us." One wisecrack, like one drink, led naturally to the next. Dos recalls that at that time he himself was known as "Muttonfish." It was a great age of cognomens. At the end of the article, Dos Passos refers to a bust of Hemingway that "some damn sculptor" had worked up, a plaster cast of the sort "that might have been carved out of soap." Because he "never took portrait sculpture very seriously," Dos "used to ring the bust with my panama hat when I came in the door. One day Ernest caught me at it. With a peevish look he picked my hat off his bust's head and dropped it in a chair. He was sour the rest of the day. Nobody said anything about the bust but after that things were never quite so good" (67). It comes across as almost, one feels inclined to say, a good story.

The last of the biographical fictions of the 1930s to feature Hemingway (to date, that is) reads somehow anticlimactically. Journalist and freelance mystery writer Patrick Kendrick, who lives in West Palm Beach, Florida, seems determined with *Papa's Problem* (2008) to ruffle the feathers of Hemingway aficionados, who will quickly detect, as any true fan would, that the times are out of joint. The date is the first of September in 1939, as newspaper headlines inform us that Hitler has invaded Poland. But by September 1939 Hemingway had left Key West behind except for a few rare visits. He had been living with Martha Gellhorn in Cuba since April of that year. The protagonist of the novel is a loner named Emmett MacWain, "displaced" Scotsman and former inspector for Scotland Yard. MacWain is dismissive of the "resident celebrity, a book writer named Hemingway" who swills too many and brags too much.[26] The first we see of Hem, he is standing outside his home on Whitehead Street, "inebriated and bellowing like a lost cow" as he invites anyone to box with him for a hundred dollars (4). As inauspicious as these opening moments are, the portrait of Ernest soon grows even uglier.

When the intoxicated author challenges Emmet to box, Ernest promptly sucker-punches him, at the same time thumbing his eye, "an age-old, dirty-fighter's trick" (5). A former amateur boxer, MacWain proves more than equal to Hem, punching him hard in his "blubbery stomach," then delivering a blow to his jaw that sends Hem to the ground "like a rhino shot dead" (6). The reader will encounter numerous hard-boiled similes of this nature. Pauline watches the scene from the second-floor bedroom window "dispassionately." Emmet, a widower haunted by memories of his wife, is soon drawn to Pauline, who appeals to him on her husband's behalf when he is accused of murder by the "cantankerous" and largely incompetent Sheriff Lauth. Despite the fact that Pauline makes several overtures to Emmet, he eventually befriends Ernest after a fishing trip on the *Pilar* during which Ernest saves him from drowning and a shark attack. And of course Emmet does solve the complex mystery, which, also of course, involves Nazi intrigue. Implausibly enough, the villain of the piece is a wealthy and prominent landowner named Bartlett who is the illegitimate grandson of Otto Von Bismarck (224).

In effect, three of the Key West novels, those of Kendrick, Erika Robuck, and Craig McDonald, and to some extent Michael Atkinson's as well, make some effort to create sympathy for Pauline. For various reasons, Hadley has generally been regarded as the most appealing of Hemingway's four wives. By all accounts, including her own, she profited by her marriage with Ernest, and her remarriage in 1933 to Pulitzer prize-winning journalist Paul Mowrer was apparently agreeable. Hadley is the subject of two book-length biographies as well as Paula McLain's biographical fiction, in which Hadley is treated quite generously, even as Hemingway treated her in *A Moveable Feast*. Both Martha, in her memoir, *Travels with Myself and Another* (1978), and Mary, in her near epic-length memoir, *How It Was* (1976), took the opportunity to tell their own side of things. But Pauline has been, at least relatively speaking, ignored, if not slighted. While a number of letters addressed to Hadley and written in the 1930s through the 1950s are included in the *Selected Letters*, only one, dated July 19, 1941, is addressed to Pauline. She is mentioned in passing (they had met only recently) in the second volume of *The Letters of Ernest Hemingway, 1923–1925* on June 21, 1925. Hadley would learn of Ernest and Pauline's affair in the spring of 1926. The two would marry on May 10, 1927. The marriage ended miserably. What followed was alimony and acrimony. Pauline did not remarry but spent the rest of her life in Key West operating a drapery and upholstery shop with longtime friend Lorine Thompson (McIver, 83). She made frequent trips to California and was there dealing with their difficult nineteen-year-old son, Gregory, when she died suddenly of a rare tumor of the adrenal gland in 1951 at the age of 56. Her death followed immediately after a bitter argument with Ernest over the telephone, and he blamed Gregory, who would tell the story from his perspective in his memoir, *Papa* (1976).[27]

In a way, Pauline Pfeiffer Hemingway might be said to deserve the revisionist story, really something of a tribute, that we encounter in Kendrick's novel, where Emmet MacWain falls in love with her and asks her to marry him more than once after she divorces Ernest. Nearly all of the romantic scenes in the novel involve Pauline and Emmet, who resists her overtures and his own temptation and the occasional erotic dream more out of lingering love for his long deceased wife than out of respect for the philandering writer. After Hemingway leaves Key West, Pauline and Emmet are frequently seen at parties or riding horses on the beach. But as Kendrick puts it in another of his reckless similes, she "was like a thoroughbred that had been put under the whip one too many times; her spirit, and so her trust, was broken" (303). In a lengthy letter dated March 2–22, 1953, to Renaissance art historian Bernard Berenson, who published nearly twenty books on that subject in his long lifetime, Hemingway famously wrote, "There are only certain words which are valid and similies [*sic*] (bring me my dictionary [apparently no one did]) are like defective ammunition (the lowest thing I can think of at this time)" (*Selected Letters*, 809).

Five

Ernest Hemingway: Our Man in Havana

Just as *A Farewell to Arms* and a new wife in the form of Pauline Pfeiffer carried Ernest Hemingway into the 1930s, so *For Whom the Bell Tolls* and another new wife, Martha Gellhorn, buoyed him into the 1940s. He would be at work on wife #4, Mary Welsh, as *The Old Man and the Sea* sailed him into the 1950s. Beginning with *The Sun Also Rises* (and Hadley Richardson) in the 1920s, he could pretty much boast one major novel per decade, along with one new wife, or muse. Despite his eventual move to Idaho, however, he could not quite claim to have established a wholly new residence with each decade. It pretty well shakes out to Paris for the Twenties, Key West for the Thirties, and Havana for the Forties and Fifties. The Finca Vigía ("Lookout Farm") was built in 1886 and is located on a hill in San Francisco de Paula, about seven miles from Havana and Ernest's favorite watering spots: the Hotel Ambos Mundos ("Both Worlds"), Sloppy Joe's Bar (recently reopened after nearly fifty years), and the Floridita (which since 2003 has housed a full-sized bronze of Papa). Hemingway remained peripatetic, touring Asia with Martha for several months in 1941, devoting nearly a year (1944–45) to covering World War II in Europe, often spending the fall in Ketchum, Idaho (starting in 1946). Then there were other venues—Venice, Wyoming, Paris, Peru, Montana, Spain on several occasions and Kenya for the ill-fated 1953–54 safari. Few important American writers have spent so many years of their lives residing outside of the United States. In April of 1959 Ernest bought the house in Ketchum, where he would commit suicide on July 2, 1961, just short of his sixty-second birthday. He and Mary had departed Cuba for the final time on July 25, 1960, Fidel Castro having driven out the dictator Fulgencio Batista at the end of 1958.

Between the signal triumphs of *For Whom the Bell Tolls* in 1940 and *The Old Man and the Sea* in 1952 came the disappointment, if not the outright disaster, of *Across the River and into the Trees* in 1950. Few of even the most devoted aficionados have been able to share Hemingway's professed enthusiasm for, and faith in, *Across the River*, which reviewers gleefully pilloried as "the poorest thing its author has ever done" and as little more than self-parody (Meyers 377). In an odd way, what redeems the novel is not so much the comeback that was to be *The Old Man and the Sea*, but two critical responses it occasioned, both of which appeared in the *New Yorker:* Lillian Ross's occasionally hilarious "Profile," published in the May 13, 1950, issue, in which Hemingway claims to have beaten *A Farewell to Arms* with *Across the River*, and E.B. White's almost uniformly hilarious parody published in the October 14, 1950, issue as "Across the Street and into the Grill." In the Ross interview, Ernest offers up the frequently quoted rhetorical question, "How do you like it now, gentlemen?" Of this inquiry Ross blandly notes, "The question seemed to have some special significance for him, but he did not bother to explain it."[1] The best comedic moment in Ross's profile, however, occurs early on when she meets a man named Myers who has been Hemingway's seatmate on the flight from Havana and who has been compelled to read the still unfinished manuscript of *Across the River:* "He read book all way up on plane," Hemingway informs Ross in his fake Indian dialect. Myers says simply "Whew!" and then walks away "unsteadily" (32, 33).

Even more transparently than in the most transparent of the Nick Adams stories, the aging Colonel Richard Cantwell of *Across the River and into the Trees* (the title refers to the dying words of Confederate general Thomas J. "Stonewall" Jackson) resembles Ernest Hemingway. Cantwell is Hemingway in his premature dotage, a sad man of fifty who romances Renata, an Italian countess of eighteen. In Ernest's case, the real-life object of his infatuation and of his fourth wife Mary's intermittent annoyance was nineteen-year-old Adriana Ivancich. Ernest also drew on his friend General Charles "Buck" Lanham's life, adding perhaps a degree of bitterness the general would not have recognized. The colonel fares better in his romance than Ernest, enjoying a predictable romp in a gondola before he expires of a heart attack near where he was wounded in the First World War. What he gains is death with dignity, death on his own terms. And what Hemingway gained from the novel, despite the mixed to negative reviews, was a best seller, running on the *New York Times* list for 21 weeks, seven of those as number one.[2]

In its best moments the novel might be considered a sort of nostalgic ode or love-song to Venice, one of Papa's favorite places. Reynolds titles his chapter on the composition of the novel in *Hemingway: The Final Years*, "Venice Preserved." By nearly all accounts Hemingway felt very much at home at the Finca Vigía and in nearby Havana, but he was well aware of how time can transform a place, even as it was transforming himself. Reynolds describes the fifty-year-old Papa as "existential to the bone, breakfasting with death as a tablemate" (206). In one of his late journalistic pieces, "A Situation Report," published in *Look* magazine on September 4, 1956, Hemingway reflects on his desire to stick with Cuba, where he had been living for the past sixteen years. "Spain and Africa are good places," he writes, "but they are being overrun."[3] Also "overrun," he reports, are Wyoming, Montana, and Idaho, "and nobody who knew them in the old days could live in them now. Those things which are necessary to develop or to rape a country ruin it for those who knew it before it was spoiled."

Something of this nostalgia for the lost good place is implicit in his incomplete short story, perhaps intended to be a short novel, "The Last Good Country," which goes back to Nick Adams as a boy in upstate Michigan, probably in his late teens. As printed in Philip Young's *The Nick Adams Stories* in 1972, the piece runs more than sixty pages. Nick's doting younger sister, called "Littless" in the rather disturbing story, with its hints of potential incestuous attraction, is said to be eleven or twelve (*Complete Short Stories*, 520). The story was apparently written around 1953, the year *The Old Man and the Sea* (1952) won the Pulitzer Prize. The Nobel Prize would follow in 1954. In addition to a powerful note of nostalgia throughout, we find Nick Adams reflecting on his intention of living ardently in the present, like so many of Hemingway's protagonists, and like Hemingway himself: "He had already learned there was only one day at a time and that it was always the day you were in" (539). "*Carpe diem*," Horace wrote more than two thousand years ago: "seize the day." And the rest of that line also deserves its moment: "*quam minimum credula postero*" ("trusting as little as possible in the next").

Any Hemingway fan reading the appropriations set in the Forties and fifties would be well aware that, despite the great success of *For Whom the Bell Tolls* in 1940 and of *The Old Man and the Sea* a dozen years later, those decades revealed the master in a state of decline as he struggled with a myriad of health problems, exacerbated by the two nearly fatal air crashes in Kenya early in 1954, and with several book manuscripts that would be published after his death without the benefit of his own editing. For that reason alone, irrespective of their contents, the posthumous volumes will, or should, remain controversial: the Paris memoir, *A Moveable Feast* (1964, 2009), least controversial because it appears to have been in nearly final form; the long, perhaps would-be epic novel *Islands in the Stream* (1970); the sports journalism book on bullfighting, *The Dangerous Summer* (1985); the heavily edited, highly controversial novel of androgyny, *The Garden of Eden* (1986); the sprawling African memoir *True at First Light* (1999) and its alternative version, *Under Kilimanjaro* (2005). Any serious critical comment on these books lies well outside the range of this particular inquiry, but I propose that the posthumous publications have contributed significantly to the ongoing production of biographical fictions dealing with Hemingway as an important character and with a profusion of what I call "Hemingway-obsessed" characters (Chapter Seven). All of these texts opened up new inquiry into, and speculation about, Ernest Hemingway's identity as person and writer, both manifest and latent. Just who was this major American author we all thought we knew so well?

At least five biographical fictions from the 1940s and 1950s feature Hemingway prominently: Henry Morgan's *Toro* (1977) and Dan Simmons' *The Crook Factory* (1999), which take us to the summer of 1942, when Hem was taking the *Pilar* in search of Nazi U-boats; Michael Atkinson's *Hemingway Deadlights* (2009), which features Hem as an amateur sleuth in 1956 Key West and Cuba; Karl Alexander's *Papa and Fidel* (1989), in which Papa joins forces with Castro in 1957 Cuba; and Cuban crime novelist Leonardo Padura Fuentes' *Adiós Hemingway* (2005), which oscillates between chapters set in October 1958, as Hemingway struggles with his writing and tries to cope with depression, and the present day, in which a detective named Mario Conde attempts to solve a murder that occurred back then at the Finca Vigía. All of these novels involve mystery or intrigue in one way or another, and four of them depict Hemingway as an action-figure. Not surprisingly, the latter three writers also portray him struggling with his writing, in some cases with writer's block generally, and in other cases with particular texts.

The presumably pseudonymous Henry Morgan, the first-person narrator of *Toro*, tells Hemingway he never read *To Have and Have Not*, so we are to presume that the shared name is coincidental.[4] The source for both Hemingway and "Morgan" is the seventeenth-century British privateer and pirate, as this Henry Morgan is well aware ("Harry" is the common nickname or informal version of "Henry"). "Toro" is the nickname Morgan foists on Ernest, who generally refers to the youthful protagonist from Chicago as "kid." The twenty-year-old Morgan is declared unfit for military service because he killed a man in a brawl in upstate Michigan (with an oar), so he has drifted down to Havana, where he runs into Hemingway, predictably enough, at a bar. He has read some of the stories and novels and thinks him "a very fine writer," but he is not particularly impressed (16). Morgan discovers that although Hemingway "enjoyed the company of beautiful and daring women" he was "no great womanizer. He was too romantic and idealistic for that" (56). This fictional observation has been voiced by some of the biographers, who have observed that contrary to the public image, Ernest tended to be shy, was often affectionate, and could be quite sentimental. We are well over a third of the way through the short novel before the intrigue involving Nazi agents in Cuba begins to enter. Hemingway believes the Germans want to kill him because of the intelligence work he has done with the *Pilar*. The skeptical Morgan is not convinced: "Hemingway was a true romantic and he never got over it; if he hadn't been one of the finest writers in the world he could easily have been a terrific bore" (98). Such is the conclusion of the mature Henry Morgan as he tells his story to a Hemingway aficionado at a Greenwich Village bar almost twenty years later when news breaks of Hem's suicide.

Of course Morgan proves to be correct. If the Germans had wanted to assassinate Hemingway there in Cuba, they might easily have done so, though just why they might have wanted the world renowned writer dead is not clear. Certainly it would not have been because of his actual adventures aboard the *Pilar*, about which more hereafter. The plot twist turns out to be even more improbable: The Nazis intend to kidnap Hemingway, take him back to the Third Reich, and convert him into a voice for the cause, perhaps in the vein of Ezra Pound, who gave radio broadcasts as an avid anti–Semite and spokesman for Mussolini's fascist Italy. Predictably, the intrigue is resolved in gunfire, after which Henry Morgan is deported back to the U.S. In the closing chapter, Ernest speaks of suicide, flatly proposing, "I think suicide defines a man's life" (229). Morgan cannot convince him otherwise. Henry Morgan's pulp novel apparently passed without comment from the reviewers. It comes off as a hastily turned out potboiler.

The same cannot be said for Dan Simmons' *The Crook Factory*, which appeared 22 years later and has drawn considerably more critical attention. The "Crook Factory" was Hemingway's term for his would-be special ops group dedicated to sniffing out any Axis spies in or around Havana and ideally to sinking a U-boat by arming the *Pilar* as a sort of Q-ship. Dan Simmons' protagonist in the sizable novel that goes by that title is an irascible FBI agent named Joe Lucas, who serves as the first-person narrator. He is not inclined to admire the author even in retrospect. The novel opens with Lucas in Cuba learning of Hemingway's suicide. As he drinks at the Floridita bar, he notices the bust of Hemingway, a "goddamned shrine" given him by his "kiss-up friends."[5] He dismisses *The Old Man and the Sea* as "that stupid fish story," though he later admits he did not read any of the fiction until 1974, just three years before he retired from the agency, and he has come to appreciate the short stories in particular (555). As it happens, thirty-year-old Lucas has even less esteem for J. Edgar Hoover, who sends him to Havana in April 1942 to check out Hemingway, whom he regards as "a liar and a phony and probably a Communist" (41). Hoover thinks the amateur spy operation is "silly," but ambassador Spruille Braden favors it.

In fact, Braden did support what many would consider a harebrained scheme involving "a bizarre combination of Spaniards: some bar tenders; a few wharf rats; some down-at-the-heels pelota players and former bullfighters; two Basque priests; assorted exiled counts and dukes; several Loyalists and Francistas. He built an excellent organization and did an A-One job'" (quoted in Reynolds, *Hemingway: The Final Years*, 60). By mid–November of 1942 the *Pilar* was in fact on armed patrol in the waters of the Caribbean. The wooden fishing boat could accommodate only light machine guns, grenades, and a bazooka, but Hemingway was confident that by deception they could get within range of a submarine's conning tower. A Marine sergeant was assigned to man the radio. As history, though not fiction, would have it, they had no luck, and by the first of February 1944 the patrols had ceased. In May Ernest was off to England, where he would cover the rest of the war for *Collier's* magazine.

The Crook Factory had drawn the most attention of the biographical fictions concerning Hemingway, at least so far as popular readership is concerned, prior to the publication in 2011 of Paula McLain's *The Paris Wife*. The book appeared at a propitious moment, coinciding with the centenary of Hemingway's birth and publication of the fifth and last volume of Michael Reynolds' highly regarded biographies, *Hemingway: The Final Years*, two chapters of which are devoted largely to the activities of the Crook Factory. Simmons' plot is fairly intricate and his protagonist is considerably more thoroughly evolved and complex than is Morgan's. Moreover, Simmons' research appears to have been far more thorough than Morgan's, and he offers Hemingway much more dimension in his supporting role. There has been talk of a film version, possibly starring Johnny Depp as Joe Lucas.[6] Author of nearly thirty novels and three collections of short fiction, Simmons earned his bachelor's degree in English from Wabash College and his master's in education from Washington University in St. Louis. He taught in elementary schools till 1989. His first book to attract attention was *Summer of Night* (1991), a horror novel in the Stephen King mode. His work has won a variety of awards in speculative fiction genres. Among the other writers dealt with in his fiction are Mark Twain and the poet John Keats, the latter in the Hugo Award–winning novel *Hyperion* (1990).[7]

The reviewer for *Publishers Weekly* admired "the zesty characters it [*The Crook Factory*] entangles" and asserted that "its intricate cross-weave of fact and fiction distinguish this celebration of the Hemingway centenary."[8] Writing for the *Library Journal*, Michael Rogers declared, "Without falling into hero worship, Simmons offers one of the best fictional portraits of Hemingway available."[9] The online reviewers have been even more commendatory: "a beautifully realized work of fierce originality," writes the reviewer for goodreads.com, "a tour de force of historical suspense."[10] Rodger Turner, writing for sfsite.com, specializing in speculative or science fiction, commended the "brilliance of the writing" and found that Simmons "captured the atmosphere of the time perfectly."[11] Adrienne Martin, writing for the *Baltimore City Paper*, a weekly alternative newspaper, suggested that while Simmons had somehow obscured his past reputation as a respected writer of genre fiction, he had nevertheless turned out with this "alternative history" a "work of speculative fiction of the purest sort," creating "a minor masterpiece here, seamlessly piecing together bits of historical fact with his own speculations."[12] Predictably, the blurbs affixed to the novel, more than a dozen of which confront the reader upon opening the book, rival those cited above on Erika Robuck's *Hemingway's Girl* (Chapter Four). English art historian, novelist, and journalist Iain Pears, writer of more than a dozen novels, particularly connecting art history with mystery, observed, "The essence of good historical fiction is not being able to tell where history ends and fiction begins." In that regard, he insists, *The Crook Factory* "succeeds extraordinarily well," and adds that the portrayal of Hemingway is "brilliantly realized."

At first resentful over his assignment, which he considers trivial, Lucas soon discovers dangerous Nazi espionage activity and corruption in the Cuban government, and he also discovers some fondness for the man he describes as possessing "a powerful sense of fun and well-being" (65). In the best of the appropriations, as in this novel, the writer, usually operating through a protagonist who is not Hemingway, offers interpretations, or reinterpretations, of the man, and sometimes of his writing as well. In writing that Ernest "could dominate any room he entered," Simmons echoes any number of his biographers and at the same time validates their perceptions. The readers-as-fans generally, but not always, know and believe that sort of thing about Hemingway, but in the biographical fiction they find their sense of the "true gen" (to appropriate Hemingway's term for the inside dope or intelligence) ratified. And more than that, they find their vision of the man, both his strengths and his weaknesses, effectually dramatized. One form of validation in novels like *The Crook Factory* is provided by a reliable narrator like Joe Lucas who will reinforce our impressions of a personage like J. Edgar Hoover, "a mean fat boy dressed in nice clothes—a vindictive sissy," and then depict our hero by way of sharp contrast as "a complex, charismatic man who could probably be simultaneously the most interesting person you'd ever met and a tiresome son of a bitch" (73). The fact that Lucas perceives both positive and potentially negative traits at this point makes him more credible to the readers. Like Erika Robuck's Mariella, he appears more objective, hence more reliable.

Readers will expect to encounter Martha Gellhorn, and Hemingway's sons, and perhaps even such "characters" as the his first mate on the *Pilar*, Gregorio Fuentes, and millionaire Winston Guest, who was a member of the Crook Factory, but they will also welcome such celebrities as Gary Cooper and Ingrid Bergman when they show up (90–107). One obligation of the writer of biographical or historical fiction is to present such personalities convincingly so that their appearance in the story does not simply come across as an opportunity for name-dropping. Cooper, for example, reflects on his part in the soon-to-be-released (1943) film version of *For Whom the Bell Tolls*, the proceeds from which would help pay for Ernest's purchase of the Finca Vigía. Ernest had sold the rights to Paramount in 1941 for what was at that time a record $150,000.[13] Cooper also mentions his role as Lou Gehrig in *The Pride of the Yankees* (1942), for which he would receive a Best Actor Academy Award nomination. Later, Joe Lucas joins Gary Cooper and others in bombarding an annoying neighbor with firecrackers.

Mostly, however, *The Crook Factory* is a novel of intrigue and action, and those who like 007 films will probably love this book. In fact, in an early chapter we find Joe Lucas flying to Miami alongside none other than Commander Ian Fleming, RN, connected with naval intelligence, who notes in passing (and with playful irony for the informed reader) that he "was never good at telling a story" (55). Although the officer describes fascinating details of ongoing espionage, the blasé Lucas claims to be "bored." Fleming was at the time ten years away from writing his first James Bond novel, *Casino Royale*. (Commander Fleming also appears near the end of the novel when Lucas is debriefed.) Ensign John F. Kennedy also gets himself read into the record, as does Marlene Dietrich, whom Hemingway called "The Kraut," sitting around the pool at the Finca with Martha Gellhorn (not a woman Joe admires) and others. But it is in offering "readings" of Hemingway via Joe Lucas that Simmons draws our closest attention, as in his observation that to go out to sea in one's own boat, out of sight of land, which Hemingway did regularly, was "a rare and challenging thing": "One could see a man's mettle in whether he treated the sea with indifference or the respect it deserved, and whether the ego blinded him to the true power that surrounded a man or men alone on a wide ocean" (252). Hemingway, he concludes, "treated the sea with an adult's respect" (253).

Simmons pays tribute to Hemingway via Lucas's long "confidential memo" to J. Edgar Hoover, in which he assures the director of the FBI that Ernest is not an enemy agent. However, he maintains a certain ambivalence in his comments. "Ernest Hemingway is a man addicted to words and thoughts," Lucas writes, but Lucas claims to have no idea what kind of writer he is (325, 326). That would come later. Hem "makes friends easily and loses them even more easily. [...] As an acquaintance, he is loyal and treacherous. In daily life, he intersperses acts of great generosity with intervals of unremitting meanspiritedness. [...] Hemingway is physically graceful and imposing, Mr. Director, while at the same time the man can be as clumsy as an ox in a phone booth" (325, 326). Nothing new here, readers of the biographies might say, but one might also say, as many have said, that there are already too many biographies of Ernest Miller Hemingway. What happens in the appropriations is that some of the best insights of the best biographers acquire new expression and emphasis. Reflecting on Hem's boasts about beating Turgenev, Tolstoy and other writers (hoping eventually "to knock Mr. Shakespeare on his ass"—not a statement I've located in the letters), Lucas calls "bullshit" (327). Lucas concludes that he does not yet know exactly "who or what Mr. Ernest Hemingway is," but he advises Hoover that "the man does not quit or fold or go away easily. [...] This man is stubborn, and tough, and used to pain, and amazingly persistent" (328). One can almost imagine Ernest rising from his grave to applaud. Not surprisingly, when Joe and Ernest later come to blows, predictably enough with two alpha males, neither man backs down and Ernest more than holds his own with the well-trained agent, who is a dozen years his junior.

As has been demonstrated, and will be hereafter, not all of the appropriators celebrate Hemingway, and few of them portray him uncritically. Most of them subordinate him in one way or another to a more experienced or savvy protagonist like Dan Simmons' Joe Lucas or Patrick Kendrick's Emmett MacWain. But in one way Simmons' Hemingway holds a major advantage over his co-protagonist, and that has to do with his writing. In perhaps his greatest tribute to Hemingway, Simmons makes him Lucas's teacher and mentor when it comes to the writing of fiction: "It's like listening to people, Lucas. If their experiences are vivid, they become part of you. [...] After a while, their experiences get to be more vivid than your own. Then you mix it all together. You invent from your own life stories and from all of theirs, and after a while it doesn't matter which is which ... what's yours and what's theirs, what was true and what was bullshit. It's all true then" (403). Hem sustains the lessons for several pages, blending a number of observations familiar to aficionados from his letters, his nonfiction, and his Nobel Prize address, and Joe appears to have reached an understanding, after which, this not being primarily a novel-of-ideas, the shooting begins (408). Proof that Joe Lucas has learned to appreciate fiction is, of course, this novel. Spoiler Alert: Ernest saves Joe's life by killing a double agent, and the *Pilar* does eventually give chase to a U-boat, but the submarine escapes.

So far as I can tell, no writer of biographical fiction has to date attempted to recount Hemingway's controversial exploits as a war correspondent in Europe after D-Day, and he made very little effort in that direction himself. Colonel Cantwell of *Across the River and into the Trees* (1950) has combat experiences similar to those of the historical Charles "Buck" Lanham, with whom Hemingway experienced the Battle of Hürtgen Forest (Hürtgenwald) in the autumn and winter of 1944-45, but other than that, only the short story "Black Ass at the Cross Roads," unpublished during his lifetime, has seen print ("black ass" was Hemingway's term for depression). Christopher Cook Gilmore captures some of Hemingway's action as "unofficial liaison officer with the French Resistance" and "irregular combatant" (Reynolds, *Hemingway: The Final Years*, 105) in his novelization, *Hemingway* (141–157), but Michael Reynolds offers a more detailed and in some ways more readable account in his biography (96–125). Elsewhere, Reynolds notes that at the Hürtgen Forest, with the 22nd Regiment of the 4th Infantry Division, Hemingway "verifiably killed a German soldier who was charging across the clearing toward Lanham's command post" ("Brief Biography," 43). Although he had to answer to a Court of Inquiry in early October 1944 on charges of bearing arms illegally as a correspondent, Ernest soldiered on. In 1947 Lanham would see to it that he was awarded a Bronze Star for his services.

Hemingway makes a pair of cameo appearances in Mark Winegardner's baseball novel, *The Veracruz Blues* (1996), about the Mexican League in 1946 when the Pasquel brothers lured a number of major league players, including New York Giants' pitcher Sal "The Barber" Maglie (1917–1992) and outfielder Danny Gardella (1920–2005), to play baseball south of the border. First-person narrator Frank Bullinger Jr. is a reporter who dreams of writing The Great American Novel. He claims to have gotten his job through "a chum of Hemingway's."[14] At the Finca Vigía Bullinger meets Ernest, who is partying with Babe Ruth and heavyweight boxer Gene Tunney, both retired. Bullinger foists off a manuscript of his novel and the evening ends with a drunken brawl; he notes in passing that the novel Hemingway was working on would eventually be published posthumously as *The Garden of Eden*. In a later scene

Bullinger drunkenly lashes out at Hemingway, who admits having lost his manuscript without having read it. Hem coldcocks the journalist but comes by his hotel the next day to apologize. At breakfast Hem rehashes the story of his own lost manuscripts (95).

A slightly more fully evolved cameo appearance by Hemingway in William Kennedy's *Changó's Beads and Two-Tone Shoes* (2011), which occurs in 1957 Havana, might prompt some question as to the pertinence of such rather slight appropriations to my study. One might argue that Winegardner's appropriations amount to hardly more than passing allusions intended to attract fan appeal and maybe to establish some credibility, or perhaps even to serve as a sort of quick tribute to an admired writer. Winegardner's Hem advises Bullinger to write "true sentences" about baseball, which he presumably does with this novel, so the scene adds some verisimilitude. But the scene about the lost valise does little to celebrate the author, as Bullinger undercuts Ernest's assertion that he "became a true writer" by learning to shrug off his "apprentice stuff" (95). Bullinger cites Gertrude Stein's version of the episode, in which Hemingway shows up "with two whores, no overcoat, a belly full of Pernod, and tears streaming down his cheeks." Ernest then makes a "showy goodbye" and disappears from the novel.

Kennedy's Hemingway appears only briefly in the novel, the eighth in his Albany cycle, when the protagonist, journalist Danny Quinn, shows up at the Floridita on March 12, 1957, to meet him. Quinn introduces himself to Ernest as a reporter who has quit his job with the *Miami Herald* in order to write a novel in the Ernest Hemingway tradition. In this, as in most of the other appropriations set in Cuba, Ernest describes Batista as "*[un] hijo de la gran puta*" (in effect, as a son of a great whore, or a son of a bitch). Also, he offers Quinn some writing advice that may strike us as more explicit than the famous "write one true sentence": "Remove the colon and semicolon keys from your typewriter" and "Shun adverbs strenuously."[15] As with his advice about similes passed along in a letter to art historian Bernhard Berenson in 1953, Hem delights here in using an adverb even as he warns against them.

Ernest and Danny hit it off, and through a friend Hemingway introduces Danny to the beautiful revolutionary Renata. (The name recalls the countess from *Across the River*.) Right after that, Ernest punches out a pesky American tourist he takes to be a "jerk." That punch eventually leads the tourist to challenge Hemingway to a duel; we learn of the inconsequential outcome of that only much later in a flashback. But Kennedy does offer, through Danny Quinn, something of a eulogy to Hemingway at the end of his career and fearless in the face of death: "He had four books going and couldn't finish any of them."

But, Danny reflects, "He could still talk, even if his ambition outdistanced what was left of his talent. He found the answer early on and kept telling us what it was, but he never got it all out. It was his iceberg principle: only the tip revealed, the rest stuck in his throat" (273). In effect, Kennedy's Hemingway ironically becomes the victim of his basic mantra of composition, as laid out in *Death in the Afternoon* (1932): "If a writer of prose knows enough about what he is writing about he may omit things that he knows and the reader, if the writer is writing truly enough, will have a feeling of those things as strongly as though the writer had stated them. The dignity of movement of an ice-berg is due to only one-eighth of it being above water."[16]

Following the chronology of the writer's life, the next biographical fiction in which Hemingway plays a major role after Simmons' novel is Michael Atkinson's *Hemingway Deadlights* (2009), a mystery set in 1956 in Key West and Cuba. "A rip-roaring, hilarious read, as brash and daring as Papa Hemingway himself," promises novelist and retired physician Tess Gerritsen in her front-cover blurb. Gerritsen is the writer of more than two dozen romantic suspense and medical and crime thrillers, including several in the *Rizzoli and Isles* series that has become popular television fare for TNT. In fact, we immediately catch something of Gerritsen's promised "read" as we learn that Ernest has been shooting at geckos (quite successfully) and that he foolhardily pursued them onto the tiled roof of his Key West home, from which he fell, breaking his ankle in the process. Inasmuch as Hem was accident prone all of his life, the episode rings credibly enough. What makes it particularly laughable, though, are Atkinson's intentionally ludicrous, heavy-handed, hard-boiled similes. The tequila-soused Hemingway, we're told, had been "rampaging around the grounds like a 230-pound kindergartner pretending to manhunt Iroquois with a pop-gun."[17]

As Atkinson presents the case in this, his debut novel, Hemingway is visiting his sons Patrick and Gregory, both of whom are in their mid-twenties and Pauline having died in 1951. Mary remains in Cuba at the Finca Vigía rather like Tam O'Shanter's wife, "nursing her wrath to keep it warm." Promptly, Hemingway gets embroiled in a murder case involving a drinking buddy who has been shot through by a "ninety-millimeter cannon harpoon" (11). Unlike Simmons' novel, this one makes no effort to develop complexity in Hemingway's character or to come to terms with his views about writing. Atkinson is a film and culture critic who has published books on pop cinema, a volume of poetry, and another Hemingway appropriation, *Hemingway Cutthroat* (Chapter Four). He teaches film at Long Island University/C.W. Post. Clearly, *Hemingway Deadlights* is intended as a jeu d'esprit. Patrick, who comes off quite well in the novel, is more successful in dealing with his father than is Gregory because he maintains "a cavalier zest about things despite his father's behemothic egomania, judgmental bullying and macho histrionics" (30). Nevertheless, he leaves for the mainland after exchanging words with Papa about his recent rereading of *A Farewell to Arms*. Simmons' Hemingway wants to be taken seriously, or perhaps it would be more accurate to say that Simmons insists that his Hemingway be taken seriously. Atkinson pretty much insists quite otherwise, making space, for example, for Hemingway to have a quick romp with a coed groupie named Germaine from the Georgia State College for Women and another with a "bizarre, long-legged Cuban woman" named Matilde (102), who, it turns out, is an agent for Batista.

And so it goes, one is tempted to say. Before long, Hemingway is confronted by three CIA agents who are aware that he is heading to Cuba in order to track down the murderers of his friend, who was apparently involved with Castro's revolt against Batista. But Atkinson will not allow Ernest to take himself seriously, even when he is in danger. When he tells Mary, back at the Finca, that he is "not just a writer and a husband and a homeowner" but "a man grappling with the real dangers of a real world," she accuses him of taking such sentiments and such phrasing out of his books: "I'm talking about ideas, meathead. You're trying to live up to these ideological notions you've picked up and used in your books." Life, Mary rages, "is not about putting yourself at preposterous risk for the sake of a vague Spartan idea about honor and machismo" (143). Like most of the appropriators, Atkinson cannot resist attempting some fairly serious efforts to come to grips with the man: "A big differentiation, Hemingway always thought, between a man's perspective and a woman's is that women most often can grow to maturity in civilized countries without ever knowing what it's like to get hit in the face so hard your nose bleeds" (144). What Hemingway "really wanted" from his wives, Atkinson asserts, is "a refuge from that life." Thinking about his lifetime of taking risks, Atkinson's Hemingway concludes, "History itself, and his tendency to become embroiled in it, allowed him to feel like the man he thought he should be" (170).

Atkinson's Hemingway subsequently tangles with the mobster Meyer Lansky and with both Fidel Castro and Che Guevara, and he ends up smoking cigars with Fidel and Che "like hunting-trip pals" (191). Spoiler Alert: Hemingway's action here probably saves the world from a serious nuclear incident. Enough said.

Enough, that is, until we once again encounter Hemingway in Cuba, this time in 1957, when he follows the lead of a journalist friend in search of a big story on Castro's guerrilla activities in the Sierra Maestras. In his brief preface to *Papa and Fidel* (1989), Karl Alexander informs us that the following story "is what might have happened, what should have happened if Ernest Hemingway and Fidel Castro had become friends."[18] Alexander has authored half a dozen novels, including the best-selling *Time After Time* (1979), in which H.G. Wells pursues Jack the Ripper into the twentieth century. It was made into a movie starring Malcolm McDowell and Mary Steenburgen. After acquiring his bachelor's degree in philosophy from Brown University, Alexander served as a Marine officer in Vietnam, and went on to gain a master's degree from San Francisco State and an MFA from the University of Iowa's Writers' Workshop. Following a family tradition of screenwriters, according to his Web site, Alexander has remained actively involved in the movie industry.[19]

How many of these writers of biographical fictions involving Hemingway have been at least quondam academics? Perhaps not surprisingly, some of them (or at least some of their characters) tend to sneer at academe, even as Hemingway was known to do from time to time. Yet few if any of the appropriators have followed Hemingway's route of eschewing a college education altogether, and more than a few of them, including Alexander, Atkinson, and Simmons, have done (or are doing) some teaching, usually at the college or university level. This is not to say that these writers tend to be conventional academics, striving to publish critical or scholarly papers in order to acquire the plum of tenure. In fact, some of them, not including Karl Alexander, tend to be rather coy about their academic credentials, as if to suggest that the possession of a graduate degree of some sort might compromise their status as popular novelists, writers of page-turning thrillers whose books might be described in such terms as hard-boiled, lurid, raucous, or the three G's—gripping, gritty, and gutsy.

Alexander's *Papa and Fidel*, which has pretty much gone by without reviews, might well be described as "all of the above," opening as it does with the nearly sixty-year-old Hemingway, suffering from liver disease, high blood pressure, and writer's block, saving the life of a journalist and getting himself seized and beaten by Batista's secret police. When Ernest recovers the presence of mind to identify himself, however, Batista himself has him released and offers him a glass of scotch. "Who the hell wants to be an old man?" Papa asks himself a couple of weeks later, lamenting that his behavior had been "very un–Hemingwayesque" (14). His journalist friend, safe in the U.S., gets him in touch with the rebels of M-26-7, and before long Hem is struggling with them into the Sierras, haunted by his apparent inability to live up to the standards of his own characters, who can embrace pain so readily.

One of several good examples of how the appropriator behaves as interpreter or literary scholar occurs early in the novel when Che Guevara tells Hemingway that none of his guerrillas in *For Whom the Bell Tolls*, not even Robert Jordan, "lived up to their ideals, their beliefs, which is why they lost. That was your intent, no?" According to Alexander, Papa is "astonished" and tells himself he had no such intention, "but yes," he thinks, "you could read *The Bell* that way, and Jesus Christ, when you think about it for a second, it damn well works" (52). Later, at Che's prompting, Fidel reads the novel in just three hours without putting it down, "not even for a cigar" (91), and subsequently claims to have used the novel in preparation for one of his successful assaults. Papa is "stunned" to learn that *For Whom the Bell Tolls*, "written in part as an antiwar statement," has been "used as a field manual," but he reacts with mixed emotions of "horror and pride" as he recognizes that something he has written has "actually made a difference" and has "affected history" (97). For the record, while there is some evidence that Castro admired the novel and learned something from it about guerrilla warfare (Meyers, 518), it appears that claims of its use as a tactical manual are apocryphal.

Fidel urges Papa to use his clout as a Nobel Prize winner to inform the world of the revolutionaries' ideals which, at that point, are not necessarily communist, but Hemingway resists political involvement. Hem unthinkingly guns down a pair of quail after Fidel has warned him not to shoot because Batista's troops are nearby, and Fidel calls him an "old fool [...] a pigheaded idiot gringo Viejo!" (60). Papa responds by socking the future dictator in the jaw and setting him down on his keister. This sort of thing can and does happen in biographical fiction, though not necessarily with much plausibility. A little over a third of the way into the novel, on January 1, 1959, Castro and his rebels march triumphantly into Havana. He and Hemingway meet again later that year, and for an instant Papa thinks he might have a great idea for a novel: "Me'n Castro, one step removed, father and son. Kid saves his country from a horrible dictatorship [...]" (182). But the inspiration fades, along with his hope for Fidel. By then Ernest has connected with Castro's illegitimate son Fidelito, introducing him to baseball and serving at times as a surrogate father.

By the time Hemingway finally left Cuba, in late July of 1960, he was a sick man still haunted by his failure to write "the big book," still struggling with the long essay for *Life* magazine that would become the unwieldy bullfight account known as "The Dangerous Summer" (published posthumously as a book in 1985), and still placing what he thought of as finishing touches on what would be *A Moveable Feast*. In Alexander's novel Papa leaves Cuba far more dramatically after the "First Annual Ernest Hemingway Marlin Tournament," held in May 1960 and actually won by Castro, who (in the appropriation) narrowly escapes an assassination attempt while fishing. In *Papa and Fidel* Alexander's Hemingway does finish his father-son novel featuring himself and Fidel, the father "redeeming himself" by saving his son from assassination (290), but there's a bit more to it. This time, though, no "spoiler alert."

Cuban mystery writer Leonardo Padura Fuentes, in *Adiós Hemingway* (2005), also focuses on Ernest's last troubled days spent at the Finca Vigía, plagued by Batista's thugs and struggling with his writing. An award-winning journalist and detective writer still residing in Cuba, Fuentes won the nation's most prestigious literary award, the National Prize for Literature, in 2012. He has been called "the best known and most widely read contemporary Cuban author."[20] In a "translator's introduction" to an excerpt from the novel, Teresa Prados-Terreira notes that Fuentes pushes "the limit of what is acceptable" in his fiction and stands as "a voice of reason, a quiet critical thinker amid many vociferous officials"; she regards his mysteries as "a pretext to explore Cuban society."[21] In his author's note, Fuentes claims to have had "a fierce love-hate relationship for years" with Hemingway, so he decided to "transfer" his "obsession" to his detective, Mario Conde, although he supposed he had closed the book on him after writing four novels featuring him between 1990 and 1997.[22] He adds that he thinks of himself as having indulged in a sort of "poetic and postmodern license" in the process (ix).

The initiating premise of the novel is that in the present time (1998) skeletal remains of an FBI agent have turned up at the Hemingway estate, Finca Vigía, now maintained as a museum, and they date back forty years, to early October 1958. Could Hemingway have committed murder? Eight years out of the police force, 45-year-old Mario Conde contents himself with buying and selling used books and trying to write. He honors Hemingway for two reasons. First, when he was a boy in 1960, his grandfather took him to Cojímar, where he saw Ernest about to leave the country for the last time. He cried out "adiós" to him, and the world famous writer responded and smiled. Second, he believes in the legitimacy, among all of the "myths" and "lies," of the bronze bust of Hemingway paid for by the fishermen of that village (7, 19). When an inspector tells him about the case, Conde somewhat reluctantly becomes involved. What sets the novel apart from most of the other appropriations is Fuentes' decision to move back and forth between unnumbered chapters with only a dingbat to signal the point of transition and with Hemingway's narrative pretty much taken up in medias res and from his perspective, which occasionally reads as if it were stream-of-consciousness. In general the seven sections that pertain to Conde's present investigation run considerably longer than those that occur with Hemingway in 1958 as he struggles with the "elusive" and "slippery" book that will be *The Garden of Eden*.

No other appropriator attempts to get us as intimately connected with Hemingway's thinking and his emotional state as Leonardo Padura Fuentes. Hemingway's depression is heightened because Mary is back in the States and because he is trying, not very successfully, to curb his drinking because of an ailing liver. As Fuentes phrases it, Papa sees "he had to forge a life for himself in order to forge a literature; he had to fight, kill, fish, live, in order to be able to write" (32). Moreover, Hemingway knows "his imagination had always been limited and unreliable" (30–31). Now, as he sees it, "with no adventures or memories, what would he write about?" He perceives that life could be defeating him, despite his famous proclamation in old Santiago's words from *The Old Man and the Sea* that "a man can be destroyed but not defeated."[23] "Absolute rubbish," Fuentes' Papa tells himself, "just rhetoric and lies" (33). At the end of Hemingway's first section, Fuentes describes what is about to happen as events "that set in motion the end of his life."

Conde, we are told, has not visited the Finca in more than twenty years, and since then he has become more critical of the writer whose life and work had once meant so much to him. More than the crime to be solved, Conde finds himself searching for "the truth—or perhaps the true lie—about Ernest Miller Hemingway" (46). Part of his disesteem of his former hero connects with the Robles-Dos Passos affair dating back to 1937 and the civil war in Spain (Chapter Four). But his "alienation" from his "literary idol" also involves his recognition that Papa was "an arrogant and violent person, unable to give love to those who loved him" and that despite his twenty years of living in Cuba the author did not "understand a damned thing about their island" (46–47). Complicating his investigation is Conde's run-in with a group that refers to itself as the "Cuban Hemingwayians," probably based on the Hemingway Society, who of course do not credit the notion that Papa was guilty of murder.

Near the midpoint of the novel Hemingway rambles around the Finca armed with his Thompson submachine gun and accompanied by Black Dog, wondering whether he should finish a rewrite on *Death in the Afternoon*, a revision of *Islands in the Stream*, a new undertaking of *The Garden of Eden*, or the possible destruction of *A Moveable Feast*—publish it, or burn it (102). In that frame of mind he pretty much confesses to the negative image that Conde has expressed: Havana remains "elusive and unfathomable" to him; "he had never known how to value, and almost never how to return the affection of those who really loved him." He attributes this to "the unsociable attitudes of his parents" with their "hypocritical puritanism" (98). In effect, Fuentes offers a portrayal of an inner, self-critical, unselfconfident Hemingway that defies the view of him as arrogant and narcissistic. Beneath the façade of public braggadocio lies genuine self-doubt. (Most analysts do in fact theorize that low self-esteem lies at the heart of pathological narcissism.) Ultimately, Ernest agonizes almost as much over his literary triumphs as he does over his apparently stillborn works in progress.

Mario Conde solves the crime easily enough, and of course Papa was not the killer. He concludes that "the real Hemingway" was, at the end, a man who "was free of the character he'd invented for himself" (217). And even though he concedes that literature is "one big lie," Conde decides he will join the Cuban Hemingwayians because "it's one of the two thousand possible and accredited ways of bullshitting" and "there are no bosses, no rules, nor anyone to keep tabs on you and you can come in and go out when you feel like it" (221–222).

The most recent novel to appropriate Ernest Hemingway's character, reminiscent in some ways of Paula McLain's *The Paris Wife* (2011) and Erika Robuck's *Hemingway's Girl* (2012), is British novelist Naomi Wood's *Mrs. Hemingway* (2014), which refracts the man through the multiple lenses of all four of his wives, each of whom is allotted meticulously measured narrative space (eighty pages apiece, more or less). Reviewers have praised the novel as "carefully written, richly imagined and emotionally wise" and "meticulously researched," and as "tension-filled, intricately structured and enormously entertaining."[24] Writing for *The Guardian*, Lara Feigel described Wood's "portrayal of Hemingway" as "enticing, maddening and haunting enough to leave us trying to solve for ourselves" the conundrum of his life: what did he need?[25] Wood presents each of the four wives on the brink of the dissolution of her marriage, Mary Welsh Hemingway's marriage to be dissolved not by the incursion of another woman and subsequent divorce, but by her husband's suicide, which she valiantly struggles to maintain, publicly at least, was an accident. In her comments on the novel, some of which are attached as a readers guide, Wood indicates that reading Hemingway's love letters prompted her to undertake the novel, and she acknowledges Bernice Kert's *The Hemingway Women* (1983) as her most important resource. She also mentions McLain's novel with respect to Hadley's time in Paris. Robuck, who offers a portrait of Pauline ("Fife") Feiffer Hemingway in her novel set in 1930s Key West, provided a blurb in which she calls Wood's novel "Obsessively readable, fascinating, and heartbreaking."[26] Wood began work on her book as part of her doctoral dissertation at the University of East Anglia. Her first novel, *The Godless Boys* (2011), is a dystopian fiction in which the Church has taken control of the England.

Wood mentions "the incident with the suitcase" (13) in each section of the novel so that it becomes something of a recurrent motif. Most of the action of the Hadley chapters takes place in Paris or the French Riviera between April and June of 1926, on the brink of publication of *The Sun Also Rises*, from which the fictional Hadley feels she has been excluded as "punishment" for having lost the "small leather suitcase" loaded with his manuscripts (37). There at Antibes, with Fife staying with them supposedly to help care for Bumby, who has suffered from whooping cough, and in the company of the wealthy Sara and Gerald Murphy, Hadley sees the breakup coming, recognizes the danger in the fact that her husband is not writing, and perceives at one point that "he is pretending to be a character in one of his stories, rather than her husband" (19). In effect, she relinquishes the marriage ruefully but without regrets or acrimony.

In the second part, or movement, in effect—the novel does at times seem symphonic in its structure, or perhaps to invite some musical reflection along the lines of "variations on a theme"—Pauline Pfeiffer Hemingway (she's called "Fife" throughout), eleven years into her marriage, awaits her husband's return from Madrid (June 1938), painfully aware of his affair with Martha Gellhorn. Fife is angry but also guilt-ridden over her role in the breakup of Hadley's marriage, as flashback chapters to Paris and Piggott, Arkansas, in 1926, inform us. But while Hadley appears pathetically resigned to her loss, Fife at least exacts the satisfaction of delivering Ernest a sock to the jaw that knocks him tumbling into the surf. Her anger is made palpable. As Wood notes in her comments on the novel, Pauline was the only wife to die before her husband and the only one who left no account or observations on their life together. She suggests that although Pauline was "badly behaved," she also "got the most rotten deal. She fell in love with someone she really shouldn't have, married him, got dumped, never remarried, and then died young" (Readers Guide 9). Pauline was also mother of two of Ernest's three sons, including the troubled Gregory, who is mentioned briefly in the final section of the novel. Mary, we are told, "counted Fife very much as her friend" (301).

Only Martha, after her divorce, remains mostly aloof from the other wives. As Wood represents Martha Gellhorn Hemingway, primarily on August 26, 1944, in Paris, she perceives herself as "different from the rest of those women, those lapdog wives" (183). In a flashback to their meeting in December of 1936 at Sloppy Joe's Bar in Key West, Martha informs Ernest she is "not a woman apt to be left" (174). She refers to him not always playfully as "Pig," and she has become exhausted by "her husband's need to self-aggrandize" (189). By 1944, just 45 years old, Hemingway seems prematurely aged and needy. After coming across his love poem to Mary Welsh. Martha concludes he "doesn't need a wife; he needs a mother!" (210). And Martha is distinctly unmotherly. In one of her more compassionate moments she thinks, "Poor Ernest. He had never loved another more than he himself was loved" (217). In fact, Wood reserves some of her most insightful observations on Hemingway for this section on Martha: "She knows he is afraid of being alone. He is scared of the brutish character of his sadness." When he tells her he wants to be both a good man and a good writer, Martha tells him to be one or the other, not both (238). After that year, Wood notes at the end of that movement, Martha never saw him again and would not "let his famous name pass her lips" (240). In his introductory note to Gellhorn's memoir, *Travels with Myself and Another* (2001, first published in 1978) Bill Buford describes Ernest Hemingway as "the forbidden subject."[27] Nevertheless, Buford writes, "she had respect for the writing" and although "she resented him for all kinds of reasons, [...] he was the only man she talked about" (xvi).

Most of the final movement, Mary's, takes place in Ketchum, late September 1961, just a couple of months after Ernest's suicide. "To lose his ability to write," Mary recognizes, "was to have lost the ability to clear his mind of itself" (245). As Bernice Kert observes, the last years were hard: "He was old and sick and she was his keeper and he resented it bitterly."[28] Mary realizes best of all the wives that "Ernest had, by default, to be shared" (275), and at fifteen years, hers was the longest lived of the marriages. Wood portrays the tempestuous nature of that marriage, beginning with their Paris courtship in 1944 when one evening, after "a silly fight," Ernest punches her on the jaw (274), an episode that recalls Fife's socking of Ernest in 1938. As in other sections of the novel, most notably Martha's, this one moves freely back and forth in time and space, from London and Paris in 1944, to Havana in 1946–47, and on to Idaho and 1961. It is Mary's lot to perceive the four wives as a "strange family" of "unlikely sisters" (302). Bernice Kert indicates it was not until 1966 that Mary "publicly acknowledged" the fact of her husband's suicide (505). "Oh, Ernest," Naomi Wood's Mary reflects, "you were a man of too many wives" (316). The thought "*almost* makes her laugh" (italics mine).

Aside from the chronological order, there's a certain rightness to the fact that Joyce Carol Oates ends her unusual book of short fiction, *Wild Nights!* (2008), stories about the afterlives or last days of Edgar Allan Poe, Emily Dickinson, Mark Twain, Henry James, and Ernest Hemingway, with her account of Hemingway's suicide. After all, the death of no other American writer has been the occasion of so much spilt ink. Writing for the *New York Times*, Brenda Wineapple hailed the book as both "hilarious and harrowing," noting that it is "also a cycle of morality tales about sexual power," or more accurately, about diminished or distorted sexual power.²⁹ Writing for the *Kenyon Review*, David S. Reynolds agreed that the stories are "sometimes funny, sometimes shattering in emotional impact," and he observes that all of the writers are "skeptics [...] who face death without the comfort of religious certainty."³⁰ Hemingway's suicide Reynolds describes as "an orgy of sensual and metaphysical delight," but he takes Oates somewhat to task for veering into "falsification," in effect, for overindulging in "distortion," even as he submits that historical fiction does necessarily involve that. Finally, he suggests that all of the stories come down to "fictional meditations" about these writers and in fact "about any artist faced with impending death."

Several writers of biographical fiction refer to the often quoted statement Hemingway makes to the Old Lady in *Death in the Afternoon:* "Madame, all stories if continued far enough, end in death, and he is no true-story teller who would keep that from you" (122). What most of those who cite that passage do not mention is his next sentence: "Especially do all stories of monogamy end in death, and your man who is monogamous while he often lives most happily, dies in the most lonely fashion." This observation applies equally in Oates's stories, both to the opening story on Poe and to the concluding story, "Papa at Ketchum, 1961," which is surely the most frightening and disturbing text in the book. Hem's references to Mary throughout as "the woman," implicitly applicable to all women, are often vicious, or even venomous: "A female is essentially a cunt, the pure purpose of the female is cunt, but a woman, a wife, is a cunt with a mouth, a man has to reckon with."³¹ Oates's story offers the reader practically no respite other than the episode in which Papa saves the life of a young buck snarled up in barbed wire. She indicates in her notes at the back of the book that her primary biographical source for Hemingway was Kenneth S. Lynn's volume, which proceeds pretty much from the premise, "thanks to the manipulations of his mother, Hemingway did not enjoy a normal childhood" and argues that he remained obsessed with her for the remainder of his life (27).

Oates's Hemingway is also obsessed with guns, and she spends some time describing his fantasy of shooting his father, reminiscent of passages involving Nick Adams in the story "Fathers and Sons." Unfortunately, her knowledge of weaponry would expose her to possible upbraiding from the true aficionado, as she refers more than once to a shotgun, as opposed to a rifle, fitted out with a scope. One must step warily when writing biographical fiction about Papa when guns are involved. In particular, Oates's Papa fantasizes about shooting Mary, more or less transferring his boyhood fantasy of shooting his father, partly because of his uxorious weakness. In the final analysis Oates's Hemingway is pathetic without being very sympathetic. Being made privy to Hemingway's mind on the eve of his suicide, the result might be predictably ugly: "What remained of his life was pent-up in him like jism clotted into his scrotum and lower gut. Pent-up so it has turned to pus. He would blow out the greeny pus" (194). One can almost hear Joyce Carol Oates sarcastically echoing Papa as quoted by Lillian Ross: "How do you like it now, gentlemen?" On the other hand, lest we suspect that Oates undervalues Hemingway's genius, we might consult her essay "Reading as a Writer," first published in 2000, where she offers the following observation on his concept of courage in both life and writing as "grace under pressure": "His was a masculinized vision of strength fortified by will, and it's as readily applicable to the art of fiction itself: grace is what we might call fluidity, smoothness, 'inevitability' of narration, and pressure is the need to keep the story as tightly crafted, as pared to its essentials, as possible."[32]

Few of the appropriators have resisted the impulse to investigate or in some way reflect on Hemingway's suicide, often comparing it to that of his father in 1928, about which, as Oates's Hemingway makes quite clear, Ernest had ambivalent if not downright contradictory feelings. Fuentes' Hemingway is "a man overcome by life," as Conde expresses it, yet in some ways triumphant. Henry Morgan's Hemingway, in his early forties but already world-weary and disillusioned (the German term *Weltschmerz* would seem to apply), insists "when you can take death into your own hands you can arrange things exactly right" (228). Dan Simmons begins *The Crook Factory* with Joe Lucas learning of Ernest's suicide and muttering irreverently, "*Sic transit hijo de puta*," which he translates to an old Cuban bellman as "there goes the son of a bitch" (2), though he doesn't bother to explain the play on the old Latin proverb that traditionally ends "*gloria mundi*" (the glory of the world). At the end of the novel, Lucas shows up at Papa's grave in Ketchum with a .38 Sig Sauer and a bottle of scotch, 85 years old and with a bad prognosis for making it to 86: his intentions are obvious. Christopher Cook Gilmore's *Hemingway* concludes simply: "He squeezed the trigger" (203). Craig McDonald, Karl Alexander, Paula McLain, and Erika Robuck all devote a concluding chapter or an epilogue to the event, which devotion comes across as a sort of eulogy.

By way of comparison, one might reflect on how a few of Hemingway's biographers concluded their volumes in response to the suicide. Carlos Baker looks back to the mantra ("maxim") cited on the first page of Chapter One, "*il faut (d'abord) durer*," proposing another one: "*il faut (après tout) mourir*." Then he moves to the scenario of the loading of the shotgun: "He slipped in two shells, lowered the gun butt carefully to the floor, leaned forward, pressed the twin barrels against his forehead just above the eyebrows and tripped both triggers" (564). From a certain perspective, the stark realism is quite appropriate. James R. Mellow also reflects on the final scene, parenthetically refers to Mary stirring in her sleep, and concludes, "Hemingway, whatever else he knew, knew for all time that the questions he had asked in a lifetime were answered, and those that remained were no longer of any consequence" (604). The last phrase looks back to Mellow's subtitle, drawn from the story "Soldier's Home": *A Life Without Consequences*. Kenneth S. Lynn offers something of a eulogy in his closing sentence: "Through the enormous curiosity and gusto with which he pursued new adventures and the valorous dedication he brought to his art, he affirmed the possibilities of life in this tough world" (593). Michael Reynolds, at the end of his five-volume biography, provides a one-page coda that begins with this sentence: "Ernest Hemingway was the embodiment of America's promise." He "set out to become the best writer of his time," or perhaps more accurately, if we were to accept Hemingway's hyperbolic confidence, "of *all* time." "With pluck and luck, talent and wit, hard work and hard living, he did just that." Reynolds concludes with an implicit nod to Greek tragedy: "It is an old story, older than written words, a story the ancient Greeks would have recognized" (*Hemingway: The Final Years*, 360).

Six

Sci-Fi Papa; or, Hemingway in Speculative Fiction

There is some justice in the fact that the first of the appropriations involving Ernest Hemingway that can clearly be identified as being connected with the realm of speculative fiction would be the product of a master of that subgenre, Ray Bradbury (1920–2012). Like Hemingway, Bradbury was educated not by college but by libraries and bookstores. He also was born in Illinois, though his family moved to Los Angeles when he was fourteen. Also like Hemingway, the writer most famous for his dystopian novel *Fahrenheit 451* (1953) was turned down for military service due to poor eyesight. Discounting his almost innumerable plays, screenplays, and teleplays, Bradbury turned out more than fifty books of fiction, primarily short story collections, many of which have been made into movies, like his 1962 novel, *Something Wicked This Way Comes* (the title is drawn from the witches in Shakespeare's *Macbeth*), or into episodes for such television series as *Alfred Hitchcock Presents* and *The Twilight Zone*. His homage to Hemingway is the short story "The Kilimanjaro Device," first printed in *Life* magazine on January 29, 1965. Coincidentally, with respect to the end of the previous chapter, it looks back to Hemingway's last days. In the editor's notes published on page three, managing editor George P. Hunt wrote that in the 28-year life of the magazine, they had run just a dozen short stories, this one being the twelfth. The articles editor likened the experience to *Life* magazine's publication of *The Old Man and the Sea* in 1952. Describing Bradbury as "the top science fiction writer in the U.S. today," Hunt notes that the author "hates freeways, admires supermarkets, refuses to drive a car or ride a plane."[1]

"The Kilimanjaro Device" is the lead story in Bradbury's 1969 collection,

I Sing the Body Electric, a title that comes from a poem by Walt Whitman (Bradbury was a lifelong poetry lover). Bradbury makes deft use of his speculative premise here, so that the staunchly realist reader may exercise the option at the end to read it that way. The unnamed first-person narrator drives into Ketchum, Idaho, and strikes up a conversation with a hunter over a beer about "that old man on the road."[2] For the most haunting photograph of Hemingway as an old man is not the headshot used on the front cover of the paperback edition of Kenneth S. Lynn's biography or the last of the photographs from his galleries (#43), which depicts the old man in winter wearing a flat cap and overcoat, his back to the camera, staring into a leafless copse (which may cause us to ponder Robert Frost's line, "The woods are lovely, dark, and deep," except for this photograph I would substitute for "lovely" the word "lonely.") No, the photo I have in mind, and that I suspect Bradbury did, too, is John Bryson's shot of Hemingway taken on February 1, 1959, along a snow-bordered road in Ketchum. The old writer is kicking a can of beer, and he is kicking it well. Wearing a flat cap and a plaid shirt with light-colored vest, he shows the athletic form of a good NFL place-kicker. The photograph appeared in *Life* magazine on July 14, 1961, just a dozen days after Hemingway's suicide.[3]

The hunter in the story asks if the man is "another of those reporters," but the narrator assures him he is not; he is "one of his readers" (4). From the opening page of the story, any Hemingway fan would detect Bradbury's understated imitation of the style or voice of the master: "I parked the truck in front of an old saloon and walked around the town and talked to a few people and breathed the air and it was sweet and clear" (3). Later the narrator admits that his voice has "without knowing, fallen into the rhythm of his way of saying" (5). The hunter agrees with the narrator that there are right and wrong places for a grave and there are good and bad times to die, and Hemingway's grave up on a mountain is not in the right place. (Actually, Hemingway's grave is not on a mountain, but right off State Route 75 near the center of Ketchum—almost too easy to access.) The narrator then reveals that he and his friends have chipped in and bought a safari truck, which is actually a time machine. For "stuff" to run it, the narrator uses not gasoline but intensive "reading" and the "love" of his fellow aficionados and "our remembering what his words did to us twenty years or twenty-five or thirty years ago" (8). At such moments Bradbury tends to flirt with allegory. The narrator then drives off.

In the second movement of the almost evenly balanced text, the narrator finds the grave on the mountain has vanished, and he then encounters "an old man in a heavy sweater" (9). At this point the story is almost entirely given over to very Hemingwayesque dialogue, but at no point does the old man actually own up to being "Papa," the nickname the narrator uses, but only sparingly. The narrator proposes to take him to the tenth of January 1954, not far from Nairobi, which would be almost exactly two weeks before the nearly fatal airplane crashes, after which, according to most biographers, Hemingway was never the same as a man or a writer. The second crash brought his fourth concussion in the past ten years. Kenneth Lynn's medical summary puts it succinctly enough:

> Even the concussion of the brain, the ruptured liver, spleen and right kidney, the temporary loss of vision in his left eye, the loss of hearing in his left ear, the crushed vertebra, the sprained right arm and shoulder, the sprained left leg, the temporary paralysis of his sphincter, and the first-degree burns on his face, arms and head [...] did not serve to wean him from the bottle [529].

Lynn's account does not differ significantly from that of Michael Reynolds in *Hemingway: The Final Years* (274). The narrator of Bradbury's story, then, proposes to save Hem from the worst years of his life by leaving him near the "frozen carcass of a leopard" on the heights of Mount Kilimanjaro, called by the Masai the "House of God," per the epigraph to "The Snows of Kilimanjaro" (*Complete Short Stories*, 39).

Bradbury's story closes with the two men racing at ninety miles an hour, both of them yelling "like boys." Toward the end, we're told, the old man says he thinks they are flying, very much as the fallen writer Harry, in his hallucination, believes he is being flown to a hospital. David Mogen includes "The Kilimanjaro Device" among Bradbury's "difficult-to-classify stories" and asserts the narrator is "obviously a surrogate for Bradbury himself."[4] Elsewhere, Mogen notes Bradbury's description of Hemingway's "clean, really fresh-water, wonderful style" (32) and suggests the influence of his "taut, dramatic dialogue, which evokes emotional intensity rather than describing it" (38). In a chapter on Bradbury's "Emerging Sense of Critical Judgment," Jonathan R. Eller indicates that Bradbury in 1944 "began to work systematically through the short stories of Hemingway, and found it tough going at times."[5] Bradbury would later speculate about the "vulnerabilities beneath the stoic exterior of Hemingway's prose" and would go on to develop a "mature sense of the complexities of Hemingway's life" (81–82). In the collection *Long After Midnight*, Bradbury would publish what Mogen calls a "comical tribute" to Hemingway with "The Parrot Who Met Papa" (132).

Two novels that grapple with Hemingway's suicide, "if that's what it was," the writers hint darkly, are William McCranor Henderson's *I Killed Hemingway* (1993) and Craig McDonald's *Print the Legend* (2010). Henderson's novel was listed as a *New York Times* Notable Book of the Year, and it drew a slew of blurbs and appreciative reviews. The protagonist is a quondam Hemingway scholar named Elliot McGuire whose lone book, *Hemingway on the Terraces*, was to have been followed by his "close-out project," *Papa Among the Piranhas: A Study of Hemingway's Attitudes Toward Biographers*, "the ultimate nihilistic project for a Hemingway biographer—a study of how he hated, feared and despised us all."[6] Instead, he got shot down at the annual Hemingway Association (HA) dinner and has turned to ghostwriting celebrity biographies. Finding that the more he haunted Hem's life, the more it haunted him, even "oppressed" him, Elliot has become "an acute Hemo-phobe" (11). His personal project is a New Age scheme called LifeForms, "a self-help system based on biographical analysis" (8). But his publisher is much more interested in the claims of an old codger from Key West called Eric "Pappy" Markham, a look-alike who claims to have known Hemingway in Paris during the 1920s, to have written or inspired much of Hem's published writing, and finally to have murdered him, making it look like suicide. Elliot soon discovers that Pappy (a sort of alter version of Papa) has written no manuscript and that he must write one himself based on his interviews with the cantankerous old cuss.

According to Pappy, it was he who gave Ezra Pound the famous motto of modernism, "make it new," and it was he who came up with Imagism, and so on. "Those early years in Paris," Pappy insists, "I literally rewrote everything he later published" (74). Elliot quickly comes to the realization that to Pappy Markham down there in Key West, the Hemingway impersonators are in fact impersonating him, and he also detects a tie-in with his LifeForms project. The concept of impersonation comes in for occasionally serious treatment here, as Elliot runs into a writer who is filled with "fear and loathing" of impersonators: "We are impersonating remote giants instead of transforming ourselves into legitimate self-creations" (67). A graduate of Oberlin College with a degree in philosophy, William McCranor Henderson has taught creative writing at the University of North Carolina and North Carolina State University. He knows something whereof he speaks on the subject of impersonation, having performed as an Elvis Presley impersonator before writing his nonfiction account, *I Elvis: Confessions of a Counterfeit King* (1997). His first novel, *Stark Raving Elvis* (1984), examines the phenomenon of rock music in American culture. In his review of *I Killed Hemingway*, Kirk Curnutt suggests it might be called "The Elvisceration of Papa" and notes more seriously that Hemingway, like such pop icons as Marilyn Monroe and Jim Morrison, shares "that sad truism that a tragic death is the ultimate good-career move."[7]

It is perhaps no great leap from impersonation to appropriation as I have employed that term in this book. Pappy not only seeks to appropriate Hemingway's thinking and writing; he also imposes on events from his life, including the famous episode of the lost valise. According to his version, it was he who encouraged Hadley to pack all of the manuscripts, carbons included, and it was he who stole the valise, and he who did Hem a "favor" by dumping it into the sewer (99). While he's at it, Pappy slips in a bit of innuendo implying that Hem might have been gay or possibly a quondam vampire. Pappy goes beyond efforts to demythologize Hemingway, asserting at one point, for instance, as reviewers did eighty years ago, that he was somehow bereft of "ideas," or, as Wyndham Lewis put it in a notorious review of *Men Without Women* (1934), that he was a "dumb ox."[8] And so it is not surprising when we encounter Wyndham Lewis in the pages of *A Moveable Feast* bearing the face of a frog, a nasty looking man with the eyes "of an unsuccessful rapist" (109). In his 2012 study, *Ernest Hemingway: Thought in Action*, Mark Cirino undertakes to correct Wyndham Lewis's argument, observing that "Hemingway himself was complicit in promoting the stereotype of his life and his work as fiercely anti-intellectual," but "the tension that defines his work" is "the internal struggle between a man of action and a man of thought."[9] Pappy Markham's game, however, is pretty much to undercut much of the Hemingway life and legend while usurping credit for the work. "No story tests credulity," Kirk Curnutt avers, "more than Pappy's claim that the Hemingway persona was lifted from his own personality," which is the reason, having lost his "voice," that Pappy Markham needs a ghostwriter (110).

In one of the more serious moments of the often comedic novel that satirizes everything from postmodernism to biography, literary scholarship, and literature itself, Elliot presents his dilemma to a fellow biographer: how important is truth to the project—"absolute objective truth," the facts, that which can be substantiated, or as Hem would have put it, "the true gen"? The fellow biographer predictably posits there's "no such thing as truth," and when he raises the question as to the most important "criterion for good biography," he shouts over his Scotch, "Entertainment!" (114). One might argue that such a view applies more to celebrity biography than it does to other subsets of the genre, like literary biography, in which one criterion, at least implicitly, is to provide the reader some reliable perspective on the writer's work. Nevertheless, Michael Reynolds' use of certain fictional techniques in his five-volume life of Hemingway, sufficient for it to be deemed at places akin to that quirky new subgenre "creative nonfiction," succeeds in providing genuine "entertainment" as well as enlightenment, and it is the former quality that sets the books apart from the other biographies. Elliot proceeds with his transcription of Pappy's ravings, justifying his decision with his new "working view": "Bottom-line veracity (whatever that has been) now paled before evident biographical verisimilitude" (198). One might detect a tautology here in the notion of "evident verisimilitude." Or perhaps the key word here is "evident" as opposed to "genuine."

After Markham's book becomes a best seller, Elliot exposes him on nationwide television as a fraud, but the public believes what it wants to believe—in effect, the better, more entertaining story. "Ultimately, y'know," a woman who teaches "Papa studies" at a university in Ohio suggests to Elliot, "everyone assembles their own custom Hemingway doll" (284).

What prompts me to identify *I Killed Hemingway* as "speculative fiction" is Henderson's fabrication of a premise that operates toward fantasy, in defiance of the sometimes admittedly rather loose verisimilitude on which most of the appropriations are founded. As the novel evolves, Pappy Markham is exposed as a writer wannabe and a plagiarist who was himself exposed by Hemingway in 1920s Paris, since which event Pappy has been on a vendetta. After reading his supposed memoir, which goes by this same title (*I Killed Hemingway*), given Henderson's playfully ironic twist, people never think of Hemingway as they did before. Biographies tend to work that same way. Most biographers are at heart historic revisionists, and this pertains particularly to those who choose to write on figures like Hemingway, who have already been the subject of multiple, substantial biographies. I'm distinguishing here between biography and personal memoir, although those writers also usually operate from the premise that they have an alternative view of the subject. In some ways Henderson does proceed like other writers of biographical fiction, however, in that he expects his audience to be drawn by the Hemingway name in the book's title and to bring with them some awareness of the genuine biographical information so they can be amused by Pappy's comments on having written "Out of Season" or tickled by his claim to have tried to kill Hem in 1928 by pushing "the goddamn skylight so it fell on his head" (154). As in all of the appropriations, the fun for the reader comes from being an insider, from being a knowledgeable fan. The novel's satire on Hemingway scholars and the critical industry they have created ironically turns on itself, as without those scholars and that industry, novels like *I Killed Hemingway* would probably have no readership.

The same applies to Craig McDonald's *Print the Legend*, which also concerns Hemingway's suicide and in which, as in Henderson's novel, Hemingway himself makes no direct appearance. McDonald's sleuth, crime writer, and longtime Hemingway pal, Hector Lassiter, serves as the protagonist for this novel, as he did for *One True Sentence* (Chapter Three) and *Toros and Torsos* (Chapter Four). The premise on which this novel is founded makes it an even more apt candidate for rating as "speculative" than *I Killed Hemingway*. Perhaps Mary Welsh Hemingway had tolerated all she could and put out a contract on her sick, crazed husband. The front cover flap lays out the plot well enough, which concerns Lassiter's discovery of some of Hemingway's lost writings: "he uncovers an audacious, decades-long conspiracy tied to the emergent art movements of 1920s Paris, the most duplicitous of Cold War espionage tactics, and J. Edgar Hoover's FBI ... a scheme to discredit and destroy not only authors but the very craft of literature itself."[10]

The novel opens with a sort of two-part prologue, two pages on Hemingway's suicide and two pages set a month later at the Finca Vigía, where Fidel Castro watches Mary pack some of her husband's "priceless manuscripts" for shipment to Ketchum (5). Standing near Castro is the villain of the piece, Donovan Creedy, agent for both the FBI and the CIA and a no-talent, bitterly envious, would-be writer whose connection with Lassiter and Hemingway dates back to Paris and the early Twenties. The most complex book of McDonald's trilogy and the second one written, *Print the Legend* is divided into eight parts and no fewer than 56 chapters, many of them very brief and some of them subdivided among the various key characters: Lassiter, Creedy, Mary Hemingway, a disreputable and abusive Hemingway scholar named Richard Paulsen, and his pregnant wife, Hannah. Each of the chapters is given a title from Hemingway's work with the exception of one, "How It Was," the title of Mary Hemingway's memoir. Each of the chapters is also affixed with a quotation from a remarkably wide variety of sources: Nietzsche, Graham Greene, J. Edgar Hoover, Jessamyn West, E.B. White, Emily Brontë, Vladimir Nabokov, Henry Miller, Sylvia Plath, Raymond Chandler, William Faulkner, Ambrose Bierce, contemporary poet David Lehman. The epigraphs alone are worth the price of admission.

The novel takes place mostly at a mythical fourth annual Hemingway conference at Sun Valley, Idaho, in 1965. Appropriately, McDonald selects for an epigraph to the first chapter Hemingway's diatribe against "professional critics," although he omits an early sentence from that 1925 letter to Sherwood Anderson, "All criticism is shit anyway" (*Selected Letters*, 162; *Letters* II, 339). In that letter, in which Ernest thanks Sherwood Anderson for promoting the book of short stories that will soon be published as *In Our Time*, he offers a rather lame apology for making cutting remarks about Anderson's novel, *Many Marriages* (1923), claims that literary critics make him "sick," and describes them as the "camp following eunochs [*sic*] of literature." Rather harsh words, one might say, for a writer not yet 26 years old and with his spurs yet to be won. But of course Hemingway's fictional longtime pal and fellow writer Hector Lassiter, "the last man standing of the Lost Generation" and reluctant keynote speaker, shares those sentiments almost exactly. Lassiter, we are told, "represents a kind of vanishing breed of martial men skilled in American letters—Hemingway-type men, that is" (11). Like Henderson then, McDonald will have his fun with the literary "establishment," if there is one. In one of his wryly self-reflexive and rather self-complimentary moments in the novel, Mary reads one of Hector's novels, which the informed reader recognizes as McDonald's *Toros and Torsos*, and thinks, "It transcended any notions of genre writing she'd ever indulged" (176).

We run into such playful moments throughout this literary thriller, or more aptly intrigue, featuring Hector Lassiter at age 65 as (we're informed three times in just one page of text and for the third time in this book) "the man who lives what he writes and writes what he lives" (11–12)—just like his old friend Hemingway, presumably. McDonald does stumble occasionally, as in a section on Donovan Creedy in 1922 Paris enviously muttering, "More Hemingway crap," hardly a plausible comment given the date (15). But for the most part, McDonald proves he has prepared himself well for this undertaking. In his acknowledgments he recommends Michael Reynolds' biographies as "definitive" (341), and perhaps they are, at least so far as such volumes can be. He also credits the late George Plimpton and Valerie Hemingway, Gregory's third wife and author of *Running with the Bulls: My Years with the Hemingways* (2004), whom he interviewed prior to writing *Print the Legend*. The title of this appropriation comes from the 1962 western *The Man Who Shot Liberty Valence*, starring James Stewart and directed by John Ford: "When the legend becomes fact," a newsman says, "print the legend." The same title has been used for a hefty biography of Ford written by Scott Eyman (2001) and for Martha A. Sandweiss's book on photography of the American West (2004).

In her review of the novel in *Hemingway Review*, Lisa Tyler describes McDonald as "a writer's writer" and finds the novel to be "improbably but effectively, a meditation on the art of writing fiction."[11] When Mary asks Hector whether as a reader he would prefer the manuscript of *Islands in the Stream* or *The Garden of Eden*, he opts for the latter because, he tells her, he thinks Ernest was "reaching there, moving from modernism into postmodernism" (98), a rather striking statement from a writer so averse to literary criticism, especially given the 1965 date. The term was rarely if ever applied to literature prior to the publication of Ihab Hassan's *The Dismemberment of Orpheus: Toward a Postmodern Literature* in 1972 (Hassan devotes a chapter to Hemingway). But the point here is not whether McDonald is guilty of a possible anachronism, but to substantiate Tyler's claim as to his unusual juxtaposition of critical commentary in the context of the hard-boiled crime novel. Mary's response, in fact, typical of her tough and profane ways, reflects the language of the latter: "And who wants to read that shit?" Mary wrinkled her nose. "A writer writing about a writer writing? What the fuck is that?" True to her own background as a journalist, not to mention her personal familiarity with some of the actual events therein, Mary Hemingway prefers the greater action of *Islands in the Stream*.

In his address to the Hemingway scholars, Hector's great revelation is that Papa was not paranoid about "being hounded by the FBI" (215), a point that Dan Simmons makes much of in *The Crook Factory*, citing evidence in his author's note of a large dossier on Hemingway in FBI files. Hector accuses Hoover and the agency of "monitoring and spying on America's novelists and poets" in general, and McDonald cites Herbert Mitgang's *Dangerous Dossiers: Exposing the Secret War Against America's Greatest Authors* (1988) in his acknowledgments. The other major revelation involves Mary. In her review Tyler describes McDonald's portrayal of the hard-drinking, crude-talking Mary Hemingway as "highly unflattering," but in some ways it is quite sympathetic. Mary tells the foolish scholar's wife, Hannah, that Ernest hit her on several occasions, and by the end of the novel we realize her erratic behavior and excessive drinking derive from his abuse and from her terrible burden, which Hannah decides not to reveal, for "the revelation that Papa was shot by a henpecking wife would mutilate the myth. [...] How would the world regard an Ernest Hemingway who was a casualty of a mercy killing?" (337).

Also connected with speculative fiction dealing with Hemingway's suicide is Roland L. Bessette's large self-published novel (nearly six hundred pages), *Sunrise at Ketchum* (2009). Bessette, who has also written a biography of renowned operatic tenor Mario Lanza, published in 1999, is an attorney from Grosse Pointe, Michigan. He not only researched his novel on Hemingway quite thoroughly, but also visited nearly all of the sites mentioned in it, from Key West to Schruns, from Paris to Pamplona, from Venice to Seville. In short, the ambitious novel is a labor of love and it has all of the strengths and weaknesses one might anticipate with such an undertaking. Ironically, perhaps, in offering up a critical observation on *For Whom the Bell Tolls*— playing literary critic is a temptation hard to resist for nearly every Hemingway appropriator—Bessette touches on one of the major problems with his own novel: "It was to be the longest novel he wrote, and length was its biggest shortcoming."[12] The premise on which *Sunrise at Ketchum* is founded is a time machine (reminiscent of Bradbury's story) intended to take the protagonist, a lawyer and former navy JAG officer named Jack Collins, back to Sun Valley just before Hemingway's suicide and then accompany him on visits to most of the places he loved and where he wrote well. The benevolent intent is to prompt the fading author to resist suicide and to return to his writing, but the scheme fails, and instead of Collins escorting Papa to Venice in 1961, they end up stuck in Venice (and subsequent locales) in 2000, often with comical results. Mostly we discover a pathetically pontificating Papa who continues to drink his way toward oblivion. For the most part this novel represents fan fiction run amok.

A far more sophisticated appropriation is offered up in Milan Kundera's *Immortality* (1990), where we encounter Ernest in the afterlife chatting with Goethe. The Czech writer—best known for his novel *The Unbearable Lightness of Being* (1984) and demonstrably an established author of "literary fiction" representative of "official culture"—introduces a first-person narrator who appears at the beginning and end of the novel in a framing role and who suggests "the one deep yearning of our lives" is "to let everybody consider us great sinners!"[13] It could be argued that this premise applies quite well to Ernest Miller Hemingway. In fact, on the next page the narrator hears on the radio that "a new biography" of Hem is being published, "the one hundred and twenty-seventh, yet this time a truly significant one because it discloses that throughout his entire life Hemingway never spoke one single word of truth" (6). The body of the novel is narrated in third person and involves characters other than the framing narrator, who is perhaps intended to be Kundera himself, as he does enter the main plot from time to time. Or *one* of the main plots, more accurately, as Goethe's relationship, in 1811 and later with the poet and singer Bettina von Arnim, plays an important part. Her husband was the poet Achim von Arnim. Goethe, 62 at the time and "a figure placed precisely in the center of European history" (75), was not afraid of immortality, Kundera's narrator tells us (48). He thus sets up the eventual dialogue with Hemingway in the hereafter, which begins quite casually: "You know, Johann," said Hemingway, "they keep bringing up accusations against me, too. Instead of reading my books, they're writing books about me." To which the elderly Goethe responds resignedly, "That's immortality. [...] Immortality means eternal trial" (81).

What did you expect, Goethe asks the American novelist, to which Ernest responds that he expected to be left to "live in peace" after he died (paradox intended). Their dialogue then turns on the point Goethe makes, which is that in writing his books, Hemingway, like all artists, sought out immortality.

Hemingway argues that he wanted only his writing to be "immortal," and he complains that when he realized he personally was in the "clutches" of immortality, "it terrified me more than death itself. A man can take his own life. But he cannot take his own immortality" (82). He then says that as he lay dead, he saw "an army of university professors all over America was busy classifying, analyzing, and shoveling everything into articles and books." Goethe sympathizes, asserting "Faust is at its most beautiful when performed as a puppet play" (83). Hemingway makes another passing appearance in the novel before showing up again in part four, "Homo Sentimentalis," this time with a youthful Goethe (the dead may appear as they please according to Kundera's narrator), who argues that their books might be in some way immortal, but they themselves definitely are not. Hemingway disagrees, protesting "our books will probably soon stop being read. All that will remain of your Faust will be that idiotic opera by Gounod" (214). Ernest proposes that at least traces of the self remain in the books, but Goethe rejects even that premise.

Goethe then tells Ernest to forget that he's an American and use his brain: "That obsession with one's own image, that's man's fatal immaturity" (214). Hemingway has been dead just 27 years, he tells Goethe, who informs him he'll need another few decades being dead to accept the truth of the matter: "Even after death it was hard for me to accept the idea that I no longer existed. [...] Man doesn't know how to be mortal. And when he dies, he doesn't even know how to be dead" (215). After that, Goethe bids Hemingway farewell, as he has decided to "go to sleep": "You see, I have come to the definite conclusion that the eternal trial is bullshit" (216). Reading that sentence, one suspects Ernest couldn't have said it better himself. Not to be overlooked in this final exchange, however, is a remarkable moment of metafiction in which Kundera self-reflexively has Goethe tell Hem not to make a fool of himself: "You know perfectly well that at this moment we are but the frivolous fantasy of a novelist who lets us say things we would probably never say on our own" (215). And that, in effect, is postmodern biographical fiction, or appropriation, in a nutshell.

As if to verify the point about the historical person (like the fictional character) being at the mercy of the novelist, Hemingway comes up for some rough handling in the brief final part of the novel, where the protagonist, Paul, declares that he no longer reads novels but finds memoir and biography "much more amusing and instructive," including a recent biography in which Hemingway is portrayed as a "fraud" and a "megalomaniac" (334). "What is revolutionary about hatred for Hemingway?" the narrator asks, to which Paul responds, "I'm not talking about hatred for Hemingway! I'm talking about his work. [...] It was necessary to say out loud at last that reading about Hemingway is a thousand times more amusing and instructive than reading Hemingway. It was necessary to show that Hemingway's work is but a coded form of Hemingway's life and that this life was just as poor and meaningless as all our lives" (336). The nihilistic view here must strike a responsive chord for those who admire such stories as "A Clean, Well-Lighted Place" with its celebration of "nada" (291).

Like Kundera's novel, Keith Abbott's short novel *Rhino Ritz* (1979), set in a futuristic San Francisco, deals with issues concerning the immortality of the writer and the writing. Abbott teaches at Naropa University in Boulder, Colorado, and has written a biography, published in 2009, of *Richard Brautigan* (1935–1984), best known for his novella, *Trout Fishing in America* (1967). The author of more than a dozen books of fiction and nonfiction and more than twenty books of poetry, Abbott regards himself essentially as "a comic writer," and he describes *Rhino Ritz*, which was translated into German in 1993, as "picaresque" in form and style.[14] In the novella he describes a Brautigan-like world in some ways reminiscent of the one we meet in *In Watermelon Sugar* (1968). *Rhino Ritz* takes place in an alter-world mostly occupied by deceased writers immortalized by their writing and their fame. All of the writers are confined to mobile and flexible boxes, inasmuch as they pretty much are what they have written. "Even though he was wearing a box," we are told, "Ernie could still move well, not as well as the years before he got packaged, but well enough."[15] Both the writer and his work have been commoditized, transformed into product. We are clearly in some postmodern realm of magic realism.

In Abbott's futuristic world, Paris has been moved to San Francisco and one can take the ferry across the bay to visit the University of Iowa at Berkeley. Abbott holds an undergraduate degree in philosophy from San Francisco State University and a master's in English from Western Washington University, so some dipping into academic satire might be predictable. (Gertrude Stein explains that the Bank of America moved Paris to San Francisco when France defaulted on a loan.) Immortalized by their books, the authors have agreed to cease writing, although they do write surreptitiously, presumably at some risk of seeing their reputations diminished with the publication of posthumous works. (Coincidentally, *Rhino Ritz* was published halfway between the appearance of two of Hemingway's posthumous novels, *Islands in the Stream* in 1970 and *The Garden of Eden* in 1986.) The major action gets underway when Gertrude reports the disappearance of Sherwood Anderson, at which point Rhino (Hemingway) and Ritz (F. Scott Fitzgerald) set up a detective agency. Subsequently, both Gertrude and Alice B. Toklas are also kidnapped by Japanese terrorists involved in a plot to set up an amusement park to be located near Kyoto and known as Writerland. The broad satire deals primarily with the academic establishment and publishers' exploitation of writers, who are shown to be always short of money. "Being immortal is great," Hemingway says, "but you still have to pay your bills like anyone else" (66).

In some ways *Rhino Ritz* hearkens to Hemingway's zany, contract-busting satire, *The Torrents of Spring* (1926). Both are seriously absurd or carnivalesque (festive) novellas. Abbott's Hemingway, for example, lives in a wigwam above North Beach "on top of Coit Tower" with his Indian wife, Ku-na-so-way, who arranges the hem of her buckskin dress and resumes the "scrubbing of the Balzac volume in front of her" (55). Later she will hang it up on the guardrail to dry on "a white Duoflex X-17 monofilament line" along with the first five volumes of Balzac's collected works. Such scenes are perhaps reminiscent of the pool hall shenanigans of Hemingway's Yogi Johnson and Chief Running Skunk-Backwards in *Torrents*. Both novellas might be said to contribute something to "The Passing of a Great Race and the Making and Marring of Americans," as the title of the fourth part of Hemingway's book, which looks back to Gertrude Stein's *The Making of the Americans*, might suggest.[16] Sherwood Anderson plays an important role in both *Rhino Ritz* and *The Torrents of Spring*. Abbott does not follow Hemingway in his overt authorial intrusions into the text for metafictional purposes, but *Rhino Ritz* is metafictional pretty much by definition, inasmuch as it is a novel about writing novels and about novelists.

Keith Abbott's most extreme fantasy (or magic realism—or perhaps satirical send-up of magic realism) occurs at the center of *Rhino Ritz* in a chapter entitled "The Temptation of Ernest Hemingway." As Ernest watches a St. Bernard peeing by Sproul Plaza at the University of Iowa at Berkeley, the dog suddenly "becomes a shelf of the most beautiful edition of Shakespeare that Ernest had ever seen" (84). At this point Ernest plans to follow his usual trophy-hunting procedure and harpoon the volumes with his "Duo-Flex X-17 spear gun," but just then the editions, including those of authors unknown to him, suddenly change into "a huge slope of white snow." As he reaches for his ski pole, however, it turns into a fly rod, and when he lets that go, it slowly melts, "filling out into the clear skin of a beautiful girl lying on her side, smiling at a book in her hands" (85). Too much peyote, one is inclined to say, too much LSD, or maybe just too much Brautigan. Another object of Abbott's satire, aside from the academic industry of American Literature, is California itself: "Ernest wondered if people lost their perspective in California from time to time, everything being so opaque, just to have something to do" (123). About Fort Point, located below the Golden Gate Bridge, he remarks, "Like all creatures of California fantasy, it never lost its air of permanent unreality" (124).

The conclusion to this short novel involves a POV (point-of-view) machine, and at the end we meet the ironically named mastermind for the operation, Michael Soul, who assures the detectives, along with Gertrude and Alice, that Sherwood Anderson signed a legitimate contract. "We just helped the market along," Soul tells them. "Interest in you here [in the U.S.] is going down, has been for years. [...] I mean, you have to make an effort to understand our point of view on the matter. You like approbation, we like money" (162). The business end of the art of writing is confronted throughout Abbott's novel. Soul elaborates that the "offer" will take Hemingway and his writer friends to a place where they'll be "appreciated." They then watch quietly as Sherwood Anderson's box is "winched up onto the deck of the Japanese freighter" (164). "Dying was bad enough," Ernest laments, "but being bought and sold too.... I thought I left all that shit behind me when we went immortal" (165).

The term "speculative fiction" most likely annoys some purists when it comes to genre, as it is intended to cover a wide range from fantasy and horror through science fiction and cyberpunk. Under this rubric, the most prominent of the appropriations would surely be Joe Haldeman's *The Hemingway Hoax*, which won both a Nebula Award in 1990 and Hugo Award in 1991 as a novella. It was first published in *Isaac Asimov's Science Fiction Magazine* in April of 1990 and has since been published with other stories and a few story poems in *None So Blind* (1996) and in *The Best of Joe Haldeman* (2013). It has been translated into Spanish, French, Italian, and Japanese. A combat veteran of the Vietnam War, Haldeman earned a BS degree in physics and astronomy from the University of Maryland and did graduate work in mathematics and computer science before moving on to take his MFA in fiction from the University of Iowa Writers' Workshop in 1974. He currently lives in Gainesville, Florida, and in Cambridge, Massachusetts, where he has taught periodically at MIT for thirty years. A prolific writer, his publications include more than two dozen novels and books of short fiction. In a review note published in *Hemingway Review* Charles M. Oliver indicates Haldeman's novel is the best he's read of at least six such appropriations: "The book is funny and a well done 'what if' sort of novel."[17] Haldeman made extensive use of the Hemingway archives at the JFK Library in Boston and, like Roland Bessette, traveled to almost every apposite site, from Key West and Havana to Sun Valley and Schruns, with Pamplona and Paris in between.

Put succinctly, the novel concerns a Hemingway scholar named John Baird—like Haldeman a Vietnam veteran who was wounded in action—who runs into a con man in Key West. The con man, who goes by the name of Castle, talks Baird and his much younger wife, Lena (all too easily, it would seem, but there are reasons), into forging manuscripts from the famous lost valise (Chapter Three). Baird is gifted with an eidetic memory, one that renders him incapable of forgetting anything that has happened to him or that he has seen or read—in effect, a super version of a photographic memory. Time travel ("timespace") is involved as are ominous forces from the "Omniverse" in the various appearances of Hemingway that inform Baird of the existence of multiple, parallel worlds (these number 120) and of the perils of his project. In fact, these mysterious, malevolent forces which appear as "the Hemingway" ("it") wish to stop the forgery, as its success would somehow save the world from an apocalyptic event. So they kill various incarnations of John Baird, but ultimately they fail. Each of the chapter titles bears the title of a story or novel by Hemingway or, in some cases, a working title he did not use.[18] McDonald may or may not have followed Haldeman's lead in this respect in *Print the Legend*.

Asked in an interview with Allie Baker conducted February 25, 2010, for "The Hemingway Project" blog how the novel was received by Hemingway scholars, Haldeman responded, "They really loved it."[19] It is one of the few biographical fictions concerning Hemingway that has drawn serious scholarly attention, notably in an essay by Donald E. Morse published in *Extrapolation* in 2004, where he refers to it as "a Möbius strip novel,"[20] drawing on a phrase near the end of *The Hemingway Hoax*, when John Baird and Hemingway, on the verge of suicide, see his life as one side of a Möbius strip "twisting [...] I suppose through various dimensions, seeing the man's life as one complex chord of beauty and purpose and ugliness and chaos" (152). In a review essay for the *New York Review of Science Fiction*, Joan Gordon traces implications of the Möbius strip quite thoroughly, suggesting that Haldeman leads us to "a definition for Möbius science fiction: science fiction which uses the genre's characteristic devices to express both interior and exterior meanings, both sides of a metaphor, progressive plot movement and hallucination, simultaneously and without hierarchy, as if these elements were arranged on a Möbius strip."[21]

Haldeman's novella is available in two versions, the 25-chapter text published as an AvoNova or Avon book by William Morrow in 1996 with short stories and story-poems as *None So Blind*, which runs about 110 pages, and the single volume, stand-alone, 31-chapter text published as *The Hemingway*

Hoax (1990), which runs 155 pages. Note: The 31-chapter figure accounts for a double-numbered chapter 28 in the 1990 edition by William Morrow. I have referred to the stand-alone edition because it appears to be the version most readily available. One advantage of this 31-chapter version of the text is that the dialogue conducted by the "inter-dimensional beings" is rendered in italics. One might argue, however, that the shorter version is tighter, more concise. The six chapters excluded, about twenty pages of text, all concern the "realistic" plot (as opposed to the speculative plot) involving Baird's wife, Lena, and Castle and Baird and a prostitute named Pansy—an erotic, if not exactly romantic, quadrangle. Also cut in the 1996 Avon version are about eight pages of rather raw backstory on Pansy's earlier life.

Perhaps the chronology of publication suggests that Haldeman himself prefers the 1996 version of his novella. One eliminated moment from the 1990 version, however, is worth noting. When Baird goes back to Boston to feel out a senior colleague on what might happen with the forgery, Baird tells him, "Hemingway scholars are a funny bunch" (38). Perhaps so. In his 2010 interview with Allie Baker, Haldeman described members of the Hemingway Society as what some might consider "fanatics," and he included himself among them. When asked what a Hemingway conference is like, he responded, "It's a fiesta with serious moments. [...] People who share a passion getting together every other year in some fascinating place. Seeing old friends you've known for decades but only get to spend time together in this venue." A pompous air of self-importance or academic pretension does not befit that world.

In the British edition, the novel bears the delightfully paradoxical subtitle *A Short Comic Novel of Existential Despair*. Following a lurid bloodbath in which Castle blows apart his three coconspirators, we enter a "timespace" in which the "inter-dimensional beings" have lost control of John Baird and must concede that "he's still around somewhen" (147). As Morse observes, in what he calls "a fifth and final Hemingway hoax," the "two aspects of Hemingway (the fictional Baird and the historical Hemingway) meld together into the author working in Paris in 1921" and the "great Hemingway stories and novels lie somewhere still to be written in the future of this universe" (235). Baird, in effect, evolves into Hemingway. The scholar-fan-fanatic becomes the author himself. The novella concludes with the presumably historical Hemingway typing out the story that will be "Up in Michigan," but he feels a "sudden cold stab of grief," not just for himself, but for all mortals (154). Readers may be justifiably confused at this point. We are told earlier that if the forgeries are published it will "prevent or at least delay the end of the world in a whole bunch of universes," but "there would be hell to pay all up and down the Omniverse" and many more will die than those who populate the planet Earth (125). At the end of the penultimate chapter an "I" who claims to be John Baird confronts himself as a young Ernest Hemingway, but then that "I" walks away from both John and Ernest and claims he is "growing to enjoy" spending "forever in the black void between timespaces." That being, presumably also interdimensional, tells us he will return "after the bloodbath that gives birth to us all" (152). So far as the historical Hemingway has in some ways melded with John Baird, that identity is erased in the last line of the novel when he (unlike Baird, who has an eidetic memory) cannot "remember" when he has ever felt that cosmic "grief" and empathy for human mortality mentioned above (154).

And then, inevitably perhaps, we have Hemingway's ghost. To date, only a few writers have stepped into the realm of the supernatural, as opposed to the world of science fiction. Layton Green has published online what he calls a "novellita" entitled *Hemingway's Ghost* (2011), and Tom Winton has self-published a short novel entitled *Four Days with Hemingway's Ghost* (2012). The typescript of *Hemingway's Ghost*, which the author kindly sent to me on my request, runs just thirty pages single-spaced, so it might be regarded as a long short story; it is not divided into chapters. Green is author of a series of mysteries featuring a detective named Dominic Grey, who specializes in cases involving religious cults: *The Summoner*, *The Egyptian*, and *The Diabolist*, all published in 2013. The characters who inhabit *Hemingway's Ghost* are four impersonators, "each more pathetic than the last," who spend their time, as Green would have it, "living another man's life." They assume the monikers Papa, Ernie, Champ, and Bumby, and they pride themselves on attracting tourists to Key West. When two others of their crew, Max and Scotty, turn up dead, they resolve to investigate, and their attempt to play detective takes them to the basement of Hemingway's home and to a Ouija board through which they do eventually manage to contact Hemingway's ghost.

Pretty soon, the four begin to be picked off themselves, apparently by the ghost of Hemingway, who shows up periodically as a first-person commentator on their inept efforts. The two surviving impersonators, Bumby and Papa, discover a trap door in the Hemingway house, and in the basement (the home is, in fact, one of few in Key West to have been so equipped) they discover a treasure trove of memorabilia. Passing through another door, they discover a cult-like ritual chamber. Lester, the caretaker, then suddenly confronts them and guns down Papa, but Bumby shoots Lester, who appears to have been guilty of all the murders. (Ernest's younger brother Leicester committed suicide in 1982.) After that, Bumby takes over as caretaker for the house, and his writing suddenly seems to be inspired. Spoiler Alert: The first-person intruder has not been Hemingway, but Lester's father, Lester Senior, who has mystical control over Hemingway's ghost, who must do his bidding. At the end of the story, Hemingway's ghost wails as he is compelled to assist Bumby (himself apparently doomed as well) with "that troublesome paragraph in chapter three."

Obviously, Layton Green's novellita, which runs about 15,300 words, makes no literary claims. It is just what it appears to be, a ghost story for Hemingway nuts. Tom Winton's self-published novel, or novella, *Four Days with Hemingway's Ghost*, may have higher aspirations, but if so, they are likely to be dashed, if only by such overeager similes as the following, which comes at the end of the opening chapter, when Jack Phelan, a Hemingway aficionado and hard-luck guy who runs a lawn care service, falls into a deep four-day coma after an accident on the job: "Peering from the corners of my eyes, I slowly turned my head.... [And] when his face came into full view I jumped as if I'd been goosed by a highly-charged, electrified thumb."[22] It turns out that God has sent Ernest to Jack's aid, so Winton manages to work in a religious angle (mostly Roman Catholic). God has informed Papa that Jack is "a very insightful, articulate person" (54), and so on. Hem's ghost wafts Jack off to Cuba, where he encounters John Dos Passos and some of Hemingway's former wives at the Floridita. All four of the wives later greet him, along with numerous other old pals like Scott and Zelda Fitzgerald, Gary Cooper, and Marlene Dietrich, for a birthday party at the Finca—even Agnes von Kurowsky shows up.

The novel that God wants Jack Phelan to write, presumably this one, is intended to show the good side of Ernest Hemingway. To borrow the back cover phrasing, "its purpose is to change the world's perception of the swaggering, hard-knuckled, macho myth he has become." Two-thirds of the way through, at Ketchum appropriately enough, Ernest disappears and Jack comes out of his coma. In the last fifty-odd pages of the novella, Jack struggles with his writing and with soaring debt and hard luck, as he is unable to go back to work and his business fails. He contemplates armed robbery. But his loyal wife, Blanche, coupled with his recognition that he is "only a middleman relaying a higher power's messages" (113), ultimately sustains him in his composition of the book, to be entitled *The Real Ernest Hemingway*. Blanche suffers a terribly painful broken leg, but Jack acquires an agent—a superagent, in fact: Bidding on his manuscript is to start at half a million dollars (156). And that is indeed the stuff of fantasy, of the supernatural writ large.

Probably the best of the Hemingway-as-ghost fiction to date is Key West writer Rick Skwiot's *Key West Story* (2012), a romance in which a struggling forty-year-old writer named Constantine Martens (Con for short) runs into Hemingway as he looked when he was also forty. Throughout the novel Skwiot allows Con to doubt whether this manifestation, who goes by the name Nick Adams, pilots a boat called the *Pilar* and is a dead ringer for Ernest, is the real thing or an inspired impersonator. The novel opens with Con's Miami lawyer girlfriend Cat taking a shot at him when she finds a red thong under his bed, left by his Key West Czechoslovakian playmate, Eva.[23] Later, helping Nick/Ernest smuggle a couple of refugees out of Cuba, Con experiences a sort of mystical fling with Aurora, who practices the West African religion of Santeria. Con (Nick/Ernest refers to him as "Conman") has experienced early success as a novelist but has squandered the money and ekes out a living teaching writing to local wannabes, including Rebecca Hemingway, a distant relative haunted by the familial association and brought to the brink of suicide in what seems to constitute a family tradition. Nick/Ernest's role consists mostly of providing writerly guidance to Con in terms that will be familiar to any Hemingway fan: "Money's at the top of the list of things that can harm a writer, along with politics, women, drink, and ambition. And the lack of money, politics, drink, and ambition" (23). The sentiment and phrasing are drawn straight out of *Green Hills of Africa* (28), as any true Hemingway fan would know. Mostly, Nick/Ernest advises hard work, and of course there's the classic aphorism out of *A Moveable Feast* (12): "All you have to do is write one true sentence. Write the truest sentence you know" (134). One thinks here of Craig McDonald's novel that goes by that title.

Skwiot earned his B.A. in sociology from the University of Missouri at St. Louis, his M.A. in English literature from the University of Missouri at Columbia, and his MFA from Old Dominion University. He has worked as a newspaper reporter and as a creative writing instructor. He is a cofounder of the Key West Writers Lab, Inc., which apparently is connected with Antaeus Books, which has published a couple of his other novels and two memoirs. In a three-and-a-half-minute video, Skwiot comments on how he "reincarnated Ernest Hemingway" in his prime, on the "sublime" qualities of the sea he attempted to capture, and on Key West as a "surreal place" where an "eclectic mix of people" have come to "remake themselves."[24] In any event, the success of Skwiot's "reincarnation" of Hemingway as a ghost lies largely in the fact that he doesn't behave in a very ghostlike manner: he's more muse than wraith, more mentor than specter. And the success of Rick Skwiot's appropriation may owe much to his mastery of contemporary media, Internet, eBooks, personal Web sites, and all.

My intention throughout this study has not been to reflect only on the best of the biographical fictions involving Ernest Hemingway, but also to offer something of an unabridged version of the lot. Hemingway appears in the speculative fiction in various guises and in various literary subgenres. These writers have opted to veer away from textbook or handbook realism with its celebration of verisimilitude. Of course one might object that virtually all of the appropriations are "speculative" in some respects, that Dan Simmons' Hemingway in *The Crook Factory* or Clancy Carlile's in *The Paris Pilgrims* or Vincent Cosgrove's in *The Hemingway Papers* is hardly more distorted or warped than what we encounter in William McCranor Henderson, Keith Abbott, or Joe Haldeman, where no effort is made to represent a credible, real-life version of events and characters. The world of popular fiction, and particularly of fan fiction, contains pretty much everything, irrespective of any supposed literary merit. That is a given. Certainly, one might question the value of such texts when it comes to Hemingway's reputation. Writers like Tom Winton, as I see it, write as well as they can, and, insofar as Hemingway appears in their work, they intend to do well by him, though the decision to treat him generously by no means constitutes a criterion for judging the potential appeal of the text. The same applies to writers whose critical presentation or re-presentation of Hemingway comes across so pejoratively that they might be described by the term I've already proposed as "fanemies." An extreme example would be Marty Beckerman's satire *The Heming Way* (2nd edition, 2012), which is memorably subtitled, *How to Unleash the Booze-Inhaling, Animal-Slaughtering, War-Glorifying, Hairy-Chested, Retro-Sexual, Legend Within…Just Like Papa!*

Beckerman is a journalist whose scathing satires have emerged from his columns in the *Anchorage Daily News* and include the likes of *Death to All Cheerleaders* (2000) and *Generation S.L.U.T.* (2004). Even the "funny bunch" (to use Joe Haldeman's phrase) of serious Hemingway scholars and certifiable "Hemingway nuts" may find themselves laughing at Beckerman's searing parody, which is not written, after all, in a benevolent spirit. On the other hand, it would not have been possible for Beckerman to have written his small book, which evolved from just eighty or so pages in the self-published 2011 edition to a little over two hundred pages, without a thorough knowledge of the writer's life and work, and a fair dose of the biographical and critical commentaries as well.[25] Some aficionados will probably cringe to discover that Beckerman has sold movie options for the book to the Gotham Group. As written up in *Variety*, the book is "a tongue-in-cheek ode to Ernest Hemingway, who Beckerman sarcastically praises for being a drunken, misogynistic, self-proclaimed war hero who'd kill himself all over again if he met today's metrosexual male."[26] Hemingway would also probably want to "kill himself all over again" if he read Beckerman's book, but only after shooting Beckerman first and perhaps mounting his head.

Hemingway would perhaps be no less censorious, or possibly homicidal, when it comes to a pair of graphic novels in which he figures prominently: Jason's *The Left Bank Gang* (2005) and Eric Peterson and Ethan Nicolle's *Jesus Christ: In the Name of the Gun, "Volume One: A Hollow Cost"* (2009). In Jason's minimalist text Hem is drawn as a slender black dog vaguely reminiscent of Walt Disney's Goofy, and he and his friends are living and writing cartoons and struggling with money in 1920s Paris. Hem wears a three-piece tan suit and Scott Fitzgerald, whose wife, Zelda, is giving him a bad time, is a white dog who wears brown knickers and a jacket. At Shakespeare and Company, Sylvia Beach offers Ernest a copy of the new translation of *War and Peace*, to which he responds that Tolstoy is "a decent cartoonist but all his characters look alike. They all have the same face, and all those Russian names.... I can never manage to keep track of who's who."[27] In a scene at Gertrude Stein's flat, Gertrude offers advice for drawing cartoons that is very much in keeping with her advice to Hem on writing. Jason (Norwegian cartoonist John Arne Sæterøy) introduces an affair involving Zelda and "Jean-Paul" (perhaps hinting at Sartre). It's Hemingway who hatches the plan to rob the cash office of the prize fights, and in addition to Fitzgerald, Ezra Pound and James Joyce get involved. All does not go well, mostly because Scott (actually Jean-Paul disguised as Scott) loses his cool and shoots a couple of the clerks. Jason even goes so far as to offer up multiple, ambiguous endings for the tale.

In Eric Peterson's *Jesus Christ: In the Name of the Gun*, illustrated in black and white by Ethan Nicolle, a highly irreverent Jesus rebels against his passive father, who seems content to let the world dissolve into violence and anarchy. Jesus emerges in the world as Hitler invades Poland, and he is about to assassinate Der Führer when, about two dozen pages into the book, an overweight, black-clad, ninja-like assassin beats him to it. When Jesus catches up to him and pulls off his mask, the assassin exclaims, "Christ! Don't you recognize me? I'm Ernest Hemingway ... and I'm on safari through time hunting mass murderers!"[28] Needless to say, Peterson's profane, homicidal Jesus is not for everyone. Hitler comes back to life as a sort of werewolf, but Jesus (with Hem in support) proves equal to the task, and in the closing pages Jesus and Ernest enjoy some beer as Hemingway plans to take his safari after Mussolini.

The only item that seems to be missing when it comes to speculative treatments of Ernest Hemingway might be something like "Hemingway and Zombies." After all, it might be argued, Seth Grahame-Smith did it in 2009 with *Pride and Prejudice and Zombies*, which appeared in April of that year as number three on the *New York Times* best-seller list. If one undertakes a Google search for "Hemingway and Zombies," one comes up with a 2012 made-for-television movie called *Rise of the Zombies* starring Mariel Hemingway, Jack's ("Bumby") daughter, and Ernest's granddaughter, born the year he committed suicide. That, of course, is sheer coincidence, but the same search also turns up on the *Psychology Today* site a short piece by Steven Schlozman, MD, entitled "Did Ernest Hemingway Dabble in a Zombie Tale?" Schlozman is an associate director of Medical Student Education in Psychiatry for the Harvard Medical School. His debut novel, *Zombie Autopsies: Secret Notebooks from the Apocalypse*, appeared in 2011. The opening paragraph of his item on Hemingway and zombies deserves quotation in full:

> While literary scholars have long known that Ernest Hemingway spent considerable time in Key West, most experts were under the now mistaken assumption that all of his Florida-based activity occurred at his famous Whitehead Street Residence. However, at last year's annual meeting of the Modern Language Association, it was revealed that Mr. Hemingway had a second and much more obscure home located in a tiny blue cottage facing the ocean. It was in the attic of this cottage that Mr. Hemingway would secretly pen what many believe to be among his most authentic and private stories. These writings include his understated and brilliant sequel "The Younger Man and the Pond," as well as his now widely celebrated Homeric epic which he had tentatively titled "Gertrude Stein Was Quite the Looker."[29]

At a recent gathering at the Library of Congress, Dr. Schlozman continues, a "half-written manuscript found tucked inside a pair of leather boxing gloves" from the attic of that cottage "represents Hemingway's first and likely only attempt at a zombie-themed novel," tentatively entitled "The Dead Sometimes Rise(s)." The good physician then offers us the first page of the purported zombie tale, tongue thoroughly lodged in cheek, beginning as follows: "There is nothing to being a zombie that anyone does not already know. You need only to bleed, but the blood must matter, must be proper and have purpose. It must be pure and strong and virile." So reads the first paragraph of the clever parody, which may remind Hemingway enthusiasts of innumerable such gestures going back to the surprisingly early effort by James Thurber that appeared in the *New Yorker* as "A Visit from Saint Nicholas in the Ernest Hemingway Manner" on Christmas Eve 1927, just a year after the publication of *The Sun Also Rises:* "It was the night before Christmas. The house was very quiet. No creatures were stirring in the house. There weren't even any mice stirring. The stockings had been hung carefully by the chimney. The children hoped Saint Nicholas would come and fill them."[30] And so it goes, one might say, and so it goes.

Seven

With Hem Obsessed

"It started off as this thing I had about Hemingway." So begins Allan Conan's 1996 novel, *The Hemingway Sabbatical*.[1] Of course, it gets better from there, one feels almost obliged to say. The fiction encountered in this chapter deals with characters who are somehow obsessed with Ernest Hemingway's life and writing, sometimes in that order and sometimes not. One might argue that all of the biographical fiction involving Hemingway is the product of writers who are Hemingway-obsessed, and most of those writers have said as much in one place or another: perhaps in a prefatory note, in reader's guides at the back of their novels, in interviews, or in their blogs. All of these appropriators, whether they treat the writer and his work reverently as fans or disparagingly as "fanemies," are well aware of Papa's clay feet, but they have remained fascinated, perhaps "morbidly fascinated" in some cases. Do they write about Hemingway and his writing in spite of the fact that he was the man that he was, or because of it? To what extent do these appropriators find themselves at all focused on the writing? That is, to what extent do they desire to draw us as readers and potential fans toward or back into Hemingway's fiction, perhaps to be read this time in some new way? Do we eventually come to celebrate this kind of fan fiction for various reasons; or to resent it because, at least in some cases, the writer abuses Hemingway in what comes across at best as a love-hate relationship with him; or because we may sense the appropriator is merely self-aggrandizing, exploiting the writer, the myths, and even at times the writing?

Such questions have been either made explicit or left implicit throughout this book. The answers, explicit and otherwise, have varied, but in the half dozen or so works of fiction taken up in this chapter, we come closer to adulation (albeit sometimes comedic in nature) than in any other chapter. More than any other appropriator, Californian MacDonald Harris (1921–1993), pseudonym for Donald Heiney, attempts extensive imitations in *Hemingway's Suitcase* (1990), which, like Gerhard Köpf's *Papa's Suitcase* (1994), looks back to Hadley's loss of the valise full of Hemingway's writings, carbons included, on December 2, 1922. In his review of Köpf's novel, Thomas A. Marshall writes, "Apparently Hadley's decision to pack the manuscripts has launched a cottage industry."[2] He was referring to these two novels and to Haldeman's *The Hemingway Hoax*, but as previous observations have indicated, that "cottage industry" has expanded considerably, the most recent case in point being Diane Gilbert Madsen's mystery, *Hunting for Hemingway* (2010). Former *Monty Python's Flying Circus* performer and televangelist behind the PBS series *Hemingway Adventure*, Michael Palin has offered probably the most comically obsessed protagonist of all in *Hemingway's Chair* (1995). Allan Conan's *The Hemingway Sabbatical* takes his main character on something of a James Bond thrill ride through Ernest's Europe, while Lauri Anderson's *Hunting Hemingway's Trout* (1990) offers a set of interrelated short stories featuring characters whose lives, like Anderson's own life, in some way connect with Hemingway.

MacDonald Harris's appropriation opens with a supposed Nick Adams story, "The Trouble with People," set in 1920s Paris, that presumably connects with the lost or stolen suitcase of his title. This one is the first of five stories that are italicized and placed strategically throughout the novel, the last story being set in Petoskey, in upstate Michigan, which brings the reader back to Nick's beginnings: "*That summer Nick lived in Petoskey in a room he rented from Dr. Schultz. He had a girl named Trudie. She worked in the café that he always went to across from the Emporium. They were together a lot that summer. He was very much in love. It was the first time and it is always better then.*"[3] Hemingway fans will, of course, recognize not only the staccato sentences, but also the setting and characters reminiscent of such stories as "Up in Michigan," "Ten Indians," and "Fathers and Sons." I would propose that the embedded stories (forgeries) do come across as imitations rather than parodies. The novel takes place in present-day Los Angeles where "a wealthy dilettante," to appropriate the description provided in the front-cover flap, named Nils-Frederik Glas has returned from Europe with an old battered suitcase that might or might not have belonged to Hemingway. The protagonist of the piece is Alan, Nils-Frederik's 34-year-old son, who is a struggling literary agent and who quickly finds himself embroiled in the scam to pass off his roguish father's forgeries as genuine Hemingway stories supposedly recovered from the lost suitcase.

As Nils-Frederik puts it, "You see, although we will never claim that the stories are genuine, we'll never admit that they're fake either. We'll just say that we got them somewhere and we've retyped them and here they are." It will turn out to be "a nice joke on the publishing establishment" and on the critics and the "great dumb brute public, that won't buy anything and won't read anything unless it's by a big-name writer, and they'll read anything by that big-name author even though it's junk" (74). One suspects in such moments one is hearing the voice of MacDonald Harris/Donald Heiney himself, offering not so much a complaint as a statement of things as they are. After graduating from the U.S. Merchant Marine Academy with a B.S. in 1943, Harris served as a naval officer in the North Atlantic and the Mediterranean as well as the Pacific theaters. In 1948 he earned a B.A. degree from the University of Redlands, during which time he began placing his short stories and articles in a wide variety of periodicals. He went on to earn his M.A. and Ph.D. in comparative literature from the University of Southern California, after which he taught for a dozen years at the University of Utah, moving to the University of California at Irvine in 1965. His first novel, published under his pseudonym, was *Private Demons* (1961). He would write eighteen novels, the best known being *The Balloonist* (1976, reprinted in 2012); the last, *The Carp Castle*, was published posthumously in 2012.[4]

The opening sentences of Harris's novel ring true to the Hemingway voice, particularly the voice of the twenties: "*There was a crowd at the Rotonde but they found a table inside looking out through the windows at the terrasse and the boulevard. It was five o'clock and already dark. It was cold outside but inside it was warm and the windows were steamy*" (11). It sounds, perhaps, like the Hemingway voice of *A Moveable Feast* (1964), which in turn sounds very much like the voice of the stories from *In Our Time* (1925) and *Men Without Women* (1927) and the novels *The Sun Also Rises* (1926) and, at least to some extent, *A Farewell to Arms* (1929). Even the elided commas contribute to the stylistic pastiche here. And one can hardly employ that term in these postmodern times without at least citing Frederic Jameson's remarkable statement on the subject: "The disappearance of the individual subject, along with its formal consequence, the increasing unavailability of the personal style, engender the well-nigh universal practice today of what may be called pastiche."[5]

In fact, the eventual product of Nils-Frederik and Alan Glas's fraud constitutes an example of yet another term promoted in Jameson's pioneering text, *Postmodernism: Or, The Cultural Logic of Late Capitalism* (1991), "simulacrum": "the identical copy for which no original has ever existed" (18). In effect, this concept connects with Jameson's important observations on what he calls the "insensible colonization of the present by the nostalgia mode"

(20). Simply put, we might regard this as our largely unconscious longing for an idyllic past that is represented in various art forms (music, architecture, painting, literature—especially historical and biographical fiction) via images that never really existed. Properly aged paper and a vintage Corona typewriter are employed to create the "discovered" lost stories, and a quasi-educated private detective named Klipspringer goes so far as to analyze the average words per sentence in one story (thirteen). He concludes that "people who wrote fictions, and people who read them, were mildly deranged but in a harmless way" (159). Alan, however, insists, paradoxically, "Fiction is true. After it's established it becomes a kind of truth, parallel to but not the same as the real world. And after that it's unchangeable" (152).

The phrasing is at least faintly reminiscent of what we have encountered in Joe Haldeman's science fiction *The Hemingway Hoax*, and the sentiment is consistent with what Hemingway wrote memorably, reflecting on *War and Peace*, in a 1934 essay published in *Esquire*: "All good books are alike in that they are truer than if they had really happened to you and afterwards it all belongs to you: the good and the bad, the ecstasy, the remorse and sorrow, the people and places and how the weather was" (*By-line: Ernest Hemingway*, 184). "For the most part," we are told, "the critics took the stories as authentic Hemingway stories" (258), and even "a very astute critic named Carleton West" hedges his bets, conceding that "whoever wrote these stories is one hell of a writer. I don't think it was Hemingway, but that doesn't matter" (259). Harris provides no gap here for what I would call a "postmodern pause," but the occasion seems to warrant as much. The "astute critic" adds, "If you like, pretend that they're Hemingway as you read them." A reviewer for the *New York Review of Books* takes it hook line and sinker, gushing over "the stunning brilliance of style, the careful control, the emotion that is all the more poignant for its expression in Nick's terse and ironic language" (252). Perhaps the most positive result of the scam is that Nils-Frederik and his son Alan are reconciled in the process.

Criminal behavior also figures in Diane Gilbert Madsen's *Hunting for Hemingway* (2010), billed as "A DD McGil Literati Mystery." Madsen's initial novel in the series was *A Cadger's Curse* (2009), in which Robert Burns factors in for DD McGil, a former English professor and now freelance insurance investigator. Madsen holds a master's degree in seventeenth-century English literature from Roosevelt University. In the author's note at the end of *Hunting for Hemingway* (not to be confused with Hilary Hemingway and Jeffry P. Lindsay's 2000 book, *Hunting with Hemingway*, which will be discussed later), following a recipe for the Papa Doble daiquiri, Madsen explains that her "interest in writing murder mysteries was sparked when she met the suspect [later exonerated] in a murder that occurred near her home."6 Following a two-page prologue that details events of December 2–4, 1922, Hadley's loss of the valise at the Gare de Lyon (railway station) in Paris, the novel opens with DD McGil, aged 39, describing herself as "female, blonde, a Scot" who works in Chicago as an insurance investigator (3).

DD's fiancé died a few years back, and she's in a rut, so a friend gives her a ticket to a Hemingway docudrama performance at Northwestern University. There she encounters her "old college flame David Barnes" (shades of Jake Barnes of *The Sun Also Rises* and David Bourne in *The Garden of Eden*, one suspects) playing the lead role. He claims someone has mailed him the long-sought lost manuscripts, but shortly after that, he is murdered, and DD becomes a suspect. She is asked at first to verify the authenticity of the few pages of the manuscripts that Barnes has provided, but eventually she finds herself being asked to prove they are fakes. Most of the 37 fast-moving chapters are affixed with epigraphs from Hemingway, the majority of which will be familiar to the aficionado, for example, "The Corona #3 is the only psychiatrist I would ever submit to" (16). One of the passages she likes so much that she uses it twice: "Never confuse movement with action" (64, 193), perhaps intending it as DD's advice to herself. The famous quote appears in A.E. Hotchner's *Papa Hemingway* (1966) near the end of the opening chapter and is passed along by Marlene Dietrich: "In those five words," she says, "he gave me a whole philosophy."7

Following MacDonald Harris and other appropriators, Madsen includes a couple of imitations to indicate the nature of the manuscripts. "First Leaves" begins as follows: "The first leaves to fall were off the trees already, and the boy remembered that soon they would slow his passage in the woods and make it dangerous" (124). The true "Hemingfan" would likely object to that single comma. The best the specialist that DD consults can say is, "If these weren't done by Hemingway, they're inspired fakes" (130). DD also consults resources at the Hemingway home and library, operated as a museum by the Ernest Hemingway Foundation of Oak Park and open for tours. She splices quite a bit of Hemingway lore into the text, particularly as it applies to Oak Park, which takes a backseat among some Hemingway fans to the more exotic site of Key West. Before all mysteries are solved, DD's life is also in jeopardy. At the end of the novel, after a couple of additional homicides and bedroom romps and following DD McGil's altercation with a Hemingway impersonator, we are left with the impression the manuscripts were in fact genuine, but they are probably lost forever.

Also connected with the missing manuscripts, but this time not involving crime, as in Henderson, Haldeman, Harris, Madsen et al., or action and intrigue as in Cosgrove's *The Hemingway Papers*, German writer Gerhard Köpf's *Papa's Suitcase* (1994) presents one of the quirkiest of all the Hemingway obsessive characters, an unnamed small-town bookseller who likes to call himself "Hemingstein," which he knows, as do all fan readers, was one of Hemingway's favorite boyhood nicknames. Unlike the more obviously plot-driven crime novels connected with the lost suitcase, this one is mostly a novel of character. Köpf's other novels include *There Is No Borges* (1991, translated into English, 1993) and *Piranesi's Dream* (1992, translated into English, 2000). The author of more than thirty books, Köpf earned his doctorate from the University of Munich in 1974, but he remains relatively unknown in Anglo-American literary circles. He has served as professor of contemporary literature and guest professor in psychiatry at the Munich Technical University and elsewhere. His novels have been praised for their surreal and fantasy elements, often bordering on magic realism, but they have also been criticized for being overly academic or complex.

Certainly that is not the case with *Papa's Suitcase*, which opens in Ketchum, Idaho, with the first-person narrator (Hemingstein) thinking, "*My big fish must be somewhere*."[8] His "big fish" is not a marlin, but the lost suitcase. The brief chapter closes on a very Hemingwayesque line: "You're really happy only when you don't think about it" (9). Hemingstein, a loner whose parents committed suicide, drops out of high school after the tenth grade, planning to become a stonecutter, but instead he becomes a bibliophile and a Hemingway addict. He describes his adolescent reading of Hemingway's short stories as being "like an infection with a lifelong high fever" (15). His favorite passage, he says, is the one at the end of "Indian Camp," where young Nick Adams, after watching his father perform a crude caesarean as the Indian father commits suicide, feels "quite sure that he would never die" (*Complete Short Stories*, 70; Köpf quotes much of the last half-page of the story in his novel). Citations from Hemingway's writing, including the journalistic pieces, occur throughout the text and are set in italics. "I not only incorporated Hemingway's stories into myself," Hemingstein informs us. "I wanted to transform myself into them. His words became my words. Reading him was beautiful" (21). We should reflect at least briefly on two points here: first, Köpf's protagonist is all but unique in his deep infatuation with the writing (consider, by way of contrast, the reluctance of Henry Morgan's and Dan Simmons' protagonists when it comes to Hemingway's writing); second, Hemingstein desires to "transform" himself not into some incarnation of Hemingway, but into his writing.

As the reviewer for *Publishers Weekly* stated, the novel is "a joyful hymn to books and literature."[9] The same anonymous reviewer notes, however, that the "intriguing parable about the necessity of art" also constitutes something of a cautionary tale "about the danger of substituting art for life." For 25 years Hemingstein worked as one of "that dying-out breed of booksellers who still read," but that compulsion has contributed to his loneliness, as he finds reading "always more sensible than wasting time with some female or other" (31). He becomes so perverse about his job, in fact, that he distributes a "decalogue" to his coworkers, the first law of which is "the bookseller is duty bound to regard the buyer as the book's enemy" (34). It seems likely that most of Köpf's readers will have encountered such a bookstore employee somewhere along the line. When he tries to insist on creating a window display in honor of Hemingway, the pathetic bookseller is fired, and at that point he begins his quest for the lost manuscripts, which may or (perhaps more likely) may not be a literal search. If in fact the geography of his quest is literal, it would have been very time-consuming and quite costly: Ketchum, Pamplona, Key West, Oak Park, Cody, Seney and Horton Bay in upstate Michigan, Toronto, Cuba, Venice, a remembered bicycle trip to Brunnenburg Castle in the Italian Tirol and on to Schruns in Austria, then Kenya, Berlin, Hong Kong, Paris.

Hemingstein does recognize that he suffers from "an illness called bibliomania" (74). He celebrates libraries and lectures his fellow employees, exhorting them to read, "for God's sake, read, otherwise you will have to become critics" (76). That is a sentiment with which his idol would almost certainly have agreed, and Köpf has him accumulate a hefty list of Hemingway's negative sentiments on literary critics, some of them implausible. Hemingstein is by no means a reliable narrator, after all. For example, he castigates biographer Kenneth S. Lynn as a female critic (Köpf, of course, knows better, as he cites Lynn's work in his afterword). Near the end of the novel Hemingstein submits that perhaps he never really did leave the small college town where he worked as a bookseller: "Maybe everything was only Hemingway's journey through my head" (233). His only friend, a high school principal named Mürzig, suffers from a compulsive (and quite comical) mania about the subjunctive mood in grammar and eventually loses his mind. "Mankind can approach God," Mürzig rants in his graduation address, "the path leads through the mysteries of the subjunctive" (199). Throughout the novel there is a quality of "if-ness" to Hemingstein's narrative, a subjunctive mood that often comes off as, "If I were Hemingway...." Indeed even in the lengthiest chapter—which recounts a boyhood memory of a Hemingway-like fishing trip combined with a sexual initiation (the girl is named Corona, like Hemingway's typewriter from the

Twenties)—readers must find themselves suspicious. At the end of the chapter, Hemingstein encounters a passage in Hotchner's *Papa Hemingway* about Marlene Dietrich's first meeting with Hemingway, which would be a prelude to a romance that would remain platonic and unconsummated.

At the end of the novel Hemingstein appears to be content, like old Santiago from *The Old Man and the Sea*, to "be in the world alone and dream about his lions" (234). But then he finds a dispatch dated December 16, 1992, in which Marlene Dietrich's daughter discovers hundreds of boxes and suitcases full of memorabilia, and "there are said to be previously unknown manuscripts found in suitcases" (236). We are told the missing Hemingway suitcase, however, was probably destroyed in Berlin during the war. In March of 2003, nine years after the publication of *Papa's Suitcase*, thirty of Dietrich's letters were donated to the Hemingway Collection of the John F. Kennedy Library in Boston by her daughter.[10] No lost manuscripts turned up. "When I was reading Hemingway," Hemingstein declares, "I myself became Hemingway" (69). The implicit wish of many appropriators is explicit in a German review of Köpf's novel: "Übrigens, man muss nicht Hemingway-Fan sein, aber man kann dabei einer warden."[11] My rough translation also draws on the previous sentence, in which Manuela Hasleberger commends the novel in warmest terms, particularly to those with a good sense of humor and some literary background: "It is not necessary, after all, that one be a Hemingway fan; however, one can become a fan by reading this novel."

Despite the comedic nature of *Papa's Suitcase*, the protagonist may strike some readers as pathetic, "almost deranged," the reviewer for *Kirkus* suggests.[12] Not much detracts, however, from the comedy of former Monty Python star Michael Palin's debut novel, *Hemingway's Chair*, which was published the next year. An Oxford graduate in modern history, Palin is best known not only for the five-year run of *Monty Python's Flying Circus* (1969–1974), but also for his numerous televised travelogues, including the four episodes of his *Hemingway Adventure* (1999), and for his travel books. He has also written several children's books. His most recent novel, *The Truth*, appeared in 2012. Although he suggests that one weakness of *Hemingway's Chair* is akin to that of the typical Monty Python sketch ("it may not mean anything when it's over"), Bruce Weber, writing for the *New York Times*, found the novel to be "an awfully strange comedy" in which the strengths include "its dry, deftly understated wit; its careful plot and character construction; its hearty, well-formed sentences; its clever, on-the-money dialogue."[13] L.D. Meagher, reviewing the novel for CNN, admired its "subtler sense of the absurdities of everyday life."[14] In his review of the novel for *Hemingway Review*, Thomas Hermann offers that one might classify the "continuously growing number of fictionalized accounts of Ernest Hemingway's life and work" by dividing them among "those in which Hemingway occurs as a character" and "those in which other characters are related in one way or another to the dead (but immortal) Hemingway."[15] Hermann further divides the titles between those, like Henderson's "Pappy" Markham, who relate to Hem as "enemies" and those, like Hemingstein and in this novel Martin Sproale, who relate to him as "admirers." Again, the fan becomes a fanatic, and as always in comedy, exaggeration lies at the heart of the comic character.

Bruce Weber aptly describes Martin Sproale, the small-town postal clerk, as "bright, decent and a little pathetic" and "a nerd obsessed with the Hemingway macho mystique." Both sets of traits might be regarded as cliché, as Weber also notes, but such cliché or stereotype lies at the heart of comedy of character. Locked into his mundane routine, Martin fantasizes a life of Hemingway-like action and adventure, and he maintains a shrine of sorts in his upstairs bedroom of the home he shares with his mother. His idol would not likely have approved. Martin's treasures amount mostly to clippings from newspapers and magazines, replicas and knockoffs—no real collector's items. He likes to toast his Papa poster with the occasional glass of grappa or some other appropriate Hemingway beverage. When would the "little people with little minds," he wonders, "realise that only through confrontation with danger could life be lived to the full?"[16] "Life everywhere furnishes an accurate observer with the ridiculous," Henry Fielding wrote in his preface to *Joseph Andrews* (1742), which he called a "Comic Epic in Prose." Hemingway adopted the passage as his epigraph for his satiric 1926 novella, *The Torrents of Spring*. Like Köpf's Hemingstein, Palin's Martin Sproale will live up to that billing.

Martin's simple life, along with his hopes for advancement to postal manager and his "romance" with the dull Elaine Rudge, who drudges along with him at the post office, undergoes a profound alteration for the worse when a new manager, Nick Marshall, is named. He is predictably young and ambitious, insensitive to the postal staff and to the needs and desires of the community, and (of course) devious, evincing "a hint of the predatory" (38). When Martin quotes the famous passage from *The Old Man and the Sea* about man being "destroyed but never defeated," Nick, who is not terribly perceptive, looks "mystified" (50). Martin observes that Elaine Rudge is not a proper Hemingway woman: "He liked them either mysterious and witty or loyal and submissive, and Elaine would have failed on both counts" (47). As for Elaine, it's tempting to imagine she's connected somehow with Dickens' Barnaby Rudge from the eponymous novel of 1841.

The impassive Elaine eventually falls into the clutches of Nick Marshall, but a new woman enters Martin's life in the form of American literary scholar Ruth Kohler, who is on sabbatical working on a book to be entitled "Admiring Ernest," drawn from Dashiell Hammett's comment to famed playwright Lillian Hellman in 1937: "Ernest has never been able to write a woman. He only puts them in books to admire them" (cited in Lynn, 452). Ruth informs Martin that she is no Hemingway fan: "[T]he more you know about Ernest Hemingway, the less of a fan you become" (84). Martin disagrees, calling him "a great man," to which Ruth contentiously responds, "Men usually do [think he's great]. I think at his best he was a great writer, but he could also be cruel, boorish and inconsiderate" (85). Martin acknowledges the author's shortcomings but is predictably disappointed in his meeting with what he hoped would be a fellow aficionado.

The "chair" of Palin's title turns out to be the one Hemingway used briefly while filming *The Old Man and the Sea* off the coast of Peru. The chair is for sale in London. Martin proves to be of some use to Ruth in her project because his hero worship in some ways balances and corrects her growing antipathy. She needs to understand why the women in Hemingway's life, "very intelligent, attractive, sensible women," would be drawn to him for any length of time. Toward that end, she enlists Martin in what turns out to be quite comical role-playing, and she uses the prospect of helping Martin purchase the fishing chair as her bait. Ironically, when she and Martin stumble into a sexual liaison, Ruth finds herself setting aside her admiration for Pauline as she slips into the role of Martha Gellhorn.

When Nick moves the post office to the back of a combination newsstand and candy shop as a step toward setting up a telecommunications hub in the village, he is able to enlist Martin's support by offering him enough of a "consultancy fee" to cover the price of the chair. By the time Martin realizes what Nick's aims are, it is too late for him to counter his moves. Martin's grassroots effort to save the local post office is in vain, and Nick forces him into early retirement. Martin believes his only option is to assume a "new role as urban guerrilla" (190). This role he eventually performs to perfection, and (Spoiler Alert) following a 007-type demolition of the telecommunications tower, Martin Sproale shows up for the final time as the winner of a Hemingway impersonation contest in Key West.

The thriller mode that informs the conclusion of *Hemingway's Chair*, minus the comedy, informs most of Allan Conan's *The Hemingway Sabbatical* (1996), which features 43-year-old Robert Aguilar, an English teacher at a private high school in San Francisco, visiting Hem's European sites while on sabbatical. His plan is to combine his research, "a little search for Papa" (9), with his honeymoon, but that falls apart when his lady friend Elizabeth declines in order to pursue work on her doctoral dissertation. We get the details on that aspect of the story later, because within the first four pages, thanks to his quick thinking, Aguilar and the other passengers escape a bomb planted in a loaf of sourdough bread. Neither this novel nor Conan's earlier thriller, *The Psi Delegation* (1989), has drawn any critical attention. While Köpf's Hemingstein and Palin's Martin Sproale are deeply, if not pathologically, engaged with Hemingway and his writing, the same cannot really be said of Conan's Robert Aguilar, whose professed intention to "follow in Papa Hemingway's footsteps" is quickly diverted (13) by a run-in with a Cuban agent who claims he can get him into Cuba to visit the Finca Vigía. The suspicious English teacher, who also happens to be writing a novel, reports the incident to the U.S. embassy, and before he knows it, he is involved in international intrigue and its attendant adventures.

By the end of the fifth chapter Robert Aguilar, now in Pamplona, has connected with a gorgeous British "tourist" who predictably finds his writing "beautiful" and "only a little reminiscent of Hemingway" (82). The CIA is keeping tabs on him and is aware that the Cuban agent is interested in working through Aguilar to get to his quondam fiancée, Elizabeth's brother, who is a computer engineering genius who runs his own small, highly specialized, top secret firm. Various incidents from Hemingway's life and writing are mentioned in passing throughout the novel, but they are clearly ancillary to the major plot action. The sabbatical occurs only during the first third of the novel, but the jet-setting continues, the intrigue builds as the Russians get involved, and references to Hemingway begin to recede. Nevertheless, in the midst of it all, Aguilar manages to find time for writing. The goal is to prevent the acquisition of "Islamic nuclear bombs" (186). Following the narrow miss of a nuclear holocaust in Chicago, Elizabeth agrees to marry Aguilar, who has nearly completed his novel and has reestablished his faith, with reference to a pair of Nobel Prize speeches, that "our hearts will endure" (Faulkner) and "the earth will abide" (Hemingway).

How important, or even valid, a novel like *The Hemingway Sabbatical* is as a kind of appropriation may be debatable. Robert Aguilar, the protagonist, is presented as a Hemingway-obsessed writer, but one could certainly argue that the novel comes closer to exploitation than it does to appropriation. I do not intend to be playing a semantic game here. The novels in which Hemingway appears as a character—technically, the biographical fictions—involve various kinds of appropriation in which his fictional character behaves well or badly. In the speculative fictions, Hemingway appears in various counter-realistic guises, often with comical intent. In the fiction involving Hemingway-obsessed characters, Hemingway appears only indirectly, as perceived by admirers whose lives are altered somehow by his writing and the legends or myths that have evolved or exploded out of his life story. Clearly, various aspects of Hemingway's life and writing are intimately connected in the fiction of MacDonald Harris, Gerhard Köpf, and Michael Palin, but no such close integration occurs in Conan's novel, where such details are pretty much relegated to the status of stage setting.

An even more obvious or egregious case of exploitation occurs in Bill Granger's spy thriller *Hemingway's Notebook* (1986). A Chicago journalist and writer of at least twenty political thrillers, Granger (1941–2012) features a former CIA agent named Devereaux, who hunts down another former agent named Harry Francis, who lives on a revolt-torn Caribbean island and who years before was a friend of Ernest Hemingway. (The name perhaps suggests Harry Morgan of *To Have and Have Not* and Francis Macomber.) Harry and Devereaux join forces in defeating a rogue ex-agent named Colonel Ready, who has turned mercenary. It turns out that Harry was the inside man on the CIA sell-out of the Bay of Pigs invasion, and in the supposed notebook, Hemingway explains how Harry used him. As Harry explains, he loved Hemingway, who was "everything I wanted to be, everything I saw in myself" (296). In the lost novel he was supposedly writing, Hemingway had Harry killed off.

Although Granger makes only a few references to the notebook, he does offer a couple of pages of Hemingway imitation (296–297). As *Hemingway's Notebook* ends, Harry is in the process of writing a novel on Hemingway in Cuba to be called "The Hemingway Assignment." The CIA is concerned, but the publisher believes it will do well. Granger does allow Harry Francis one very Hemingwayesque moment: "He had written the truth for a change and it had freed him and he did not care" (358). This sentence imitates the early, terse style both in form (note the lack of commas) and in ironic backspin. Heavy on action and light on character, this novel does not rate nearly as many stars on Amazon.com as others by Granger, like *November Man* (also 1986) and *Henry McGee Is Not Dead* (1988).

"Many may claim to detect the narrative voice of Hemingway behind my staccato sentences," Cuban author Edmundo Desnoes writes in his introduction to the new translation and publication of his influential novella, *Memories of Underdevelopment* (2004), which appeared in Spanish as *Memorias del subdesarollo* in 1966 and in its first English translation (his own work) the next year as *Inconsolable Memories*. In his introduction to the 2004 edition Desnoes suggests that conceptually more significant with respect to the complex theme and to the psychology of the protagonist were such novels as Dostoyevsky's *Notes from the Underground and* Camus' *The Stranger*. In reflecting on the supposed Hemingway influence, Desnoes writes, "Caramba!" (one might translate that expletive loosely as "good grief!"). What established the fame of the short novel was the award-winning 1968 film directed by Tomás Gutiérrez Alea.

The Hemingway moment in the novella occurs when the first-person narrator (Sergio in the film) and his young girlfriend, the would-be actress Elena, encounter a group of Russian tourists while visiting the Hemingway museum at the Finca Vigía. The very important ten-page episode occurs at the center of the 76-page novella (the length as printed in Al Schaller's 2004 translation). As the narrator sees it, the "great world power" is visiting one of its "colonies," and he likens the Russians' attitude to what he conceives to have been Hemingway's: "All that the backward countries are good for is indulging the instincts, for killing savage animals, for fishing or lying in the sand to catch some sun. For enjoying life."[17] He then becomes furious when he sees that Elena, "the little tart," is flirting and "enjoying her role as exotic, underdeveloped beast of prey." The mulatto tour guide, who had been employed at the Finca, then comments on the trophy head of a gazelle. The analogy is obvious, and the narrator turns away, finding the "litany" to be "repulsive" (38). The guide turns out to be René Villarreal, who regarded himself as Hemingway's "Cuban son," which is the title of his memoir, published in 2009. The narrator complains that Hemingway found Villarreal in the streets and "molded him to meet his needs, the well-bred faithful dog of the gran señor. The colonizer and his Gungha Din" (41).

The narrator finds the Russians to be just like the Americans, admiring Hemingway more than they do Castro, and he believes Hemingway's home shows the writer's "profound disdain for life," that it provides evidence of how "people squander and waste and spend lavishly when they have things in abundance" (40). He finds everything to be "stiff" and "rigid and even "austere." As the tour continues, the narrator finds himself increasingly angered by the guide's "idolatry" (42), and he thinks of him as a "marionette" (44). Recognizing that Mary Hemingway took all of the original art with her, he reflects bitterly, "This is all we deserve, copies, we are nothing but a bad imitation of the powerful, civilized countries, a caricature, a cheap reproduction" (45). But in practically the same instant, the narrator admits his "conflicted feelings": "I feel both love and hate towards Hemingway; I admire him and at the same time he makes me feel ashamed." This perspective is similar to that of Leonardo

Padura Fuentes' detective, Mario Conde, in *Adiós Hemingway* (see Chapter Five). Also like Fuentes, Desnoes' narrator concludes resentfully that Hemingway "never gave a damn about Cuba" but used it only as "a place of refuge" where he could write without being pestered, receive guests, and "fish in the Gulf Stream" (45). At the end of the episode the narrator finds himself falling in love with Elena, even though he resists the temptation, partly because of their great difference in age. In effect, he feels similarly confused emotions with respect both to her and to Hemingway.

The Hemingway name is obviously one to conjure with. Witness Paula Huntley's 2003 memoir, *The Hemingway Book Club of Kosovo*, which opens with a prefatory statement about finding a copy of *The Old Man and the Sea* that will suit her students because of its "simple" prose and "will resonate with these brave young people" (Albanians).[18] She reminds herself to be "alert for Hemingway macho, though. God knows this country doesn't need any more macho." As Lisa Tyler notes in her review for *Hemingway Review*, "Hemingway and his work do not feature nearly as prominently in this work as the title might suggest."[19] Whether this book, or any nonfiction, constitutes an "appropriation" may be debatable, but what about *Hunting with Hemingway* (2000)? Much of the text Hemingway's niece Hilary claims to have composed from an audiocassette recorded by her father, Leicester (1915–1982), Ernest's younger brother by about sixteen years. Leicester's nickname was "Baron." A journalist who would write a novel and a notable memoir, *My Brother Ernest Hemingway*, Leicester committed suicide by gunshot about 21 years after Ernest. Hilary and her coauthor, her husband, Jeffry P. Lindsay, claim to have chucked the audiocassettes overboard after listening to them with their children.[20]

Leicester's wild stories are interrupted periodically by a supposed "professor" who may at times resemble George Plimpton in his interview published in the spring 1958 issue of *Paris Review*, albeit this professor is more naïve and more irksome by a long shot. Plimpton would never speak the academic lingo of Hemingway and Lindsay's imagined prof, later referred to as a "Hemingleech" (273), and neither would most actual professors, for that matter. In that context the writers make an important appeal to those who would "turn Ernest into a kind of religion": "read his books." While the real-life Leicester (Les) did not participate in safaris or other great adventures with his older brother, most biographers would agree with Michael Reynolds that Ernest "was a role model and hero" for him (*Hemingway: The Final Years*, 45). Hemingway and Lindsay's book makes an effort to assert Leicester's identity by way of his fanciful tales, which include a highly improbable set-to with an irate ostrich, a supposed encounter with a huge king cobra in India (Papa saves Les's life), and

Les's being fired on by a U-boat off Costa Rica. Not every appropriation or biographical fiction on Hemingway has been reviewed in *Hemingway Review*, but it is a little surprising that this book is among those that have not been so served, regardless of what one decides to make of Leicester's supposed comments on his adventures with his big brother. The anonymous reviewer for *Publishers Weekly* dismissed the book as a "disappointing narrative," the entirety of which "seems apocryphal."[21] She or he also described the professor as stereotypical and "overdone."

At the end, Professor Leech, who is reminiscent in some ways of the Old Lady in *Death in the Afternoon*, proves impossible to locate and Hilary decides to regard her father's stories as just that, as fiction, so she tosses the tape into the ocean, reminding her husband and children that those stories were intended to remind them of her father's "love of life and adventure…. The stories are for you, for me, for everyone, to know my dad as he really was, a man who had the courage to love life" (314–315). Hilary also finds personal consolation in the stories, which she says have helped her deal with the pain of her father's suicide. The Library of Congress classifies the book as biography, but some librarians will doubtless categorize it as fiction, thinking most likely of that elusive subgenre of biographical fiction or the almost equally elusive nonfictional subgenre of memoir. A journalist and screenwriter, Hilary Hemingway has coedited with Carlene Brennen *Hemingway in Cuba* (2003) and has also cowritten with her husband, Jeffry Lindsay, a pair of fantasy novels.

In fact, I might have placed *Hunting with Hemingway* in the chapter on speculative fiction, but it seemed right, all things considered, to regard Leicester Hemingway, and his daughter, too, among the "obsessed" characters. At times, in fact, the term "possessed" seems applicable. The book deserves some attention here because Ernest does play an important role, and he is significantly "appropriated." Reviewing the book for *Journal of Popular Culture*, Marc Seals observes, "The perception of literary academics by the Hemingways is funny and at times painfully accurate."[22] One irony that occurs in this book, however, and really throughout the appropriations, is that while the characters delight in their disparagement of academics, and certainly Les follows his brother Ernest in this respect, surely the primary readership of such texts will be those very academics who are treated with such open, albeit sometimes comical, contempt. One must stop somewhere when it comes to deciding what does or does not qualify as an "appropriation." Ernest's granddaughter Lorian Hemingway, Gregory's daughter, has written a well-received memoir of fishing and drinking, *Walk on Water* (1998), and other books. Although she does reflect on a deep-sea fishing adventure with Gregory, on which Paul Hendrickson comments in *Hemingway's Boat*, she does not seek to appropriate her renowned grandfather as a fictional character. As he appears in the pages of *Hunting with Hemingway*, however, Papa is mostly a product of the imagination.

The characters in Lauri Anderson's collection of interrelated short stories in *Hunting Hemingway's Trout* (1990), however, are quite obviously Hemingway-obsessed. The first two pieces that make up the slim volume are nonfiction essays reflecting on Anderson's personal obsession with Hemingway as well as observations on his Finnish heritage. Anderson has served as the chair of humanities and English at Finlandia University in Hancock, Michigan, a small (600 or so students) liberal arts institution in the Upper Peninsula. He has published six short-story collections and a novel, including *Mosquito Conversations* and *Misery Bay*. His most recent book is a memoir, *From Moosehead to Misery Bay* (2013). *Hunting for Hemingway's Trout* did not draw much critical attention when it appeared about two dozen years ago, partly because of its unusual blending of brief nonfiction inter-chapters on Hemingway (subjects like "Hemingway and Women" or "Hemingway and War"), conventional fiction, and what would now be called "creative nonfiction," personal essays in narrative form. Anderson chose as subjects for the vignettes aspects of Hemingway he believes have been "romanticized": "I unromanticize them."[23] The impact of Hemingway in some of the texts is fairly slight, but in the title story and such others as "A Short Unhappy Life" we encounter characters whose fascination with Hemingway's life and writing deeply influences their own behavior.

In "Hunting Hemingway's Trout" the first-person narrator, a college student doing summer work, and his "book dumb and undisciplined" cousin are logging birch and drinking Stroh's beer in northern Michigan.[24] It's a Finnish family, but somehow a very American story. The town of Gaylord, which is mentioned in the story, is located about 35 miles southeast of Hemingway's Petoskey and Horton Bay. The only Hemingway that Cousin Toivo has read is "Big Two-Hearted River," twice, and he admires it and is determined to fish that river, which in Hemingway's story is located near Seney. The cousins locate Seney and talk with an old clerk who remembers taking a day off in 1919 to show a guy named Wemedge and a couple of his pals where to fish on the Fox, which pretty much runs through the small township. But ironically, as it happens, Cousin Toivo insists on fishing the river of the story, unaware that Hemingway actually fished the Fox and changed its name for lyrical reasons, borrowing the moniker of a river on the Upper Peninsula. Anderson, then, offers a conflict between art (fiction) and reality.

The narrator, who is more interested in a day off work than he is in trout fishing anyway, knows about Hemingway's alteration but does not tell his cousin, and the two never fish the Two Hearted River, which is located about 25 miles north and east, even though they do drive 26.5 miles due north. Instead, they see an elderly couple broadside a moose, an episode that Anderson employs in somewhat altered form in his memoir, the subtitle of which is "The Moose in the VW Bug." The cousins briefly tend to the pair, who are not badly injured, and send another car for help, after which Toivo cuts a haunch from the moose, and they return home and to the hard work of logging. In Hemingway's story, the lone Nick Adams memorably avoids fishing in the swamp at the end because he believes it would be "a tragic adventure" (*Complete Short Stories*, 180). Anderson's story comes across as more of a comical misadventure through which the Hemingway fan, including the college-boy cousin, is reminded of the distance that separates art from life.

Following a one-page inter-chapter entitled "Hemingway and Sports," in which Anderson debunks some of the fables of Hemingway's "athletic prowess" (44), he offers the story "A Short Unhappy Life," featuring a first-person narrator who admires Hemingway's life and writing but is himself "indecisive, cowardly, unathletic, uncreative, and almost obsessively clumsy" (46). The narrator was introduced to Hemingway's fiction as a college freshman via "The Short Happy Life of Francis Macomber" on the eve of Kennedy's assassination in November 1963. He regards himself as a "panophobe" who prefers his world to be "quiet and safe"; accordingly, he pursued his doctorate in literature at a "third-rate" university in the Midwest, where he still teaches (47). He has a "girlfriend of sorts" named Tiffany, "a crashing bore with a degree in developmental education." Tiffany is not a reader, but she dislikes Hemingway because she has heard he was "a male chauvinist pig" and is "overrated" as a writer (51). When the narrator gets too depressed, he escapes "into the world of Hemingway's fiction" and consequently has "read the complete works at least fifty times" (48). Haunted by memories of his boyhood hero JFK and "trapped" with the "entwined" images of Kennedy's and Francis Macomber's deaths, the narrator claims to have read the story "five hundred times" and to have taught it every year since 1969 (50). He remains obsessed, however, with a desire to discover a "definite answer," at least to the mystery surrounding Macomber's death.

To acquire that answer the narrator decides to reenact the ending to Hemingway's story with the reluctant Tiffany playing Margot. Not surprisingly, the National Endowment for the Humanities denies his grant application for this undertaking. The comic highlight of the story takes place in a gun shop where the narrator goes to buy a costly Mannlicher 6.5, in keeping with the story (*Complete Short Stories*, 28), and the store owner annoys him with his insistence that "of course she murdered him. She blew the brains right out of that yuppie son of a bitch!" (58). The store owner explains that his love of Hemingway and of firearms began with his boyhood reading of *Green Hills of Africa*. The two men debate the interpretation of the story along lines familiar to most readers who know the extensive secondary commentary on it. Paul Smith estimated that at least 120 commentaries on the story had been published by 1985.[25] Or perhaps the most comical episode occurs at a zoo where the narrator pays a keeper to time a charging African buffalo, which expires in the process, due to its age and the uncustomary exertion.

But the final scene, when the narrator uses a whistle to time Tiffany's response to the expected charge of the buffalo, provides maybe the most comical of all moments in the fiction involving Hemingway-obsessed characters. Tiffany shoots a hole in the floor of the rented open Jeep. On her next effort she shoots out the windshield. Meanwhile, the distraught narrator confuses Margot with Lee Harvey Oswald, obviously revealing his own muddled mental state. He tells Tiffany the experiment has given him new admiration for Margot, but Tiffany isn't impressed. She doesn't want to see him again. She has an upcoming date with the zookeeper.

"Sooner or later," the front cover flap of *Hunting Hemingway's Trout* tells us, "every writer in America must address the work, the life, and the legend of Ernest Hemingway." As the generations pass, however, those of us involved in all of that must wonder: How long will it last? Will the Hemingway hoopla, from widely respected writing awards like the PEN/Hemingway, given annually since 1976 for a first novel or book of short fiction, to the often disdained impersonation contests held during the Hemingway Days festival in Key West never end? One can purchase Hemingway cigars (Arturo Fuente), Hemingway pens (Montblanc), Hemingway furniture (Thomasville), Hemingway sandals (Neil M Footwear). One may, in effect "Live the Legend."[26] In a recent piece in the *Wall Street Journal* about ongoing efforts to sell William Faulkner's leavings, Stephanie Cohen notes in passing that Hemingway's heirs hired Marla Metzner of Fashion Licensing of America to provide "an alternate revenue stream," as the copyrights on many of his earlier works, as on Faulkner's, will elapse in just a couple of decades. And "Ms. Metzner says the line [of Hemingway merchandise] has grossed over $750 million in retail sales since 1999."[27] Somewhere along "the line" one should probably read the books.

Hemingway's self-commoditization is a matter of record. As a celebrity, he was much in demand by the commercial world, and as Matthew J. Bruccoli's *Hemingway and the Mechanism of Fame* (2006) demonstrates, he was willing on occasion to shill for such products as Parker pens, Ballantine ale, and Pan American Airlines. Bruccoli states succinctly, "The camera loved him."[28] And perhaps the opening statement on the front cover flap says it all: "Ernest Hemingway was famous for being famous." Near the end of his biography, Jeffrey Meyers confidently asserts that Hemingway "has survived his decline, his death and his detractors. He is now recognized as the most important American novelist of the twentieth century as well as a seminal influence on the modern American character" (570). Those words were written nearly thirty years ago, and the present study amounts in part to a commentary on the assertions stated so confidently above. One does wonder, though, just what "seminal influence" Hemingway might be said to have had on "the modern American character." The Hemingway obsession, which does not, after all, necessarily require blind adulation either of the man or of his writing, appears to be something of a sustained phenomenon. At least twenty Hemingway appropriations to date have been published in the 21st century.

Eight

Hemingway on Stage, Screen and Television

For various reasons, no actor's rendition of Ernest Hemingway on the stage is likely ever to rival Hal Holbrook's Mark Twain or Julie Harris's Emily Dickinson, but that would not be for want of effort. Near the end of his study of Hemingway's appropriation in men's magazines of the 1950s, David M. Earle lists a few of the novels in which Hemingway is fictionalized and a few of the plays as well: John de Groot's *Papa: The One-Man Play*, Brian Gordon Sinclair's *Hemingway on Stage*, James Mitchell Lear's *Hemingway Reminisces*, and Ben Pleasants' *The Hemingway/Dos Passos Wars*. The availability of these and similar items varies considerably, but de Groot's *Papa* (1987) has been printed, and a two-and-a-half minute clip of Adrian Sparks' February 2008 performance, which won him a nomination for an Ovation Award, is currently available on YouTube. De Groot's *Papa* ought not to be confused with Ken Vose and Jordan Rhodes' play of the same title but different subtitle, released in a DVD version in 2010 but not presently available, which Rhodes performed with Lynn Moore throughout the Southeast in the summer of 2002. The text of Pleasants' *The Hemingway/Dos Passos Wars* (1977) is also in print, as is Michael Hollinger's *An Empty Plate in the Café du Grand Boeuf* (2003, premiered in 1994), which is billed as a "'comic tragedy in seven courses' celebrating the joys of cooking, sex, bullfighting and the collected works of Ernest Hemingway" (back cover).

Hemingway makes a brief appearance in Tennessee Williams' *Clothes for a Summer Hotel*, which has been described as an "uneven 'ghost play'" (Williams' term for it) that "pits the alcoholic, repressed Scott [Fitzgerald] against the intense, overly sensual Zelda."[1] The play ran on Broadway for just two weeks in 1980 and did not fare much better when the White Horse Theater Company made another effort at the Hudson Guild Theatre in 2010. The most obvious contribution to the dramatic appropriations, however, and surely the most intriguing one, would be Frederic Hunter's *The Hemingway Play*, which debuted at Harvard University's Loeb Dramatic Center in the summer of 1975. As Tom Wright, reviewing the performance for *Harvard Crimson*, observed, Hunter's play "allows four Hemingways to appear onstage at once. Four separate personalities, each from a different phase of Hemingway's life, meet one another in a Madrid café. The complexity of the man is revealed through characters who share common memories but cannot sort out the truth from the self-perpetuated myth."[2] The play appeared on public television in the "Hollywood Television Theater" series and was revived by the Arts and Entertainment Network in 1986.

Briefly, the two-act play is set on the day of Hemingway's suicide, and the premise, as Hunter states it in his foreword, is that "a play about Hemingway's life would need to show multiple phases of him simultaneously."[3] The four "phases" interact with each other unaware that they are the same self at different points in one man's life. Wemedge is Hemingway at 19 on his return from World War I and very much in love with his former nurse, Agnes von Kurowsky; Hem is Hemingway as the writer at the peak if his early career, nearly 28 years old and about to marry Pauline, so for him the present moment is the spring of 1927 and the stories of *In Our Time* and *Men Without Women* are accomplished, along with his first novel, *The Sun Also Rises;* Ernest is Hemingway as "a world personality writer" at age 55, just six months after his narrow escape from a pair of airplane crashes in Africa, so for him the present moment would be the summer of 1955; Papa is the disoriented, paranoid Hemingway in the spring of 1960, struggling with the text of his article based on the mano-a-mano bullfights he witnessed in Spain during the "dangerous summer" of 1959. The various avatars turn out to be quite critical of one another. Hem, for example, is particularly hard on Ernest, calling him "King of the windbags" (31). Wemedge, who is very critical of his father, undertakes to interview Ernest on the subject of the two plane crashes. Hem waxes nostalgic about Paris in the vogue of *A Moveable Feast* and picks on Ernest for pontificating in his writing, for being overly autobiographical, and for preaching art but practicing commerce (123). But Ernest is also "on to" Hem, whom he castigates as a writer with "impressive talent" who is also "a mean, ambitious shit" (131). In short, the ironies are at least potentially amusing, but Papa's pathetic, suicidal presence tends to loom over the play, casting an ominous shadow.

Before reflecting further on the appropriation of Hemingway on stage, however, it might prove worthwhile briefly to consider his own foray into theater. As numerous commentators have observed, he had a flair for the dramatic, generally preferring to occupy center stage himself, whether at a private party, a literary salon, or the more familiar stage of a bar or tavern. In *Hemingway and His Conspirators* (1997), Leonard J. Leff reminds us that, from the first, Hemingway "needed the approbation of the crowd," that he was "acutely aware of audience," and that he "cultivated publicity even as he pretended to scorn it."[4] Describing his impact on the world of expatriates in 1920s Paris, Leff reflects on Ernest's infectious smile, his "mercurial and abrasive" behavior, and his casual good looks: "He was the real thing costumed as the real thing. He was the performer par excellence, most content when active and, above all, when watched" (8). That was how he was even before his writing made him into a celebrity.

Although *The Fifth Column*, set in Madrid during the Spanish Civil War and first published in 1938 with his *First Forty-nine Stories*, is generally regarded as Hemingway's only foray into playwriting, one could make a good argument for "Today Is Friday," published among the stories of *Men Without Women* in 1927, as a very brief one-act play. The three-page text is set up in dramatic form and features three Roman soldiers and a Hebrew wine-seller named George (a favorite Hemingway moniker) on the evening of the Crucifixion. The quick play acts as a sort of ironic epilogue to the event, with the soldiers speaking in distinctly American vernacular and describing Jesus as if he were a boxer who "was pretty good in there today" (*Complete Short Stories*, 272). Mary Magdalene comes off as "a nice-looker" (273). A three-act adaptation of *A Farewell to Arms* was produced in 1930, script by Leonard Stallings, but reviews were poor and the play held on for just three weeks.[5] A.E. Hotchner wrote an adaptation of *The Fifth Column* for television and adapted several of the stories for television, including "Fifty Grand," "The Gambler, the Nun and the Radio," "The Killers," and "Snows of Kilimanjaro," all produced between the fall of 1959 and the spring of 1960. "Soldier's Home" was adapted for television in 1977 by Robert Geller, and there have been many others.

Nearly everyone who has taught such stories as "Cat in the Rain," "Hills Like White Elephants," or "A Clean, Well-Lighted Place," stories driven by powerfully understated dramatic dialogue, will have found it nearly impossible to resist parceling out roles among their students for what amounts to impromptu script-reading. Hilary Hemingway, Ernest's niece through his brother, Leicester, wrote a play based on Hemingway's life in 1920s Paris with her husband, Jeffry P. Lindsay, that was performed in Key West during the Hemingway Days festival in July 1987. More recently, she was cowriter of the script for the movie *Hemingway and Fuentes*, currently in production and featuring Anthony Hopkins as Ernest. The film concerns the long friendship between Ernest and Gregorio Fuentes, the Cuban who served as first mate or captain of his beloved boat, the *Pilar*. Born in the Spanish Canary Islands, Fuentes, who died in 2002 at age 104, is often regarded as the model for old Santiago, the protagonist of *The Old Man and the Sea*. Either directly or indirectly, much of Hemingway's writing has been reconfigured for stage, television, and film, and he has been a stage presence himself as well, whether willingly or not. In an article published in the *North Dakota Quarterly* (2003), Richard Allan Davison chronicles Hemingway's "enduring affection for theater," takes note of his important role in his high school's senior class play in 1917, *Beau Brummell*, and accounts for details pertaining to the staging of *The Fifth Column*.[6]

Hemingway's only significant effort at dramatic writing, in fact, remains *The Fifth Column*, which was adapted and heavily edited by Benjamin Glazer and first staged by the Theater Guild of New York, starring Lee J. Cobb and Franchot Tone, in the spring of 1940. The play showed to mixed reviews and closed after 87 performances (Oliver 97). It was revived and staged using Hemingway's original script by the Mint Theater in New York in the spring of 2008, but reviews remained "mixed." In his review of the 1969 publication of the play along with four stories from the Spanish Civil War, Philip Young called it an "autobiographical drama," finding Hemingway's "dominating presence" to be ubiquitous: "This is immediate, unmistakable Hemingway."[7] Young pretty much equates the protagonist, a journalist and Loyalist agent named Philip Rawlings, with Hemingway, as have most commentators on the play. Peter L. Hays refers to Rawlings as "a fictional Hemingway alter ego."[8] Other commentators, including Hays, have also, generally, conceded that except for "her unbelievable stupidity," as Young puts it, Rawlings' Vassar-educated mistress, Dorothy Bridges, "is an accurate portrait of fellow journalist Martha Gellhorn." Just why the Bryn Mawr–educated Martha Gellhorn (1908–1998), nine years younger than Ernest, would have agreed to marry him after having read the script of the play might remain one of the unsolved mysteries of Hemingway lore.

Over the past couple of dozen years, the play has attracted more serious critical attention, with Raymond Conlon hailing it as Hemingway's "only truly ideological work" and in fact as something of a "political morality play."[9] In an essay published as the lead piece in the fall 1998 issue of *Hemingway Review* John Raeburn reflected on Hemingway's misgivings about the play as printed in 1938 and especially as produced in 1940, after the collapse of the Loyalist cause to Franco and the Nationalist forces. Raeburn emphasizes that like the documentary *The Spanish Earth*, which appeared the same year as the play was written and for which Hemingway wrote the script, *The Fifth Column* was "propagandistic."[10] Never was Hemingway, before or after the civil war in Spain, as much of a political insider, but the play demonstrates that he was not politically astute. Raeburn compares it unfavorably with George Orwell's *Homage to Catalonia*, also written in 1937, and asserts the play "would have utterly undermined his credibility as a writer with a clear-eyed grasp of political issues" had it not been superseded by the novel *For Whom the Bell Tolls*, published three years later (15). With his epic novel of the Spanish Civil War, Raeburn concludes, Hemingway "transformed himself from a propagandist with Stalinist inclinations into a political novelist of the first magnitude" (16),

At one extreme of critical response to the play one might cite Stephen Koch's comments in *The Breaking Point* (2005) to the effect that it is "an exceptionally nasty piece of work and the moral nadir of Hemingway's entire career" (240). He describes the journalist turned counterinsurgent Philip Rawlings as a "Popular Front assassin who, motivated by antifascism, kills not for money but for goodness; a real man who, in contrast to the lily-livered liberals around him, understands the necessity for complicity in the necessary murder" (240). "Every characterization of Martha" via Dorothy, Koch observes, "is insulting" (242). In fact, in order to deny his personal infatuation with her and commit himself unreservedly to the Republican cause, Philip brutally rejects Dorothy at the end of the play, spurning her as a "commodity" that he "can't afford."[11] Perhaps it should go without saying that Philip's cruelty here makes dramatic sense only if he does truly love Dorothy despite her many shortcomings: she's "lazy and spoiled and rather stupid" (58), but she also constitutes a beautiful and dangerous distraction. At the heart of the play is the dilemma of the tension between personal and political (and perhaps, in a way, "moral") commitment. When he addressed that dilemma again in *For Whom the Bell Tolls*, Hemingway would fashion a far more sympathetic pair of lovers in Robert Jordan and Maria.

In an essay published in *Hemingway Review* following the 2008 revival of the play, Noël Valis suggests *The Fifth Column* "is too morally confused" to be either "political propaganda or political morality play," and she questions the extent to which Hemingway himself "was aware of the play's muddled ethical core."[12] Her essay appears to call for a more thoughtful, if not necessarily more sympathetic, consideration of the "moral quicksand" in which Philip Rawlings (and perhaps ipso facto Ernest Hemingway) finds himself (29). In her review of the 2008 production, Verna Kale praises not only its "faithfulness to Hemingway's text" but also the fact that "it acknowledges the complexity of the main characters."[13]

From its initial performance on March 6, 1940, it was obvious to reviewers, as it was to Hemingway, that the ideal moment for *The Fifth Column* had passed. The world war that Hemingway and many others believed would be heralded by the civil war and fascist victory in Spain had become manifest in Hitler's invasion of Poland on the first of September 1939; and by early March of 1940 the Russo-Finnish Winter War was coming to a bitter end, Stalin having concluded a nonaggression pact with Hitler with that end (among others) in mind. Theatergoers on March 16 soon learned of the German air raid on the British fleet at Scapa Flow, and two days later Mussolini declared war on France and Britain. In early April a fifth column movement in Norway led by former defense minister Vidkun Quisling contributed to that country's rapid fall to the Nazis, and by the date the play closed, May 18, German troops had occupied the Benelux countries and invaded France. The immediate relevance of the play had been lost. In her review of the play's 2008 revival Verna Kale writes, "Now that the Spanish Civil War is history and not just old news, the play can receive the attention it deserves" (132), and she finds the Mint Theater production to be "smart, violent, sexy, and surprisingly funny" (133). Other reviewers were not so welcoming, however, and in her concluding paragraph Kale, while noting that scholars may at last "recognize it as one of Hemingway's important experiments with genre," submits that it has been reduced, after all, to "an interesting artifact" (134).

What, then, might be said of Ben Pleasants' two-act play, *The Hemingway/Dos Passos Wars*, first staged at Al's National Theater in Los Angeles on March 12, 1995? Also known as "Al's Bar National Theater," the former saloon was recognized for providing a stage for eclectic stage productions. Pleasants (1940–2013) was a longtime public-school teacher and a contributor of book and theater reviews to the *Los Angeles Free Press*. His published work includes a memoir of poet Charles Bukowski, a couple of independently published short novels, poems, and several plays, including *"Contentious Minds": The Mary McCarthy/Lillian Hellman Affair* (2002). That is, if one proceeds from the premise that *The Fifth Column* has been reduced to the status of historic or literary artifact, devoid of interest except to Hemingway enthusiasts and possibly to historians, what does that say of a play set during the same period (late 1930s in Key West and Madrid) and involving personalities connected with historic events? A "revised and reinterpreted" version of the play opened on August 27, 1999, at the Hollywood Court Theatre for a one-month run connected with the Hemingway centennial. In all likelihood the play would have passed into oblivion had it not appeared as an apparently self-published text in 1997, but like the novels and stories featuring Hemingway as a character—and along with the films, to be considered hereafter—*The Hemingway/Dos Passos Wars* has entered the abyss of the popular literary infatuation with Ernest Hemingway.

Not surprisingly, given what has been said above about the relationship between Dos Passos and Hemingway (see Chapter Four), Pleasants' two-hour play diminishes Hemingway. In fact, one might argue that most fictional treatments of the broken friendship show Hemingway in a bad light, but to what ostensible end? One suspects some writers simply take malicious pleasure in undercutting the giant. Even presumably objective biographers appear to take some satisfaction in noting that by the time he was in his forties, Hemingway had begun to gain weight and his hairline was beginning to recede, as if such transformations were exceptional in his case. What did Henry James look like at age 45? Even though one of his professed aims in writing *Hemingway's Boat* was "to try to help rescue Hemingway from his seemingly set-in-stone image of immortal writer and immortal bitch of a human being" (299), Paul Hendrickson cannot resist the gratuitous observation that at fifty "Hemingway looked old enough to be somebody's grandfather" (465). As a matter of fact, he *was* "somebody's grandfather," as his son Jack's first child, a daughter, was born in 1950. Perhaps if Hemingway had been less of public figure, less demonstrative, less conflicted, less greedy for fame, less macho, less photogenic—less himself, that is—he would not have been such a likely subject for all sorts of appropriation. One might easily project an alternative Ernest Hemingway, one who would be modest and easygoing, temperate if not abstemious in his drinking, monogamous, camera shy—in short, someone not at all like the man he was, someone not nearly as interesting or as complex.

But the bad boy makes the best copy, and that is clearly the case with Hemingway as Ben Pleasants configures him from the outset, coming on to his boyhood girlfriend Katy Dos Passos, belittling critics as "one step below hemorrhoids,"[14] punching out the besotted poet Wallace Stevens, and moving in on Martha Gellhorn as his current wife, Pauline, struggles with his tendency to "put real people" in his fiction and hurt them in the process (41). Any student of Hemingway will be aware that, like other writers of biographical fiction, Pleasants did not just make up those events. "Your characters are real," Pauline rails. "You're the fiction" (41). The second act takes place mostly in Madrid, where Papa courts Martha, struggles with Dos Passos over the missing José Robles, and shrugs off the accusation of having missed the bombing of

Guernica as just another battle that will "soon be forgotten" (58). Of course, thanks to Picasso's colossal painting in gray, black, and white, completed in June 1937, the tragedy of Guernica would not be forgotten. In his heated argument about Robles with Dos Passos, it is Dos who takes the high ground, pointing out that "as a journalist" Hem is there "to write about the truth. Not just some Stalinist fantasy of the truth" (67). "You don't care about the people of Spain," Dos Passos challenges. "It's their war you want. It arouses you in a sexual way" (69).

Significantly, Hemingway has no response to his friend's contention here. In the seventh scene of Act Two we encounter Dos Passos and Katy at a café in Paris, with Dos expressing remorse for his failure to have perceived there was "a civil war inside a civil war" that undermined the Loyalist side, as he has been informed by a "man named Eric Blair," or George Orwell, as the audience is expected to recognize (70). Hemingway's argument that Dos has lost "perspective on the whole war over one little guy" (73), José Robles, rings very hollow. Katy brands him an "opportunist" (75). In the eighth scene, Pleasants reduces Hem to a stumbling, vomiting drunk. He is roundly rejected by his scornful wife, Pauline, who rips at him for the success of his novel *To Have and Have Not*, which sold some 38,000 copies in its first five months. "Those people are real," she insists. "Dos and Katie and me and Jane [Mason]. They're so real they'll know themselves in a second" (77). When he tries to maintain that these "people" are fictional, Hemingway retches, as if sickened by his own argument. After that, he boasts, "I'm a hero and I'll always be one." The boast rings hollow.

As the scene ends, however, Hem tells himself he "should have listened to the man on the Blue Guitar," obviously a reference to Wallace Stevens' 1937 poem, which includes, among many passages that might resonate here, the following from the fifteenth section: "Things as they are have been destroyed. / Have I?"[15] In the ninth scene, leftist playwright Lillian Hellman celebrates Hemingway's narration of the film *The Spanish Earth* and joyously anticipates a visit to the Plaza Hotel, "where love and liquor triumph" (80). The tenth and final scene, described as an epilogue, takes place at the screening of the film in Carnegie Hall, where Hemingway is dressed in a bullfighter's costume. His final words dissolve into confused and empty rhetoric, but Dos Passos gets the last words in the play: "We all loved him, Papa Hem, and we all hated him. One of those bad boy artists who never grew up." He pronounces his former friend to have been "always a hero and a buffoon" (82). Dos Passos then proceeds to summarize the lives of others who appear in the play, so that, as Hemingway promised the Old Lady in *Death in the Afternoon*, "all stories, if continued far enough, end in death" (122). Writing for the *Los Angeles Times* on April 7, 1995, Scott Collins hailed Pleasants' play for "sheer campy fun," describing it as a "melodrama of sex, socialism and the Spanish Civil War."[16] Although he called it "a handsome revival" when he reviewed its rerun at the Hollywood Court Theatre on September 2, 1999, Philip Brandes concluded "this furtive, craven, smaller-than-life portrait misses any sense of the immense experiential appetites that compensated for Hemingway's excesses."[17]

John de Groot's one-man play, *Papa*, which debuted in its final form in Boise in 1988, has made a considerably larger splash in the theatrical world, having been staged from Key West to San Francisco and from Los Angeles to New York City. Reviewing George Peppard's performance in the role at the Royal-George Theatre for the *Chicago Tribune* on August 3, 1988, Richard Christiansen called it "piercing," the portrait of "a proud but ruined man, looking back with wry humor, black anger and increasing alcoholic bravado on his life and work."[18] The play depicts Hemingway at the Finca Vigía in 1959, his sixtieth year. De Groot describes it as "not a play about Ernest Hemingway's enduring legacy as a writer. Rather, it is a theatrical encounter with a 19th-century American Ulysses who became lost in the 20th century, as he struggled to discover what it is to be a man" (de Groot, "Note from the Playwright").[19] De Groot credits novelist Kurt Vonnegut Jr. with the analogy to Ulysses.

The subtitle of the ninety-minute play is often overlooked by reviewers but is important: *A Play Based on the Legendary Lives of Ernest Hemingway*. Emphasis might fall either on the plural of "lives" or on the qualifier "legendary." De Groot is a Pulitzer Prize–winning journalist (or quondam journalist) now living in Florida. George Peppard (1928–1994), a recovering alcoholic who at the time (like Hemingway) had been married four times, claimed to have felt "an adrenaline rush" on first reading the script.[20] Len Cariou took over the role when the play was performed at the Douglas Fairbanks Theater in New York in June 1996. In *Hemingway Review* Robert J. Kirkpatrick opened his comments thusly: "As soon as Len Cariou stalks onstage bellowing his opening line, 'Goddamn it, Mary!,' the audience can guess what type of Hemingway will be portrayed."[21] De Groot's Hemingway, Kirkpatrick writes, "is vulgar, boastful, hypocritical, and spiteful—certainly an affront to the Hemingway apologist who would see the author's work as representing his life." The role was later picked up by Adrian Sparks, who received a Best Actor nomination for it in 2005 from the Los Angeles Ovation Awards.

Considerably different in tone is another one-man performance, that of Boise, Idaho, native L.E. (Erv) Johnson in *E. Hemingway*, which opened in Boise in 1984. While de Groot's Hemingway indignantly quarrels with the audience as trespassers at the Finca, Johnson's seems rather congenial as he directly addresses the audience as if it were some stranger, most likely a fan, who has barged in on him: "Who the hell let you in here?" he asks. What do "you" know about boats, deep sea fishing, and so on? Okay, he agrees, I'll give you an hour, "but don't you ask me one goddamned thing about writing."[22] Then he grouses about "kids these days," and before long he is talking all about writing, about how happy he was in 1920s Paris. He quotes the opening paragraph of *A Farewell to Arms* and reflects on Cézanne's influence on his writing. He complains (predictably) about literary critics, and he argues against symbolic interpretations of his writing. He rambles, but he rambles affably. In the VHS tape of the performance in Boise, the live audience laughs often throughout. The theater notes indicate that Act One occurs at the Finca Vigía in 1951, several years earlier than the date of de Groot's Hemingway, and Act Two, following a twenty-minute intermission, takes places at Sun Valley in 1961.

In the first act, Johnson's Hemingway is dressed in khaki shorts and a short-sleeved shirt, and he wears a sun-visor; in the second act, he wears a brownish, long-sleeved shirt and green trousers stuffed into brown boots. He slips into a fishing vest and takes out a pair of slippers, to suggest that he is at home in Idaho. He boasts of his sales and claims "The Snows of Kilimanjaro" is his personal favorite among his short stories. He reminisces about war, bullfighting, "Miss Mary," fishing and hunting, notably in the vicinity of Ketchum and Sun Valley, and finally, as he takes off the fishing vest and dons a dark-brown sweater, about the necessity for the writer to maintain his "integrity." He worries over the drying up of his creative juices, but he insists he'll be content to stand on his six novels. The play ends serenely with the passage from *The Old Man and the Sea* when old Santiago is "dreaming of lions." Introducing an upcoming performance of the play at the old Ramp Theatre in Los Angeles in the fall of 1985, Lawrence Christon quoted Johnson to the effect that the play is intended as "a dialogue with the audience": "The piece makes no apology for his strongly masculine persona. It pulls no punches in regard to terminology either. My wife, Ginger Scott, who directs, didn't want to do it at first; she couldn't accept the kind of personality he was. But eventually I convinced her that he was the expression of an era. We can understand what it's like these days for someone to devote as much time to one's public figure as to one's art. Hemingway had no use for anybody he thought weak. But he wasn't a phony. He lived the way he believed."[23]

One problem with that sentiment, or premise, is that it tends to reduce Hemingway, and ipso facto his writing, to the status of historical artifact. Erv Johnson's performance, then, becomes a reenactment. In his review of the performance for the *Los Angeles Times*, Christon lamented that Johnson did not commit himself to any one of many directions he might have gone with his portrayal. Noting Johnson's background in public relations, Christon asserts "it's a public relations Hemingway who greets us," and he finds the tone to be too "modulated, avuncular." The tone "doesn't let us in on the furies that charged the engine of Hemingway's ambition—the force that made him write with such discipline also gorged him with nasty jealousies." He concludes that *E. Hemingway* "is a pleasant enough experience in the theater, but we part strangers." (Johnson performed the play in Boise as recently as March 24, 2012.)

For those who might hold that a one-man performance of Hemingway should be more unsettling than "pleasant," one might turn again to John de Groot's *Papa*, which was first performed in September 1987 in Miami, Hemingway being played by Bill Hindman (1922–1999). In his review of that performance, Jack Zink notes that part of de Groot's attraction to Hemingway had to do with the fact that he, too, had struggled with alcoholism.[24] Hemingway's "tragic flaw," de Groot says in his prefatory note, was his belief "in the myth of external answers to the questions of his life." He calls the one-man play "a deliberate metaphor," for it concerns "a creative giant driven to eat what he killed and destroy what he loved." The play opens to "a musical montage of Bach, Scott Joplin, George M. Cohan and Mozart," followed by a rattling of typewriter keys and Fats Waller singing "I'm Gonna Sit Right Down and Write Myself a Letter" and revealing "an absolute clutter of things to suggest both a strange museum and a boy's room, complete with the head of a large Cape buffalo" (1). When the Waller recording gets stuck at the phrase "make believe," Hemingway shouts the play's first words from offstage: "Goddamn it!" (2). He then "explodes" onto the stage holding his cat Boise and directly addresses the audience, angrily informing them that the sign in Spanish means they are not welcome.

De Groot's Hemingway invests much of his vitriol in his mother, but his father also gets a fair dose for being a "coward" and "a sorry son of a bitch" (10). Ernest then moves to his wounding in World War I and his unsuccessful courtship of Agnes von Kurowsky. His narration softens when he recounts the years in Paris with Hadley, but, significantly, that happy interlude absorbs only four or five pages of the seventy that comprise the text of the play. He does pay tribute to Mary, who is "the least jealous of all my wives" and who "understands my occasional need for a younger woman to stir the creative juices" (30). But he soon gives over to anxieties about sexual inadequacy and impotence. The first act ends with Cuban children calling on Papa to play baseball with them. Act Two begins with a shotgun blast as the kids have lost the "damn baseball," so he has taken to a new game: "killing famous living authors," including Faulkner, Dos Passos, and Norman Mailer (44). Right away he contemplates suicide, which had been a motif in Act One, when he mentioned his father's suicide and that of Hadley's father as well. His drinking, which has been ongoing, seems to occupy him more fully in the second act. He relives painful memories of his convalescence in Milan and of the nearly fatal air crashes in Africa, and he lashes out against the FBI and J. Edgar Hoover. Then he drops back to his exploits in World War II, when he claims to have shot and killed an "SS son of a bitch" he was interrogating (59). Soon after that tale, Papa begins to drink gin straight from the bottle.

De Groot's Hemingway ends the play by quoting roughly from "The Snows of Kilimanjaro" about the "frozen body of a great male leopard": "What drove this proud creature to these fatal heights seems a mystery—to nearly everyone" (70). In de Groot's adaptation of the passages, it is clear that Papa identifies himself with the "great male leopard," which, presumably, does understand life's mystery. In his last line, Papa declares, "Now there, by god, is a metaphor!" (71). In Adrian Sparks' performance of the play in July 2006 at the Eureka Theatre in San Francisco, "a *Life* magazine photographer has set up an appointment for a photo shoot," so the audience takes on a slightly different role. Richard Connema described it as "a ferocious performance as the no-nonsense titan American author": "He strides about the stage as a person who is on the edge of a physical and emotional collapse."[25] Sparks also won strong reviews for a "reprise limited engagement" as a benefit for the Vox Humana Theatre Company in September 2009. In his review of George Peppard's performance at Chicago's Royal-George Theatre, published August 11, 1988, however, Anthony Adler applauds Peppard but complains that de Groot fails utterly in his understanding of Hemingway: "The trouble with *Papa* is that de Groot thinks he knows the answer to Ernest Hemingway. But in fact he hasn't any real grasp of the question. He supposes that a pattern of compulsion"—whereby Hemingway is depicted as "a repressed homosexual with oedipal conflicts thanks to Mom's lethal mind games" and so fabricates "a he-man mystique in self-defense"—amounts to "the same thing as a view of the soul."[26] De Groot, Adler concludes, "hasn't even scratched the surface."

It may well be that any effort to appropriate Ernest Hemingway as a solo stage act is doomed to failure. In his review of the 1987 Miami production of de Groot's *Papa*, Jack Zink observes that "one-character biographical plays are a difficult breed in modern theater. An immense challenge to the performer, they can also test an audience's mettle." He apparently agrees with actor Bill

Hindman's observation that de Groot makes very little use of the "published prose" in his text, but attempts to capture "the whole man, complete with the contradictions. You understand Hemingway not just as a great storyteller, but also as a wonderfully entertaining human being." Not at all, counters Anthony Adler, who found the first act "hard to take," as Papa comes across as "Hemingwayesque," too "comfortably ensconced in his legend, narrating his life with vast bluster and no self-knowledge at all." In the second act, Adler maintains, as Papa's drinking increases, he begins "throwing mean tantrums, confessing to ugly little acts of private cowardice, and exposing the hurt child inside."

But to what extent, if at all, is it fair to evaluate the impact or significance, even in the realm of popular literature and culture, of what amounts to a performance medium? Does the text of a play like John de Groot's *Papa* bear any determinable connection to its performance? Do the reviews constitute reliable, or at least useful, commentaries on either the text of the play or the performance of it? These and other questions arise with respect to James Mitchell Lear, who performed *Hemingway Reminisces* throughout Europe; to Brooklyn-born actor Ed Metzger, noted for his performance of *Albert Einstein: Practical Bohemian* and for "his stirring and dynamic one man show, *Hemingway on the Edge*"[27]; and particularly to Canadian performer and playwright Brian Gordon Sinclair, who has been described as "the foremost dramatic interpreter of Ernest Hemingway in the world today."[28] In all three instances, ample online information in the form of reviews and personal Web sites exists, but apparently no complete texts or DVD versions of their performances are available. Sinclair, however, offers at least a partial exception, inasmuch as his thoroughly developed Web sites include excerpts from each play in his six-part chronological sequence, *Hemingway on Stage*, and a comical minute-and-a-half bit is available on YouTube from part five *The Death Factory*, which concerns Hemingway in the 1940s.[29] The first play in the sequence, *Sunrise: The Early Years*, premiered in Key West during the Hemingway Days festival of 2003. It was sponsored by the Key West Art and Historical Society, with proceeds donated to the Hemingway collection in the Customs House Museum.

Born in Brantford, Ontario, to an Irish mother, Sinclair graduated from the National Theatre School of Canada and earned his master of arts in theatre from the University of Denver. He has performed plays from the sequence all over Europe and frequently in Key West and Cuba. He is a dual citizen of Canada and Ireland. Unlike John de Groot in *Papa*, Brian Sinclair draws heavily on the fiction in composing his plays, as the excerpts published on his Web site demonstrate. In the first part of the sequence, for example, *Sunrise: The Early Years*, the excerpts transform the Nick Adams of stories like "Indian

Camp" and "Big Two-Hearted River" to Ernest's first-person reminiscences. In the former case, Sinclair summarizes the story and only slightly alters a line of dialogue near the ending after Nick asks whether it's hard to die: "No, son, I think it's pretty easy. It all depends." In the story, Hemingway wrote, "No, I think it's pretty easy, Nick. It all depends" (*Complete Short Stories*, 70). The major excerpt from the second play of the sequence, *The Lost Generation*, features a guilt-plagued Hemingway kneeling in a cathedral as he struggles with his love for Pauline, who will insist that he convert to Roman Catholicism when they marry. The two excerpts from the third play, *Death in the Afternoon*, look back to the bullfights and Pamplona and then to his easygoing life in Key West. The fourth play, *The Man-Eaters*, draws on *The Spanish Earth* and the Spanish Civil War, and the pair of excerpts representing the fifth play, *The Death Factory*, look back to World War II, Hemingway's turbulent marriage to Martha Gellhorn, and a war story drawn from "Black Ass at the Cross Roads," one of Hemingway's less familiar stories. The last play in the sequence, *In Deadly Ernest*, which debuted in Havana in June of 2011, is represented by an excerpt concerning Mary Welsh Hemingway's near death connected with a tubal (ectopic) pregnancy in the summer of 1946 in Casper, Wyoming. In her memoir, *How It Was*, Mary directly asserts, "He [Ernest] alone had saved my life" (190).

Sinclair also includes an excerpt from a separate play featuring Hemingway that lies outside the sequence, *Hemingway's HOT Havana*, which reflects on Ernest's friendship with the wealthy, beautiful, and flirtatious Jane Mason. His conclusion to the excerpt reveals something of Sinclair's talents as a writer of dramatic comedy: "Oh, there is one more thing to clear up. Some people say that I had sex with Jane Mason. Other people say that I did not have sex with Jane Mason. Are you familiar with the expression, 'kiss and tell'? Well, then here's the truth. Yes. Yes I kissed Jane Mason. And I will not tell you what happened that time she climbed in the balcony of my room at the Hotel Ambos Mundos and found me lying there with a great big.... Never you mind what she found!" He then takes a drink. In a lengthy interview published online in the Hemingway Project on May 2, 2010, by Allie Baker, Sinclair speaks to the value of introducing humor into his scripts, and he declares, "I truly wanted to find a noble Hemingway. Anyone, in examining a life so vast, can find anything that satisfies a particular end or interpretation. My end was nobility and I found it. My Hemingway is a hero!"

One might propose that the next step from a one-man play would be a two-person play, as is the case with Ken Vose and Jordan Rhodes' *Papa: The Man, the Myth, the Legend* (2002), in which Hemingway, as Lynn Trenning, a reviewer for the *Charlotte Observer* wrote, appears "in turn daunting, gleeful, frustrated and arrogant."[30] The play features Rhodes as Papa in five scenes throughout his life, beginning and ending on the day of his suicide in Ketchum, Idaho: Italy and Toronto, 1917–1920; Paris-Spain-Toronto, 1921–1930; Key West and Cuba, 1930–1935; Spanish Civil War–Hollywood and World War II, 1936–1944; and Africa-Spain-Paris-Idaho, 1945–1961. An intermission separates the first three scenes from the latter two. Lynn Moore "appears in brief but illuminating cameos," Trenning notes, first as nurse Agnes von Kurowasky, and then as each of Hemingway's four wives. Although a DVD made of the performance appears to be no longer available, it won the New York International Independent Film Festival Award as Best Historical Drama in the summer of 2010. As of fall 2013 the writers were pursuing publication of the script.

Hemingway appears in only a single scene of the four that comprise Tennessee Williams' late two-act play, *Clothes for a Summer Hotel* (1980), which drew not only on the writings of F. Scott Fitzgerald and on Zelda's novel, *Save Me the Waltz* (1932), but also on Hemingway's posthumously published memoir of 1920s Paris, *A Moveable Feast* (1964). Scott, in 1940, the last year of his life, presumably hoping for some sort of reconciliation, is visiting the asylum in North Carolina where Zelda has been institutionalized. But these "ghosts" are themselves beset by ghosts like Gerald and Sara Murphy and the French aviator Edouard, with whom Scott was convinced Zelda had had an affair. Ernest and Hadley arrive in the middle of 2.1, and nearly the first words out of his mouth are, "Zelda's a crazy, Scott's a rummy, so speculation is useless and interest is wasted."[31] As in the essays from *A Moveable Feast*, Ernest has no sympathy for the "lunatic" Zelda. He is soon drunk. The British actress known as "Mrs. Patrick Campbell," who died in 1940, appears briefly and sets up what may be Hemingway's best line, albeit a tad vicious: "Old bitches never die, just smell bouillabaisse" (267). But the most telling moments between Scott and Ernest occur in an exchange on how they create characters, male and female:

> Scott: You are fortunate in having such an inexhaustibly interesting and complex nature, Hem, that regardless of how often you portray yourself in a book—Hemingway: Don't be a bitch. [...] Fuck it!—You know as well as I know that every goddam character an honest writer creates is part of himself. Don't you? [269].

To that challenge, Scott submits that all writers "have multiple selves as well as what you call dual genders," and then he begs Ernest to "admit" that they are.... But here he breaks off and says simply "friends."

Williams' stage directions are laced with homosexual innuendo: "[He approaches Scott. For a moment we see their true depth of pure feeling for each other. Hemingway is frightened of it, however.]" (268). When Scott looks back to a scene from the essay entitled "F. Scott Fitzgerald," the longest piece by far in *A Moveable Feast*, Hem admits that he found his friend "touchingly vulnerable" and that he was "disturbed" by some of his physical features (149): "the skin of a girl, the mouth of a girl, the soft eyes of a girl" (270). In that context, Scott recalls the story "A Simple Enquiry," which of course is not such a simple inquiry at all. Hem counters with his story "The Sea Change," which also refers to homosexuality, and he insists that as a writer it is his "profession" to "observe and interpret all kinds of human relations" (271). In this passage near the end of 2.1, easily the longest speech by any character in the play to that point, Hem clearly seeks to distance himself from any suggestion that he might harbor latent homosexual inclinations. Later, he tells Scott, he will write about him and reveal "embarrassing aspects" of his characters because "I can betray even my oldest close friend" (271). Then, stressing the anachronistic nature of the "ghost play," Hem reflects on having "executed" himself not long after having written that story by "blasting" his "exhausted brains out with an elephant gun." By some extension, the reader of the text, if not the viewer of the play, might speculate that with his suicide Hemingway also slays any notion of repressed or closeted homosexuality.

Tennessee Williams had high regard for Hemingway's writing and considered him, in fact, "unquestionably the greatest" American author and "without any question" the writer who was the "greatest" influence on his own work.[32] As to the issue of homosexuality, Williams reflected, "Hemingway had a remarkable interest in and understanding of homosexuality, for a man who wasn't a homosexual. I think both Hemingway and Fitzgerald had elements of homosexuality in them. I make quite a bit of that in my rewrite of *Clothes for a Summer Hotel*" (Devlin, *Conversations*, 347). In his commentary on the play, William Prosser observes, "Williams suggests that both Hemingway and Fitzgerald had a homosexual component in their natures, which, while totally repressed, caused both men to be remote and unfeeling, as well as tortured."[33] In his review of the play's Broadway debut, John Simon called it "not embarrassing. Neither, however, is it good." He speculated that Williams had in fact "long since written himself out."[34] A dozen years after Williams' death in 1983, Wilborn Hampton described it as his "last, futile attempt to kindle one more dramatic blaze on Broadway" and its failure "devastated Williams" (Crandell, *Critical Response*, 275). Interest in the play, however, has been sustained by Tennessee Williams scholars, so, unlike many dramatic appropriations, this text will likely remain generally accessible to readers.

Frederic Hunter's *The Hemingway Play* (1975) might be said to vie for the title of most inventive stage appropriation with the recent (summer of 2013) farce playing off-off-Broadway, James Rutherford and Elliot B. Quick's *The Importance of Being Ernest Hemingway*. The director (Rutherford), who received his MFA in directing from Columbia University, describes it as "a rollicking macho-queer tragedy of disappointed love" involving Oscar Wilde and Ernest Hemingway.[35] The play has drawn generally positive reviews. John Hutt describes the play as a "mashup" of Oscar Wilde's and Ernest Hemingway's writing in which all of the dialogue has been drawn from their work and "nothing new was added."[36] The script was created by Elliott B. Quick and James Rutherford, and in his interview with the playwrights, Hutt notes that spoken "in a gruff, manly voice, Wilde's witticisms seem more like Hemingway's disconnected musings on war; and Hemingway's short sharp sentences delivered effeminately and whimsically flow perfectly with the witty banter." Rutherford indicates the intentional juxtaposition "started to become very interesting" when the two voices were run together and it began to become unclear which was which: "it doesn't exactly reconcile, we're putting these things next to each other because it becomes complicated." The play follows the structure and characterization of Wilde's *The Importance of Being Earnest*, first performed in 1895, and some familiarity with that comedy would seem all but essential. Rutherford and Quick's play is set in Paris in 1926 and includes passages from *The Sun Also Rises* and *A Moveable Feast* along with other Hemingway texts. The play concerns "artistic heroism and the human cost of Art," Rutherford comments, observing that "the macho Hemingway male and the Wildean dandy are both kinds of male drag, and our play explores the dangers [of] a life built on posturing and deception." Regardless of whether one supposes Hemingway to have harbored latent homosexual urges, it should be fairly obvious that in the manifest sense of things, he would not have been even slightly amused. As one blogger put it, "The Importance of Being Ernest Hemingway Would Have Hemingway Digging Out of His Grave."[37]

At least one theatrical production might be said to parallel the published fiction that features what I have called "Hemingway-obsessed" characters (see Chapter Seven), and that is Michael Hollinger's *An Empty Plate at the Café du Grand Boeuf*, which premiered in Philadelphia on November 10, 1994, and in New York City a little over five years later. A 1984 graduate of Oberlin Conservatory (performance—viola) with a master of arts in theater from Villanova in 1989, Hollinger has since that time written seven more full-length plays, including *Opus* (2006), which involves the psychodynamics of a string quartet, and more recently *Ghost Writer* (2010), a one-act play set in 1919 involving three characters. It won the 2011 Barrymore Award for Outstanding New Play. Hollinger teaches in the theater department of Villanova University. "Plays are music to me," he has said. "Characters are instruments, scenes are movements; tempo, rhythm and dynamics are critical; and melody and counterpoint are always set in relief by rests—beats, pauses, the spaces in between."[38] The simple but important stage direction "Beat" occurs frequently throughout *An Empty Plate*, which reviewer John Moore has described as "a whimsically sad little play" about a "great connoisseur of life, love, food and all things Ernest Hemingway" who owns supposedly the finest restaurant in Paris and as its lone patron has decided to die of starvation.[39]

The play is set three days following Hemingway's suicide in Ketchum on July 2, 1961, but unlike Ernest, the protagonist of the play, a wealthy American expatriate and Hemingway aficionado named Victor, intends to commit suicide gradually, perhaps over some months, as he starves himself. The main character's name may or may not be intended ironically, and the same may be said of the play's title, as the restaurant's name as Victor translates it comes off as "The Big Ox Café,"[40] perhaps a squint reference to Wyndham Lewis's notorious essay, "The Dumb Ox: A Study of Ernest Hemingway," published in the June 1934 issue of *American Review*. Victor is determined to kill himself because the love of his life, Louise Berger, has rejected his marriage proposal, presumably because, like Jake Barnes of *The Sun Also Rises*, Victor has been left impotent, though in his case from having contracted mumps as a child. Hemingway enthusiasts will immediately recognize most of the obvious passages drawn from that novel and from such stories as "A Clean, Well-Lighted Place" and "A Very Short Story." The chef and waiters insist on preparing a sumptuous seven-course gourmet dinner for Victor, but he refuses to eat a bite. About three-quarters of the way through the play Victor tells of Hemingway's suicide: "He wasn't cleaning his shotgun; he was cleansing his palate" (49).

Shortly after that, Victor and one of the waiters stage a mock bullfight reminiscent of that which occurs in "The Capital of the World" but without the tragic results. (In *The Hemingway Play* Frederic Hunter also stages a mock bullfight, with Hem as the bull and Dana, one of the young women, taking the part of the matador.) After the "bullfight" in *Empty Plate*, Victor tells of his marriage proposal to Louise while at the bullfights in Madrid. Then the chef offers the dessert, Victor's favorite, an exquisite crème brûlée. As he breaks down and eats it, Louise enters, most likely prompting the audience to anticipate a reconciliation of some sort. Instead, she reveals that she is terminally ill, presumably from some sort of brain cancer, and she turns the tables on the pathetic Victor by accurately quoting a passage from the end of *For Whom the Bell Tolls:* "The world is a fine place and worth the fighting for and I hate very much to leave it" (Hemingway, 467; Hollinger, 58). "For all his faults," Louise submits, "the man did have a way with words." The two dance briefly and kiss, and with that, Louise agrees they are "married," pretty much as Marie and Robert Jordan marry in Hemingway's epic novel. After she leaves, Victor is surprised to see that his appetite has returned, but at that point Hollinger engineers a dark surprise ending: the chef, hoping to ease Victor into his death, has poisoned the crème brûlée. At this news Victor absurdly and comically replies, "I thought it seemed runnier than usual" (60). As John Moore, reviewing a performance in Denver, wrote, "It's all very funny, despite the underlying sadness."

The play concerns longing and loss, and Victor's Hemingway fixation is generally threaded through ably enough. In a largely negative review of the play's 2007 revival at the Arden Theatre in Philadelphia, where all of Hollinger's plays have premiered, Tim Dunleavy commends his "rich, evocative use of language" but complains that the play comes off as "cute" and "a little too trivial for its own good." He finds the ending "funny, but frustratingly implausible," and overall, he sees the play as "clever, but little more."[41] In effect, a script has simultaneous advantages and disadvantages over literary text, and while these may be obvious enough, a quick summary of some additional reviews of the performances may be pertinent. Robert Hofler, writing for *Variety* on March 8, 2000, suggested that everyone "acts much giddier and nuttier than Hollinger's dialogue ever suggests they should."[42] Does such a comment suggest a quirky production, or some uncertainty as to Hollinger's intent with what appears to be an absurdist comedy? Jenn Goddu, for chicagoreader.com on October 4, 2001, wrote, "Michael Hollinger's intelligent comedy benefits from its soupcon of tragedy." She adds, "Witty philosophy and genuine heartache temper this light, funny 90-minute work."[43] Presumably, she was bearing witness to quite a different production than that which caused Charles McNulty of the *Los Angeles Times* to write on June 2, 2009, that he could not bring himself to emit "a single chuckle throughout the 90 minutes of Michael Hollinger's innocuous yet inert comedy." McNulty blamed "playwriting faults" and the "farfetched premise," and, of significance, he proposed that the play amounts to a confused jumble of "old-fashioned French farce," "absurdist homage to [Samuel] Beckett," and a "literary vignette" concerning Hemingway, among other things.[44] This survey of theater reviews accounts for only the tip of the iceberg, and perhaps one should end it with a positive note: Jimmy Ferraro's rave notice: "This is a FIVE STAR production! And the cast is superb!"[45]

Live theater productions involving Hemingway, whether one-man performances like that of Brian Sinclair or those involving a cast of actors like Frederic Hunter's *The Hemingway Play* or Michael Hollinger's *An Empty Plate at the Café du Grand Boeuf*, sustain the man, the myth, and in some cases (and in quite various ways) the writing as well. In the interview with Allie Baker cited above, Sinclair laments that "a recent U.S. poll of secondary school students found that less than 14 percent could even identify the famous author." In a personal communication Sinclair listed more than a dozen invitations he is considering, from Key West to Cuba, from Canada to Bulgaria. He indicated "the Cuban Ministry of Education is currently making plans to publish all [his] plays in bilingual editions for use in all Cuban schools." Just how or where the next generations encounter the writing of Ernest Hemingway surely does matter, but perhaps most important is that they do encounter that writing. On August 30, 2013, Garry Trudeau's popular *Doonesbury* comic strip portrayed a character who was struggling with writer's block. In the process, the writer analogizes his dilemma to that of a baseball player who "used to be able to knock'em out of the park." His friend promptly commends his "slick baseball analogy" he "tossed off," and points out in the last panel, "like a freakin' Hemingwad!" Will such a moment draw readers into the world of Nick Adams or Robert Jordan? Probably not, but thanks to the widely varied media of popular culture, no other American writer remains so incessantly present and available. Sooner or later, one suspects, the casual reader or theatergoer or moviegoer will investigate the writing and discover the "secret," as Hemingway wrote "of his own writing": "The secret is that it is poetry written into prose and it is the hardest of all things to do" (Mary Hemingway, *How It Was*, 305).

Of course no consideration of how Ernest Hemingway and his writing have been appropriated would be complete without at least some reference to the video world, the world of film and television that embraced his novels and stories from the outset, starting with *A Farewell to Arms*, with Gary Cooper and Helen Hayes in 1932, and that has continued to do so. In a 2007 blog for slate.com David Haglund refers slightingly to most of the films from the Fifties as "a peculiar subgenre one might call Hollywood Hemingway."[46] Several books speak to the subject of Hemingway and the movies, including Gene D. Phillips' *Hemingway and Film* (1980) and Frank M. Laurence's *Hemingway and the Movies* (1981). Hemingway, Leonard J. Leff asserts in *Hemingway and His Conspirators* (1997), "saw authorship as a blood sport" (9), and he intended to establish for himself a broad readership. Leff is among the few commentators to suggest that Ernest saw his contract-breaking parody of Sherwood Anderson, *The Torrents of Spring*, to be "marketable.... [H]e obviously hoped to reach beyond the literary clique to the general reader" (26). Although Hemingway disdained nearly every Hollywood version of his fiction that the likes of Darryl F. Zanuck and David O. Selznick could produce, they contributed significantly to his economic well-being (despite his frequent complaints of penury), and they added incalculably to his popularity, attracting readers who would not otherwise have been likely to embark on one of his print stories or novels.

Hemingway has been the subject of many documentaries, some of which are exceptional. For example, there are the A&E Biography Series production, *Ernest Hemingway: Wrestling with Life* (100 minutes), produced in 1998 (Home DVD, 2005), and the PBS film from the American Masters series, *Ernest Hemingway: Rivers to the Sea* (90 minutes), which appeared in 2005. In October 2013 a full-length documentary, *Cooper and Hemingway: The True Gen*, written and directed by John Mulholland and featuring 45 interviews with the likes of Kirk Douglas and Charlton Heston, premiered at the Quad Cinema in New York to considerable fanfare. Sam Waterston narrates the film, with Len Cariou speaking for Ernest. It was a *New York Times* Critic's Pick for the week of October 14.[47] But what concerns us here are what might be described as "biopics," movie or television versions of what amounts to biographical fiction, several of which have gained some prominence in recent years: *Hemingway* (1988 TV miniseries), *The Moderns* (1988), *In Love and War* (1996), *Midnight in Paris* (2011), and *Hemingway and Gellhorn* (2012). Two of these films, *Hemingway* and *Hemingway and Gellhorn*, could be said almost to qualify as documentaries. One might even make a case for *In Love and War*, which is based on Henry S. Villard's memoir cowritten with James Nagel and including "The Lost Diary of Agnes von Kurowsky" and her letters, *Hemingway in Love and War* (1989). In *The Moderns* and *Midnight in Paris* Hemingway makes brief but memorable appearances. What qualifies these films for at least passing comment here, as I see it, is that in each of them Hemingway is presented as a character, and that character is interpreted by a congeries of scriptwriters, directors, and, most important, actors. In what follows, I do not intend to pose as a film scholar or critic, but simply to reflect briefly on each of the five films indicated.

An extensive commentary on the filming of *In Love and War*, produced and directed by Richard Attenborough and shot on location in Vittorio Veneto, Venice, and Montreal, is presently available online (http://www.film-scouts.com/scripts/matinee.cfm?Film=lov-war&File=productn). In his review published in the *New York Times*, Gioia Diliberto remarks that the "$40 million soap opera" takes considerable liberties with what is known about the romance between Lieutenant Ernie Hemingway (age 19) of Oak Park and Nurse Agnes von Kurowsky of Philadelphia, "but it does prove that the Hemingway myth is alive and well."[48] Attenborough had won a pair of Academy Awards for *Gandhi* in 1983 and had presided over a more recent success with *Shadowlands* (1993), concerning the amour of Oxford don C.S. Lewis and American poet Joy Davidman (Debra Winger won an Academy Award in that role). But while *In Love and War* fared well enough at the box office, it was not (and has not been) a critical success. The relative failure can hardly be blamed on the casting, which featured Sandra Bullock as Agnes and Chris O'Donnell as Ernie, or on the hype, which was considerable. Bullock is about six years older than O'Donnell, who was 25 at the time of the filming, so the age disparity nearly simulates that of the historical Agnes and Ernest. Agnes was about seven and a half years older than Ernest, and as her letters and diary entries indicate, she was concerned about the difference. Unfortunately, or possibly otherwise, Ernest's many letters to Agnes have been lost, but he mentions her directly or indirectly fairly often in letters home, beginning with the declaration on August 29, 1918, to his mother he is "in love again" (*Letters,* 136). He had been wounded on July 8. In subsequent letters he refers to her as "Ag," "my girl," and "the Missus."

Most Hemingway biographers are convinced that the love was never consummated, and Agnes insisted that was the case. But in the movie, predictably, at a dilapidated hotel/brothel near the front, Agnes and Ernie make passionate love. In her devastating letter to him dated March 7, 1919, (he received it on the 30th), Agnes explains that she remains "still very fond of you, but, it is more as a mother than as a sweetheart."[49] Considering the lifelong tension that existed between Grace Hemingway and her son, no analogy could have hurt him worse. She concludes her letter with the "sudden" declaration that she expects "to be married soon." That marriage, to an aristocratic doctor named Caracciolo, Ernest's rival for her affections in the film, did not come to pass. On the day he received the letter, Ernest wrote his boyhood friend William D. Horne Jr. that he was "smashed by it" and he claims she had been his "ideal," that he "forgot all about religion and everything else" because he had "Ag to worship." "Now," he declares, "the bottom has dropped out of the whole world" (*Letters,* 177). But, after all, Ernest Hemingway was still several months short of his twentieth birthday, and youth is nothing if not resilient. Not even three weeks later, he was able to write another pal, James Gamble, "now it's over I'm glad" (*Letters,* 181). He would eventually "cauterize" the wound Agnes inflicted, as he informed another buddy on June 15 (*Letters,* 193); and on July 2 he informed Bill Horne that her name "doesn't recall any image to mind at all" (*Letters,* 195).

Indeed, if it were not for his composition of "A Very Short Story" about four years later, in which the unnamed male, who closely resembles Hemingway's surrogate Nick Adams, receives a similar Dear John letter after a similar romance at a hospital in Padua, one might be more inclined to credit his boast that Ernest had successfully put her out of his mind. Apparently he wrote to Agnes sometime after his marriage to Hadley on September 3, 1921. Perhaps her response to that letter on December 22, 1922, prompted him to write the story, which ends with the man contracting gonorrhea "from a sales girl in a loop department store while riding in a taxicab through Lincoln Park" (*Complete Short Stories*, 108). One might regard this bitter story as a form of penance or self-punishment, cauterizing with a vengeance. Agnes's 1922 letter mentions "the very biting letter you wrote" to a fellow nurse about her (Villard and Nagel, 164). The movie ends quite un-historically with Agnes visiting Ernest at his retreat in upstate Michigan, and in this Hollywood version, Ernest rejects Agnes. One might, or might not, argue that Hemingway's infatuation or obsession with Agnes was resolved only with the novel *A Farewell to Arms* (1929), in which Agnes von Kurowsky is idealized—and fictionalized—as the nurse, Catherine Barkley, and dies what might be taken as a martyr's death in childbirth.

In the FilmScouts.com interview much is made of Chris O'Donnell's "aggressively" pursuing the part of young Ernest and of Sandra Bullock welcoming the opportunity to be featured in a serious role after her success in various comedies. She describes Ernest as "a completely innocent, beautiful, egocentric, cocky, fun-loving, witty, sharp young man" who is idealistic and "eager for adventure." Certainly his letters home from that period tend to confirm her sense of the man. As for Agnes, Bullock plays her as she describes her: "somewhat repressed. She never dealt with passion because she was there to heal and help, and not to delve into her own emotions. Then suddenly she was confused with somebody who came across at first as a beautiful, sweet younger man. He just opened up everything that was raw about her." But the interviewer concludes that finally, Agnes was "too conventional to marry him," if only because of the age difference. In her Dear John letter of March 7, 1919, Agnes writes, "I somehow feel that some day I'll have reason to be proud of you, but, dear boy, I can't wait for that day, & it is wrong to hurry a career" (Villard and Nagel, 163). In her letter of December 22, 1922, with publication of *Three Stories and Ten Poems* just months away and *In Our Time* about two years ahead, she writes, "How proud I will be some day in the not-very-distant-future to say 'Oh yes, Ernest Hemingway. Used to know him quite well during the war'" (167).

Although Michael Wilmington, reviewing *In Love and War* for the *Chicago Tribune*, found the movie a failure in various ways (albeit "an interesting one"), he conceded it had been directed "with some warmth and sensitivity" and was "very well acted." He refers to Sandra Bullock and Chris O'Donnell as "incredibly empathetic and photogenic."[50] The same, unfortunately cannot be said for the epic, five-part, six-hour biopic concocted for television and released in May 1988. In her March 29, 2002, review of the DVD release of *Hemingway* for DVDTalk.com, Holly E. Ordway wrote "what is surprising is that a series about such an adventurous life could manage to be so absolutely dull."[51] A great admirer of Hemingway's writing who "carried a footlocker of books by him and about him" as he traveled from Kenya to Paris to Key West to Idaho in making the movie, Stacy Keach does "look something like the writer," as *Christian Science Monitor* reviewer Alan Bunce observed.[52] That is, Keach looks something like Hemingway when he was in his forties or fifties, and he was successfully made up to look like him in his last years, but even the best Hollywood makeup artists could not make Keach at age 47 look anything like Hemingway at 23 (or like Chris O'Donnell at 25, for that matter). Consequently, the first couple of hours of the movie demand from the viewers a suspension of disbelief they may well not be willing to grant.

Hemingway's room-brightening smile and boyish charm simply do not come across, and the charisma of which Keach speaks in his interview with Bunce also falters, even though Keach struggles to express "the sensitivity of the man" and even though his physical likeness comes through more convincingly as Hemingway ages. Ordway faults not only the acting but also the screenplay, which too often becomes "tedious." In the early scenes in Paris, at Gertrude Stein's salon and at various bistros, the dialogue should crackle with wit and energy, and the background should be a jazzy din. It is not. Hemingway famously described the 1957 production of *The Sun Also Rises* as a "splashy Cook's tour of Europe's Lost Generation bistros, bullfights, and more bistros" (Laurence, 116), but at least Zanuck's version of Twenties Paris offers music, noise, and vitality. Occasionally somewhat subtle efforts are made to weave Hemingway's fiction into the film, as when Hadley (played by Geraldine Chaplin) watches from her hotel window a cat sheltering from the rain. Later, at Schruns, Ernest reads her a passage from "Cat in the Rain." The sets, exotic (and costly) locations, and costuming achieve the desired effects, but they cannot carry the burden. Ordway asserts that what "kills" the film is "the combination of terrible acting and a dreadful script," and she concludes "the film or television treatment that will bring his [Hemingway's] character alive and engage us with his life has yet to be made."

Of course the challenges undertaken in a film like *In Love and War*, which focuses narrowly on just a couple of years of Hemingway's life, cannot justly be compared with those that the director, Bernhard Sinkel, faced with *Hemingway*, which, after a prologue featuring Ernest and Mary in Ketchum as he struggles with his writing (one of Keach's better moments), we move quickly to the marriage with Hadley in 1922, and from there across four decades, four wives, many locales, and a complex character undergoing a daunting range of traumas and transformations. One might argue that it simply could not be done and perhaps should not even have been attempted. And indeed, none of the other films that attempt to capture or appropriate Hemingway has tried to go where wise men fear to tread.

Like Chris O'Donnell in Attenborough's *In Love and War*, Kevin J. O'Connor was just 25 when he appeared as Hemingway in *The Moderns*, which made a small splash when it appeared in 1988, the same year as Keach's *Hemingway*. The director and cowriter of the screenplay, Alan Rudolph, was not undertaking a biopic of even a portion of Hemingway's life but a period piece on the Lost Generation of 1920s Paris in which just a handful of historical characters, including Gertrude Stein, make an appearance. The film concerns an American expatriate artist named Nick Hart (perhaps intentionally reminiscent of Nick Adams) who is attracted to an art patroness coincidentally, à la *Hemingway*, played by Geraldine Chaplin. Keith Carradine plays the part of Nick Hart, and the cast is also graced with the presence of Genevieve Bujold as a gallery owner. Unlike such films as *In Love and War* and *Hemingway*, this one was shot on a proverbial "shoestring budget," with Montreal standing in for Paris, which seems appropriate to a plot that involves art forgery and other forms of deception. The film is also "about" modernism in art and literature, with all of its self-infatuation and self-promotion.

Thanks to the Internet, one might mine movie reviews almost ad infinitum, but in this case three will suffice. Roger Ebert described it as "not a great movie" and conceded it was "fairly sloppy and unsatisfying," but rather incongruously he concluded that he "never found a moment of it uninteresting."[53] Vincent Canby, writing for the *New York Times*, panned it as a movie of "muddled aspirations" and for its "lame sendup of 'art.'" He complained, "Just what the film is really about is anybody's guess." He also found the acting below par.[54] Writing for the *Washington Post*, Rita Kempley described it as "a languid, liars' film, rich with red lipstick and faux Cézanne."[55] At its best, she writes, *The Moderns* provides "an ingenuous mix of sight, sound and snappy repartee"; at its worst, "it's an inconclusive display of cryptic virtuosity." It is "snappy repartee," in fact, that we find all too little of in Bernhard Sinkel's

Hemingway. Kempley describes Hemingway as portrayed in *The Moderns* as "a sort of brilliant clod irreverently played by Kevin O'Connor, who turned what was originally a three-line part into an integral role." Those familiar with the recent Woody Allen hit, *Midnight in Paris* (2011), which won both a Golden Globe and an Academy Award in 2012 for best screenplay, may detect similarities in the way Hemingway is played in these films.

Midnight in Paris, both a critical and a box office success, features Corey Stoll as Ernest. Writing for laweekly.com, Mark Olsen commented on the similar roles Alan Rudolph's and Woody Allen's Hemingways are compelled to play. [56] Both of them tend to converse in phrases and sentences that reflect Hemingway's early prose style, which an anonymous reviewer for the *New York Times Book Review*, writing back in the fall of 1925, described perhaps as well as anyone has: "Ernest Hemingway has a lean, pleasing, tough resilience. His language is fibrous and athletic, colloquial and fresh, hard and clean; his very prose seems to have an organic being of its own" (Stephens, *Critical Reception*, 7). Except, as both Rudolph and Allen recognized, when a person actually talks in that manner, the results are quite comical. Olsen draws attention to a pair of humorous moments from the two movies. In *The Moderns*, Ernest (Kevin O'Connor) "moodily declares Paris 'a portable banquet,'" which prompts a journalist to advise, "You should work on that." In *Midnight in Paris* Ernest describes the flapper Adriana, whose name Allen probably borrowed from Adriana Ivancich, object of Hemingway's late-in-life infatuation, as "a movable feast." Hemingway aficionados are probably aware of his fascination with that metaphor, based on feast days of the church, like Easter. Not only is Paris "a moveable feast" in his famous memoir, but also "happiness" in *Across the River and into the Trees* (68) and "love" in *True at First Light* (262). Woody Allen's Hemingway goes him one better with Adriana.

The most recent appropriation is the 2012 made-for-television movie, *Hemingway and Gellhorn*, which, similar to *In Love and War*, focuses on his courtship of Martha Gellhorn, which began when Ernest was still married to Pauline. The film spans the Spanish Civil War and World War II and covers Hemingway and Gellhorn's rocky marriage, which culminated in a bitter divorce. Most biographers consider it the unhappiest of Hem's four marriages. The HBO movie, starring Nicole Kidman as Martha and Clive Owen as Ernest, has received mixed reviews at best. Both actors were nominated for a number of television movie or miniseries awards, as was the movie, but it won only for outstanding music composition and outstanding sound editing (an Emmy in both cases). Reviewing the movie for the *New York Times*, Mike Hale slammed it as "a disheartening misfire: a big, bland historical melodrama built on platitudes about honor and the writing life."⁵⁷ Mostly he faults the screenplay "that has nothing new to tell us about Hemingway or Gellhorn or the times they lived in." But "worst of all," Hale asserts, "is the fake poetic dialogue, which ranges from Hemingwayesque to actual Hemingway." Because such lines as "a man can be destroyed but not defeated" are taken out of context and imposed on the script that intends high seriousness, they ring false. Woody Allen's Hemingway, on the other hand, is mostly played for laughs. So when Corey Stoll pontificates to the effect that "no subject is terrible if the story is true and if the prose is clean," and "that's what war does to men and there's nothing fine and noble about dying in the mud unless you die gracefully," and so on, the sentiments and expression run so contrary to the context that the Hemingwayisms come across as funny. On the other hand, Hale objects to Clive Owen's Hemingway (or perhaps, more accurately, director Philip Kaufman's) as too "loud" and "slightly buffoonish."

By the end of the movie, Nicole Kidman's Gellhorn has pretty much taken over the show as "the real action hero of the piece," but Hale complains Kidman is not well fitted to that sort of role, namely that of "the profanity-spewing, danger-courting protagonist" that she becomes. Hemingway aficionados will likely object that Martha Gellhorn's prominence in the latter portions of the film comes too obviously at Ernest's expense. James Wolcott began his commentary for *Vanity Fair* as follows: "None of the reviews quite prepared me for the unchained malady of Hemingway & Gellhorn.... [I]t's as if Kaufman answered the call of the wild and it turned out to be a loon."⁵⁸ Remarkably, Wolcott's evaluation of the movie goes down from there, and he saves most of his vitriol for Clive Owen's portrayal of Ernest, whom he likens early on to "a strapping Groucho Marx": "He writes like he fucks and he fucks like he drinks and he drinks like he fights and he fights like he fucks, and all this ferocity do get wearisome." At the end, Wolcott does concede that the viewer "won't be bored."

About an hour of the movie occurs in Spain, where we watch an incongruous but credible enough medley of torrid romance, combat (Ernest actually participates in a Loyalist attack), and political intrigue. Various episodes recall John Dos Passos' painful attempt to solve the disappearance of his Spanish translator José Robles, the filming of the propaganda movie *The Spanish Earth*, and moments that Hemingway would splice into the play *The Fifth Column*. As Robert Lloyd writes in his more temperate review, as the movie unfolds it becomes clear that Ernest is "the conventional one who needs a base and a gang," while Martha is "the footloose free spirit who wants to be where the action is."⁵⁹ When she becomes involved as a war correspondent in China,

Finland, and Europe, Hemingway "grows clownish, petty and belligerent." The movie ends with Martha being interviewed after Ernest's suicide. She boldly declares her autonomy, grabs her backpack, and heads out on her next assignment. Ernest Hemingway is pretty much left in the dust. Some comparison with the conclusion to *In Love and War* suggests itself here. In a major distortion of the actual events, Richard Attenborough's Agnes von Kurowsky, her romance with the Italian doctor having come to naught, follows Ernest to his retreat in upstate Michigan, where he rejects her, presumably out of hurt pride. Like Philip Kaufman's Martha, Agnes is given the final words: "Some say he lived with the pain of it all his life. The hurt boy became the angry man, a brilliant, tough adventurer who was the most famous writer of his generation." The "eager, idealistic, and tender" kid he had been, Agnes laments, would live on "only in my heart."

And what of Ernest Miller Hemingway in all of his complexity? Surely there is more than a little irony in the fact that he lives on largely as appropriated, interpreted, re-presented, misconstrued, and occasionally distorted by the very medium he so often and so vociferously disparaged. And in that respect, the irony is doubled, given his own long infatuation with movies and actors, dating at least to a letter from Kansas City he wrote to his sister Marcelline ("Ivory") dated February 12, 1918, claiming to be romantically involved with silent movie star Mae Marsh (*Letters*, 81), and including later friendship with such actors as Gary Cooper, Ingrid Bergman, and Marlene Dietrich. Hemingway profited considerably from his involvement with theater and film, and by all accounts stage and Hollywood have profited from their involvement with Hemingway's life and fiction. Perhaps the relationship might be described as symbiotic. What must disturb admirers of Hemingway and his writing, however, is the predominance of what must be called not simply negative, but antagonistic, portrayals. Was the real Ernest Hemingway all that utterly boorish, self-absorbed, arrogant, misogynistic, sexist, violent, angry, belligerent, drunken, clumsy, petulant, clownish, foolhardy, defensive, pathetic (rarely sympathetic)? And if so, does his talent as a writer, even if classified as genius, excuse or at least mitigate the offenses? The obvious answer to the latter might be "to some extent" or "at times," and to the former something in the way of a rebuttal: Hemingway could be all of that, but he could also be affectionate, kind, generous, clever, witty, serious, courageous, idealistic, charismatic, sensitive, perceptive, intelligent.

In setting out to write *By Force of Will: The Life and Art of Ernest Hemingway* (1977), Scott Donaldson offers that he wished to "construct a mosaic of his mind and personality" from many "disparate fragments."[60] Donaldson found Hemingway to be "a complicated man, with a difficult, a quirky, and frequently a contradictory mind" (xiii). Hemingway worked hard at his writing, at his craft, and he believed in writing as hard work. He refers to his writing as "work" often in the pages of *A Moveable Feast*, the memoir he had nearly completed at his death. Even if one were to discount the other writing he had underway at the time, much of which has now been published, an objective judge should be careful about accepting the notion that he could no longer write, or even the premise that he could no longer write well, despite his own avowed declarations to that effect in his last year. Only in his final months, it would seem, was there absolutely nothing, nada, and he could not live with that. In the coda to the final volume of his five-part biography, Michael Reynolds writes:

> Ernest Hemingway was the embodiment of America's promise: the young boy from Oak Park who set out to become the best writer of his time. With pluck and luck, talent and wit, hard work and hard living, he did just that. In the process he told us that pursuit was happiness, that man alone was no fucking good, and that any story followed far enough would end badly. [...] He remodeled American short fiction, changed the way characters speak, confronted the moral strictures confining the writer, and left behind a shelf of books telling us how we were in the first half of this [the twentieth] century. [...] His ambition, intensity, creative drive, sense of duty, belief in hard work, and faith in the strenuous life carried him to the pinnacle of his profession, provided him with wide recognition and considerable wealth, before destroying him when he could no longer meet their demands [*Hemingway: The Final Years*, 360].

As previously noted, Reynolds ends with a sentence suggesting that the biography constitutes a tragedy of the sort "the ancient Greeks would have recognized."

Reflecting on the efforts of a remarkable range of playwrights, writers of screenplays, producers and directors, and actors, perhaps what strikes us most forcibly is that, despite decades of hard work and good intentions, usually by persons professing serious interest in Hemingway's life and legend and great admiration for his writing, so little of what has been stated in the previous two paragraphs has been achieved on stage, screen, or television. The stage and film appropriations of Hemingway often focus on aspects of his life as a writer, more consistently and intently than in most of the stories or novels in which he appears. But such character traits as genius, talent, wit, and creative drive are nearly impossible to stage or film, while the drunken, angry sexist or the bitter, paranoid, old man make for titillating drama. Nothing in these genres has been accomplished so far that would indicate great success. One might posit that the complex and contradictory person that Hemingway was has simply proven too challenging to present on stage or screen. Perhaps the stage has some advantages, setting aside the problem of limited audience, over screen or television. In the meantime, both media have continued to make important contributions to the sustaining of interest in, and curiosity about, both Hemingway and his writing. What should concern Hemingway fans, scholars and aficionados alike, about Reynolds' concluding paragraph, above, is that statement about the "shelf of books telling us how we were" in the twentieth century. Here, in the midst of the postmodern moment, the modernist enthusiasm for the presence of the past, in the mode of T.S. Eliot's "Tradition and the Individual Talent" or William Faulkner's assertion in *Requiem for a Nun* that "the past is never dead. It's not even past," seems to have vanished, to have been obliterated.[61] At issue is whether, or more accurately to what extent, Hemingway's writing is pertinent in the present century.

Nine

Hem Among the Poets[1]

Only the most hard-boiled of Hemingway aficionados have spent much of their time and energy dealing with his poems, even though his first book, what we would now call a chapbook, was *Three Stories and Ten Poems*. Typically, biographers cite the opening sentence of renowned critic Edmund Wilson's review to the effect that "Mr. Hemingway's poems are not particularly important, but his prose is of the first distinction" (Stephens, *Critical Reception*, 1). Six of the poems, the composition of which apparently dated back to 1920, appeared (at the prompting of Ezra Pound) in the January 1923 issue of Harriet Monroe's influential *Poetry* magazine. The revised edition of Hemingway's *Complete Poems* (1992), edited by Nicholas Gerogiannis, opens with a baseball poem written several months before Ernest was thirteen years old and includes the haunting "Poem to Mary (Second Poem)," which begins, "Now sleeps he / With the old whore Death."[2] Written in the fall of 1944, the strange, prosy rant rambles on for more than six pages and is available in an audio version (http://www.youtube.com/watch?v=Af17jSIkQCs). Gerogiannis' volume numbers 89 poems, including the recently discovered "Critical Intelligence," written from Paris around 1927. Gerogiannis' edition is carefully annotated and includes both an introduction and an afterword. He concludes his introduction as follows: "They [the poems] are direct, often quick, ribald, but sometimes moving reflections of the man. They lack the subtlety, psychological complexity, and beauty of the prose. But there is no mistaking their messages" (xxiv).

In their study of his library, James D. Brasch and Joseph Sigman wrote that Hemingway was "throughout his life a reader of poetry," and they found the 229 volumes of poetry in his collection to be "remarkably diverse."[3] Their essay refers specifically to nine modern poets (his contemporaries) whose poems are represented by at least four volumes each: Ezra Pound, of course, T.S. Eliot, Archibald MacLeish, W.H. Auden, William Butler Yeats, William Carlos Williams, Marianne Moore, Edna St. Vincent Millay, and E.E. Cummings. But in an essay published in *Hemingway Review* in 2007, Verna Kale draws attention to Hemingway's "repeated moves to disown his work" in that genre.[4] Kale's particular interest is in showing how the poems helped him to formulate the "stylistic and thematic elements that would come to characterize his prose" (60). She also observes that readers tend to concur that Hemingway's best poetry appears as prose, a point Donald Junkins stressed in a 1985 essay, the title of which might have suggested something else: "Hemingway's Contribution to American Poetry." In that essay and in "Hemingway's Bullfighter Poems," published two years later, Junkins, himself a poet of some note, describes the poems as "passionless, choppy, often sentimental halflines," and sets up passages from the prose, most notably from *Death in the Afternoon*, as if they were lines of verse.[5] In the former essay Junkins reflects on the poetic or lyrical elements (notably repetition) in "The End of Something," concluding that "the story is composed of a series of melodic gestures; it is a tone poem based on repetition of archetypal images and sounds within the implicative structures of unstated but implicit meanings" (21).

Verna Kale offers brief but perceptive commentaries on eight poems: "They All Made Peace—What Is Peace," "Ultimately," "Mitrailliatrice," "Neothomist Poem," "Riparto d'Assalto" (on the elite Italian troops known as the Arditi), "The Age Demanded" (which looks to Ezra Pound's *Hugh Selwyn Mauberley*), "The Earnest Liberal's Lament" (with an obvious pun on his own name), and the two-line "Valentine," which is printed in Mary Hemingway's *How It Was* (428). In that bizarre epigram dated February 14, 1956, and written from the Finca Vigía, Ernest threatens to hang himself from her Christmas tree if she won't be his valentine. In his notes on "Mitrailliatrice" Gerogiannis indicates some confusion over Hemingway's spelling of the title, which appears to indicate the French word for "machine-gun fire" (137). The poem, written in Chicago in 1921 and published in the January 1923 issue of *Poetry*, ends with the one-word line, "Mitrailleuse," or "machine gun." Curiously, it appears in *Three Stories and Ten Poems* with the title in Italian, "Mitraigiatrice" (not French as Gerogiannis suggests), also meaning "machine-gun." For the record, Hemingway was never celebrated for his orthography. In the seven short lines that comprise the poem, Hemingway pleads that his typewriter (his Corona) be metamorphosed into a machine gun wielded by the gods (37).

As many readers have observed, Hemingway would often reflect his musical sense, his tonality, and his remarkable sense of rhythm in his prose. Consider briefly the first two sentences from the story "In Another Country" set up as lines of "poetry":

> In the fall the war was always there,
> But we did not go to it any more.
> It was cold in the fall in Milan
> And the dark came very early
> [*Complete Short Stories*, 206].

Even an elementary glance or listen will reveal the assonance and rhyme that connects "fall" and "always," "war" and "more." The scansion of such lines can be tricky, but most readers would surely agree (at least) that the first line opens with an anapestic foot and follows with three iambic feet, and the third line runs to three "perfect" anapests. Joan Didion has conducted a rather elaborate celebration of what one might call the "poetics" of the opening paragraph of *A Farewell to Arms*, commenting on what she calls its "liturgical cadence."[6] After all, "Anyone who breathes is in the rhythm business," poet William Stafford (1914–1993) memorably wrote, and that applies not only to poets but also to serious writers of prose.[7]

Hemingway was to be connected personally with various poets, starting with Carl Sandburg, whom he met at a party in Chicago early in 1921. In the biography *Along with Youth*, Peter Griffin notes that the 21-year-old journalist read aloud from *The Rubaiyat of Omar Khayyam* on that occasion, and Sandburg "praised Ernest's sensitive interpretation and style."[8] In Paris the next year Ernest would fall into the orbit of the most influential poet of the day, Ezra Pound, "the man who had taught me to distrust adjectives as I would later learn to distrust certain people in certain situations" (*A Moveable Feast*, 134), and through Pound he would discover the poems of T.S. Eliot and others. Archibald McLeish would become a close friend, at least for a while, and in the pages of *A Moveable Feast* Hemingway also writes of his encounters with minor poet Ernest Walsh (1895–1926): "dark, intense, faultlessly Irish, poetic and clearly marked for death as a character is marked for death in a motion picture" (123). In the next couple of essays he writes admiringly of Evan Shipman (1904–1957), "a truly fine poet and who truly did not care if his poems were ever published" (146) and Ralph Cheever Dunning (1878–1930), "a poet who smoked opium and forgot to eat" (143). The target of one of Hemingway's crueler stories, "Mr. and Mrs. Elliot," is not, as some readers might suspect, T.S. Eliot and his neurasthenic wife, Vivienne, but Chard Powers Smith (1894–1977), who "wrote very long poems very rapidly" (*Complete Short Stories*, 123). Hem's peculiar antipathy appears to derive from the fact that Smith (Hubert Elliot in the story) was a prosperous lawyer. In the story Hemingway asserts that Elliot pays to have his book published, and he implies that Elliot's considerably older wife, Cornelia, is involved in a lesbian relationship.

Allusions to Ernest Hemingway appear in predictable places in poetry—in Ezra Pound's *Cantos*, for example, most notably in #XVI, where Hemingway is listed among other writers and artists who went off to battle in the Great War.[9] The canto was written around 1925; Hemingway met Pound in Paris, through Sherwood Anderson's letter of introduction, in February of 1922. About halfway through the canto, Pound turns specifically to the war, lashing out at Franz Josef of Austria and naming several writers and artists who got taken up in combat, including the sculptor Henri Gaudier-Brzeska, killed in action in 1915, and British writer and artist Wyndham Lewis (1882–1957), whom Hemingway would viciously describe in *A Moveable Feast* as having the eyes of "an unsuccessful rapist" (109).

Allusions to Hemingway appear in the poems of his sometime friend Archibald MacLeish, who also wrote several poems for or about Hemingway, and among the works of such poets as Derek Walcott, James Wright, Charles Wright, Kenneth Koch, Robert Penn Warren, and Ai. The indefatigable Ogden Nash even had his day with Hemingway in "Roll On, Thou Deep and Dark Blue Copy Writer—Roll!" (*Versus*, 1949). Byron fans will recognize this title as a parody of a line from the fourth canto of *Childe Harold's Pilgrimage:* "Roll on, thou deep and dark blue Ocean—roll!" (stanza 179). Nash draws an epigraph for his 28-line poem from an advertisement for the movie *The Macomber Affair*, in which "GREGORY PECK makes that HEMINGWAY kind of love to JOAN BENNETT." In the most comically quotable quatrain, Nash manages to hyphenate and thereby to rhyme up "Heming-" with "lemming"; more conventionally, to the point of being intentionally trite, he rhymes "love" with "dove."[10] Of course, no rule requires every allusion to Hemingway to be reverent, or even respectful, and as I will demonstrate hereafter, some of the best poems, like some of the best fiction, plays, and movies concerning Hemingway, are humorous and highly irreverent.

Another case in point would be E.B. White's "The Law of the Jungle," which took its point of departure from a news item in the *New York Herald Tribune* about Hemingway's successful safari in Africa in 1933–34. White is better known today as the author of the children's books *Stuart Little* (1945) and *Charlotte's Web* (1952) and as coauthor of *The Elements of Style* (1918). He takes an epigraph from the news piece: "Mr. Hemingway said that he shot only lions that were utter strangers to him." Of course, that is not quite what Ernest said, his point being that he never shot at animals they had been photographing. The poem, composed in two ten-line stanzas of tetrameter couplets, opens with the suggestion that the typical novelist, when he is keen to kill, will simply shoot "at will"—but not Ernest Hemingway.[11] Ernest, White protests, obeys the laws of the jungle and guns down only strangers. Who but a bounder, the playfully offended White asks in the second stanza, would meet a beast over tea one day and shoot him the next? One suspects Ernest did not relish the wit. E.B. White (1899–1985) would later indulge his penchant for irritating Hemingway in his parody of *Across the River and into the Trees*, published in *New Yorker* as "Across the Street and into the Grill" (October 14, 1950).

The poems in which Hemingway appears, sometimes as a fictionalized character, fall into three categories: (1) responses to Hemingway or his work, including reminiscences (not always positive in nature) and what might be described as testimonials; (2) elegies, epitaphs, and eulogies—in effect, reactions to his suicide; (3) imaginative reconstructions—those poems in which the poet, sometimes with the postmodernist's playful sense of the vulnerability of history, creates scenarios or narratives in which Hemingway or characters from his fiction appear or reappear as though they were present before us.

The poems in the first category, responses to Hemingway or his work, may be divided among those by poets who draw upon personal acquaintance (sometimes fleeting) with the writer and those by poets who comment on the work, the man, or the legend from a more distant perspective. Among the former are several poems by MacLeish, most of them eulogistic in nature, the most noted of which is an eleven-line elegy simply entitled "Hemingway," to be considered hereafter. One of the most striking poems that reflects on a run-in with Hemingway (very likely an imaginary one) is Russian poet Yevgeny Yevtushenko's "Encounter," also translated under the title "A Meeting in Copenhagen," in which Yevtushenko describes the novelist as if he were old Santiago himself. The poet is sitting with friends drinking beer at the airport terminal in Copenhagen when "that old man" suddenly appears and, like an old ship's captain, confidently strides through the room, rejects the offer of vermouth and a Pernod, and takes up a glass of Russian vodka.

The earth itself, the poet continues, appears to quake as he enters the room, and at this point one of the speaker's friends declares that the man is the spitting image of Ernest Hemingway. Then the old man walks away, appearing to be, as Yevtushenko describes it, the living embodiment of his style, with terse expression reflecting a fisherman's stride, all of it seemingly carved out of granite (100–101). The man moves, we are told, as men have moved through battlefields over the centuries, crouched low as bullets fly and shoving aside whatever gets in their way. When Yevtushenko comments on Hemingway's style, both as a man and as a writer, his lines are nearly uniform in length, suggesting rhetorical control and careful craftsmanship. Only in the last three lines of the poem does the speaker declare that the old man not only looks just like Hemingway, but in fact is the writer himself. For the record, no such encounter appears to have occurred. The poem, composed in 1960, constitutes a tribute to Hemingway and the great impact of his modern voice on traditional ways of writing.

Although his longtime friend Archibald MacLeish (periodically rejected, as so many were) left a number of poems in which Hemingway appears, none is so apt and striking a tribute as "Poet" (dedicated "for Ernest Hemingway"), which appears to be both a comment on fishing and on the kind of perception or insight required of any good writer. Running fourteen lines, the poem resembles a sonnet despite McLeish's use of tetrameter. The first-person speaker describes a deep-sea fisherman who laughs as he fights and lands a large fish, most likely a tuna or marlin. The latent message of the poem, however, concerns not so much the fighting of the fish, but the insight of the angler whose keen eyes penetrate the depths of the sea in order to land "the heavy silver of his wish."[12] Scott Donaldson connects this poem with Hemingway's winning of the Nobel Prize in 1954, an event that brought at least a temporary reconciliation between the old friends, who had drifted apart during the 1930s (441). MacLeish's *Collected Poems* won the Pulitzer Prize for poetry in 1953, the same year Hemingway won it in fiction for *The Old Man and the Sea*. Clearly, the poem depicts not only old Santiago, but also Hemingway himself, fishing and peering into the depths of life, from which he draws the wished-for treasure taken with considerable physical exertion as he boats the "bloody," "shivering fish."

In "Years of the Dog," which appeared in his 1948 collection, *Actfive and Other Poems*, MacLeish looks back on Paris of the 1920s with mixed emotions, noting that everyone there was scrabbling after fame (376). The 27-line poem opens with six prefatory lines wherein MacLeish suggests that fame back then could be flushed from hiding like a quail. He then devotes nine rather playful lines to James Joyce (by name), balanced by eight lines to Hemingway, whom he does not name but refers to as a "lad" living in a carpenter's loft and looking like a "sleepy panther." Then he asks what became of that lad, and answers his own question: "Fame became of him" (377). The poem ends with a sort of four-line epilogue composed of questions asking where they live now and what has become of their fame. John Raeburn would appropriate the title of his 1984 book from MacLeish's poem: *Fame Became of Him: Hemingway as Public Writer*. The cover features an image of Hemingway in 1953 posed with a leopard, perhaps a conscious decision by the book designer to look back to the line likening the young author to "a sleepy panther." In the prose of *A Continuing Journey* (1968) MacLeish refers to that passage in his 1961 tribute commenting, "I don't suppose any writer since Byron has been as famous as Hemingway was when he died, but fame is a young man's passion."[13] MacLeish was in his mid-fifties when he wrote "Years of the Dog."

The many poems in which poets who never encountered him respond to Hemingway or his work range from Irish poet Basil Payne's "An Answer to Allegory," where the speaker watches the Spencer Tracy movie *The Old Man and the Sea* "on telly" with his son, after which the boy weeps for twenty minutes "for fish; man; boy; lost Paradise; him; me,"[14] to Paiute poet Adrian C. Louis's "The Hemingway Syndrome," in which the speaker is dropped off by a friend at the Indian cemetery in Lovelock, Nevada, where he drinks, takes up his rifle, and despises himself for thinking of suicide as an escape.[15] In Ai's appropriation of Elvis, "The Resurrection of Elvis Presley," the immortal rock star gets hooked and finds at the end of his line not God but Ernest Hemingway, who has been banished to an island "in the stream of unconsciousness."[16] Elvis claims to have yielded to death because God promised resurrection, but as the poem ends, Papa advises him to forget God and fish for something more within reach "even if it's just sweet time," for that is "better than nothing" (35–36).

Distinctive among the poems concerning Hemingway that do not at least purport to concern personal encounters are the forty-eight in Gerald Locklin's *Hemingway Colloquium: The Poet Goes to Cuba* (1999). The prolific Locklin (he lists more than eighty books, most published by small presses), who taught at California State University at Long Beach from 1964 through 2007, provides a poetic journal in prosaic free verse that recounts his experiences during a conference of Hemingway scholars scheduled to celebrate the opening of the museum at the Finca Vigía, July 15–21, 1995. Many of Locklin's poems are among those wherein the poet's focus is less on Hemingway than on himself. In "soul brothers," for example, Locklin likens himself to Hemingway, "not claiming to be / the great writer and adventurer / that he was," but, like him, inclined to "get mean with people" when his work is "being frustrated," then "apologetic" after the project is finished.[17] Although he no longer drinks, Locklin reflects upon his ability in the past to "consume a great deal / for long periods of time / without getting really drunk." Again like Hemingway, Locklin declares, "i try to be loyal to my friends, / and i expect loyalty in return," and "like him i had wives and women," but he confesses not to have Hemingway's "accumulation of wounds / because i didn't lead as brave a life." Most of the poems in this collection concern Locklin's travel experiences; "they don't make it easy," for example, which runs more than 240 lines, mentions Hemingway only in passing.

A simple measure of the value of Hemingway poems for students and admirers of him and his writing might be to inquire whether the poem is concerned at least as much with Hemingway as it is with the poet. In such poems as "his local pub," for example, Locklin comments on his own visit to the Floridita, concluding with a passage that reflects on Hemingway and himself and his fellow conferees:

> hemingway would say of us,
> as colonel cantwell did in Venice,
> "call me when the riffraff have left."
>
> i have good company at my table, though:
> bill and harvard (his real name).
> we agree that hemingway was really
> only a prick
> when his time and space for writing
> were being invaded, lost,
> which is when we find ourselves
> at our worst also [11].

In such passages Locklin, who wrote a memoir in 1995 of his long friendship with poet Charles Bukowski (1920–1994), becomes something of an apologist for Hemingway, a role that is not uncommon for poets who write on the man and his writing; and the poem concerns Hemingway in at least a proportionate ratio to Locklin himself. In "a prophet with honor" Locklin's adulation may seem ingenuous, but it is apparently sincere:

> i do not mind that hemingway
> is a god to the cubans.
> i do not find this excessive.
> he is a god to me also,
> the greatest of all american writers,
> and a great man as well [14].

Such celebratory passages may strike the reader as ingenuous, but they ring with what might be described as a boyish candor, and they are framed in diction and syntax almost certainly intended to echo the terse clarity of the early Hemingway style.

A subset of sorts could be compiled from poems in which the writers connect with Hemingway via his Key West home, a National Historic Landmark. Ernest and Pauline visited Key West in April 1928 and purchased the house on Whitehead Street early in 1931; they would reside there through most of 1939. Richard Eberhart's "Key West" notes in passing that Hemingway's house is "more elegant than you would have thought of him,"[18] but Philip Schultz's "The Hemingway House in Key West," appearing in *Deep Within the Ravine*, for which he won the Lamont Prize for 1984, is a more engaging and thoughtful poem that begins with the first-person speaker's recognition that when his father left him "a book of Hemingway's stories [...] he meant this as an explanation."[19] A year later, the speaker drives to Hemingway's grave in Ketchum and visits the house where he killed himself; twenty years after that, he visits the house in Key West, where he meets a guide who provides "the real dope on Papa." The speaker in the poem sees himself, like Hemingway, as one of "the sons of failed fathers" and as a man who has "something dark" in his nature (44). Schultz, founder of the Writers Studio in New York City, suggests at the end of the poem that the father (presumably his own), who went bankrupt and appears with "fire fading / in his eyes like a pilot light," also committed suicide. The speaker's father attempts to say something but fails at that as well, and in the morning he is found dead, "as if asking a last question the silence would never answer." For the rest of his life, the speaker concludes, "I have wondered what he meant to tell me."

For Iowa poet Robert Dana (1929–2010), too, in "Key West: Looking for Hemingway," Hemingway is not just an important literary or historical figure: he is a "ghost-fish." Dana thinks of Papa's head mangled into "perfect prose," and he calls out "silently" into the "terrible" emptiness left by his absence.[20] These three Key West poems reflect the range of poets' encounters with Hemingway, from the passing and somewhat slighting reference of Eberhart to the haunted reflections of Dana. Both Schultz and Dana attempt in some way to understand the mysteries of Hemingway's life and death.

Also connected with Key West is Brooklyn-born Latino poet Martin Espada's "The Man Who Beat Hemingway," which takes up the story of Kermit "Battling Geech" Forbes (better known in 1930s Key West as "Shine"), who punched Papa when he was refereeing a match between Forbes and a Cuban fighter named Alfred "Black Pie" Colebrook. The account offered in Stuart McIver's *Hemingway's Key West* (1993) makes better history, but Espada's poem makes better reading. According to McIver, the much smaller Forbes' punches landed harmlessly, and when police intervened, Hemingway refused to let him be arrested, but instead lined him up as a sparring partner at the boxing ring he set up in his backyard. "I thought he was some bum trying to pick up a dollar," Forbes said years later. Forbes would go on to be a ranking lightweight in the army. The year before he died in 2000 at age 84, he told the *Miami Herald* that Papa wasn't much of a fighter: "What he was was big. You'd run into him and just the weight of it would knock you down. But he never tried to hurt us. He always pulled his punches." "That big poke I took at Ernest Hemingway? Oh man, that was the greatest thing that ever happened to me in my life. [...] It kinda got me famous." In his poem, Espada, who teaches at the University of Massachusetts at Amherst, connects Forbes in 1937 with legendary blues guitarist Robert Johnson, who died mysteriously in 1938, and recounts the story Forbes liked to tell "the amazed tourists," that he was "the man who beat Hemingway."[21] Ernest Hemingway's prowess as a boxer remains a bone of contention, but one should probably not credit Kermit Forbes as a reliable source on the subject—all those years and tourists later—any more than one should credit Papa himself.

Surely the most ambitious of the Key West poems must be that of John Logan (1923–1987), who taught nearly twenty years at SUNY–Buffalo and authored more than a dozen books of poems. In "Papa's House, Son's Room," which appeared in *The Bridge of Change* (1979), he opens by referring to poinciana trees that "bloom flamboyant red" in the yard, "bright as the blood from Papa's head."[22] The seven-part poem, however, quickly shifts focus to a myriad of details about the furnishing of the house, from "Pauline's beloved chandeliers" and "Picasso's gift ceramic cat" to the infamous "cracked, old urinal" from Sloppy Joe's Bar (to water the cats) and "the custom king-sized bed, its broken-hinged headboard / fashioned from a mahogany gate he'd brought from Spain" (423). As the poem evolves, the title's suggestion of tension between Ernest and his difficult son Gregory, who was briefly Logan's student in Maryland (St. John's College) and who "never spoke of his father," takes over. Anticipating Paul Hendrickson's tribute in *Hemingway's Boat*, Logan salutes Gregory at the end of the poem as "a smart and beautiful man." In a reference to the "Lenten tree" Logan draws attention to the process of self-denial and penitence connected with Lent and implicitly necessary for Papa, whose demands have overshadowed the lives and the needs of his family. The house in this poem, per the title, is distinctively "Papa's"; Gregory's room is diminished, "filled with pictures of him / and his friends, and souvenirs from all over the world" (423).

Similar to Schultz's, Dana's—and Logan's—poems in the use of Hemingway or his possessions as symbol or metaphor (in this case, technically, "metonymy") is British poet Vicki Feaver's "Hemingway's Hat," which appeared in the *New Yorker* in 1996. The first-person speaker puts on an imitation of the cap Hemingway wore at the Finca Vigía, a cap her lover's mother gave him so he would "look dashing, nerveless."[23] Into the nine quatrains, Feaver pours a rich thematic (mostly gender-connected) stream. The hat makes her feel like a Shakespearean heroine, a boy costumed as a woman, which causes her to wonder how it would be for her if she were a man. Hemingway's curiosity about such matters has been well documented in various scholarly studies, including Mark Spilka's *Hemingway's Quarrel with Androgyny* (1990) and Nancy R. Comley and Robert Scholes's *Hemingway's Genders* (1994). To be a man, Feaver's speaker asserts, would involve not just being brave, but "'needing / to be seen to be brave' like Hem." Feaver's critique of the Hemingway Code here is rather subtle and is similar in some ways to Eberhart's observation that Hemingway's house (not "home") in Key West is "more elegant than you would have thought of him." Numerous biographers have commented on the striking inelegance of Hemingway's dress, which likely began with his residence in the hyper-casual Key West of the early 1930s.

Feaver then shifts to her father, "gentle, nervous," but unmanly as seen by her mother, who wanted a replacement for her brother who was killed in Burma in the last years of World War II. Significantly, the speaker, unlike her mother, considers her father's gentle, nervous nature to be an acceptable identity for a man. Readers familiar with Hemingway's biography might associate the strained relationship between the speaker's parents with that of Clarence and Grace Hemingway. At the onset of puberty, the speaker attempted gender transformation by getting her hair cut short like a boy's, but later, she changed herself back "into a girl," with "nylon petticoats, a perm." The focus of the poem then shifts to her lover, who "travelled from war to war" before coming home, where he encountered "a silence like the silence at Plei Me," a battle in Vietnam in October of 1965, where he saw ghosts rising from the battlefield. The poem ends with the speaker's comments upon their hat-changing games, with her "riding" him in their lovemaking, but with him, in the last stanza, bathing her in the morning "with a woman's tenderness." Hemingway's hat, therefore, becomes something of a symbol for transformation, particularly as the changes pertain to gender.

The ghost of Ernest Hemingway also haunts four poems in *Paris* (1997) by Jim Barnes, who is of Choctaw descent, founder of Chariton Review Press, and the longtime editor of *Chariton Review* at Truman State University in Missouri. In "Looking for Hemingway's Ghost at the Crillon," Barnes visits the famous restaurant where Hemingway drank when he could afford it, discovering that many boasts and lies still haunt the place.[24] He and his wife pay homage, disregarding exaggerations about his life and well aware of having "lost a generation of giants." Barnes effectually expands the frame of reference from the personal to the universal realization that people delude themselves about the lives of others because their own lives have become too bland. Part of the appeal of Hemingway, Barnes implies here, is that, unlike theirs, his life was in fact rich enough to "rival reality." In the closing lines the speaker and his wife lament, not just for themselves but for the present generation, because their lives have become too vague to be captured in enduring poetry.

John Logan, Philip Schultz, Vicki Feaver, and Jim Barnes borrow (or steal, as T.S. Eliot would have it) from Hemingway both tangibly (the home, the cap, the restaurant) and conceptually, and they are drawn, presumably, by the personal coincidence between some event in their own lives and that of Ernest Hemingway. In John Updike's "Meditation on a News Item" the first stanza also focuses on a cap, this time the one not worn by Fidel Castro, who stands beside Hemingway in a 1960 photograph from *Life* magazine (shown in Norberto Fuentes' *Hemingway in Cuba*, facing page 97). In this playful poem, first published in the July 16, 1960, issue of *New Yorker*, the focus does not shift away from Hemingway and back to the poet or his first-person speaker. Although we are well aware of Updike's voice and point of view throughout the poem, the focus remains on Hemingway. The subject of the photo is Castro's winning first place in a fishing tourney in Havana sponsored by Ernest not long before he left Cuba in May of 1960. What attracts the speaker is how these two faces have become familiar and at the same time magnified, as if the photographs of Papa and Fidel have somehow managed to establish their identities. Updike likens the strangeness of this fact to someone discovering a woodcut of Shakespeare awarding a prize to Queen Elizabeth for winning a baking contest.[25]

The speaker then playfully proceeds to speculate on how the tournament came about. Did Hemingway depart from his writing routine (Updike spells out the details) and suddenly decide to sponsor a fishing tournament? And did he receive an application form from "Fidel Castro, Dictator," who proceeded to don his waders and hook the prize-winning fish? At the end of the poem, the speaker speculates on their very different kinds of fame. In the photograph, he suggests that both seem saintly. Finally, the speaker expresses his delight with the ironic discrepancies implied in the photograph, which he likens to opening up a copy of *Alice in Wonderland* and finding that Alice actually won the Queen of Hearts' croquet match (312). The consummate author and the consummate politician meet on neutral grounds (the game, the fair competition), and the writer presents an award to the dictator (perhaps not universally recognized as such in 1960). Art, both that of the writer and that of the photographer, defines or interprets the individual (the "lucky novice") and confers recognition.

While the poems that comment on Hemingway as writer, personality, and myth vary in tone from the outright comic to the downright reverential, those which might best be described as elegies, eulogies, and epitaphs occasioned by his July 1961 suicide are more uniformly somber and deferential, at times even ceremonious. Of course it could be argued that all of the poems written since Hemingway's suicide are de facto elegiac in nature—"Every poem an epitaph," Eliot wrote in "Little Gidding"—but the event gave rise to a number of poems specifically focused on that event. MacLeish's "Hemingway" is perhaps the most familiar of these, and it bears an epigraph from Mary Hemingway: "In some inexplicable way an accident," to which the opening line immediately responds, that such a death is not actually "inexplicable," but that only death can explain that kind of death.[26] MacLeish treats Death as a movie camera operator who "rewinds remembrance" to the place where the action started. He concludes the poem grimly, with two terse sentences presented as a couplet: "The gun between the teeth explains. / The shattered mouth foretells the singing boy." (The gun placed "between the teeth" is an error—it was aimed above the eyebrows.) Scott Donaldson, who has written biographies of both Hemingway and MacLeish, suggests that the poem emphasizes "the troubling chiaroscuro" of Hemingway's personality.[27] MacLeish's "Voyage" (dedicated "for Ernest Hemingway" and appearing in *Poems, 1924–1933*) is also elegiac, a funeral poem in the heroic mode, but obviously, given the period of its composition, it does not concern Hemingway's death.

One of the most elaborate tributes written for Hemingway is the triptych "To Ernest Hemingway," by Iraqi poet Abdul Wahab Al-Bayati (1926–1999). The poem, first published in Arabic in 1964, reflects on Spain, one of several places where Al-Bayati lived (he died in exile in Syria) and connects Hemingway in the first line with "Death in Madrid" and later in the stanza with the Spanish Civil War and Federico García Lorca, who was executed by the Falangists in 1936. The short lines impart a dirge-like rhythm, and the opening lines of the first section, "In Spain," set the tone and image patterns for the whole poem—blood and roses—as the speaker asks rhetorically "for whom the bell tolls."[28] The images of blood and roses in the first section recur in the second, entitled, "On the Verge of Death," as "wine in the leather bottle the rose in the garden" and as "a bloody struggle between the forces of darkness and man" (39). The imagery is reiterated in the third section, "The End," which begins with the one-word line, "Death," as flowers burned by the departing gypsies and "a song bleeding" (40).

Thomas Merton's prose poem, "An Elegy for Ernest Hemingway," also puns on such titles as *For Whom the Bell Tolls* and *The Sun Also Rises*. The poem appears early in his 1963 collection, *Emblems of a Season of Fury*, and it might best be described as an "equivocal elegy," for it soon becomes apparent that the Trappist monk detects a certain justness to the fact that only upon his death is Ernst Hemingway's name "mentioned in convents."[29] Now, Merton proposes, the "true bell" will ring out the end of the story of his life, and at this moment the famous writer stands "anonymous," his writings *not* having been consulted. Hemingway has passed through only "briefly." Yet, Merton allows, some "look up" to recognize "a friend once known in a far country," and for those "the sun also rose." They have not forgotten him, and for them he remains famous, "no ritual shade." Like Al-Bayati, Merton (1915–1968) seizes on the tolling bell, which achieves yet another variation, having first appeared in the seventeenth meditation of John Donne's *Devotions Upon Emergent Occasions* in 1624, from which it was revived for the title of Hemingway's novel of 1940. The bell at the monastery tolls slowly "for a whole age," but no sooner does Merton suggest Hemingway's enduring fame than he calls into question the value of Hemingway's legacy. The "bell tolls" for a "brave illusion: the adventurous self!" The unaided individual, the self without community, whether looking back to Harry Morgan of *To Have and Have Not* or perhaps to Santiago of *The Old Man and the Sea*, is a brave, but also fragile, illusion: "For with one shot the whole hunt is ended!" In effect, Merton's poem is both praise and critique, both lament and warning.

John Berryman's "Dream Song #235," which begins, "Tears Henry shed for poor old Hemingway," also provides what turns out to be an ironic critique of Hemingway's suicide.[30] Berryman compares Hemingway's suicide with that of the poet's father, who, like Hem's father, also shot himself: "Save us from shotguns & father's suicides." Although Berryman—who describes Hemingway as "that cruel & gifted man"—writes "a bad example, murder of oneself," he committed suicide by throwing himself from a bridge in 1972.

A brief lament cast in Hemingwayesque sentences that seem especially terse because of the trimeter lines, Paul Ramsey's "Elegy for Ernest Hemingway" appears in the first issue of *Hemingway Notes*. Ramsey (1924–1994) taught at the University of Tennessee at Chattanooga:

> Out in the killing woods
> He taught a gun to sound,
> Learning the lesson well.
> The dying quarry failed.
> He bided what he saw
> Until a speechless day.
> Silence lasts around
> What cast itself away.[31]

The stoic tone of this dirge allows for nothing in the way of the consolations conventionally offered in most elegies. One might hazard the surmise that Hem would have appreciated the stark simplicity of Ramsey's poem pared down to just 35 words cast in four sentences.

Charles Bukowski's "the fighter" also constitutes what might best be called a lament, which opens with lines proclaiming that Hemingway "feels it from the grave" when the bulls run in Pamplona.[32] Bukowski concludes the poem simply, likening the beauty of the young bulls to that of Ernest, regardless of what "they" now say. In effect, Bukowski's poem is a critique not of Hemingway but of those who have sought to undermine his reputation and attack his character. Given Bukowski's preference for Hemingway's early fiction, his setting of the poem in Pamplona is particularly apt.

Washington poet David Wagoner's "At the Hemingway Memorial" is also a lament, but images replace the flat assertions of Bukowksi's poem. On a bone-dry summer day the first-person speaker visits the bronze bust of Hem beside Trail Creek, a tributary of the Big Lost River outside Sun Valley and Ketchum, Idaho.[33] Wagoner quotes from the inscription on the memorial, which is drawn from Hemingway's eulogy for his friend and hunting partner Gene Van Guilder. Those lines may constitute Hemingway's finest "poem":

> Best of all he loved the fall,
> The leaves yellow on the cottonwoods,
> Leaves floating on the trout streams
> And above the hills, the high blue windless skies.
> Now he will be a part of them forever.[34]

Wagoner finds the road along the creek to be "as hard, / as shimmering, straight, and spare" as Hemingway's early prose, and he adds, "The style is still the man when it deserts him." The poem ends with the speaker reflecting on "the husk of a cicada nymph [...] / The back split open, / And nothing to be brave about."

Maybe the most poignant of the elegiac poems, however, is University of Wisconsin at Milwaukee emeritus philosophy professor John Koethe's simply titled "E.H.," published as a Poem-A-Day on September 20, 2013, the online Web site of the Academy of American Poets. The first-person speaker in the poem appears at times to conflate Koethe himself with Hemingway, but perhaps not in the opening line, which reads like straight Hem: "I like to get drunk and I like to write."[35] The 32-line poem is set up in three stanzas, the first of which introduces Hemingway as a lost soul, unable any longer to find "the life between the words." The stanza concludes with familiar phrases: "in our time," "in another country," a swamp "where the fishing was tragic." His feelings, E.H. tells us, now seem "diminished in the telling."

In the second stanza Koethe directly blends himself as the speaker with Hemingway as he comments on watching a recent revival of Stephen Sondheim's musical *Follies*, which was first staged on Broadway in 1971. In the play, 49-year-old Sally Weismann, a former Ziegfeld girl and "a prisoner of rage and her imagination," returns to the stage of a theater slated for demolition, where "all she can find is her age." In the third stanza E.H. asks himself, "Why do I get so angry? Why do I assume / The characters I love, the characters I love and hate?" Unable now to distinguish "the mask or the face," he finds himself "here" (in Ketchum) "in a home that isn't home," neither his beloved boat *Pilar* nor the Finca Vigía. As he moves toward his suicide, Hemingway reflects in the closing line, paralleling Sally's phrasing at the end of the second stanza, "I'm sixty-two. That's all I am." In his comments on composing the poem, Koethe reports he had been reading Paul Hendrickson's best seller *Hemingway's Boat* (2011) and had recently attended a Broadway performance of *Follies*: "Hemingway and Sondheim's character Sally seemed to me pathetic and heartbreaking in different ways, and I wound up putting them together in this poem."

The future for poems about Hemingway, other than passing references or allusions, most likely resides with verse of the third variety, which I have described as "postmodernist reconstructions." Koethe's "E.H." might be said to bestride the border between the elegiac poems and the reconstructions. Chicago poet Campbell McGrath's playful "Hemingway Dines on Boiled Shrimp and Beer" is one such poem, in which the speaker assumes the character of Hemingway in a sort of dramatic monologue wherein Hem portrays himself as rambunctious self-parody swaggering and brawling his way through Key West.[36] Perhaps drawing on the episode recounted early in A.E. Hotchner's *Papa Hemingway*, in which the journalist is welcomed into "the Royal Order of Shrimp Eaters" (7), McGrath depicts Hemingway eating shrimp in the Catalonian style, shells and all. His Hemingway offers himself up as a sort of human embodiment of Sandburg's "Chicago," paying his respects at Sloppy Joe's Bar, and then staggering off to the beach where he pisses mightily into the ocean. First published in the summer 1991 issue of *Paris Review* and later in his *Florida Poems* (2002), McGrath's fourteen-line poem comes across as a free-wheeling sonnet. It is available online at the Academy of American Poets Web site: http://www.poets.org/viewmedia.php/prmMID/16373.

Although Charles Bukowski has long been recognized as an admirer of Hemingway's earlier writing and as having fallen under his influence in various ways, I have not found any evidence that they ever met. Bukowski intimates as much, however, in his typically prosaic "Hemingway's Shadow," which appeared in a chapbook issue of *Wormwood Review* in 1988. The first-person speaker, presumably Bukowski, claims to have met Hemingway on one occasion after the writer had fallen into all of the "traps" of fame, the big advances from his publishers, the interviews and talk-shows.[37] Although Papa appears to be well-off, Bukowski observes that he is no longer writing, or at least is not writing well, but he claims to have liked him as a man. Such a declaration constitutes a reversal of how some would judge Hemingway, but the judgment here might say as much about Bukowski, or his persona in the poem, as it does about the later Papa. The only part of Hemingway the speaker claims not to have admired during their day and night together was, ironically, that Hem didn't drink very much.

As the night wears on, Hemingway simply watches as Bukowski (or his doppelgänger) drinks, looking at him as if he were some kind of "freakazoid" (62). The speaker finds Hem to be a real gentleman, and he toasts him succinctly: "we are / all piss-ants." The poem ends with the speaker's (in effect, Bukowski's) declaration that he truly liked Papa and found him to be "the old heavyweight champ" (63). In some ways this poem recalls Yevgeny Yevtushenko's "Encounter" or "A Meeting in Copenhagen," but Yevtushenko's poem constitutes more of a tribute to Hemingway than it does a personal appropriation, almost, one might say, an "expropriation." Bukowski has been likened to Hemingway (some details are listed in Gaylord Brewer's *Charles Bukowski*),[38] and along with such poets as Robinson Jeffers, Walt Whitman, and William Carlos Williams, Hemingway importantly influenced his work.

Gaylord Brewer's poems on Hemingway include "Brief Hemingway Encounter" from *Devilfish* (1999), in which the speaker reflects on a supposed run-in with the old writer on a bus in Spain, also similar in some ways to Yevtushenko's "Encounter." But Hemingway never acknowledges the speaker's presence; and as the poem unwinds, Papa seems to fade away until "the body disintegrates," leaving only "an old man's pudgy face," and finally, "the saddest, clearest eyes I've ever seen."[39] The imaginary encounter has the aura of a dream. Hemingway's eyes wish to join the dead, and they seem to speak out in the final line: "I went as far as I could and didn't quit. Don't look at me" (72). In a very different sort of poem, "The Hemingway Look-alike Society Meets Bimini Bay Developers," from *Barbaric Mercies* (2003), Brewer, who teaches at Middle Tennessee State University and is founder of the magazine *Poems and Plays*, imagines "what He would have done" to the developers who served up weak rum punch and promises of a segregated colony complete with 18-hole golf course.[40]

Guyana-born poet Cyril Dabydeen, who left South America in 1970 to attend college in Canada, where he earned MA and MPA degrees at Queens University, connects with the spirit of Hemingway while in Havana, but his encounter is considerably more congenial than Brewer's as he imagines himself in Havana sipping mojitos with Papa.[41] With Hemingway he strolls the streets in the evening, eyeballing young Cubans as they promenade "by the seawalls, hand in hand, much in love"; and also with him he reflects on the proletarian revolution, wondering whether he too might find a home in Cuba. Hemingway, Dabydeen suggests, never really left Cuba.

Like Dabydeen, Lowell Mick White, who teaches at Pittsburg State University in Kansas, shares what one might describe as a "virtual drink" with Ernest in "I Bought Hemingway's Ghost a Drink," which appeared in an anthology of poems from Texas in 2007. Initially White's first-person speaker dismisses the "ghost" as "crazy and impotent," a "tiresome asshole, a sad delusional bully," but he cannot resist the opportunity.[42] He buys a round of drinks and talks of fishing the Clark Fork of the Yellowstone under clouds that remind him of an Albert Bierstadt painting—"shafts of sunlight like / angels screaming down, like Manifest / Destiny, like floating Truth revealed." When the speaker describes himself "shivering amid water hailstones mayflies / trout" and "gazing into gauzy gold air," Hemingway's ghost gets "excited," and the speaker tells him he "learned to see it from him."

In "Poem for Hemingway & W.C. Williams," Raymond Carver (1938–1988), better known for his short stories than for his poems, but an accomplished poet as well, brings together two writers who had considerable influence on his work in both genres and imagines them as friends discovering "3 fat trout'" in a pool.[43] Carver depicts Hemingway as a former heavyweight boxer wearing a hunter's cap and eager to catch and eat the trout, while Williams is identified as a physician who would prefer simply to admire the fish in the clear stream. Critics mention Hemingway as an influence on Carver's prose style almost invariably, and according to Adam Meyer, William Carlos Williams was of great importance for Carver's poetry.[44] Carver may or may not have been aware of the notorious, prolonged tennis match pitting Williams against Hemingway in Paris in 1924. According to Williams' biographer Paul Mariani, they played four sets, "with neither Hemingway nor Williams being willing to give in and neither man able to beat the other," although Hem was sixteen years younger.[45]

Bukowski's and Brewer's imaginative renderings of Hemingway encounters, into which they project themselves in some way, and those of Koethe, McGrath, Dabydeen, and Carver, in which they develop a scenario based on what they have read about Hemingway, place a fairly high premium on credibility or verisimilitude. It might be argued that they do not differ greatly in their approach to the man and myth from David Ray in the 107 poems that comprise *Hemingway: A Desperate Life* (2011). Part of what distinguishes Ray's poems involving Hemingway as a character is that, along with a few other poets, he has featured Hemingway throughout an entire collection. Author of more than twenty books of poetry, Ray is a professor emeritus from the University of Missouri at Kansas City. In a brief online review, Willard Manus describes Ray's poems in terms early book reviewers used to describe Hemingway's prose style: "terse" and "lapidary."[46] The poems are generally understated, somewhat prosaic at times, rarely offering up much in the way of images or metaphors.

In effect, what Ray offers is a biography in poetic form stripped of dates and of what might be considered superfluous details, leaving us with a streamlined version of the life and the myth and touching on a broad range of topics. Following a pair of short prefatory poems, Ray proceeds, with some exceptions, in chronological, linear fashion, starting with "Just Out of High School," which takes Hemingway to Kansas City. In the next poem, "Falstaff in Oak Park," Ernest is back from the war, showing off his souvenirs and allowing a local reporter to embellish the facts of his military exploits: "And thus the mythic Hemingway was launched."[47] The run of nine poems, in which Ray gives ample space to Ernest's relationship with Agnes von Kurowsky, culminates in the notorious letter of reprimand his mother sent him in the spring of 1920 (see Chapter Three). The next fifteen poems pertain to Ernest's marriage with Hadley and their sojourn in Paris, including a poem on Hemingway's long tennis bout with William Carlos Williams mentioned above and three poems on Scott and Zelda Fitzgerald. The poems in this section end with one that registers Grace Hemingway's disapprobation of her son's writing.

The poem ironically entitled "An Industrial Accident" introduces Pauline into the mix and reflects on the dissolution of Hemingway's marriage to Hadley, whose presence lingers even after their divorce. Echoes from *A Moveable Feast* resound throughout the nine poems of the previous section and many of the twenty that make up this second major movement in the book, which soon segues into Key West. In "A Literary Friendship," also ironically titled, Ray perpetuates a couple of myths regarding the brawl that occurred in February 1936 between the poet Wallace Stevens and Ernest, namely that Ernest broke Stevens' jaw (actually Stevens broke his hand when he punched Hem's jaw) and that Sunny (Madelaine) was the sister who had been "in a huff" about what the tipsy poet said (according to a letter he wrote right after the event, it was his sister Ursula). Ray also introduces Sun Valley into the mix, but the Key West world is disrupted soon enough when Martha Gellhorn shows up in "Windfall or Wife." Only five poems concern that brief, turbulent relationship and marriage, but while two of them deal with their trip to China in early 1941, none of the poems attends to events during the civil war in Spain.

Following a sort of transitional poem, "Ernest's Brave Bull," which refers to a very short story entitled "The Faithful Bull," published in *Holiday* magazine in 1951, Ray offers a medley of a dozen or so poems in which Mary Welsh Hemingway plays an increasingly important role. But in these the chronological order of events is frequently scrambled, with poems like "The Long Hot Summer," which deals with the 1959 Ordóñez-Dominguín mano-a-mano bullfights that would be recorded in the nonfiction book *The Dangerous Summer*, preceding poems about Ernest's submarine hunting during World War II. Similarly, the killing of Hem's favorite Black Dog by Batista's men in 1957 appears a couple of poems before "In Normandy," which looks to Ernest's post–D-Day experiences as a war correspondent in Europe, and prior to a couple of poems on the nearly fatal second African safari of 1953–54.

Such interruptions of the chronological flow probably affect some readers only slightly, if at all, but the issue itself prompts one to inquire as to the readership of such a book. Was it aimed at fans of David Ray's poetry or at admirers (or more likely detractors) of Hemingway's life and writing? In a review in the *Tucson Weekly* entitled "Picking on Papa" and subtitled "David Ray's Hemingway Biography-in-verse Sermonizes on a Great Writer's Failings," Jarret Keene proceeds from the premise that "Hemingway's moral and creative standing fluctuates on an article-by-article basis."[48] An admirer of Ray's verse, Keene regards this book as "a misstep" and "the slightest of Ray's customarily rewarding collections": "From the start, it's clear Ray has no intention of treating Hemingway like a real human being; better to tear down a myth, to rip apart a cartoon."

Beginning with "Written of and to Write," however, Ray devotes roughly the latter third of the poems to at least somewhat sympathetic observations on Hemingway's anxiety about his writing and his fear of approaching death. Even being awarded the Nobel Prize in the fall of 1954 seems to bring him no genuine pleasure. "It wasn't fun anymore," Ray writes in "Marks on a Wall" (93), echoing Nick Adams' statement in the poignant story "The End of Something" from *In Our Time*. But while Nick's statement refers to his feelings for Marjorie (*Complete Short Stories* 81), Ray's assertion on Ernest's behalf clearly refers to writing, and beyond that to life itself. At least a dozen poems lead Hemingway inexorably to his suicide, and in the last eight or nine poems in the collection, Ray reflects on the dark aftermath: the shotgun cut into fragments and buried, the Finca and the *Pilar* lost, the life and myth compromised by commoditization of various kinds ("As Icon"), even the literary achievement undercut ("Reports of Hemingway's Failure Greatly Exaggerated").

Ray's most ambitious effort is what was published originally as a three-part poem entitled "Hemingway's Garden," first in *New Millennium Writings* and subsequently in *The Best American Poetry, 1999*. In his book it is printed as three separate poems, with others breaking up the sequence, but I will comment on the poem as it appeared in *Best American Poetry* (the guest editor that year was Robert Bly). The second page number listed refers to the version that appears in Ray's book. The poem draws on an episode involving Hemingway's gardeners at the Finca Vigía, recounted in Norberto Fuentes' *Hemingway in Cuba* (1984), Ray's apparent source, given similarity in phrasing, including the title of the first part, "Dead Man's Water." The narrative tells of Hemingway's first gardener, Pedro, who was offended at being told he was not to prune the trees and walked off the job. By the time he returned, Hemingway had hired José Pichilo as his gardener, and the disconsolate Pedro reacted by drowning himself in one of the wells on the Finca. When Hemingway asks, "Why [...] did this man come to kill himself at my farm?" (a verbatim quotation from Fuentes[49]), Pichilo explains, in the poem, it was not Hemingway's fault "that Pedro had owned no farm / of his own, with no well for the jumping" (136, 94). In Fuentes' account the details are slightly different, as Pichilo claims he "couldn't explain it to him," nor could he remind Hemingway "that Pedro did not own a farm and therefore, for his grim purpose, he had to use someone else's. But then, it wasn't Hemingway's fault that old Pedro didn't have his own farm."

In the second part of the poem, "The Interim Gardener," Ray recounts the story of how, at Mary's request, Pichilo cut a root from a ceiba (kapok) tree that was destroying the floor tiles. In Fuentes' account, the gardener is unnamed (not Pichilo, who tells the story), but other details are close, including Mary's description of her husband as "spoiled and bad-tempered" (Ray, 136, 95; Fuentes, 53). When he observes what has been done, the furious Hemingway grabs a twelve-gauge shotgun and pursues the gardener, who leaps out the window and escapes. Mary is required to do penance for some time thereafter "each day by kneeling before the ceiba / and asking forgiveness, saying the prayer / that her husband prescribed" (137, 96). The "famous root" now "hangs as a trophy over the door" of the Venetian Room at the Finca.

In the third part, "An Abrazo" (an embrace), Hemingway bids Pichilo good-bye in July 1960, citing a proverb: "He who says / goodbye often, never leaves" (Ray, 137, 100; Fuentes, 57). In the poem, however, Hemingway says he does not think the proverb is true. In both versions, he tells Pichilo that he feels sick and the "Cuban doctors can't find out what's wrong with me" (Fuentes 57). Then Hemingway tells Pichilo of his father's suicide (in Ray's poem, the weapon, actually a .32, is given as a .38 Smith and Wesson—poet's license, perhaps). In both accounts Hemingway tells Pichilo "neither animals nor humans / should die in bed or be allowed / to suffer or make others suffer" (Ray, 138, 100; Fuentes, 57). Of various ailments from which Hemingway was suffering at the time, kidney and liver disorders appear to have been most prominent. After a strong embrace (abrazo) Hemingway says adios and gives Pichilo a handful of Cuban money, "saying / he no longer had any use for it." The theme of Ray's poem is that trees, and presumably humans as well, "should always be allowed to grow / without restraint" (136, 94) and to die with dignity.

The poems of Yevtushenko, McGrath, Bukowski, Brewer, and Carver are based on imagined events; they are "reconstructions," often in the postmodern mode that tends to defy or repudiate history—what Frederic Jameson refers to as "fantastic historiography" or "fabulation" and describes as "free play with the past" (368–369). I recall here an episode of the *Monty Python Show* in which an interviewer discusses current events with Caligula, Attila the Hun, and who else? Hitler? Stalin? In short, it is as if the old premise of "historical inevitability" had given way to "historical implausibility." Perhaps no poet has mined this lode more rigorously than Diane Wakoski, who in the mid–1970s introduced George Washington, tongue-in-cheek, as a character into many of her poems. Spokane-Coeur d'Alene writer Sherman Alexie often slips Crazy Horse into his poems and fiction as if he were alive and well, just passing through the rez.

David P. Reiter's book, *Hemingway in Spain: Words and Images* (1997, 2nd edition, 2007) offers a kaleidoscopic portrayal of Ernest Hemingway in that postmodern vein touring contemporary Spain accompanied by his girlfriend Maria, presumably borrowed from his 1940 novel *For Whom the Bell Tolls*. As director of Interactive Press in Brisbane, Australia, Reiter, who was born in Cleveland, Ohio, and holds a Ph.D. in creative writing from the University of Denver, has seen to the publication of several of his own books, and on the IP Web site he describes the "several 'Hemingways'" that make up the sequence as "voices from the past and present, real and imagined" in a mode he calls "fusion poetry."[50] In a DVD based on the book and released in late 2006, available through Amazon.com, Reiter fuses his reading of most of the poems (only sixteen of the 61 are not included) and an elaborate pastiche of images and videos pertinent to the texts. We can sample the variety of these Hemingway voices by reflecting on a few of the poems, starting with the first one, "At Plaza de España, Madrid," where we hear a voice sounding very much like Hemingway addressing Cervantes:

> You were their best, Miguel,
> but you only got it right once.
> Is that why they bronzed
> the myths before the man?[51]

The presumably rhetorical question might apply equally to Hemingway. Hemingway—or more accurately David Reiter, speaking through that mask or persona—then rips on Franco, whom he reduces to no more than "wet sand" between the toes of the *peónes*. In the DVD, Reiter provides images ranging from statues of Cervantes and Franco on horseback to a quick clip of a donkey. Throughout he occasionally inserts lines of text from the poems, in this case the description of Franco as "no more than wet sand between their toes."

As the poem ends, Reiter looks back to a piece of dialogue near the conclusion of *The Sun Also Rises*, when Brett says, "It's sort of what we have instead of God" (249). The neuter pronoun's antecedent may or may not be regarded as ambiguous. It would seem from the context that she means simply "deciding not to be a bitch" is what we have instead of God. But Jake proposes they have a martini, so one might surmise that alcohol is "what we have," and in a broader context, perhaps "it" refers to love, or perhaps to feeling "rather damned good." In appropriately postmodern fashion, Reiter's Hemingway offers "irony's what we have instead of God" (4). Addressing Cervantes again, he writes, "You took up a pen to escape the war; / I took up battle to escape an uncertain / pen." In the closing line, he declares flatly, "Things haven't changed a hell of a lot." The opening poem is set opposite a familiar photograph of Hemingway from the early 1930s. Another twenty or so photos of scenes from Spain are distributed throughout the book, and most of those also appear in the film.

The second poem in the book, "A Clean Well-lighted Place," opens with a three-line passage from *A Moveable Feast* and follows with a quatrain very much in synch with the style and tone:

> It's easier when you come back in winter,
> in the half-life. The sun's more sympathetic
> to grey and you can sip a cheap rosé without
> regretting those stories you left too quickly [5].

Hemingway then notices a wooden bust of himself, and he comments on how a waiter told tales of how Papa composed *A Moveable Feast* there in Madrid and he made out so well with the tips that he was able to open his own place, which he called "Not the Hemingway Restaurant / and all the postmodern pretenders go there" (6). Ernest claims not to be able to understand a word the postmodernists say. In the third poem, "At the Hotel Florida," the first-person speaker signs the register as "E. Hemingway, / Ketchum, Idaho," and in the lobby he encounters Maria, who will accompany him throughout the rest of his visit to Spain (7). In that poem we watch him struggle with his writing. Maria joins him in the next poem, "No Writers in the Prado." There and elsewhere in the book the dictator Franco, who ruled Spain from 1939 until his death in 1975, is conjured up and repudiated as a man incapable of appreciating art or literature.

Some sense of how the poems affect the reader can be gained by citing a few opening stanzas in which the historical past (sometimes the Spanish Civil War, sometimes events from much more distant history—Reiter provides explanatory endnotes) mingles with the present:

> It took days for our troops to reach
> Toledo through all the sniper fire
> and land mines but just a few hours
> for Maria's old Renault
> ["The Walls of Toledo," 15].

> I couldn't help but think of Robert Cohen
> as we walked by that pathetic synagogue
> scrunched between souvenir shops
> ["In the Barrio de la Juderia," 25].

> Charles was tapping his scepter in the dust
> as we passed the ticket counter. "I suppose,"
> he said, "that Boabdil asked you to intervene
> with me on his behalf. The man has no shame.
> He gives the crown—or whatever he wore—
> a bad name." [Boabdil, or Muhammad XII, was the last
> Muslim ruler of Granada, the last Muslim-ruled city in Spain]
> ["Charles V Sets the Record Straight," 65].

> It would have been pure hell for Scott—
> a Hollywood without martinis and olives—
> but old Clint never looked so fit.

> "You won't believe your eyes, Hemingway,"
> he said, "but they've done it up in spades.
> Look at this—it's a base away from home!"
> ["Clint Eastwood at Tabernas," 73].

Some of the poems are more subtle, and in some Hemingway appears nonexistent, or perhaps more completely blended into a first-person speaker who seems more akin to David Reiter lowering the mask. In the credits at the end of the film, Reiter states simply, "David Reiter was Ernest Hemingway."

True to the postmodern premise of the poems, anything can happen. For example, in "Bluffing at Gibralfaro" (Lighthouse Hill in Málaga, per Reiter's endnote—a castle-like fortification on a hill that rises about 427 feet over the Mediterranean) a gypsy attempts to force Hemingway to pay a parking fee, an obvious scam. "Here was another gypsy / who didn't recognize Hemingway!" he grouses (48). When the gypsy returns with a shillelagh, Hemingway, slipping into the role of his own character, Robert Jordan from *For Whom the Bell Tolls*, regards him as "one of the faceless ones I shot down / before I passed out above the bridge." Then, just as a fight seems inevitable, Teddy Roosevelt shows up with "a mean bull-whip" and the gypsy turns tail. "Get tough, / Hemingway," TR advises, "that's the ticket to ride" (50). In that gesture, Reiter connects what was most likely an unpleasant contretemps he experienced as a tourist in Málaga with Hemingway, with the fictional character of Robert Jordan, with Theodore Roosevelt (as Rough Rider), and with the Beatles via the allusion to their 1965 hit "Ticket to Ride." Viewing the bullring from the ramparts of the Gibralfaro, TR scoffs at bullfighting, but Hemingway suggests, "Maybe that's what they have instead of God" (51).

Near the end of the book Maria parts company with Ernest, ending their relationship "quick / as a bullet" and reminding him, "If you have to turn the page / the ending was wrong!" (105). In the final two poems Hemingway first visits the Escorial, where Philip II (1527–1598) welcomes him and Ernest likens writers to kings: "The veins we mine are the only ore / worth a sentence. Yet who else loses sleep / over the marrow behind the architecture?" (107). He then visits the Valley of the Fallen, a monument to the dead from the Spanish Civil War. Here he feels the presence of Franco, who had the site constructed by prisoners of war, but Franco is not there:

> I walked further and further into the mountain
> but I couldn't find him among the statues.
> Maybe he'd decided not to interrogate the myth [110].

Of course, both the film and these poems, most of them driven through with lines and characters drawn from Hemingway's prose, invite just such an interrogation.

My own poems on Hemingway, seventeen of which were published as *The Hemingway Poems* (2001), a chapbook that won the Pecan Grove Press competition held in 2000, contribute something to this reconstructive mode, though they rarely approach the seriousness of David Ray's or David Reiter's appreciations and appropriations. Perhaps inevitably how one decides to appropriate or reconfigure Ernest Hemingway in one's writing, whether as fiction, script, screenplay, or poetry, has everything to do with one's personality, one's outlook on life. I'm inclined to comedy, so at times my send-ups or parodies of Hemingway may come across as irreverent as that of Marty Beckerman in *The Heming Way* (Chapter Six), but like Beckerman and most other appropriators, my writing proceeds from admiration for the work, from no small respect for the man, and from considerable curiosity about the legends and myths, some self-perpetuated and some not.

"What would Hemingway think about this?" I've asked myself this question on finishing this or that poem, one I've also asked myself with respect to the texts I've dealt with in this book. Certainly I would not describe my poems as "dark and deconstructive," as Jarret Keene objected in his review of David Ray's book. Hemingway could be, and so far as I can tell often was, an affable and convivial guy. We have numerous photographs of Hemingway smiling broadly, obviously laughing. Old friends have remarked in documentary films how Ernest could brighten up a room the moment he walked in. We have the evidence of his own fondness for parody in the novella *The Torrents of Spring* (1926). Yet Beckerman prefaces his book with a negative passage on that subject taken from A.E. Hotchner's *Papa Hemingway:* "The parody is the last refuge of the frustrated writer. [...] The greater the work of literature, the easier the parody. The step up from parodies is writing on the wall above the urinal" (70). So with full awareness of those caveats and feeling akin to the lawyer who has himself for a client, I will proceed with a few observations on my own efforts.

The poem "Altercation" was initially published in the spring 1997 issue of *Hemingway Review*. It revisits the infamous brawl with renowned poet Wallace Stevens on February 19, 1936, which Jeffrey Meyers connects with "The Short Happy Life of Francis Macomber" (274). My main sources, in addition to Ernest's letter to Sara Murphy dated February 27, 1936, were James R. Mellow's account in *Hemingway: A Life Without Consequences* (466–467) and Peter Brazeau's *Parts of a World: Wallace Stevens Remembered* (96–99). Apparently the cause was an insulting remark made by the inebriated poet in the presence of the novelist's sister Ursula, who was upset and reported the incident to her brother. Ernest, then thirty-six years old, confronted Stevens outside after the party and knocked the sixty-year-old poet into a puddle a few times before Stevens, who was a sizable man himself and had also boxed as an amateur, connected with Hemingway's jaw and broke his own hand in the process. Six years later Stevens invited Hemingway to lecture on poetry at Princeton, so apparently the fences were mended.

For a truly negative take on the episode, see act one, scene three, of Ben Pleasants' play, *The Hemingway / Dos Passos Wars* (Chapter Eight). In my version of the fracas, told from Stevens' viewpoint, the poet is careful to keep the news from his teetotaler wife, Elsie, and the reader probably gets the impression that Stevens, Hemingway, and Judge Powell were actually drinking together: "He and the judge and Hem fishing and drinking / at Long Key, pretending to be good ol' boys."[52] (Judge Arthur G. Powell of Atlanta has been credited with giving Stevens the memorable title of one of his less memorable poems, "No Possum, No Sop, No Taters.") I imagine Hemingway throwing a "roundhouse right winging in from somewhere / out in the Gulf of Mexico" and knocking Stevens "staggering flat on his derrière" (Stevens was fond of spicing up his poems with French words and phrases). The poet counters with "a wild punch / drawn from some radio broadcast of Jack Dempsey / cracking into the author's jaw," but "what cracks / is his own hand." The poem ends with Stevens conceding, "Hemingway had the makings of a fine poet." As Ezra Pound wrote about eighty years ago in his *ABC of Reading*, "Gloom and solemnity are entirely out of place in even the most rigorous study of an art originally intended to make glad the heart of man."[53] I think the same applies not just to criticism, but to that art itself.

Another of my published contributions to the evolving canon of Hemingway-in-poetry is an altogether imaginary reconstruction entitled "Hemingway in Africa: The Untold Story," which first appeared in a special Hemingway centennial issue of the *North Dakota Quarterly*. What prompted this little poem was simply my reading in Michael Reynolds' *Hemingway: The 1930s* of the tally of his bag while on safari in Africa in 1933, figures which I report faithfully, up to a point, in the opening lines:

> During his first trip to the Serengeti
> Hemingway killed more than thirty
> wild animals, including three lions,
> and one uncelebrated parakeet [10].

In this poem the reconstruction is quite liberal with the facts. The parakeet turns out to have belonged to "the only woman he ever met / but never wrote or talked about," and I assume she must have betrayed him in some way. One afternoon, therefore, "buoyed on Beefeater's," he pops open the cage and the bird flies out. The true Hemingway buff might object that Papa tended to prefer Gordon's when it came to gin, but I decided to give my poetic license free rein here for the sake of alliteration. I assume later in the poem that she "must have been beautiful," maybe even "more gorgeous than The Kraut herself." I am assuming the true aficionado will recognize The Kraut as Marlene Dietrich, whom he met on his return trip from Africa. Finally, I pilfer the "shockingly big-bored .505 Gibbs" (phrasing included) from "The Short Happy Life of Francis Macomber" so that Papa can "blow that parakeet to smithereens."

My poems on Hemingway, now numbering more than two dozen, several of which have appeared in print since the publication of the chapbook, are what Susan Beegel in her blurb described as efforts at catching Hemingway's "doubleness," his "simultaneous status in our culture as an icon of swaggering boorishness and of amazing grace." They are far removed from the sometimes eloquent elegies and laments already mentioned. My poems trade on the myths and legends as well as the "true gen," on Hemingway's writings, and on a "fabulous" disrespect for history, and they proceed from my curiosity about all of that. In "Hemingway Meets Evangeline," for example, the two "characters" get together romantically, but they "get in the way of each other," "grow sullen," and eventually "they have, and they have not" (9). Most poems, after all, begin in fact and go elsewhere. In three "Virtual Hemingway" poems distributed throughout the chapbook, the reader is addressed as "you" and is invited to "be" Ernest Hemingway at various periods of his career.

Some traditionalists might object that the genre of poetry by definition runs counter to the currents of popular culture. To some extent the general view of the poet is still haunted by the pronouncements of poets like Percy Bysshe Shelley to the effect that "he is the author to others of the highest wisdom, pleasure, virtue, and glory" and "the greatest poets have been men of the most spotless virtue, of the most consummate prudence."[54] Given his own irregular life, Shelley promptly proceeds to exculpate himself from any "calumny," for, after all, he will conclude at the end of his essay that "poets are the unacknowledged legislators of the World" (297). Some poets and lovers of poetry will agree with Shelley that "poetry is indeed something divine" (293). That vision may fade, but it will not likely vanish.

We do live in a different era, though. We live, for instance, in the age of "slam-poetry." The project of most poets over the past several decades has been to make their work accessible, to promote the reading of poetry in the public schools and in public places. Essays like Joseph Epstein's "Who Killed Poetry?" in *Commentary* (August 1988) and Dana Gioia's "Can Poetry Matter?" in the *Atlantic Monthly* (May 1991) turned many heads. "However healthy poetry may appear within its professional subculture," Gioia wrote, "it has lost this larger audience, who represent poetry's bridge to the general culture."[55] Dana concluded his essay by offering half a dozen "modest proposals" for how that lost audience might be recovered. At the risk of trivializing what Dylan Thomas celebrated as his "craft or sullen art" ("sullen" in the sense of "solitary"), anyone who reads poems today must be aware that not all poetry requires gravitas. Many today look to the observations of such poets as Montana's Richard Hugo (1923–1982), who reminded us that "words love the ridiculous areas of our minds" and "you have to be silly to write poems at all."[56] William Stafford, who famously described a poem as "a serious joke" or "a truth that has learned jujitsu," would surely concur.[57] The poems in which Ernest Hemingway makes an appearance represent the gamut from serious to capricious, from tragedy to comedy.

Conclusion

Critics and scholars who write solely on Ernest Hemingway's writing may be said to possess a distinct advantage over those who write about his life and legends. After all, in the final analysis, the writing is what it's all about, and what Ernest Hemingway was all about. Moreover, those who produce commentaries on the texts are dealing with substance, matter, form. There it is, in all its tangible thereness: "Cat in the Rain." Whatever this or that reader derives from the story, the story itself has certifiable existence. Of course, as countless reams of critical commentary demonstrate, it's not as simple as that, for as any serious writer or reader would agree, that's where the fun begins.

Not least among the challenges for the biographer or memoirist is distinguishing details of the life from those of the various legends or myths, particularly from those that Hemingway himself helped to propagate. For example, as I observed in the opening chapter, the question as to whether he carried a wounded Italian soldier to safety near Fossalta despite his own badly injured leg, thereby justifying some claim to heroism, remains unresolved and perhaps unresolvable. The same may be said of some of his exploits (or shenanigans) during the civil war in Spain and in Cuba and Europe during World War II.

For the writers of biographical fiction, however, for the appropriators, whether they intend to celebrate or to denigrate the life or writings might be argued to be subordinate to their primary intention: to produce a good novel or story, play, film or poem. What they acquire by introducing Hemingway into their writing is a certain kind of validation. Some appropriators in each of the genres take apparent pride in sharply critiquing the life and legend or in outright diminishing it, although a majority offer some sort of homage in their writings. But surely all are motivated to a certain extent by the halo effect. They have enlisted in Hemingway's army, and, while they may have their doubts about the worthiness or reliability of their commanding officer, they do take some pride in having served under him.

I have an uncle who served under General Patton during World War II (my uncle was wounded at the Battle of the Bulge), and he considers Patton to have been a son of a bitch. Nevertheless, Uncle Stony takes a sort of perverse pride in having been personally chewed out on one or two occasions by one of the war's most controversial generals. If he were to write a novel in which Patton appeared as a character, I wonder how Uncle Stony would configure or reconfigure him? Perhaps the term "halo effect" does not fit exactly when it comes to an army private's connections with Patton or with the appropriator's connections with Hemingway. But the appropriators surely recognize that connecting their narrative to Hemingway will potentially provide some enhancement, even as they must be aware of the risks. It may well be, for instance, that Americans, more than those of any other nationality, tend toward admiration of the moderate in personalities and characters, even tending toward the bland. Vivid sports figures like Mohammed Ali or Howard Cosell acquired broad popularity, but for every person who was attracted to their ostensible charisma, there were perhaps ten who, like my father, were alienated.

My father was fifteen years old when *A Farewell to Arms* was published in 1929, but he wasn't reading Hemingway back then. A solid Midwesterner, an Ohioan, he was reading Booth Tarkington, whose humorous stories and sketches published as *Penrod* appeared the year he was born. My own baptism by Hemingway came the way many, if not most, readers of my generation encountered his fiction—a high school English class in which *The Old Man and the Sea* was foisted upon us. As it happens, I still have that hardback copy with the blue cover featuring a huge marlin leaping from the sea beside old Santiago. It's a "Special Student's Edition" and it includes such valuable marginal notes as "first time Santiago really talks of the sea." I was working as an assistant at the Cocoa Public Library in Florida when news came that Hemingway had killed himself the day before (July 2, 1961), and I remember checking out copies of his books as fast as our patrons could get to them. The last to go, as I recall for some reason, was *Death in the Afternoon*. Perhaps under the circumstances the title was too ominous.

Looking back over the many texts I've touched upon in this book, I propose now to suggest my personal favorites. I am basing these admittedly subjective selections on three criteria I have employed along the way: (1) preference to texts (mostly novels) in which Hemingway acquires considerable attention as a character as opposed to those in which he makes only a cameo appearance, although I do have my favorites among those; (2) preference to texts in which writers present Hemingway thoughtfully, whether as a character or as perceived through an "obsessed" character, and this does *not* necessarily mean "favorably"; (3) preference to texts in which writers introduce characters, in many cases a protagonist who is not Hemingway, and develop them with some complexity and particular appeal in their own right.

Leonardo Padura Fuentes' *Adiós Hemingway* (2005), Paula McLain's *The Paris Wife* (2011), and Clancy Carlile's *The Paris Pilgrims* (1999) constitute a triad of works in which the authors make serious efforts to come to grips with Hemingway both as a person and as a writer, but they differ wildly from each other. Carlile treats Hemingway harshly, but his grasp of the 1920s Paris scene with its vibrant personalities is impressive. McLain limits her scope and subordinates Ernest to Hadley in her narrative, but she offers a nicely balanced portrayal of their life together, and her sympathetic characterization of Ernest appears consistent with what we know of Hadley's views later in her life. Fuentes offers us a portrait of the aging, troubled Hemingway blended with a mystery that features a protagonist whose attitude toward the writer remains conflicted throughout. Moreover, more successfully than most of the writers of biographical fiction, Fuentes credibly depicts Hemingway's inner struggle with his writing.

Joe Haldeman's *The Hemingway Hoax* (1990) and William McCranor Henderson's *I Killed Hemingway* (1993) best represent the treatment of Hemingway by writers of speculative fiction, the former in science fiction and the latter in what I might describe as fantasy-intrigue. Henderson engages the tension between literal and emotional truth, which borders on what I might call "virtual" truth as he probes the limits of memoir. Simultaneously he inquires into the American literary scene, the conflict between "literature" and "best sellers," and particularly into the Hemingway "business." "Americans like to be tickled," Pappy Markham tells the protagonist of the novel, whose interest in LifeForms amounts to a send-up of New Age therapy. Americans "like to believe what feels good. Doesn't make any difference whether it's *true* or not" (254). In some respects, Haldeman's intricate little novel involving fraud and deception on the quotidian side and a threatening Omniverse on the sci-fi side also investigates the limits of reality and the nature of fictional truth.

Dan Simmons' *The Crook Factory* (1999) and Karl Alexander's *Papa and Fidel* (1989) represent Papa-in-action, as do a number of the other appropriations. Alexander's novel stands out among most of the others because he deploys an aging Hemingway as his protagonist, though one suspects that Papa at sixty would not likely have been able to endure the hardships he undergoes here. Some credit goes to an intriguing premise that might qualify the novel as "speculative," depending on how one decides to read it, and some credit, too, for Alexander's portrayal of Castro. Simmons' novel, set in Cuba during World War II, combines all the intrigue of the classic tale of espionage with fast-paced action in a well-contrived historical context and setting. He devoted considerable research to his portrayal of Hemingway as a co-protagonist. Most of the appropriators, understandably, I think, develop protagonists that interest them, and presumably engage their readers as well. But in the process, Hemingway is subordinated, sometimes almost shunted aside, sometimes rather rudely. Credit goes here, then, to this pair of notable exceptions.

MacDonald Harris's *Hemingway's Suitcase* (1990), Gerhard Köpf's *Papa's Suitcase* (1994), and Michael Palin's *Hemingway's Chair* (1995) constitute a triad of novels concerning what I call Hemingway-obsessed characters. Fraud is involved in Harris's novel as in Henderson's *I Killed Hemingway* and Haldeman's *The Hemingway Hoax*, and in all three the circumstances concern the lost manuscripts. But while the other two novels enter the realms of speculative fiction, as I see it, Harris plays it straight, the result being an ingenious "web of intrigue and mystery," to employ phrasing from the front cover flap. Again, as in Henderson's novel, we encounter conflict between appearance and reality and some digs at the academic and publishing enterprises. Köpf's and Palin's novels are a kick: amidst the mystery, intrigue, and action-adventure, we encounter two novels in which the comical protagonists, neither of whom come across as buffoons as I read them, are delightful.

Among the many cameo appropriations, none has affected me as powerfully as Milan Kundera's in *Immortality* (1990). Among the other novels, for sheer fun it's hard to beat Keith Abbott's *Rhino Ritz* (1979), and I still laugh out loud at places in Lauri Anderson's story "A Short Unhappy Life" in *Hunting Hemingway's Trout* (1990). Hemingway idolaters might wish to steer clear of Marty Beckerman's biting satire, *The Heming Way* (2012), but I confess to getting a kick out of it. My wife would probably say that it appeals to my inner junior high school boy. Some recognition for precedence might be owing to Henry Morgan's *Toro* (1977) and Michael Murphy's *Hemingsteen* (1978), though they might not be credited with having had any apparent influence on the stream of biographical fictions dealing with Papa, and to Vincent Cosgrove's *The Hemingway Papers* (1983), which received more notice and might have helped prompt the tidal wave of the 1990s. Also recommended are Craig McDonald's *Toros and Torsos* (2008) and Michael Atkinson's *Hemingway Deadlights* (2009).

Among the plays, I prefer Frederic Hunter's *The Hemingway Play* (1975, 2009) and Michael Hollinger's *An Empty Plate in the Café du Grand Boeuf*

(1994, 2003), although Brian Gordon Sinclair's one-man performances appear attractive. Theatrical appropriations are divided between single-actor plays and those with a full cast, and my choices are complicated by the fact that printed texts are not available for many of these. Finally, in addition to the books by David Ray, *Hemingway: A Desperate Life* (2011), and David P. Reiter, *Hemingway in Spain* (2nd ed., 2007), I would particularly recommend five poems, all of which were dealt with in Chapter Nine: Archibald MacLeish's "Poet," Yevgeny Yevtushenko's "Meeting in Copenhagen" (or "Encounter"), Gaylord Brewer's "Brief Hemingway Encounter," John Logan's "In Papa's House, Son's Room," and Campbell McGrath's "Hemingway Dines on Boiled Shrimp and Beer."

At this writing, I am struck by two very different, recent examples of how completely Ernest Hemingway has been absorbed into American culture. This morning's paper ran a Dear Abby column written by Jeanne Phillips, daughter of Pauline, who founded the column in 1956. The lead item is entitled, "Husband Enlists Hemingway in Campaign to Have an Affair." The husband, planning to indulge himself in some extramarital affairs, informed his wife of ten years that he should be permitted to do so because he knew his wife found Hemingway "interesting," and Hemingway was known to have had affairs. Ms. Phillips informed the wife, "Unsure in Washington," that Hem was also known for drinking and big game hunting, and she asked whether her husband was contemplating similar adventures. She also suggested marriage counseling.

On the evening of January 22, 2014, *The Colbert Report* devoted half an hour on the Comedy Channel to a mock book club session on *A Farewell to Arms*. The logo was reminiscent of Oprah's Book Club. The setting featured Stephen Colbert in hunting regalia, indulging in various alcoholic beverages and seated in a den complete with trophy heads and a painting of Colbert himself posed to resemble Papa in the famous Karsh photograph. Guests for the show included Pulitzer Prize–winning novelist Michael Chabon, a Hemingway admirer, whose most recent novel was *Telegraph Avenue* (2012), and Mariel Hemingway, Ernest's granddaughter (Jack's daughter), whose book *Running with Nature*, written with her partner, Bobby Williams, was published in 2013. Both Chabon and Mariel offered some serious appreciation of the man and his writing, and both Colbert and Mariel claimed they received an A on book reports they wrote at about age twelve on *The Old Man and the Sea*. Although the focus was largely fixed on light, playful comedy, both guests offered serious observations on Hemingway's importance as a writer and on his understanding of male-female relations.

About the time the proofs for this book arrived, a former student told me of the upcoming screening (May of 2015) of Orson Welles' last film, *The Other Side of the Wind*, principal photography for which was completed by 1976. The experimental film features John Huston (1906–1987) in the role of aging movie director Jake Hannaford, who dies in a possibly suicidal car crash right after his seventieth birthday party. As described in an extensive Wikipedia entry, Welles (1915–1985) modeled the main character on Ernest Hemingway, apparently taking the first name from Jake Barnes and reflecting the surname with the initial letter H and a rhythm matching the rhythm of *Hemingway*.[1] Welles claimed to have gotten the idea for the film shortly after Hemingway's suicide in 1961. Jake Hannaford had been struggling to make a comeback, presumably reflecting Hemingway's efforts. Apparently laced with homosexual males and heavy with innuendo, the film appears most unlikely to have appealed to Ernest.

Four or five minutes of a half-hour interview with Welles conducted with Michael Parkinson in 1974 is currently available on YouTube.[2] Welles was originally intended to narrate the film *The Spanish Earth*, but Hemingway ended up performing in that capacity. In the interview Welles speaks of coming to blows with Hem in the screening room, sparring in the dark, as it were, but ending up collapsing in laughter. He tells Parkinson Hem was "a very close friend of mine," but theirs was "a very strange relationship." "I made fun of him," Welles says, "and nobody ever made fun of Hemingway." He observes, as others have, that "there's hardly a word of humor in a Hemingway book," but "when he relaxed he was riotously funny." The men shared a love of bullfighting and a close personal relationship with Marlene Dietrich. Coincidentally, Welles could have scored fairly well in a Hemingway lookalike contest.

Surely Hemingway himself must speak the last words in this book, albeit in properly appropriated form. Early in *Coffee with Hemingway* (2007), Kirk Curnutt's delightful "fictional dialogue based on biographical facts," a querulous Papa, in an imaginary meeting at the Closerie des Lilas, complains about readers who "only care about personality." But the interviewer counters his "fiction is so transparently autobiographical that readers are naturally intrigued by the life that inspired it."[3] Hemingway responds here, as elsewhere in the small book, in phrases similar to those we find strewn throughout his letters and other prose: "The only writing that's any good is what you make up, out of your imagination." Writing for *Hemingway Review*, Timothy Galow described the small book in Duncan Baird Publishers' Coffee With series ("coffee with" everyone from Plato to Groucho) as a "thoroughly engaging" treatment that "does not sacrifice complex insights to the challenges of the form."⁴ "Nothing kills the fiction faster than psychoanalyzing the writer," Papa informs the interviewer. "Biography besieges a guy—it's invasive and inhibiting" (49). Near the end of the dialogue Papa insists, "*Work*'s the word I want you to walk away with—not personality, not fame, not reputation. [...] The only thing that matters is the work" (132–133).

Chapter Notes

Preface

1. Kirk Curnutt, *Literary Topics: Ernest Hemingway and the Expatriate Modernist Movement*, vol. 2 (Detroit: Gale Group, 2000), 192.
2. Milan Kundera, *Immortality*, tr. Peter Kussi (New York: Harper Perennial, 1992), 334.
3. Wallace Stevens, *The Collected Poems* (New York: Vintage, 1954), 59.

Chapter One

1. Nathan P. Heller, "Hemingway: How the Great American Novelist Became the Literary Equivalent of the Nike Swoosh," posted on slate.com, March 16, 2012, http://www.slate.com/articles/arts/assessment/2012/03/emest_hemingway_how_the_great_american_novelist_became_the_literary_equivalent_of_the_nike_swoosh.html.
2. Carlos Baker, *Ernest Hemingway: A Life Story* (New York: Macmillan, 1969), vii.
3. Debra A. Moddelmog, *Reading Desire: In Pursuit of Ernest Hemingway* (Ithaca: Cornell University Press, 1999), 23–24.
4. Ernest Hemingway, *The Complete Poems*, ed. Nicholas Gerogiannis, rev. ed. (Lincoln: University of Nebraska Press, 1992), 45.
5. John Raeburn, *Fame Became of Him: Hemingway as Public Writer* (Bloomington: Indiana University, 1984), 1. Raeburn takes his title from Archibald MacLeish's poem "Years of the Dog" in answer to the question, "What became of him?" (see Chapter Nine).
6. Joli Jenson, "Fandom as Pathology: The Consequences of Characterization," in *The Adoring Audience: Fan Culture and Popular Media*, ed. Lisa A. Lewis (London: Routledge, 1992), 9.
7. Michael Reynolds, "Ernest Hemingway, 1899–1961: A Brief Biography," in *A Historical Guide to Ernest Hemingway*, ed. Linda Wagner-Martin (New York: Oxford University Press, 2000), 15.
8. David M. Earle, *All Man! Hemingway, 1950s Men's Magazines, and the Masculine Persona* (Kent, OH: Kent State University Press, 2009), 23.
9. Ernest Hemingway, *Ernest Hemingway: Selected Letters, 1917–1961*, ed. Carlos Baker (New York: Scribner's, 1981), 22. Cited in the text as *Selected Letters*. This volume would eventually be superseded by the multivolume complete letters, but that event lay several years in the future.
10. Toni Morrison, *Playing in the Dark: Whiteness and the Literary Imagination* (Cambridge: Harvard University Press, 1992), 85.
11. Terry Eagleton, *Literary Theory: An Introduction* (Minneapolis: University of Minnesota, 1983), 197.
12. T.S. Eliot, "The Metaphysical Poets," in *Norton Anthology of English Literature*, vol. F, 8th ed., ed. Stephen Greenblatt (New York: W.W. Norton, 2006), 2330.
13. Ernest Hemingway, *The Letters of Ernest Hemingway*, vol. 1, 1907–1922, ed. Sandra Spanier and Robert W. Trogdon (Cambridge: University Press, 2011), 112 (cited in the text as *Letters*).
14. George McClellan, *The Mexican War Diary and Correspondence of George B. McClellan,* ed. Thomas W. Cutrer (Baton Rouge: Louisiana State University Press, 2009), 18.

15. Michael Reynolds, *The Young Hemingway* (New York: Basil Blackwell, 1986), 35.
16. Robert W. Lewis, "Hemingway in Italy: Making It Up," *Journal of Modern Literature* 9.1 (May 1982), 212.
17. Cynthia Maziarka and Donald Vogel, Jr., eds., *Hemingway at Oak Park High* (Oak Park, IL: Oak Park and River Forest High School, 1993), 117.
18. Ernest Hemingway, *The Complete Short Stories*, Finca Vigía ed. (New York: Scribner, 1987), 111. All references to the short stories pertain to this edition.
19. Paul Smith, *A Reader's Guide to the Short Stories of Ernest Hemingway* (Boston: G.K. Hall, 1989), 60–70.
20. Frederick Voss, *Picturing Hemingway: A Writer in His Time* (New Haven: Yale University Press, 1999), 45.
21. A.E. Hotchner, *Hemingway and His World* (New York: Vendome, 1989), 9.
22. Ernest Hemingway, *Under Kilimanjaro*, ed. Robert W. Lewis and Robert E. Fleming (Kent, OH: Kent State University Press, 2005), 113.
23. Christopher Cook Gilmore, *Hemingway* (New York: St. Martin's, 1988), 28.
24. Craig McDonald, *Toros and Torsos* (Madison, WI: Bleak House Books, 2008), front cover flap.
25. Deborah Kaplan, "Construction of Fan Fiction Character Through Narrative," in Karen Hellekson and Kristina Busse, eds., *Fan Fiction and Fan Communities in the Age of the Internet* (Jefferson, NC: McFarland, 2006), 136.
26. Carl Sandburg, "Chicago," *Complete Poems*, rev. ed. (New York: Harcourt Brace, 1970), 3.

Chapter Two

1. The scrapbooks are now available online through the JFK Library: http://www.jfklibrary.org/About-Us/News-and-Press/Press-Releases/Hemingway-Scrapbooks-Made-Available-to-Public-for-First-Time.aspx.
2. Madelaine Hemingway Miller, *Ernie: Hemingway's Sister "Sunny" Remembers* (New York: Crown, 1975), 28.
3. Marcelline Hemingway Sanford, *At the Hemingways*, centennial ed. (Moscow: University of Idaho, 1999), 128. This is an expanded version of the 1961 edition, with foreword by Michael Reynolds.
4. Although *this* Michael Murphy was born in 1930, as was the founder of the Esalen Institute, officials in Big Sur, where the institute was founded in 1962, informed me that *their* Michael Murphy, whose published work includes several novels, most notably *Golf in the Kingdom* (1971) and its sequel, *The Kingdom of Shivas Irons* (1997), has never heard of *Hemingsteen* (St. Louis: Autolycus, 1978).
5. Kenneth Lynn, *Hemingway* (New York: Fawcett Columbine, 1987), 27.
6. Carlos Baker, *Ernest Hemingway: A Life Story* (New York: Macmillan, 1969), 6.
7. Susan F. Beegel, "Eye and Heart: Hemingway's Education as a Naturalist," in *A Historical Guide to Ernest Hemingway*, ed. Linda Wagner-Martin (New York: Oxford University Press, 2000), 70.
8. Paul Hendrickson quotes an omitted excerpt from Marcelline's memoir in Morris Buske's 2002 essay, "Hemingway Faces God," attesting to Clarence Hemingway's use of the strap (quote is found in *Hemingway's Boat* (New York: Vintage, 2012), 383.
9. Stephen Koch, *The Breaking Point: Hemingway, Dos Passos, and the Murder of José Robles* (New York: Counterpoint, 2005), 224.
10. Joseph Blotner, *Faulkner: A Biography*, vol. 1 (New York: Random House, 1974), 211.
11. Townsend Ludington, *John Dos Passos: A Twentieth Century Odyssey* (New York: E.P. Dutton, 1980), 231.
12. Gioia Diliberto, *Paris Without End: The True Story of Hemingway's First Wife* (New York: Harper Perennial, 2011), xv (originally published by Ticknor & Fields in 1992 as *Hadley*).
13. Paula MacLain, *The Paris Wife* (New York: Ballantine, 2011), 53.
14. Robert O. Stephens, ed., *Ernest Hemingway: The Critical Reception* (New York: Burt Franklin, 1977), 168–170; 178; 174–176; 179–180 (cited hereafter as *Critical Reception*).
15. Denis Brian, *The True Gen: An Intimate Portrait of Ernest Hemingway by Those Who Knew Him* (New York: Delta, 1988), 127.
16. Mary Welsh Hemingway, *How It Was* (New York: Alfred A. Knopf, 1976), 221.
17. Bernice Kert, *The Hemingway Women* (New York: Norton, 1986), 486.
18. Ernest Hemingway, *To Have and Have Not* (New York: Scribner Classic/Collier, 1987), 138.
19. John Dos Passos, *Chosen Country* (Boston: Houghton Mifflin, 1951), 58, 60.
20. http://www.pulpfest.com/pulp-history/.
21. Arthur Mizener, review of *Chosen Coun-*

try, in *New York Times Book Review* (December 2, 1951), 7.

22. Charles J. Rolo, "Reader's Choice," *Atlantic* 189 (January 1952), 88.

23. John Dos Passos, *The Best Times: An Informal Memoir* (New York: New American Library, 1966), 143.

24. Joli Jenson, "Fandom as Pathology: The Consequences of Characterization," in Lisa A. Lewis, ed., *The Adoring Audience: Fan Culture and Popular Media* (London: Routledge, 1992), 27.

25. Burness E. Moore, "Narcissism," in *Psychoanalysis: The Major Concepts*, ed. Burness E. Moore and Bernard D. Fine (New Haven: Yale University Press, 1995), 247.

26. Peter Griffin, *Along with Youth: Hemingway, the Early Years* (New York: Oxford University Press, 1985), 22.

27. Reuben Fine, *Narcissism, the Self, and Society* (New York: Columbia University, 1986), 67.

28. *Diagnostic and Statistical Manual of Mental Disorders*, 4th ed. (Washington, DC: American Psychiatric Association, 1994), 658, 661.

29. One may purchase a 22" × 28" "Hemingway Mirror" from Amanti Art for about $140. Caravaggio's oil painting of Narcissus (ca. 1595), measures about 43" × 36" and is on display at the National Gallery in Rome.

30. E.B. White, "Across the Street and into the Grill," *New Yorker* 26 (October 14, 1950), 28.

Chapter Three

1. Hemingway's grandson Sean (via Pauline) presided over the restored edition, deleting passages that were unflattering to his mother; Hemingway's granddaughter Mariel (via Hadley), owns the TV and film rights to the book, http://articles.latimes.com/2011/mar/19/entertainment/la-et-0319-book-20110319.

2. Henry S. Villard and James Nagel, *Hemingway in Love and War: The Lost Diary of Agnes von Kurowsky* (New York: Hyperion, 1989), 163.

3. John Fiske, "The Cultural Economy of Fandom," in *The Adoring Audience: Fan Culture and Popular Media* (London: Routledge, 1992), 31.

4. Paul Hendrickson, in *Hemingway's Boat* (2011), devotes considerable attention to Samuelson and his book *With Hemingway: A Year in Key West and Cuba*, published posthumously in 1984.

5. Ernest Hemingway, *By-line: Ernest Hemingway*, ed. William White (New York: Scribner's, 1967), 218.

6. http://www.nytimes.com/1988/04/25/arts/review-television-stacy-keach-as-ernest-hemingway.html?pagewanted=print&src=pm.

7. Paula McLain, *The Paris Wife* (New York: Ballantine, 2011), ix; Ernest Hemingway, *A Moveable Feast* (New York: Touchstone, 1996), 211.

8. Janet Maslin, review of *The Paris Wife* in *New York Times*, February 27, 2011, http://nytimes.com/2011/02/28/books/28book.html?_r=0.

9. Brenda Wineapple, review of *The Paris Wife* in *New York Times Book Review*, March 18, 2011. http://www.nytimes.com/2011/03/20/books/review/book-review-the-paris-wife-by-paula-mclain.html?_r=0.

10. Susan Salter Reynolds, Review of *The Paris Wife*. *Los Angeles Times*. March 19, 2011. http://articles.latimes.com/2011/mar/19/entertainment/la-et-0319-book-20110319.

11. Gail Sinclair, "An Interview with Paula McLain, author of *The Paris Wife*," *Hemingway Review* 32.1 (Fall 2012), 119.

12. http://readingisfashionable.com/2011/06/author-interview-with-paula-mclain.html.

13. http://articles.washingtonpost.com/2011-04-17/entertainment/35231454_1_paris-wife-ernest-hallmark-version.

14. http://www.washingtontimes.com/news/2011/may/20/book-review-the-paris-wife/.

15. http://www.writersdigest.com/writing-articles/by-writing-goal/improve-my-writing/mclain-1.

16. http://www.randomhouse.com/rhpg/features/paula_mclain/author/.

17. Ernest Hemingway, *A Farewell to Arms* (New York: Scribner, 1929, 2006), 115.

18. John Donne, *The Complete Poetry and Selected Prose of John Donne*, ed. Charles M. Coffin (New York: Modern Library, 2001), 16.

19. J. Gerald Kennedy, "Hemingway, Hadley, and Paris: The Persistence of Desire," in *The Cambridge Companion to Ernest Hemingway*, ed. Scott Donaldson (New York: Cambridge, 1996), 199.

20. Michael Reynolds, *Hemingway: The Paris Years* (New York: W.W. Norton, 1989), 3.

21. William White, "For the Collector," *Hemingway Review* 4.1 (Fall 1984), 58.

22. Vincent Cosgrove, *The Hemingway Papers* (New York: Bantam Books, 1983).
23. Clancy Carlile, *The Paris Pilgrims* (New York: Carroll & Graf, 1999), 1.
24. Christopher Lehman-Haupt, "Books of the Times: Fleshing Out Hemingway with Literary License," *New York Times*, July 7, 1999, http://www.nytimes.com/1999/07/07/books/books-of-the-times-fleshing-out-hemingway-with-literary-license.html.
25. Scott Donaldson, *By Force of Will: The Life and Art of Ernest Hemingway* (New York: Viking, 1977), 182.
26. In a letter F. Scott Fitzgerald dated about December 24, 1925, Hemingway claims "Out of Season" is the only story from *In Our Time* "in which Hadley figures" and that it was triggered by "a row" he had with her (*Selected Letters*, 180; *Letters* 2, p. 455). He adds that the pathetic guide was fired and subsequently hanged himself, but he left that out of the story.
27. Tony Hays, *Murder in the Latin Quarter* (Bell Buckle, TN: Iris Press, 1993).
28. Craig McDonald, *Toros and Torsos* (Madison, WI: Bleak House, 2008), 31.
29. Craig McDonald, *One True Sentence* (New York: Minotaur Books, 2011), 227.
30. Ernest Hemingway, *The Sun Also Rises* (New York: Scribner, 1926, 1954), 30.
31. http://therapsheet.blogspot.com/2011/02/story-behind-story-one-true-sentence-by.html.
32. Walter Satterthwait, *Masquerade* (New York: St. Martin's, 1998), 194.
33. Howard Engel, *Murder in Montparnasse* (Woodstock, NY: Overlook, 1992).
34. http://www.thestar.com/news/2007/02/21/order_of_canada_recipients.html. Australian mystery writer Kerry Greenwood has a novel by the same title published in 2004 (a Phryne Fisher mystery), which features Australian soldiers in the Paris of 1918 and Australia during the 1920s. Engel's novel might also be confused with Cara Black's recent (2013), mystery, *Murder Below Montparnasse*. Apparently Montparnasse was a prime site for homicide.
35. Ernest Hemingway, *Hemingway: The Homecoming* (New York: W.W. Norton, 1992), 220.

Chapter Four

1. Scott McIver, *Hemingway's Key West* (Sarasota, FL: Pineapple, 1993), 30.
2. Philip Roth, *The Great American Novel* (New York: Holt, Rinehart and Winston, 1973), 24.
3. Alfredo José Estrada, *Welcome to Havana, Señor Hemingway* (Miami: Vista, 2004). Citations refer to the 47-chapter edition.
4. Steve Paul, review of *Welcome to Havana, Señor Hemingway*, *Hemingway Review* 24.1 (Fall 2004), 110.
5. Alfredo José Estrada, *Havana: Autobiography of a City* (New York: Palgrave Macmillan, 2008), 5.
6. http://www.ask.com/wiki/Gelett_Burgess?qsrc=3044.
7. Erika Robuck, *Hemingway's Girl* (New York: New American Library, 2012), n.p.
8. Eric Weiner, "Why Women Read More Than Men," September 5, 2007, http://www.npr.org/templates/story/story.php?storyId=14175229.
9. http://www.theguardian.com/books/booksblog/2013/oct/08/literary-fiction-improves-empathy-study.
10. Milton Wolff, *Another Hill* (Urbana: University of Illinois Press, 1994), 57.
11. James R. Mellow, *Hemingway: A Life Without Consequences* (New York: Houghton Mifflin, 1992), 487.
12. Donald Pizer, "The Hemingway-Dos Passos Relationship," *Journal of Modern Literature* 13.1 (March 1986), 117–118.
13. Robert E. Fleming, "The Libel of Dos Passos in *To Have and Have Not*," *Modern Literature* 15.4 (Spring 1989), 601.
14. Stephen Koch, *The Breaking Point: Hemingway, Dos Passos, and the Murder of José Robles* (New York: Counterpoint, 2005), 77.
15. http://www.youtube.com/watch?v=dufYM6f9pOg.
16. http://therapsheet.blogspot.com/2008/10/running-with-bulls.html.
17. Craig McDonald, *Toros and Torsos* (Madison, WI: Bleak House Books, 2008), 124.
18. Michael Atkinson, *Hemingway Cutthroat* (New York: Minotaur Books, 2010).
19. Michael Atkinson, *Hemingway Deadlights* (New York: Minotaur, 2009), back cover.
20. John Dos Passos, *Century's Ebb* (Boston: Gambit, 1975), vii-ix.
21. Ernest Hemingway, *The Fifth Column* (New York: Bantam, 1970), 93.
22. John Dos Passos, *The Fourteenth Chronicle: Letters and Diaries of John Dos Passos*, ed. Townsend Ludington (Boston: Gambit, 1973), 597.

23. Donald Pitzer, "The Hemingway-Dos Passos Relationship," *Journal of Modern Literature* 13.1 (March 1986), 117.
24. Jeffrey Meyers, *Hemingway: A Biography* (New York: Harper & Row, 1985), 310.
25. John Dos Passos, "Old Hem Was a Sport," *Sports Illustrated* 20 (June 29, 1964), 58.
26. Patrick Kendrick, *Papa's Problem* (Jacksonville, FL: Bluewater, 2008), 2.
27. Paul Hendrickson offers substantial comments on Pauline along with very sympathetic reflections on Gregory in *Hemingway's Boat* (2011).

Chapter Five

1. Lillian Ross, *Portrait of Hemingway* (New York: Avon, 1961), 51 (includes a fifteen-page introduction).
2. Michael Reynolds, *Hemingway: The Final Years* (New York: W.W. Norton, 1999), 229.
3. Ernest Hemingway, *By-line: Ernest Hemingway*, ed. William White (New York: Scribner's, 1967), 471.
4. Henry Morgan, *Toro* (New York: Tower, 1977), 61.
5. Dan Simmons, *The Crook Factory* (New York: HarperTorch, 1999), 4.
6. http://movies.nytimes.com/movie/461495/The-Crook-Factory/overview.
7. http://www.ask.com/wiki/Dan_Simmons?o=2800&qsrc=999. In his author's note, Simmons claims that the "incredible story" of Hemingway's Crook Factory is "95 percent true" (559). If one discounts the 95 percent in the novel that is obviously fiction, there is some validity to his assertion, as Reynolds' biography attests.
8. http://www.publishersweekly.com/978-0-380-97368-2.
9. Michael Rogers, review of *The Crook Factory*, *Library Journal* 124.1 (January 1, 1999), 158.
10. http://www.goodreads.com/book/show/11535.The_Crook_Factory.
11. http://www.sfsite.com/05a/cro56.htm.
12. http://www2.citypaper.com/arts/review.asp?rid=5217.
13. Frank M. Laurence, *Hemingway and the Movies* (New York: Da Capo, 1981), 14.
14. Mark Winegardner, *The Veracruz Blues* (New York: Viking, 1996), 4.
15. William Kennedy, *Changó's Beads and Two-Tone Shoes* (New York: Viking, 2011), 8.

16. Ernest Hemingway, *Death in the Afternoon* (New York: Scribner, 1932, 1960), 192.
17. Michael Atkinson, *Hemingway Deadlights* (New York: Minotaur, 2009), 1.
18. Karl Alexander, *Papa and Fidel* (New York: Tom Doherty, 1989), n.p.
19. http://www.karlalexander.net/index.htm.
20. http://www.plutojournals.com/leonardo-padura-fuentes-cubas-man-of-letters/.
21. Teresa Prados-Terreira, "Translator's Introduction" (excerpt from *Adiós Hemingway*) *Raritan* 24.1 (Fall 2004), 159.
22. Leonardo Padura Fuentes, *Adiós Hemingway*, tr. John King (Edinburgh: Canongate, 2005), viii.
23. Ernest Hemingway, *The Old Man and the Sea* (New York: Scribner Classic, 1952, 1986), 103.
24. Jon Day, Review of *Mrs. Hemingway*. *The Telegraph* (February 18, 2014). http://www.telegraph.co.uk/culture/books/fictionreviews/10638451/Mrs-Hemingway-by-Naomi-Wood-review.html; Kate Braithwaite, "Talking *Mrs Hemingway* with Naomi Wood." http://historicalnovelsociety.org/talking-mrs-hemingway-with-naomi-wood/.
25. Lara Feigl, Review of *Mrs. Hemingway*. *The Guardian* (February 20, 2014). http://www.theguardian.com/books/2014/feb/20/mrs-hemingway-naomi-wood-review/print.
26. Naomi Wood, *Mrs. Hemingway* (New York: Penguin, 2014) front matter.
27. Bill Buford, "Foreword," *Travels with Myself and Another*, Martha Gellhorn (New York: Tarcher/Penguin, 2001) xv.
28. Bernice Kert, *The Hemingway Women* (New York: W.W. Norton, 1983) 487.
29. http://www.nytimes.com/2008/04/20/books/review/Wineapple-t.html?_r=0.
30. https://www.kenyonreview.org/writer/david-s-reynolds/.
31. Joyce Carol Oates, *Wild Nights!* (New York: Ecco, 2008), 201.
32. Joyce Carol Oates, "Reading as a Writer: The Artist as Craftsman," in *The Faith of a Writer: Life Craft, Art* (New York: Ecco, 2003), 121.

Chapter Six

1. http://books.google.co.uk/books?id=00gEAAAAMBAJ&pg=RA1PA3&dq=%22ray+bradbury%22&hl=en&ei=XWiOTZiQDMKyhAfIreS7Dg&sa=X&oi=book_

result&ct=result&resnum=1&ved=0CC4Q6AEwAA#v=onepage&q=%22ray%20bradbury%22&f=false.

2. Ray Bradbury, "The Kilimanjaro Device," in *I Sing the Body Electric* (New York: Knopf, 1969), 4.

3. Among other places, the photograph appears in Boris Vejdovsky and Mariel Hemingway's *Hemingway: A Life in Pictures* (Buffalo, NY: Firefly, 2011), 182.

4. David Mogen, *Ray Bradbury*, Twayne U.S. Authors Series (Boston: G.K. Hall, 1986), 132.

5. Jonathan R. Eller, *Becoming Ray Bradbury* (Urbana: University of Illinois Press, 2011), 81.

6. William McCranor Henderson, *I Killed Hemingway* (New York: Picador, 1993), 87.

7. Kirk Curnutt, review of *I Killed Hemingway*, *Hemingway Review* 13.1 (Fall 1993), 108.

8. Jeffrey Meyers, ed., *Hemingway* (London: Routledge & Kegan Paul, 1982), 186.

9. Mark Cirino, *Ernest Hemingway: Thought in Action* (Madison: University of Wisconsin, 2012), 4, 9.

10. Craig McDonald, *Print the Legend* (New York: Minotaur, 2010).

11. Lisa Tyler, review of *Print the Legend*, *Hemingway Review* 31.1 (Fall 2011), 134.

12. Roland L. Bessette, *Sunrise at Ketchum: A Biographical Novel of Ernest Hemingway* (CreateSpace, 2009), 322.

13. Milan Kundera, *Immortality*, tr. Peter Kussi (New York: Harper Perennial, 1991), 5.

14. http://www.elephantjournal.com/2009/02/keith-abbot-brilliant-naropa-writing-teacher-writer-calligrapher/.

15. Keith Abbott, *Rhino Ritz* (Berkeley, CA: Blue Wind, 1979), 30.

16. Ernest Hemingway, *The Torrents of Spring* (New York: Scribner's, 1972), 71. The section title also satirizes Madison Grant's study in eugenics, *The Passing of the Great Race*, essentially a study in Nordic racism. Scott Fitzgerald takes a potshot at the book in *The Great Gatsby* when Tom Buchanan promotes a book entitled *The Rise of the Colored Empires*.

17. Charles M. Oliver, review note of *The Hemingway Hoax*, *Hemingway Review* 10.1 (Fall 1990), 75.

18. Joe Haldeman, *The Hemingway Hoax* (New York: William Morrow, 1990).

19. http://www.thehemingwayproject.com/interview-with-joe-haldeman-author-of-the-hemingway-hoax/.

20. Donald E. Morse, "Hoaxing Hemingway: Ernest Hemingway as Character and Presence in Joe Haldeman's *The Hemingway Hoax* (1990)," *Extrapolation* 45.3 (Fall 2004), 229. Morse erroneously locates Hemingway's suicide in Utah rather than in Ketchum, Idaho.

21. Joan Gordon, "Autobiographical Science Fiction and Möbius Strips: Joe Haldeman's *The Hemingway Hoax*," *New York Review of Science Fiction* 4.46 (June 1992), 9.

22. Tom Winton, *Four Days with Hemingway's Ghost* (self-published, 2012), 10.

23. Rick Skwiot, *Key West Story* (Key West: Antaeus Books, 2012), 5.

24. http://www.antaeusbooks.com/antaeus-books-authors/key-west-story/death-in-mexico-rick-skwiot/.

25. In an e-mail note dated August 4, 2013, Marty Beckerman wrote, "I couldn't have written a parody that required so much research if I weren't a Hemingway fan myself. Yeah, I make fun of the public image that he cultivated, but I read thousands of pages of his writing for a reason—because *they're really fucking good*—and recommend that others do the same."

26. http://variety.com/2011/film/news/gotham-group-options-heming-way-1118039465/ Writer Jeff Sneider notes that the book became Amazon.com's bestselling parody over the July 4 weekend in 2011.

27. Jason [John Arne Sæterøy], *The Left Bank Gang* (Seattle: Fantagraphics Books, 2005), 6.

28. Eric Peterson and Ethan Nicolle, *Jesus Christ: In the Name of the Gun*, vol. 1, *The Hollow Cost* (no city indicated: Bad Karma Productions, 2009), n.p.

29. http://www.psychologytoday.com/blog/grand-rounds/201107/did-ernest-hemingway-dabble-in-zombie-tale.

30. http://www.mondaymorningmemo.com/page/thurber-hemingway.

Chapter Seven

1. Allan Conan, *The Hemingway Sabbatical* (Minneapolis: Mid-List, 1996), 1.

2. Thomas A. Marshall, review of *Papa's Suitcase*, *Hemingway Review* 15.1 (Fall 1995), 112.

3. MacDonald Harris, *Hemingway's Suitcase* (New York: Simon & Schuster, 1990), 270.

4. http://www.physics.upenn.edu/~heiney/harris/index.html. This website is

maintained by Philip Heiney, son of the author.
5. Frederic Jameson, *Postmodernism; or, The Cultural Logic of Late Capitalism* (Durham, NC: Duke University, 1991), 16.
6. Diane Gilbert Madsen, *Hunting for Hemingway* (Woodbury, MN: Midnight Ink, 2010), 277.
7. A.E. Hotchner, *Papa Hemingway* (New York: Random House, 1966), 26.
8. Gerhard Köpf, *Papa's Suitcase*, tr. A. Leslie Willson (New York: George Braziller, 1994), 7.
9. http://www.publishersweekly.com/978-0-8076-1342-9.
10. http://www.nytimes.com/2007/03/30/books/30hemi.html?_r=0.
11. http://www.amazon./de/Papas-Koffer-Gerhard-Köpf/dp/363086807X.
12. http://www.kirkusreviews.com/book-review/gerhard-kopf/papas-suitcase.
13. http://www.nytimes.com/books/98/05/24/reviews/980524.524weber.html.
14. http://www.cnn.com/books/reviews/9805/20/index.html.
15. Thomas Hermann, review of *Hemingway's Chair*, *Hemingway Review* 15.1 (Fall 1995), 114.
16. Michael Palin, *Hemingway's Chair* (New York: St. Martin's, 1995), 16.
17. Edmundo Desnoes, *Memories of Underdevelopment*, tr. Al Schaller (Pittsburgh: 2004), 37.
18. Paula Huntley, *The Hemingway Book Club of Kosovo* (New York: Jeremy P. Tarcher/Putnam, 2003), 1.
19. Lisa Tyler, review of *The Hemingway Bookclub of Kosovo*, *Hemingway Review* 23.1 (Fall 2003), 122.
20. Hilary Hemingway and Jeffry P. Lindsay, *Hunting with Hemingway* (New York: Riverhead, 2000), 314.
21. http://www.amazon.com/Hunting-Hemingway-Hilary/dp/productdescription/1565113845/ref=dp_proddesc_0?ie=UTF8&n=283155&s=books.
22. Marc Seals, review of *Hunting with Hemingway*, *Journal of Popular Culture* 37.4 (May 2004), 745.
23. Personal e-mail correspondence of July 29, 2013: "Often people believe that parts of my book are unadulterated autobiography, but actually the stories are all fiction mixed with elements of real events and journalism."
24. Lauri Anderson, *Hunting Hemingway's Trout* (New York: Atheneum, 1990), 12.

25. Paul Smith, *A Reader's Guide to the Short Stories of Ernest Hemingway* (Boston: G.K. Hall, 1989), 333–334.
26. http://www.ernesthemingwaycollection.com/Products-Services/Default.aspx. Arturo Fuente cigars start with the tasty Hemingway Short Story, Maduro or Cameroon wrapper, at $5.60. Beneath the clutter of my desk rests a 4-ounce Darsee and David's Hemingway jar candle that will "fill your home or office with the sophisticated spicy mixture of woods and musk." On a more respectful plane, in 1989 the USPS issued a commemorative stamp (#2518, 25¢), featuring the Karsh photograph.
27. Stephanie Cohen, "Faulkner for Sale." *Wall Street Journal*, July 26, 2013, pp. D1–D2.
28. Matthew J. Bruccoli, ed., with Judith S. Baughman, *Hemingway and the Mechanism of Fame* (Columbia: University of South Carolina, 2006), xix.

Chapter Eight

1. http://www.backstage.com/review/ny-theater/off-off-broadway/clothes-for-a-summer-hotel/.
2. Tom Wright, "The Hemingway Playwright," *Harvard Crimson*. August 1, 1975, http://www.thecrimson.com/article/1975/8/1/the-hemingway-playwright-pbibn-the-usually/.
3. Frederic Hunter, *The Hemingway Play* (Santa Barbara: Nebbadoon Press, 2009), n.p.
4. Leonard J. Leff, *Hemingway and His Conspirators: Hollywood, Scribners, and the Making of American Celebrity Culture* (Lanham, MD: Rowman & Littlefield, 1997, 1999), xii, xvi, xvii.
5. Charles M. Oliver, *Ernest Hemingway A to Z* (New York: Checkmate Books [Facts on File], 1999), 92.
6. Richard Allan Davison, "Hemingway and the Theater," *North Dakota Quarterly* 70.4 (Fall 2003), 175.
7. Philip Young, review of *The Fifth Column*, *New York Times* September 21, 1969, http://www.nytimes.com/books/99/07/04/specials/hemingway-fifth.html.
8. Peter L. Hays, *Ernest Hemingway* (New York: Continuum, 1990), 80.
9. Raymond Conlon, "*The Fifth Column*: A Political Morality Play," *Hemingway Review* 6.2 (Spring 1987), 11.
10. John Raeburn, "Hemingway on Stage: *The Fifth Column*, Politics, and Biography," *Hemingway Review* 18.1 (Fall 1998), 7.

11. Ernest Hemingway, *The Fifth Column and Four Stories of the Spanish Civil War* (New York: Bantam, 1970), 132–134.
12. Noël Valis, "Hemingway's *The Fifth Column*, Fifthcolumnism, and the Spanish Civil War," *Hemingway Review* 28.1 (Fall 2008), 19, 20.
13. Verna Kale, review of *The Fifth Column* (a play by Ernest Hemingway, directed by Jonathan Bank), Mint Theater, March 26–May 18, 2008, *Hemingway Review* 27.2 (Spring 2008), 133.
14. Ben Pleasants, *The Hemingway/Dos Passos Wars* (Los Angeles: Engadine Books, 1997), 32.
15. Wallace Stevens, *The Collected Poems* (New York: Vintage, 1982), 173.
16. Scott Collins, "'Dos Passos Wars' is Good, Campy Fun," *Los Angeles Times*, April 7, 1995, http://articles.latimes.com/1995-04-07/entertainment/ca-51922_1_dos-passos.
17. Philip Brandes, "A Literary 'Hemingway' Tells of Egotism, Hypocrisy," *Los Angeles Times*, September 2, 1999, http://articles.latimes.com/1999/sep/02/entertainment/ca-5863.
18. Richard Christiansen, "Peppard Does a Piercing Hemingway," *Chicago Tribune*, August 3, 1988, http://articles.chicagotribune.com/keyword/george-peppard/recent/2.
19. John de Groot, *"Papa": A Play Based on the Legendary Lives of Ernest Hemingway* (Boise: Hemingway Western Studies Center, 1984).
20. Marilyn Beck, "George Peppard Plays 'Papa' with a Passion," *Chicago Tribune*, May 5, 1988, http://articles.chicagotribune.com/1988-05-05/features/8803140512_1_george-peppard-garry-shandling-boris-and-natasha.
21. Robert J. Kirkpatrick, theater review of *Papa*, *Hemingway Review* 16.1 (Fall 1996), 121.
22. L.E. (Erv) Johnson, *E. Hemingway*, Boise State University Theatre, September 29–30, 1984, VHS tape, http://scholarworks.boisestate.edu/cgi/viewcontent.cgi?article=1096&context=theatre_programs.
23. Lawrence Christon, "Stage Review: One Man's 'Hemingway': He's Still a Stranger," *Los Angeles Times*, October 11, 1985. http://articles.latimes.com/1985-10-11/entertainment/ca-17351_1_ernest-hemingway.
24. Jack Zink, "'Papa': A One-man Play Deals with a Singular Man," *Palm Beach (FL) Sun-Sentinel*, September 27, 1987, http://articles.sun-sentinel.com/1987-09-27/features/8703160126_1_papa-character-ernest-hemingway.
25. Richard Connema, "Adrian Sparks Gives a Gung Ho Performance in John de Groot's *Papa*," http://www.talkinbroadway.com/regional/sanfran/s799.html.
26. Anthony Adler, Review of Papa. August 11, 1988, http://www.chicagoreader.com/chicago/papa/Content?oid=872604.
27. http://www.einstein-hemingway-shows.com/hemingway.html.
28. http://www.youtube.com/watch?v=HfmnGXCYbPU.
29. http://www.youtube.com/watch?v=tKFrjhNi1TI.
30. Lynn Trenning, "Actor Brings 'Papa' to Life," *Charlotte Observer*, November 8, 2003, http://hemingwayonstage.com/reviewchob.htm.
31. Tennessee Williams, "Clothes for a Summer Hotel," *Theatre of Tennessee Williams*, vol. 8 (New York: New Directions, 1992), 260.
32. Albert J. Devlin, *Conversations with Tennessee Williams* (Jackson: University Press of Mississippi, 1986), 222, 245.
33. William Prosser, *The Late Plays of Tennessee Williams* (Lanham, MD: Scarecrow Press, 2009), 185.
34. George W. Crandell, ed., *The Critical Response to Tennessee Williams* (Westport, CT: Greenwood Press, 1996), 273.
35. http://www.nytheatre.com/Preview/james-rutherford-the-importance-of-being-ernest-hemingway.
36. John Hutt, "The Macho Fops of 'The Importance of Being Ernest Hemingway." out.com August 27, 2013, http://www.out.com/entertainment/popnography/2013/08/27/oscar-wilde-importance-being-ernest-hemingway-m34.
37. http://www.t2conline.com/the-importance-of-being-ernest-hemingway-would-have-hemingway-digging-out-of-his-grave/.
38. http://en.wikipedia.org/wiki/Michael_Hollinger.
39. John Moore, "'Empty Plate' a Feast of Wordplay, Hemingway," *Denver Post*, April 28, 2011, http://www.denverpost.com/ci_17942838.
40. Michael Hollinger, *An Empty Plate at the Café du Grand Boeuf* (New York: Dramatists Play Service, 2003), 47.
41. http://www.talkinbroadway.com/regional/philly/phil61.html.
42. Robert Hofler, "Review: 'An Empty Plate in the Café du Grand Boeuf,'" *Variety*, March 8, 2000, http://www.variety.com/2000/legit/reviews/am-empty-plate-in-the-cafe-du-....
43. Jenn Goddu, review of *An Empty Plate*

at the *Café du Grand Boeuf*, *Chicago Reader*, October 4, 2001, http://www.chicagoreader.com/chicago/an-empty-plate-in-the-cafe-du-grand-boeuf/Content?oid=906619.

44. Charles McNulty, review of *An Empty Plate in the Café du Grand Boeuf*, *Los Angeles Times*, June 2, 2009, http://latimesblogs.latimes.com/culturemonster/2009/06/review-an-empty-plate-in-the-caf%C3%A9-du-grand-bouef-at-laguna-playhouse.html.

45. http://www.broadwayworld.com/tampa/sacramento/article/BWW-Reviews-AN-EMPTY-PLATE-AT-THE-CAFE-DUE-GRAND-BOEUF-a-Bountiful-Feast–20130217.

46. David Haglund, "Hollywood Hemingway: How the Movies Mangled Great Fiction," *Slate Magazine*, April 13, 2007, http://www.slate.com/articles/arts/dvdextras/2007/04/hollywood_hemingway.html.

47. http://cooperhemingway.com/.

48. Gioia Diliberto, "A Hemingway Story, Just as Fictional," *New York Times*, January 26, 1997, http://www.nytimes.com/books/99/07/04/specials/hemingway-diliberto.html.

49. Henry S. Villard and James Nagel, *Hemingway in Love and War: The Lost Diary of Agnes Von Kurowsky* (New York: Hyperion, 1989), 163.

50. Michael Wilmington, "'In Love and War': A Skewed Tale About Hemingway," *Chicago Tribune*, January 24, 1997, http://articles.chicagotribune.com/1997-01-24/entertainment/9701240223_1_agnes-domenico-caracciolo-bell-tolls.

51. Holly E. Ordway, film review of *Hemingway* (DVD), March 29, 2002, http://www.dvdtalk.com/reviews/3608/hemingway-miniseries/.

52. Alan Bunce, "In Pursuit of a Legend: Stacy's Keach's Role as Hemingway," *Christian Science Monitor*, April 26, 1988, http://www.csmonitor.com/1988/0426/lhem.html/%28page%29/2.

53. Roger Ebert, film review of *The Moderns*, May 6, 1988, http://www.rogerebert.com/reviews/the-moderns-1988.

54. Vincent Canby, film review of *The Moderns*, *New York Times*, April 15, 1988, http://www.nytimes.com/movie/review?res=940DE3DE1E3EF936A25757C0A96E948260.

55. Rita Kempley, film review of *The Moderns*, *Washington Post*, April 30, 1988, http://www.washingtonpost.com/wp-srv/style/longterm/movies/videos/themodernsnrkempley_a0ca12.htm.

56. Mark Olsen, "*Midnight in Paris* vs. *The Moderns*," laweekly.com, January 12, 2012, http://www.laweekly.com/2012-01-12/film-tv/midnight-in-paris-vs-the-moderns/full/.

57. Mike Hale, "Literary Lions Stalk Each Other Through Wars and Across the World," *New York Times*, May 27, 2012, http://www.nytimes.com/2012/05/28/arts/television/hemingway-gellhorn-has-its-premiere-on-hbo.html.

58. James Wolcott, "No Time for Tulips: On *Hemingway and Gellhorn*," *Vanity Fair*, September 6, 2013, http://www.vanityfair.com/online/wolcott/2012/05/No-Time-for-Tulips-On-Hemingway-Gellhorn.

59. Robert Lloyd, "'Hemingway and Gellhorn's' Third-Rate Romance," *Los Angeles Times*, May 28, 2012, http://articles.latimes.com/2012/may/28/entertainment/la-et-hemingway-gellhorn-20120528.

60. Scott Donaldson, *By Force of Will: The Life and Art of Ernest Hemingway* (New York: Viking, 1977), xi.

61. William Faulkner, *Sanctuary: and Requiem for a Nun* (New York: Signet, 1954, 1961), 229.

Chapter Nine

1. In order to avoid the excessive costs of acquiring permission to quote even a few lines of many of the poems referred to in this chapter, it has often been necessary for me simply to summarize the contents. I am most grateful to a few poets and publishers who have granted me permission to quote from the poems, and I regret the necessity of having to eliminate passages that would substantiate or illustrate my observations. The copyright rules of "fair use" remain unequally applied when it comes to quotation of poetry.

2. Ernest Hemingway, *Complete Poems*, ed. Nicholas Gerogiannis, rev. ed. (Lincoln: University of Nebraska Press, 1992), 107.

3. James D. Brasch and Joseph Sigman, "Hemingway's Library: Some Volumes of Poetry," *College Literature* 7.3 (Fall 1980), 282.

4. Verna Kale, "Hemingway's Poetry and the Paris Apprenticeship," *Hemingway Review* 26.2 (Spring 2007), 58–59.

5. Donald Junkins, "Hemingway's Contribution to American Poetry," *Hemingway Review* 4.2 (Spring 1985), 18.

6. Joan Didion, "Last Words," *New Yorker* 74.34 (November 9, 1998), 74–80.

7. William Stafford, *Writing the Australian Crawl: Views on the Writer's Vocation* (Ann Arbor: University of Michigan Press, 1978), 3.

8. Peter Griffin, *Along with Youth: Hemingway, the Early Years* (New York: Oxford University Press, 1985), 152.

9. Ezra Pound, *The Cantos* (New York: New Directions, 1972), 72.

10. Ogden Nash, "Roll On, Thou Deep and Dark Blue Copy Writer—Roll!," in *Versus* (Boston: Little, Brown, 1949), 80.

11. E.B. White, "The Law of the Jungle," *New Yorker* (April 14, 1934), 31.

12. Archibald MacLeish, *Collected Poems, 1917–1982* (Boston: Houghton Mifflin, 1985), 427.

13. Archibald MacLeish, *A Continuing Journey* (Boston: Houghton Mifflin, 1968), 307.

14. Basil Payne, "An Answer to Allegory," in *Love in the Afternoon* (Dublin: Gill and Macmillan, 1971), 35.

15. Adrian C. Louis, "The Hemingway Syndrome," in *Songs from the Earth on Turtle's Back*, ed. Joseph Bruchac (Greenfield Center, NY: Greenfield Review, 1983), 146.

16. Ai, "The Resurrection of Elvis Presley," in *Fate* (Boston: Houghton Mifflin, 1991), 34.

17. Gerald Locklin, *Hemingway Colloquium: The Poet Goes to Cuba* (Palm Springs: Event Horizon, 1999), 2.

18. Richard Eberhart, "Key West," in *Collected Poems, 1930 to 1986* (New York: Oxford University Press, 1988), 396.

19. Philip Schultz, "The Hemingway House in Key West," in *Deep Within the Ravine* (New York: Viking, 1984), 43.

20. Robert Dana, "Key West: Looking for Hemingway," in *Starting Out for the Difficult World* (New York: Harper and Row, 1987), 59.

21. Martin Espada, "The Man Who Beat Hemingway," *Clockwatch Review* 10.1, 2 (1995–96): 4–5, http://sun.iwu.edu/~jplath/10no1-2poems.html#Espada, reprinted in *Motion: American Sports Poems*, ed. Noah Blaustein (Iowa City: University of Iowa, 2001).

22. John Logan, "Papa's House, Son's Room," in *Collected Poems* (Brockport, NY: BOA Editions, 1989), 421.

23. Vicki Feaver, "Hemingway's Hat," *New Yorker* 72 (December 23–30, 1996), 108.

24. Jim Barnes, "Looking for Hemingway's Ghost at the Crillon," in *Paris* (Champaign: University of Illinois Press, 1997), 15.

25. John Updike, "Meditation on a News Item," in *Collected Poems, 1953–1993* (New York: Alfred A. Knopf, 1993), 311.

26. Archibald MacLeish, "Hemingway," in *Collected Poems, 1917–1982* (Boston: Houghton Mifflin, 1985), 482.

27. Scott Donaldson, *Archibald MacLeish: An American Life* (New York: Houghton Mifflin, 1992), 463.

28. Abdul Wahab Al-Bayati, "To Ernest Hemingway," *Modern Poetry of the Arab World*, Tr. and ed. Abdullah al-Udhari (New York: Penguin, 1986), 38.

29. Thomas Merton, "An Elegy for Ernest Hemingway," *Selected Poems*, enlarged ed. (New York: New Directions, 1967), 122.

30. John Berryman, "Dream Song #235," in *His Toy, His Dream, His Rest: 308 Dream Songs* (New York: Farrar, Straus, Giroux, 1968), 164.

31. Paul Ramsey, "Elegy for Ernest Hemingway," *Hemingway Notes* 1 (Spring 1971), 16.

32. Charles Bukowski, *Septuagenarian Stew: Stories and Poems* (Santa Rosa: Black Sparrow, 1995), 214.

33. David Wagoner, "At the Hemingway Memorial," in *Collected Poems, 1956–1976* (Bloomington: Indiana University, 1978), 212.

34. Lloyd Arnold, *Hemingway: High on the Wild* (New York: Grosset and Dunlap, 1977), 162.

35. John Koethe, "E.H.," September 20, 2013, http://www.poets.org/viewmedia.php/prmMID/23697.

36. Campbell McGrath, "Hemingway Dines on Boiled Shrimp and Beer," *Paris Review* 33 (Summer 1991), 243.

37. Charles Bukowski, "Hemingway's Shadow," *Wormwood Review* 110/111 (1988), 61.

38. Gaylord Brewer, *Charles Bukowski* (Boston: Twayne, 1997), 6–8.

39. Gaylord Brewer, "Brief Hemingway Encounter," in *Devilfish* (Los Angeles: Red Hen, 1999), 72.

40. Gaylord Brewer, "The Hemingway Look-alike Society Meets Bimini Bay Developers," in *Barbaric Mercies* (Los Angeles: Red Hen, 2003), 25.

41. Cyril Dabydeen, "Hemingway," in *Poetry of Men's Lives: An International Anthology*, ed. Fred Moramarco and Al Zalynas (Athens: University of Georgia, 2004), 338.

42. Lowell Mick White, "I Bought Hemingway's Ghost a Drink," in *The Weight of Edition: An Anthology of Texas Poetry*, ed. Randall Watson (Houston: Mutabilis Press, 2007), 253.

43. Raymond Carver, "Poem for Hemingway and W.C. Williams," in *Fires: Essays, Poems, Stories* (New York: Vintage, 1989), 114.

44. Adam Meyer, *Raymond Carver* (Bos-

ton: Twayne, 1995), 168. For observations on Hemingway's influence on Carver's writing, see Carol Sklenicka, *Raymond Carver: A Writer's Life* (New York: Scribner, 2009).

45. Paul Mariani, *William Carlos Williams: A New World Naked* (New York: McGraw-Hill, 1982), 237.

46. http://www.lively-arts.com/books/2012/03/hemingway.htm.

47. David Ray, *Hemingway: A Desperate Life* (Shawnee, KS: Whirlybird, 2011), 14.

48. Jarret Keene, "Picking on Papa," *Tucson Weekly*, October 20, 2011, http://www.tucsonweekly.com/tucson/picking-on-papa/Content?oid=3168626.

49. Norberto Fuentes, *Hemingway in Cuba* (Secaucus, NY: Lyle Stuart, 1984), 52.

50. http://www.ipoz.biz/Titles/HIS.html.

51. David Reiter, *Hemingway in Spain*, 2nd ed. (Brisbane, Australia: Interactive Press, 2007), 3.

52. Ron McFarland, *The Hemingway Poems* (San Antonio: Pecan Grove, 2001), 11.

53. Ezra Pound, *ABC of Reading* (New York: New Directions, 1934, 1960), 13.

54. Percy Bysshe Shelley, "A Defence of Poetry," in *Shelley's Prose*, ed. David Lee Clark (Albuquerque: University of New Mexico, 1954), 295.

55. Dana Gioia, "Can Poetry Matter?," in *Can Poetry Matter?* (St. Paul: Graywolf, 1992), 19.

56. Richard Hugo, *The Triggering Town: Lectures and Essays on Poetry and Writing* (New York: Norton, 1979), 19, 10.

57. William Stafford, *Writing the Australian Crawl: Views on the Writer's Vocation* (Ann Arbor: University of Michigan Press, 1978), 3.

Conclusion

1. http://en.wikipedia.org/wiki/The_Other_Side_of_the_Wind

2. https://www.youtube.com/watch?v=6dAGcorF1Vo. The entire interview is also available on YouTube as of this date (November 3, 2014).

3. Kirk Curnutt, *Coffee with Hemingway* (London: Duncan Baird, 2007), 45, foreword by John Updike. Curnutt has written more than a dozen books, including two novels, and is chair of the English department at Troy University in Montgomery, Alabama.

4. Timothy Galow, review of *Coffee with Hemingway*, *Hemingway Review* 27.2 (Spring 2008), 141.

Works Consulted

Primary Sources

Ernest Hemingway and Family or Personal Memoirs

Brian, Denis. *The True Gen: An Intimate Portrait of Hemingway by Those Who Knew Him*. New York: Delta, 1988 (Interviews with such persons as Hadley Hemingway Mowrer, Buck Lanham, A.E. Hotchner, Archibald MacLeish, Michael Strater, Leicester Hemingway, Jack (Bumby) Hemingway, and many others including several critics and biographers).

Hemingway, Ernest. *Across the River and Into the Trees*. New York: Scribner, 1950, 1996.

———. *By-line: Ernest Hemingway*. Edited by William White. New York: Scribner, 1967.

———. *The Complete Poems*. Edited by Nicholas Gerogiannis. Rev. ed. Lincoln: University Press of Nebraska, 1992.

———. *The Complete Short Stories of Ernest Hemingway*. Finca Vigía ed. New York: Scribner, 1987 (all references to the short stories pertain to this edition).

———. *Death in the Afternoon*. New York: Scribner, 1932, 1996.

———. *Ernest Hemingway: Selected Letters, 1917–1961*. Edited by Carlos Baker. New York: Scribner, 1981.

———. *A Farewell to Arms*. New York: Scribner, 1929, 2006.

———. *The Fifth Column and Four Stories of the Spanish Civil War*. New York: Bantam, 1970.

———. *For Whom the Bell Tolls*. New York: Scribner, 1940, 1995.

———. *The Garden of Eden*. New York: Scribner, 1986.

———. *Green Hills of Africa*. New York: Scribner, 1935, 1996.

———. *Hemingway at Oak Park High: The High School Writings of Ernest Hemingway*. Introduction by Michael Reynolds. Edited by Cynthia Maziarka and Donald Vogel, Jr. Oak Park, IL: Oak Park and River Forest High School, 1993.

———. *The Letters of Ernest Hemingway, 1923–1925*. Vol. 2. Edited by Sandra Spanier, Albert J. DeFazio III, and Robert W. Trogdon. Cambridge: University Press, 2013 (cited as *Letters* II).

———. *The Letters of Ernest Hemingway, 1907–1922*. Edited by Sandra Spanier and Robert W. Trogdon. Cambridge: University Press, 2011 (cited as *Letters*).

———. *A Moveable Feast*. New York: Touchstone, 1964, 1996. Restored ed. New York: Scribner, 2009.

———. *The Old Man and the Sea*. New York: Scribner, 1952, 1995.

———. *The Sun Also Rises*. New York: Scribner, 1926, 2006.

———. *To Have and Have Not*. New York: Scribner, 1947, 1996.

———. *The Torrents of Spring*. New York: Scribner, 1926, 1998.

———. *True at First Light*. New York: Scribner, 1999.

———. *Under Kilimanjaro*. Kent, OH: Kent State University Press, 2005.

———. "Who Murdered the Vets?" *New Masses*. September 17, 1935: 9–10 (the article, for which Hemingway refused reimbursement, was set in triple-column).

Hemingway, Gregory. *Papa: A Personal Memoir*. Boston: Houghton Mifflin, 1976.

Hemingway, Hilary, and Jeffry P. Lindsay. *Hunting with Hemingway*. New York: Riverhead Books, 2000.
Hemingway, Jack. *Misadventures of a Fly Fisherman: My Life With and Without Papa*. New York: McGraw-Hill, 1986.
Hemingway, John. *Strange Tribe*. Guilford, CT: Lyons, 2007.
Hemingway, Leicester. *My Brother, Ernest Hemingway*. New York: World, 1962.
Hemingway, Lorian. *Walk on Water: A Memoir*. New York: Harvest Books, 1999.
Hemingway, Mary Welsh. *How It Was*. New York: Alfred A. Knopf, 1976.
Hemingway, Valerie. *Running with the Bulls: My Years with the Hemingways*. New York: Ballantine, 2004.
Hotchner, A.E. *Papa Hemingway*. New York: Random House, 1966.
Miller, Madelaine Hemingway. *Ernie: Hemingway's Sister "Sunny" Remembers*. New York: Crown, 1975.
Sanford, Marcelline Hemingway. *At the Hemingways*. Centennial ed., expanded version of the 1961 edition with foreword by Michael Reynolds. Moscow: University of Idaho Press, 1999.

Biographical Fiction, Plays and Poems

Abbott, Keith. *Rhino Ritz*. Berkeley: Blue Wind, 1979.
Ai. "The Resurrection of Elvis Presley." *Fate*. Boston: Houghton Mifflin, 1991.
Al-Bayati, Abdul Wahab. "To Ernest Hemingway." *Modern Poetry of the Arab World*. Translated and edited by Abdullah al–Udhari. New York: Penguin, 1986.
Alexander, Karl. *Papa and Fidel*. New York: Tom Doherty, 1989.
Anderson, Lauri. *Hunting Hemingway's Trout*. New York: Atheneum, 1990.
Atkinson, Michael. *Hemingway Cutthroat*. New York: Minotaur, 2010.
_____. *Hemingway Deadlights*. New York: Minotaur, 2009.
Barnes, Jim. "Looking for Hemingway's Ghost at the Crillon." *Paris*. Champaign: University of Illinois Press, 1997.
Beckerman, Marty. *The Heming Way*. 2nd ed. New York: St. Martin's Griffin, 2012.
Berryman, John. "Dream Song #235." *His Toy, His Dream, His Rest: 308 Dream Songs*. New York: Farrar, Straus, Giroux, 1968.
Bessette, Roland L. *Sunrise at Ketchum: A Biographical Novel of Ernest Hemingway*. CreateSpace, 2009.
Bradbury, Ray. "The Kilimanjaro Device." In *I Sing the Body Electric*. New York: Knopf, 1969.
Brewer, Gaylord. "Brief Hemingway Encounter." In *Devilfish*. Los Angeles: Red Hen, 1999.
_____. "The Hemingway Look-alike Society Meets Bimini Bay Developers." In *Barbaric Mercies* Los Angeles: Red Hen, 2003. 25.
Bukowski, Charles. "The Fighter." In *Septuagenarian Stew: Stories and Poems*. Santa Rosa: Black Sparrow, 1995. 214.
_____. "Hemingway's Shadow." *Wormwood Review* 110/111 (1988): 61–63.
Carlile, Clancy. *The Paris Pilgrims*. New York: Carroll & Graf, 1999.
Carver, Raymond. "Poem for Hemingway and W.C. Williams." In *Fires: Essays, Poems, Stories*. New York: Vintage, 1989.
Conan, Allan. *The Hemingway Sabbatical*. Minneapolis: Mid-List, 1996.
Cosgrove, Vincent. *The Hemingway Papers*. New York: Bantam, 1983.
Curnutt, Kirk. *Coffee with Hemingway*. Foreword by John Updike. Distributed through Starbuck's Coffee Company. London: Duncan Baird, 2007.
Dabydeen, Cyril. "Hemingway." In *Poetry of Men's Lives: An International Anthology*. Edited by Fred Moramarco and Al Zalynas. Athens: University of Georgia, 2004.
Dana, Robert. "Key West: Looking for Hemingway." In *Starting Out for the Difficult World*. New York: Harper and Row, 1987. 59.
de Groot, John. *"Papa": A Play Based on the Legendary Lives of Ernest Hemingway*. Boise: Hemingway Western Studies Center, 1984.
Desnoes, Edmundo. *Memories of Underdevelopment*. Translated by Al Schaller. Pittsburgh, 2004.
Dos Passos, John. *The Best Times: An Informal Memoir*. New York: New American Library, 1966.
_____. *Century's Ebb*. Boston: Gambit, 1975.
_____. *Chosen Country*. Boston: Houghton Mifflin, 1951.
_____. *The Fourteenth Chronicle: Letters and Diaries of John Dos Passos*. Edited by Townsend Ludington. Boston: Gambit, 1973.
_____. *John Dos Passos: The Major Nonfictional Prose*. Edited by Donald Pizer. Detroit: Wayne State University, 1988.
_____. "Old Hem Was a Sport." *Sports Illustrated* 20 (June 29, 1964): 58–67. http://

sportsillustrated.cnn.com/vault/article/magazine/MAG1076075/index.htm
Eberhart, Richard. "Key West." In *Collected Poems, 1930 to 1986*. New York: Oxford University Press, 1988. 396.
Engel, Howard. *Murder in Montparnasse*. Woodstock, NY: Overlook, 1992.
Espada, Martin. "The Man Who Beat Hemingway." *Clockwatch Review* 10.1, 2 (1995–96): 4–5. http://sun.iwu.edu/~jplath/10no1-2poems.html#Espada. Reprinted in *Motion: American Sports Poems*. Edited by Noah Blaustein, Iowa City: University of Iowa, 2001.
Estrada, Alfredo José. *Havana: Autobiography of a City*. New York: Palgrave Macmillan, 2008.
_____. *Welcome to Havana, Señor Hemingway*. Miami: Vista, 2004 (the hardcover 2005 version is published by Planeta Press, also of Miami, Florida).
Feaver, Vicki. "Hemingway's Hat." *New Yorker* 72 (December 23–30, 1996): 108.
Fuentes, Leonardo Padura. *Adiós, Hemingway*. Translated by John King. Edinburgh: Canongate, 2005.
Gilmore, Christopher Cook. *Hemingway*. New York: St. Martin's, 1988.
Granger, Bill. *Hemingway's Notebook*. New York: Warner Books, 1986.
Haldeman, Joe. *The Hemingway Hoax*. New York: William Morrow, 1990.
_____. "The Hemingway Hoax." In *None So Blind*. New York: Avon, 1996.
Harris, MacDonald [Donald Heiney]. *Hemingway's Suitcase*. New York: Simon & Schuster, 1990.
Hays, Tony. *Murder in the Latin Quarter*. Bell Buckle, TN: Iris Press, 1993.
Henderson, William McCranor. *I Killed Hemingway*. New York: Picador, 1993.
Hollinger, Michael. *An Empty Plate at the Café du Grand Boeuf*. New York: Dramatists Play Service, 2003.
Hunter, Frederic. *The Hemingway Play*. Santa Barbara: Nebbadoon Press, 2009.
Huntley, Paula. *The Hemingway Book Club of Kosovo*. New York: Jeremy P. Tarcher/Putnam, 2003.
Jason [John Arne Sæterøy]. *The Left Bank Gang*. Seattle: Fantagraphics Books, 2005.
Johnson, L.E. (Erv). *E. Hemingway*. Boise State University Theatre, September 29–30, 1984. VHS tape. http://scholarworks.boisestate.edu/cgi/viewcontent.cgi?article=1096&context=theatre_programs.

Kendrick, Patrick. *Papa's Problem*. Jacksonville, FL: Bluewater, 2008.
Kennedy, William. *Changó's Beads and Two-Tone Shoes*. New York: Viking, 2011.
Koethe, John. "E.H." September 20, 2013. http://www.poets.org/viewmedia.php/prmMID/23697.
Köpf, Gerhard. *Papa's Suitcase*. Translated by A. Leslie Willson. New York: George Braziller, 1994.
Kundera, Milan. *Immortality*. Translated by Peter Kussi. New York: Harper Perennial, 1991.
Logan, John. "Papa's House, Son's Room." In *Collected Poems*. Brockport, NY: BOA Editions, 1989.
Louis, Adrian C. "The Hemingway Syndrome." *Songs from the Earth on Turtle's Back*. Edited by Joseph Bruchac. Greenfield Center, NY: Greenfield Review, 1983: 146.
MacLeish, Archibald. "Hemingway," "Poet," "Voyage," "Years of the Dog." In *Collected Poems, 1917–1982*. Boston: Houghton Mifflin, 1985.
Madsen, Diane Gilbert. *Hunting for Hemingway*. Woodbury, MN: Midnight Ink, 2010.
McDonald, Craig. *One True Sentence*. New York: Minotaur, 2011.
_____. *Print the Legend*. New York: Minotaur Books, 2010.
_____. *Toros and Torsos*. Madison, WI: Bleak House Books, 2008.
McFarland, Ron. *The Hemingway Poems*. San Antonio: Pecan Grove, 2001.
McGrath, Campbell. "Hemingway Dines on Boiled Shrimp and Beer." *Paris Review* 33 (Summer 1991): 243.
McLain, Paula. *The Paris Wife*. New York: Ballantine, 2011.
Merton, Thomas. "An Elegy for Ernest Hemingway." In *Selected Poems*. Enlarged ed. New York: New Directions, 1967.
Morgan, Henry. *Toro*. New York: Tower Publications, 1977.
Murphy. Michael. *Hemingsteen*. St. Louis: Autolycus, 1978.
Nash, Ogden. "Roll On, Thou Deep and Dark Blue Copy Writer—Roll!" In *Versus*. Boston: Little, Brown, 1949.
Oates, Joyce Carol. "Papa at Ketchum, 1961." In *Wild Nights!* New York: Ecco, 2008.
Palin, Michael. *Hemingway's Chair*. New York: St. Martin's, 1995.
Payne, Basil. "An Answer to Allegory." In *Love in the Afternoon*. Dublin: Gill and Macmillan, 1971.

Peterson, Eric, and Ethan Nicolle. *Jesus Christ: In the Name of the Gun.* Vol. 1, *A Hollow Cost.* Toronto (?), Canada: Bar Karma Productions, 2009.

Pleasants, Ben. *The Hemingway/Dos Passos Wars.* Los Angeles: Engadine Books, 1997.

Ezra Pound, #XVI. In *The Cantos.* New York: New Directions, 1972.

Quick, Elliott B., and James Rutherford. *The Importance of Being Ernest Hemingway.* 2013. No text available. See http://www.out.com/entertainment/popnography/2013/08/27/oscar-wilde-importance-being-ernest-hemingway-m34.

Ramsey, Paul. "Elegy for Ernest Hemingway." *Hemingway Notes* 1 (Spring 1971): 16.

Ray, David. *Hemingway: A Desperate Life.* Shawnee, KS: Whirlybird, 2011.

Reiter, David. *Hemingway in Spain.* 2nd ed. Brisbane, Australia: Interactive Press, 2007.

———. http://www.ipoz.biz/Titles/HIS.html.

Robuck, Erika. *Hemingway's Girl.* New York: New American Library, 2012.

Roth, Philip. *The Great American Novel.* New York: Holt, Rinehart and Winston, 1973.

Satterthwait, Walter. *Masquerade.* New York: St. Martin's, 1998.

Schlozman, Steven. "Did Ernest Hemingway Dabble in a Zombie Tale?" *Psychology Today* (July 14, 2011). http://www.psychologytoday.com/blog/grand-rounds/201107/did-ernest-hemingway-dabble-in-zombie-tale.

Schultz, Philip. "The Hemingway House in Key West." In *Deep Within the Ravine.* New York: Viking, 1984.

Simmons, Dan. *The Crook Factory.* New York: HarperTorch, 1999.

Sinclair, Brian Gordon. Excerpts from *Hemingway on Stage.* http://www.briangordonsinclair.com/hemngwayexcerpts.htm#part1.

———. http://www.youtube.com/watch?v=tKFrjhNi1TI.

Skwiot, Rick. *Key West Story.* Key West: Antaeus Books, 2012.

Thurber, James. "A Visit from Saint Nicholas in the Ernest Hemingway Manner." *New Yorker* (December 24, 1927). http://www.mondaymorningmemo.com/page/thurber-hemingway.

Updike, John. "Meditation on a News Item." In *Collected Poems, 1953–1993.* New York: Alfred A. Knopf, 1993.

Wagoner, David. "At the Hemingway Memorial." In *Collected Poems: 1956–1976.* Bloomington: Indiana University Press, 1978. 212.

White, E.B. "Across the Street and into the Grill." *New Yorker* 26 (14 October 1950), 28.

———. "The Law of the Jungle." *New Yorker* (April 14, 1934), 31.

White, Lowell Mick. "I Bought Hemingway's Ghost a Drink." In *The Weight of Edition: An Anthology of Texas Poetry.* Edited by Randall Watson. Houston: Mutabilis Press, 2007.

Williams, Tennessee. "Clothes for a Summer Hotel." In *The Theatre of Tennessee Williams.* Vol. 8. New York: New Directions, 1992.

Winegardner, Mark. *The Veracruz Blues.* New York: Viking, 1996.

Wolff, Milton. *Another Hill.* Introduction by Cary Nelson. Urbana: University of Illinois Press, 1994.

Yevtushenko, Yevgeny. "Encounter." In *Collected Poems, 1952–1990.* Translated by Albert C. Todd. New York: Henry Holt, 1991.

———. "A Meeting in Copenhagen." In *The Poetry of Yevgeny Yevtushenko, 1953–1965.* Translated by George Reavey. New York: October House, 1965.

Secondary Sources

Adler, Anthony. Review of *Papa.* August 11, 1988. http://www.chicagoreader.com/chicago/papa/Content?oid=872604.

Arnold, Lloyd. *Hemingway: High on the Wild.* New York: Grosset & Dunlap, 1977 (first published as *High on the Wild with Hemingway* by Caxton Press, Caldwell, Idaho [1968]).

Baker, Allie. "Hemingway on Stage: An Interview with Brian Gordon Sinclair." The Hemingway Project. May 2, 2010. http://www.thehemingwayproject.com/hemingway-on-stage-an-interview-with-brian-gordon-sinclair/.

———. "Interview with Joe Haldeman, Author of *The Hemingway Hoax.*" The Hemingway Project. February 25, 2010. http://www.thehemingwayproject.com/interview-with-joe-haldeman-author-of-the-hemingway-hoax/.

Baker, Carlos. *Ernest Hemingway: A Life Story.* New York: Macmillan, 1969.

Beck, Marilyn. "George Peppard Plays 'Papa' with a Passion." *Chicago Tribune,* May 5, 1988. http://articles.chicagotribune.com/1988-05-05/features/8803140512_1_george-peppard-garry-shandling-boris-and-natasha.

Beegel, Susan F. "Eye and Heart: Hemingway's

Education as a Naturalist." In *A Historical Guide to Ernest Hemingway*. Edited by Linda Wagner-Martin. New York: Oxford University Press, 2000.

Blotner, Joseph. *Faulkner: A Biography*. Vol. 1. New York: Random House, 1974.

Brandes, Philip. "A Literary 'Hemingway' Tells of Egotism, Hypocrisy." *Los Angeles Times*, September 2, 1999. http://articles.latimes.com/1999/sep/02/entertainment/ca-5863.

Brasch, James D., and Joseph Sigman. "Hemingway's Library: Some Volumes of Poetry." *College Literature* 7.3 (Fall 1980), 282–288.

Brewer, Gaylord. *Charles Bukowski*. Boston: Twayne, 1997.

Bruccoli, Matthew, ed., with Judith S. Baughman. *Hemingway and the Mechanism of Fame*. Columbia: University of South Carolina, 2006. (This book includes Hemingway's public statements, blurbs and introductions, prefaces, reviews, and product endorsements along with illustrations.)

Bunce, Alan. "In Pursuit of a Legend: Stacy's Keach's Role as Hemingway." *Christian Science Monitor*, April 26, 1988. http://www.csmonitor.com/1988/0426/lhem.html/%28page%29/2.

Burgess, Anthony. *Hemingway and His World*. 1978. New York: Scribner's, 1985.

Canby, Vincent. Film review of *The Moderns*. *New York Times*, April 15, 1988. http://www.nytimes.com/movie/review?res=940DE3DE1E3EF936A25757C0A96E9482 60.

Carr, Virginia Spencer. *Dos Passos: A Life*. New York: Doubleday, 1984.

Christiansen, Richard. "Peppard Does a Piercing Hemingway." *Chicago Tribune*, August 3, 1988. http://articles.chicagotribune.com/keyword/george-peppard/recent/2.

Christon, Lawrence. "Stage Review: One Man's 'Hemingway': He's Still a Stranger." *Los Angeles Times*, October 11, 1985. http://articles.latimes.com/1985-1011/entertainment/ca-17351_1_ernest-hemingway.

_____. "Stage Week: Outrage and Loving It." *Los Angeles Times*, September 29, 1985. http://articles.latimes.com/1985-09-29/entertainment/ca-18548_1_martin-magner.

Cirino, Mark. *Ernest Hemingway: Thought in Action*. Studies in American Thought and Culture. Madison: University of Wisconsin Press, 2012.

Cohen, Stephanie. "Faulkner for Sale." *Wall Street Journal*, July 26, 2013, pp. D1-D2.

Collins, Scott. "'Dos Passos Wars' Is Good, Campy Fun." *Los Angeles Times*, April 7, 1995. http://articles.latimes.com/1995-04-07/entertainment/ca-51922_1_dos-passos.

Comley, Nancy R., and Robert Scholes. *Hemingway's Genders*. New Haven: Yale University Press, 1994.

Conlon, Raymond. "*The Fifth Column*: A Political Morality Play." *Hemingway Review* 6.2 (Spring 1987): 11–16.

Connema, Richard. "Adrian Sparks Gives a Gung Ho Performance in John de Groot's Papa." http://www.talkinbroadway.com/regional/sanfran/s799.html.

Crandell, George W., ed. *The Critical Response to Tennessee Williams*. Westport, CT: Greenwood Press, 1996.

Curnutt, Kirk. *Literary Topics: Ernest Hemingway and the Expatriate Modernist Movement*. Vol. 2. Detroit: Gale Group, 2000.

_____. Review of *I Killed Hemingway*. *Hemingway Review* 13.1 (Fall 1993): 108–112.

Davison, Richard Allan. "Hemingway and the Theater." *North Dakota Quarterly* 70.4 (Fall 2003): 166–177.

Deutsch, Stephanie. Review of *The Paris Wife*. *Washington Times*, May 20, 2011. http://www.washingtontimes.com/news/2011/may/20/book-review-the-paris-wife/.

Devlin, Albert J. *Conversations with Tennessee Williams*. Jackson: University of Mississippi, 1986.

Diagnostic and Statistical Manual of Mental Disorders. 4th ed. Washington, DC: American Psychiatric Association, 1994.

Didion, Joan. "Last Words." *New Yorker* 74.34 (November 9, 1998), 74–80.

Diliberto, Gioia. "A Hemingway Story, Just as Fictional." *New York Times*, January 26, 1997. http://www.nytimes.com/books/99/07/04/specials/hemingway-diliberto.html.

_____. *Paris Without End: The True Story of Hemingway's First Wife*. 1992. New York: Harper, 2011 (originally published by Ticknor & Fields as *Hadley*).

Donaldson, Scott. *Archibald MacLeish: An American Life*. New York: Houghton Mifflin, 1992.

_____. *By Force of Will: The Life and Art of Ernest Hemingway*. New York: Viking, 1977.

Donne, John. *The Complete Poetry and Selected Prose of John Donne*. Edited by Charles M. Coffin. New York: Modern Library, 2001.

Eagleton, Terry. *Literary Theory: An Introduction*. Minneapolis: University of Minnesota, 1983.

Earle, David M. *All Man! Hemingway, 1950s Men's Magazines, and the Masculine Persona. Kent, OH: Kent State University Press, 2009.

Ebert, Roger. Review of *The Moderns*. May 6, 1988. http://www.rogerebert.com/reviews/the-moderns-1988.

Eliot, T.S. "The Metaphysical Poets." In *Norton Anthology of English* Literature. Vol. F, 8th ed. Edited by Stephen Greenblatt. New York: W.W. Norton, 2006.

Eller, Jonathan R. *Becoming Ray Bradbury*. Urbana: University of Illinois Press, 2011.

Faulkner, William. *Sanctuary: and Requiem for a Nun*. New York: Signet, 1954, 1961.

Fenton, Charles A. *The Apprenticeship of Ernest Hemingway: The Early Years*. New York: Farrar, Straus & Cudahy, 1954.

Fine, Reuben. *Narcissism, the Self, and Society*. New York: Columbia University, 1986.

Fiske John. "The Cultural Economy of Fandom." In *The Adoring Audience: Fan Culture and Popular Media*. Edited by Lisa A Lewis. London: Routledge, 1992.

Fleming, Robert E. "The Libel of Dos Passos in To Have and Have Not." *Modern Literature* 15.4 (Spring 1989): 597–601.

Flowers, Fifi. "Author Interview with Paula McLain." Reading Is Fashionable. June 13, 2011. http://readingisfashionable.com/2011/06/author-interview-with-paula-mclain.html.

Fuentes, Norberto. *Hemingway in Cuba*. Secaucus, NY: Lyle Stuart, 1984.

Galow, Timothy. Review of *Coffee with Hemingway*. Hemingway Review 27.2 (Spring 2008): 141–143.

Gioia, Dana. *Can Poetry Matter?* St. Paul: Graywolf, 1992.

Goddu, Jenn. Review of *An Empty Plate at the Café du Grand Boeuf*. Chicago Reader (October 4, 2001). http://www.chicagoreader.com/chicago/an-empty-plate-in-the-cafe-du-grand-boeuf/Content?oid=906619.

Gordon, Joan. "Autobiographical Science Fiction and Möbius Strips: Joe Haldeman's *The Hemingway Hoax*." New York Review of Science Fiction 4.46 (June 1992): 1, 8–9.

Griffin, Peter. *Along with Youth: Hemingway, the Early Years*. New York: Oxford University Press, 1985.

Haglund, David. "Hollywood Hemingway: How the Movies Mangled Great Fiction." Slate (April 13, 2007). http://www.slate.com/articles/arts/dvdextras/2007/04/hollywood_hemingway.html.

Hale, Mike. "Literary Lions Stalk Each Other through Wars and Across the World." New York Times, May 27, 2012. http://www.nytimes.com/2012/05/28/arts/television/hemingway-gellhorn-has-its-premiere-on-hbo.html.

Hassan, Ihab. *The Dismemberment of Orpheus: Toward a Postmodern Literature*. Rev. ed. Madison: University of Wisconsin Press, 1982.

Hays, Peter L. *Ernest Hemingway*. New York: Continuum, 1990.

Hellekson, Karen, and Kristina Busse, eds. *Fan Fiction and Fan Communities in the Age of the Internet*. Jefferson, NC: McFarland, 2006.

Heller, Nathan P. "Hemingway: How the Great American Novelist Became the Literary Equivalent of the Nike Swoosh." Posted on Slate.com, March 16, 2012. http://www.slate.com/articles/arts/assessment/20 12/03/ernest_hemingway_how_the_great_american_novelist_becametheliterary_equivalent_of_the_nikeswoosh.html.

Hendrickson, Paul. *Hemingway's Boat*. New York: Vintage, 2011.

Hermann, Thomas. Review of *Hemingway's Chair*. Hemingway Review 15.1 (Fall 1995): 114–116.

Hofler, Robert. "Review: 'An Empty Plate in the Café du Grand Boeuf.'" *Variety* (March 8, 2000). http://www.variety.com/2000/legit/reviews/am-empty-plate-in-the-cafe-du- ....

Hotchner, A.E. *The Good Life According to Hemingway*. New York: Ecco, 2008.

———. *Hemingway and His World*. New York: Vendome, 1989.

Hugo, Richard. *The Triggering Town: Lectures and Essays on Poetry and Writing*. New York: W.W. Norton, 1979.

Hutt, John. "The Macho Fops of 'The Importance of Being Ernest Hemingway.'" out.com, August 27, 2013. http://www.out.com/entertainment/popnography/2013/08/27/oscar-wilde-importance-being-ernest-hemingway-m34.

Jameson, Fredric. *Postmodernism; or, The Cultural Logic of Late Capitalism*. Durham, NC: Duke University, 1991.

Jenson, Joli. "Fandom as Pathology: The Consequences of Characterization." In *The Adoring Audience: Fan Culture and Popular Media*, ed. Lewis, Lisa A. London: Routledge, 1992, 9–29.

Kale, Verna. Theater review of *The Fifth Column: A Play by Ernest Hemingway*. Directed by Jonathan Bank. Mint Theater.

March 26–May 18, 2008. *Hemingway Review* 27.2 (Spring 2008): 131–134.

Kaplan, Deborah. "Construction of Fan Fiction Character Through Narrative." In *Fan Fiction and Fan Communities in the Age of the Internet*, ed. Hellekson and Busse. Jefferson, NC: McFarland, 2006, 134–152.

Keene, Jarret. "Picking on Papa." *Tucson Weekly*, October 20, 2011. http://www.tucsonweekly.com/tucson/picking-on-papa/Content?oid=3168626.

Kempley, Rita. Film review of *The Moderns*. *Washington Post*, April 30, 1988. http://www.washingtonpost.com/wpsrv/style/longzterm/movies/videos/themodernsnrkempley_a0ca12.htm.

Kennedy, J. Gerald. "Hemingway, Hadley, and Paris: The Persistence of Desire." In *The Cambridge Companion to Ernest Hemingway*. Edited by Scott Donaldson. New York: Cambridge, 1996. 197–220.

Kert, Bernice. *The Hemingway Women*. New York: Norton, 1986.

Kirkpatrick, Robert J. Theater review of *Papa*. *Hemingway Review* 16.1 (Fall 1996): 121–123.

Klems, Brian A. "Historical Spotlight: Paula McLain." *Writer's Digest* (January 20, 2011). http://www.writersdigest.com/writing-articles/by-writing-goal/improve-my-zwriting/mclain-1.

Koch, Stephen. *The Breaking Point: Hemingway, Dos Passos, and the Murder of José Robles*. New York: Counterpoint, 2005.

Lamb, Robert Paul. *Art Matters: Hemingway, Craft, and the Creation of the Modern Short Story*. Baton Rouge: Louisiana State University Press, 2010.

Laurence, Frank M. *Hemingway and the Movies*. New York: Da Capo, 1981.

Leff, Leonard J. *Hemingway and His Conspirators: Hollywood, Scribners, and the Making of American Celebrity Culture*. Lanham, MD: Rowman & Littlefield, 1997, 1999.

Lehman-Haupt, Christopher. "Books of the Times: Fleshing Out Hemingway with Literary License." *New York Times*, July 7, 1999. http://www.nytimes.com/1999/07/07/books/books-of-the-times-fleshing-out-hemingway- with-literary-license.html.

Lewis, Lisa A., ed. *The Adoring Audience: Fan Culture and Popular Media*. London: Routledge, 1992.

Lewis, Robert W. "Hemingway in Italy: Making It Up." *Journal of Modern Literature* 9.1 (May 1982): 209–236.

Lloyd, Robert. "'Hemingway and Gellhorn's' Third-Rate Romance." *Los Angeles Times*, May 28, 2012. http://articles.latimes.com/2012/may/28/entertainment/la-et-hemingway-gellhorn- 20120528.

Ludington, Townsend. *John Dos Passos: A Twentieth Century Odyssey*. New York: E.P. Dutton, 1980.

Lynn, Kenneth. *Hemingway*. New York: Fawcett Columbine, 1987.

MacLeish, Archibald. *A Continuing Journey*. Boston: Houghton Mifflin, 1968.

Manus, Willard. Review of *Hemingway: A Desperate Life*. http://www.lively- arts.com/books/2012/03/hemingway.htm.

Mariani, Paul. *William Carlos Williams: A New World Naked*. New York: McGraw-Hill, 1982.

Marshall, Thomas A. Review of *Papa's Suitcase*. *Hemingway Review* 15.1 (Fall 1995): 111–113.

Maslin, Janet. Review of *The Paris Wife*. *New York Times*, February 27, 2011. http://nytimes.com/2011/02/28/books/28book.html?_r=0.

McClellan, George B. *The Mexican War Diary and Correspondence of George B. McClellan*. Edited by Thomas W. Cutrer. Baton Rouge: Louisiana State University Press, 2009.

McFarland, Ron. "Recent Fictional Takes on the Missing Hemingway Manuscripts." *Journal of Popular Culture* 44.2 (April 2011): 314–332.

_____. "Three Novels on Hemingway in Cuba." *North Dakota Quarterly* 76.1 and 2 (Winter and Spring 2009): 151–160.

_____. "The World's Most Interesting Man." *Midwest Quarterly* 54.4 (Summer 2013): 414–430.

McIver, Stuart B. *Hemingway's Key West*. Sarasota: Pineapple, 1993.

McNulty, Charles. Theater review of *An Empty Plate in the Café du Grand Boeuf*. *Los Angeles Times*, June 2, 2009. http://latimesblogs.latimes.com/culturemonster/2009/06/review-an-empty-plate-in-the-caf%C3%A9-du-grand-bouef-at-laguna-playhouse.html.

Meagher, L.D. Review of *Hemingway's Chair*. CNN-Books, May 20, 1998. http://www.cnn.com/books/reviews/9805/20/index.html.

Mellow, James R. *Hemingway: A Life Without Consequences*. New York: Houghton Mifflin, 1992.

Meyer, Adam. *Raymond Carver*. Twayne U.S. Authors Series. Boston: G.K. Hall, 1995.

Meyers, Jeffrey. *Hemingway: A Biography*. New York: Harper & Row, 1985.

———. ed. *Hemingway: The Critical Heritage*. London: Routledge & Kegan Paul, 1982.

Mitgang, Herbert. *Dangerous Dossiers: Exposing the Secret War Against America's Greatest Authors*. New York: Dutton, 1988.

Mizener, Arthur. Review of *Chosen Country*. *New York Times Book Review*, December 2, 1951.

Moddelmog, Debra A. *Reading Desire: In Pursuit of Ernest Hemingway*. Ithaca: Cornell University Press, 1999.

Mogen, David. *Ray Bradbury*. Twayne's U.S. Authors Series. Boston: G.K. Hall, 1986.

Moore, Burness E. "Narcissism." In *Psychoanalysis: The Major Concepts*. Edited by Burness E. Moore and Bernard D. Fine. New Haven: Yale University Press, 1995.

Moore, John. "'Empty Plate' a Feast of Wordplay, Hemingway." *Denver Post*, April 28, 2011. http://www.denverpost.com/ci_17942838.

Morrison, Toni. *Playing in the Dark: Whiteness and the Literary Imagination*. Cambridge: Harvard University Press, 1992.

Morse, Donald E. "Hoaxing Hemingway: Ernest Hemingway as Character and Presence in Joe Haldeman's *The Hemingway Hoax* (1990)." *Extrapolation* 45.3 (Fall 2004): 227–236.

Oates, Joyce Carol. "Reading as a Writer: The Artist as Craftsman." In *The Faith of a Writer: Life, Craft, Art*. New York: Ecco, 2003.

O'Connor, John. "Review/Television: Stacy Keach as Ernest Hemingway." *New York Times*, April 25, 1988. Arts. http://www.nytimes.com/1988/04/25/arts/review-television-stacy-keach-as-ernest-hemingway.html.

Oliver, Charles M. Review note of *The Hemingway Hoax*. *Hemingway Review* 10.1 (Fall 1990): 74–75.

Olsen, Mark. "*Midnight in Paris* vs. *The Moderns*." laweekly.com, January 12, 2012. http://www.laweekly.com/2012-01-12/film-tv/midnight-in-paris-vs-the-moderns/full/.

Ordway, Holly E. Review of *Hemingway* (DVD). March 29, 2002. http://www.dvdtalk.com/reviews/3608/hemingway-miniseries/.

Paul, Steve. Review of *Welcome to Havana, Señor Hemingway*. *Hemingway Review* 24.1 (Fall 2004): 110–113.

Pizer, Donald. "The Hemingway-Dos Passos Relationship." *Journal of Modern Literature* 13.1 (March 1986): 111–128.

Plath, James. *Historic Photos of Ernest Hemingway*. Nashville, TN: Turner, 2009.

Pound, Ezra. *ABC of Reading*. New York: New Directions, 1934, 1960.

Prados-Terreira, Teresa. "Translator's Introduction" (excerpt from *Adiós Hemingway*). *Raritan* 24.1 (Fall 2004): 159–160.

Prosser, William. *The Late Plays of Tennessee Williams*. Lanham, MD: Scarecrow Press, 2009.

Pustienne, Jean-Pierre. *Ernest Hemingway*. Paris: Fitway, 2005.

Raeburn, John. *Fame Became of Him: Hemingway as Public Writer*. Bloomington: Indiana University Press, 1984.

Rahv, Philip. Review of *Across the River and into the Trees*. *Commentary* 10 (October 1950): 400–402. In *Ernest Hemingway: The Critical Reception*. Edited by Robert O. Stephens. New York: Burt Franklin, 1977.

Reynolds, David S. Review of *Wild Nights!* *Kenyon Review* (Spring 2009). https://www.kenyonreview.org/writer/david-s-reynolds/.

Reynolds, Michael. "Ernest Hemingway, 1899–1961: A Brief Biography." In *A Historical Guide to Ernest Hemingway*. Edited by Linda Wagner-Martin. New York: Oxford University Press, 2000: 15–50.

———. *Hemingway: The Final Years*. New York: W.W. Norton, 1999.

———. *Hemingway: The Homecoming*. New York: W.W. Norton, 1992.

———. *Hemingway: The 1930s*. New York: W.W. Norton, 1997.

———. *Hemingway: The Paris Years*. New York: W.W. Norton, 1989.

———. *The Young Hemingway*. New York: Basil Blackwell, 1986.

Reynolds, Susan Salter. Review of *The Paris Wife*. *Los Angeles Times*, March 19, 2011. http://articles.latimes.com/2011/mar/19/entertainment/la-et-0319-book-20110319.

Rifkind, Donna. Review of *The Paris Wife*. *Washington Post*, April 17, 2011. http://articles.washingtonpost.com/2011-04-17/entertainment/35231454_1_paris-wife-ernest-hallmark-version.

Rogers, Michael. Review of *The Crook Factory*. *Library Journal* 124.1 (January 1, 1999): 158.

Rolo, Charles J. "Reader's Choice." *Atlantic* 189 (January 1952), 87–88.

Ross, Lillian. *Portrait of Hemingway*. New York: Avon, 1961. http://www.newyorker.com/archive/1950/05/13/1950_05_13_036_TNY_CARDS_00022 3553.

Rutherford, James. Self-interview. nytheatre. com, August 27, 2013. http://www.nytheatre.com/Preview/james-rutherford-the-importance-of-being-ernest-hemingway.

Sandburg, Carl. "Chicago." In *Complete Poems*. Rev. ed. New York: Harcourt Brace, 1970.

Seals, Marc. Review of *Hunting with Hemingway*. *Journal of Popular Culture* 37.4 (May 2004): 744–745.

Sinclair, Gail. "An Interview with Paula McLain, Author of *The Paris Wife*." *Hemingway Review* 32.1 (Fall 2012): 119–127.

Smith, Paul. *A Reader's Guide to the Short Stories of Ernest Hemingway*. Boston: G.K. Hall, 1989. (Although after more than two decades this reference work is showing its age, it remains a valuable, if not invaluable, resource.)

Sneider, Jeff. "Gotham Group Options 'Heming Way.'" *Variety* July 5, 2011. http://variety.com/2011/film/news/gotham-group-options-heming-way-1118039465/.

Sokoloff, Alice Hunt. *Hadley: The First Mrs. Hemingway*. New York: Dodd, Mead, 1973.

Spilka, Mark. *Hemingway's Quarrel with Androgyny*. Lincoln: University of Nebraska Press, 1990.

Stafford, William. *Writing the Australian Crawl: Views on the Writer's Vocation*. Ann Arbor: University of Michigan Press, 1978.

Stephens, Robert O., ed. *Ernest Hemingway: The Critical Reception*. New York: Burt Franklin, 1977 (cited as *Critical Reception*).

Stevens, Wallace. *The Collected Poems*. New York: Vintage, 1954, 1982.

Trenning, Lynn. "Actor Bings 'Papa' to Life." *Charlotte Observer*, November 8, 2003. http://hemingwayonstage.com/reviewchob.htm.

Tyler, Lisa. Tyler. Review of *The Hemingway Bookclub of Kosovo*. *Hemingway Review* 23.1 (Fall 2003): 120–123.

———. Review of *Print the Legend*. *Hemingway Review* 31.1 (Fall 2011): 133–135.

Valis, Noël. "Hemingway's *The Fifth Column*, Fifthcolumnism, and the Spanish Civil War." *Hemingway Review* 28.1 (Fall 2008): 19–34.

Vejdovsky, Boris, and Mariel Hemingway. *Hemingway: A Life in Pictures*. Buffalo, NY: Firefly Books, 2011.

Villard, Henry S., and James Nagel. *Hemingway in Love and War: The Lost Diary of Agnes Von Kurowsky*. New York: Hyperion, 1989.

Voss, Frederick. *Picturing Hemingway: A Writer in His Time*. Foreword by Michael Reynolds. New Haven: Yale University Press, 1999.

Weber, Bruce. "Not the Full Monty" (Review of *Hemingway's Chair*). *New York Times*, May 24, 1998. http://www.nytimes.com/books/98/05/24/reviews/980524.524weber.html.

White, William. "For the Collector." *Hemingway Review* 4.1 (Fall 1984): 58.

Wilmington, Michael. "'In Love and War': A Skewed Tale About Hemingway." *Chicago Tribune*, January 24, 1997. http://articles.chicagotribune.com/1997-01-24/entertainment/9701240223_1_agnes-domenico-caracciolo-bell-tolls.

Wineapple, Brenda. Review of *The Paris Wife*. *New York Times Book Review*, March 18, 2011. http://www.nytimes.com/2011/03/20/books/review/book-review-the-paris-wife-by-paula-mclain.html?_r=0.

———. Review of *Wild Nights! New York Times Sunday Book Review*, April 20, 2008. http://www.nytimes.com/2008/04/20/books/review/Wineapple-t.html?_r=0.

Winter, Jim. "Running with the Bulls: Interview with Craig McDonald." *The Rap Sheet*, October 30, 2008. http://therapsheet.blogspot.com/2008/10/running-with-bulls.html.

Wolcott, James. "No Time for Tulips: On Hemingway and Gellhorn." *Vanity Fair*, September 6, 2013. http://www.vanityfair.com/online/wolcott/2012/05/No-Time-for-Tulips-On-Hemingway-Gellhorn.

Wright, Tom. "The Hemingway Playwright." *Harvard Crimson*. August 1, 1975. http://www.thecrimson.com/article/1975/8/1/the-hemingway-playwright-pbibn-the-usually/.

Young, Philip. Review of *The Fifth Column*. *New York Times*, September 21, 1969. http://www.nytimes.com/books/99/07/04/specials/hemingway-fifth.html.

Zink, Jack. "*Papa*: A One-man Play Deals with a Singular Man." *Palm Beach (FL) Sun-Sentinel*, September 27, 1987. http://articles.sun-sentinel.com/1987-0927/features/8703160126_1_papa-character-ernest-hemingway.

Index

A&E Network, Biography Series 169, 188
Abbott, Keith 19, 26, 138–140, 146, 230
ABC, abecedarios 81
ABC of Reading 224
Abraham Lincoln Battalion 19, 89
Academy of American Poets 212, 213
Academy Awards 111, 189, 193
Achebe, Chinua 2
Across the River and into the Trees 48, 64, 105, 113, 114, 193, 202
"Across the Street and into the Grill" (White) 48, 105, 202
Actfive and Other Poems 203
Adiós Hemingway 26, 81, 107, 119–121, 162, 229
Adler, Anthony 179–180
Africa 10, 24, 25, 39, 77, 80, 88, 106, 145, 166, 169, 179, 182, 201, 224–225
African 20–21, 56, 74, 77, 107, 145, 166, 217
African American 64
Agassiz, Louis 31, 34
Agassiz Club 34
"The Age Demanded" 199
Ai 204
Albanians 162
Albany, New York 114
Al-Bayati 210, 211
Albert Einstein: Practical Bohemian 180
Alexander, Karl 25, 104, 117–119, 125, 229–230
Alexie, Sherman 219
Alfred Hitchcock Presents 127
Alger, Horatio, Jr. 31
Ali, Mohammed 228
Alice in Wonderland 209
All Man! Hemingway, 1950s Men's Magazines, and the Masculine Persona 28–29
All Quiet on the Western Front 15
Allen, Woody 23, 57, 193–194
Along with Youth 200
Al's Bar National Theater 173
"Altercation" (McFarland) 223–224

Alvarez del Vayo, Julio 93
Amazon.com 58, 83, 84, 160, 219
Ambos Mundos Hotel 104, 181
American Airlines 167
American Masters *see* PBS
American Review 185
An American Tragedy 49
Americano 81
Americans 7, 16, 20, 21, 22, 24, 25, 32, 49, 50, 63, 64, 71, 72, 77, 78, 79, 81, 85, 92, 93, 96, 98, 100, 104, 107, 113, 114, 123, 130, 134, 136, 137, 139, 154, 158, 161, 164, 167, 170, 176, 179, 183, 185, 187, 188, 192, 196, 199, 205, 212, 213, 218, 228, 229, 231
Amherst, Massachusetts 207
Anastasia (Russian grand duchess) 64
Anastasia (film) 64
Anchorage Daily News 146
Anderson, Lauri 150, 164–165, 230
Anderson, Sherwood 26, 38, 45, 90, 101, 133, 138–140, 187, 201
Another Hill 19, 88–89
"An Answer to Allegory" (Payne) 204
anti–Semite 65, 108
The Apprenticeship of Ernest Hemingway: The Early Years 9, 20, 40
Arabic 210
Arden Theatre (Philadelphia) 186
Arditi 17, 65, 199
Arnim, Achim Von 136
Arnim, Bettina Von 136
Arnold, Lloyd 20–21
"Ars Poetica" (Horace) 82
Arts and Entertainment Network *see* A&E
Arturo Fuente cigars 166, 239n
"As Icon" (Ray) 219
Associated Press 84–85
"At Plaza de España, Madrid" (Reiter) 220
"At the Hemingway Memorial" (Wagoner) 212
At the Hemingways 30–31, 32, 41

255

"At the Hotel Florida" (Reiter) 221
Atkinson, Michael 26, 80, 95–96, 102, 107, 115–117, 230
Atlanta, Georgia 224
Atlantic 151
Atlantic (magazine) 44, 225
Attenborough, Richard 188, 189, 192, 195
Attila the Hun 219
Auden, W.H. 199
Austria 24, 74, 155, 201
Autolycus Press 32
AvoNova, Avon Book 141–142
Axis 108

Babbitt 54
Bach, Johann Sebastian 178
Bahamas 5, 24, 86
Baker, Allie 141, 142, 181, 187
Baker, Carlos 7, 9, 10, 18–19, 20, 34, 44, 50, 53, 63, 125
Ballantine ale 167
The Balloonist 151
Baltimore City Paper 110
Balzac, Honoré de 139
Bank of America 138
Barbaric Mercies 214
Barcelona, Spain 89
Barnaby Rudge 157
Barnes, David (character in Diane Gilbert Madsen's *Hunting for Hemingway*) 153
Barnes, Djuna 67
Barnes, Jake (character in *The Sun Also Rises*) 23, 57, 68, 73, 85, 153, 185
Barnes, Jim 208–209
Barrymore Award for Outstanding New Play 185
Barthes, Roland 14
Basque 109
Batista, Fulgencio 81, 104, 114, 116–119, 217
Battle of Argonne Forest 88
Battle of Hürtgen Forest 113
Battle of the Bulge 228
"The Battler" 33
Bay of Pigs 160
Beach, Sylvia 65, 68, 73, 90, 147
Beau Brummell 171
Beckerman, Marty 146, 223, 230, 238n
Beckett, Samuel 186
Beefeater's gin 224
Beegel, Susan F. 34, 85, 225
Beethoven, Ludwig van 54
Benelux countries 173
Bennett, Joan 201
Berenson, Bernard 103
Bergman, Ingrid 64, 111, 195
Berlin, Germany 24, 155, 156
Berryman, John 211
Bessette, Roland L. 26, 135, 140
Best American Poetry, 1999 218
The Best of Joe Haldeman 140

Best Short Stories 61
The Best Times 45, 48
Bierce, Ambrose 133
Bierstadt, Albert 215
Big Lost River (Idaho) 2121
Big Money 39, 91
"Big Two-Hearted River" 18, 23, 72, 164, 181
Bimini, Bahamas 5, 20, 86, 88, 214
Bismarck, Otto von 102
"Black Ass at the Cross Roads" 113, 181
Blake, William 69
Blondie 95
Bloom, Harold 5
"Bluffing at Gibralfaro" (Reiter) 222
Blum, Jenna 83
Bly, Robert 218
Boabdil 221
Boise, Idaho 176–177
Bolshevik 64
Boni and Liveright 25
Bookclub-in-a-Box 15
Borden, Lizzie 72
Boreth, Craig 9
Boston 5, 56, 84, 140, 142, 156
Boston University 83
Boulder, Colorado 138
Boyle, T. Coraghessan 14
Boyne City, Michigan 52
Bradbury, Ray 19, 27, 127–129, 136
Braden, Spruille 109
Brandes, Philip 176
Brantford, Ontario 180
Brasch, James D. 198–199
Brautigan, Richard 19, 138, 139
Brazeau, Peter 223
The Breaking Point: Hemingway, Dos Passos, and the Murder of José Robles 92, 93, 172
Brennen, Carlene 163
Brewer, Gaylord 214–215, 219, 231
Brian, Denis 46, 56, 72, 76, 95, 97, 100
The Bridge of Change 207
"Brief Hemingway Encounter" (Brewer) 214
Brisbane, Australia 219
Britain 84, 173
British 21, 68, 107, 121, 142, 159, 173, 182, 201, 207
Broadway 98, 77, 168–169, 183, 184, 213
Brontë, Emily 133
Bronze Star 20, 113
Brown University 117
Bruccoli, Matthew 166–167
Brumback, Ted 16–17, 52
Brunnenburg, Italy 24, 155
Bryher, Winifred Ellerman 66
Bryn Mawr College 79, 94, 171
Brynner, Yul 64
Bryson, John 128
Buford, Bill 123
Bujold, Geneviève 192

Index

Bukowski, Charles 173, 205, 212, 213–214, 215, 219
Bulgaria 187
Bullock, Sandra 23, 189–191
Bunce, Alan 191
Burgess, Anthony 21
Burgess, Frank Gillet 83
Burma 208
Burns, Robert 152
Burwell, Rose Marie 85
Busse, Kristina 27–28
By Force of Will: The Life and Art of Ernest Hemingway 195–196
By-line: Ernest Hemingway 152
Byron, George Gordon, Lord 201, 204

A Cadger's Curse 152
California 63, 83, 103, 139–140, 151, 204
California State University at Long Beach 204
Caligula 219
Call Me Zelda 83
Cambridge, Massachusetts 140
Cambridge University Press 10
Camus, Albert 161
"Can Poetry Matter?" (Gioia) 225–226
Canada 73, 84, 180, 187, 215
Canadian 59, 72
Canadian Army 37, 42
"A Canary for One" 70, 76
Canary Islands 171
Canby, Vincent 192
Cantos 201
"The Capital of the World" 77, 95, 185
Caracciolo, Domenico 189
Caribbean 109, 160
Cariou, Len 176, 188
Carlile, Clancy 11, 55, 59, 62–67, 74, 90, 99, 146, 229
Carnegie Hall 35, 94, 175
The Carp Castle 151
Carradine, Keith 192
Carver, Raymond 215, 219
Casino 63
Casino Royale 111
Casper, Wyoming 181
Castro, Fidel 25, 104, 107, 116–119, 133, 161, 209, 229, 230
"Cat in the Rain" 58, 170, 191, 227
Catalonian 213
Century's Ebb 41, 80, 97–101
Cervantes, Miguel de 220
Cézanne, Paul 177, 192
Chabon, Michael 231
Chandler, Raymond 133
Chango's Beads and Two-Toned Shoes 19, 114
Chaplin, Charlie 9
Chaplin, Geraldine 191, 192
Chariton Review 208
Charles Bukowski 214

"Charles V Sets the Record Straight" (Reiter) 221
Charlotte Observer 182
Charlotte's Web 201
Chaudhry, Lakshmi 85
Cherokee 64
"Chicago" (Sandburg) 29, 213
Chicago, Illinois 24, 29, 30, 37, 38–39, 41–43, 53, 73, 81, 107, 153, 159, 160, 176, 179, 186, 191, 199, 200, 213
Chicago Tribune 37, 176, 191
chicagoreader.com 186
Chicote's Café 89
Childe Harold's Pilgrimage 201
Children of the Dust 64–65
China 15, 194, 217
Chosen Country 31, 38, 40–41, 44–46, 68, 80, 91, 97–101
Christian Science Monitor 191
Christiansen, Richard 176
Christon, Lawrence 177–178
CIA 116, 133, 159, 160
Cicero 12
Cirino, Mark 131
Clancy, Tom 14
Clark Fork River (Montana) 215
"A Clean, Well-Lighted Place" 77, 138, 170, 185
"A Clean Well-Lighted Place" (Reiter) 220–221
Cleveland, Ohio 219
"Clint Eastwood at Tabernas" (Reiter) 221
Closerie des Lilas 232
Clothes for a Summer Hotel 168–169, 182–183
CNN 156
Cobb, Lee J. 77, 171
Cocoa, Florida 228
Cody, Wyoming 24, 155
Cohan, George M. 178
Cohen, Stephanie 166
Cojímar, Cuba 119
The Colbert Report 231
Colebrook, Alfred "Black Pie" 206
Collected Poems (MacLeish) 203
Collier's (magazine) 109
Collins, Scott 176
Columbia University 92, 184
Columbus, Ohio 44
Comley, Nancy R. 208
Commentary (magazine) 225
communism 39, 68, 92, 93, 96, 98, 109, 118
The Complete Short Stories of Ernest Hemingway 18, 32, 36, 39, 58, 62, 70, 106, 129, 154, 165, 166, 170, 181, 190, 200, 217
Conan, Allan 149, 150, 158–159, 160
Conch Republic 78
Confederate 105
Confessions of Nat Turner 11
The Confidential Agent 82
Conlon, Raymond 171
Connema, Richard 178

"Construction of Fan Fiction Character Through Narrative" (Kaplan) 27–28
"Contentious Minds": The Mary McCarthy/Lillian Hellman Affair 173
A Continuing Journey 204
Conversations with Tennessee Williams 183
Cooper, Gary 21, 22, 23, 77, 111, 144, 187, 188, 195
Cooper and Hemingway: The True Gen 23, 188
Copenhagen, Denmark 202–203
Cornell University 37
Corona typewriter 152, 153, 155, 199
Cosell, Howard 228
Cosgrove, Vincent 1, 7, 55, 62–64, 68, 73, 82, 146, 154, 230
Costa Rica 162
Covarrubias, Miguel 22
Cowley, Malcolm 40
Crandell, George W. 183
Crane, Stephen 77
Crazy Horse 219
Crime Writers of Canada 73
"Critical Intelligence" 198
The Critical Response to Tennessee Williams 183
Crook Factory, *The Crook Factory* 3, 11, 25, 107, 108–111, 125, 135, 146, 229
Crowley, Aleister 70–71
Crucifixion 170
Crumley, James 94
Cuba 3, 9, 24, 26, 81, 85, 102, 104–121, 125, 144–145, 155, 159, 160–162, 163, 171, 178–179, 182, 187, 204, 205, 206, 209, 215, 218–219, 227, 230
Cuban-American 85
"The Cultural Economy of Fandom" (Fiske) 53
Cummings, E.E. 199
Curnutt, Kirk 1, 10, 130, 232–233
Customs House Museum (Key West) 180
Czech, Czechoslovakian 136, 145

Dabydeen, Cyril 214–215
The Dain Curse 69
Dana, Robert 206, 207
Dangerous Dossiers: Exposing the Secret War Against America's Greatest Authors 135
The Dangerous Summer 10, 107, 118, 217
Dante (Alighieri) 54
Dateline: Toronto 51
Davidman, Joy 189
Davison, Richard Allan 171
D-Day 113, 217
"The Dead" (Joyce) 48
Dear Abby 231
The Death Factory 180, 181
Death in the Afternoon 10, 16, 22, 23, 39, 77, 115, 120, 124, 163, 175–176, 181, 199, 228
"Death in the Gulf Stream" (Peirce) 22
Death to All Cheerleaders 146
Deep Within the Ravine 206
DeFazio, Albert J., III 10

"The Defense of Poesy" (Sidney) 82
De Groot, John 168, 176–180
DeLillo, Don 14
De Maupassant, Guy 13, 54
Dempsey, Jack 224
Denver, Colorado 186
Depp, Johnny 109
Desnoes, Edmundo 160–162
Deutsch, Stephanie 58
Devilfish 214
Devlin, Albert J. 183
Devotions Upon Emergent Occasions 211
DeVoto, Bernard 40, 77
The Diabolist 143
Diagnostic and Statistical Manual of Mental Disorders 47
Dickens, Charles 2, 14, 31, 157
Dickinson, Emily 123, 168
Didion, Joan 200
Dietrich, Marlene 111, 153, 156, 195, 225, 232
Diliberto, Gioia 38–30, 43, 56, 188–189
Dior, Christian 19
The Dismemberment of Orpheus: Toward a Postmodern Literature 134
Doctorow, E.L. 14
Donaldson, Scott 195–196, 203, 210
Donne, John 12, 60, 211
Doonesbury 187
Dorman-Smith, Eric Edward ("Chink") 63
Dos Passos, Elizabeth ("Betty") 100
Dos Passos, John 3, 31, 38–46, 48, 49, 50, 68, 73, 76, 77, 80, 89–101, 120, 144, 168, 173–175, 179, 194, 224
Dos Passos, Kate Smith *see* Smith, Katherine
Dostoyevsky (Dostoevsky), Fyodor 13, 54, 161
Douglas, Kirk 188
Douglas Fairbanks Theater (New York) 176
Dracula 31
"Dream Song #235" (Berryman) 211
Dreiser, Theodore 49
"The Dumb Ox: A Study of Ernest Hemingway" (Wyndham Lewis) 185
Dunleavy, Tim 186
Dunning, Ralph Cheever 200
Dutch 15, 65, 92, 97
DVDTalk.com 191

E. Hemingway 177–178
Eagleton, Terry 14
Earle, David M. 12, 28–29, 168
"The Earnest Liberal's Lament" 199
Eastman, Max 22
Eastwood, Clint 64, 221
Eberhart, Richard 206, 208
Ebert, Roger 192
The Egyptian 143
"E.H." (Koethe) 212–213
Einstein, Albert 180
Eisenhower, Dwight "Ike" 97

"An Elegy for Ernest Hemingway" (Merton) 210–211
"Elegy for Ernest Hemingway" (Ramsey) 211–212
The Elements of Style 201
Eliot, T.S. 14, 197, 199, 200, 209, 210
Elizabeth II 209
Eller, Jonathan R. 129
Ellis, Havelock 65
Emblems of a Season of Fury 210
An Empty Plate in the Café du Grand Boeuf 168, 184–187, 230–231
"Encounter" (Yevtushenko) 202, 214
"The End of Something" 199, 217
Engel, Howard 55, 72–74
England 109, 121
English 31, 42, 57, 68, 82, 83, 109, 110, 138, 145, 152, 154, 158, 159, 160, 164, 228
Epstein, Joseph 225
Ernest Hemingway: A Life Story 9
Ernest Hemingway and His World 21
Ernest Hemingway: Complete Poems 198–199
Ernest Hemingway Foundation of Oak Park 153
Ernest Hemingway House 78, 84, 206
Ernest Hemingway: Rivers to the Sea 22, 188
Ernest Hemingway: Selected Letters, 1917–1961 10, 13, 16, 17, 32, 38, 39, 40, 41, 49, 54–55, 61, 90, 92, 93, 103, 133
Ernest Hemingway: The Critical Reception 48, 50, 76, 77, 88, 183, 193, 198
Ernest Hemingway: Thought in Action 131
"Ernest's Brave Bull" (Ray) 217
Ernie: Hemingway's Sister "Sunny" Remembers 9, 20
Escorial (Spain) 222
Espada, Martin 206–207
Esquire (magazine) 39, 54, 77, 92, 152
Estrada, Alfredo José 80–82
Eureka Theatre (San Francisco) 179
Europe 37, 104, 113, 150, 180, 191, 195, 217, 227
European 2, 136, 158
Everglades 62
"The Extasie" (Donne) 60
Extrapolation 141
"Eye and Heart: Hemingway's Education as a Naturalist" (Beegel) 34
Eyman, Scott 134

"F. Scott Fitzgerald" 183
"The Faithful Bull" 217
Falangists 210
"Falstaff at Oak Park" (Ray) 216
Fame Became of Him: Hemingway as Public Writer 8–9, 203–204
fan, fandom, fanemy, fanfic, fan fiction 1, 3, 11, 26–28, 32, 33, 41, 45–46, 48, 51, 53, 57, 58, 59, 65–66, 68, 69, 70, 71, 72, 75, 78, 82, 84, 86, 102, 106, 110, 114, 128, 132, 136, 142, 145, 146, 149, 150, 153, 154, 156, 157, 158, 165, 177, 197, 201, 217

Fan Fiction and Fan Communities in the Age of the Internet 27
fantasize, fantasy 3, 67, 124, 132, 137, 139, 140, 149, 154, 157, 163, 175, 229
A Farewell to Arms 3, 15, 22, 25, 33, 45, 50, 59, 74, 77, 84, 85, 91, 104, 105, 116, 151, 170, 177, 187, 190, 200, 228, 231
The Farm (painting) 45
Fashion Licensing of America 166
"Fathers and Sons" (Hemingway) 81, 124, 150
Fathers and Sons (Turgenev) 65
Faulkner, William 2, 14, 38, 54, 65, 68, 69, 147, 203
Faust 137
FBI 108, 112, 119, 133, 135, 179
Feaver, Vicki 207–208, 209
Feigel Lara 121
Fenton, Charles A. 9, 20, 40–41
Ferraro, Jimmy 186
Fielding, Henry 54, 157
Fifth Column, *The Fifth Column* 77, 79, 89, 98, 170, 171–174, 194
"Fifty Grand" 170
"the fighter" (Bukowski) 212
FilmScouts.com 190
Finca Vigía 26, 36, 40, 78, 81, 88, 104, 106, 107, 111, 113–116, 119–120, 133, 144, 159, 161, 176–177, 199, 204, 207, 213, 218
Fine, Reuben 47–48
Finland 195
Finlandia University 164
Finnish 164
First Forty-Nine Stories 170
Fiske, John 53, 56
Fitch, Noel Riley 10
Fitzgerald, F. Scott 15, 22, 26, 38, 49, 50, 63, 83, 101, 138, 144, 147, 168, 182, 183, 216, 238n
Fitzgerald, Zelda 63, 83, 144, 147, 168, 182, 216
.505 Gibbs 225
Flaubert, Gustave 2, 54
Fleming, Ian 111
Fleming, Robert E. 91
Florida 50, 79, 102, 140, 148, 176, 228
Florida (hotel in Madrid) 89, 95, 97, 221
Florida Poems 213
Floridita (bar in Havana) 10, 81, 104, 108, 114, 144, 205
Flowers, Fifi 58
Follies 213
For Whom the Bell Tolls 20, 25, 78, 96, 104, 105, 106, 111, 118, 135, 172, 186, 210, 219, 222
Forbes, Kermit "Battling Geech" 206–207
Ford, Ford Madox 70–71
Ford, John 134
Fort Doniphan, Missouri 37
The 42nd Parallel 39
Fossalta, Italy 227
Four Days with Hemingway's Ghost 143–144
4th Infantry Division 113

The Fox (Lawrence) 49
Fox River (Michigan) 164
France 24, 37, 138, 173
Francistas 109
Franco, Francisco 93, 172, 220–222
Franz Josef of Austria 201
French 15, 69, 71, 140, 182, 186, 199, 224
French Resistance 113, 122
French Riviera 113
Frost, Robert 128
Fuentes, Gregorio 111, 171
Fuentes, Leonardo Padura 26, 81, 119–121, 125, 162, 229
Fuentes, Norberto 209, 218–219

Gainesville, Florida 140
Galow, Timothy 232
Gamble, James 189
"The Gambler, the Nun, and the Radio" 77, 170
Gandhi 189
Gardella, Danny 113
The Garden of Eden 22, 23, 51, 59, 62, 107, 113, 120, 134, 138, 153
Gardner, Ava 22
Gaudier-Brzeska, Henri 201
Gaylord, Michigan 164
Gehrig, Lou 111
Geller, Robert 170
Generation S.L.U.T. 146
George, David Lloyd 68
Georgia State College for Women 116
German, Germans 15, 24, 55, 64, 108, 113, 125, 138, 154, 156, 173
Gerogiannis, Nicholas 198–199
Gerritsen, Tess 115
Ghost Writer 184–185
Gide, André 66
Gilmore, Christopher Cook 11, 25, 27, 33, 55, 62, 74, 79–80, 87, 93–94, 125
Gingrich, Arnold 92
Gioia, Dana 225–226
"Giovinezza" ("Giovanezza," Italian fascist song) 93
Glazer, Benjamin 171
Goddu, Jenn 186
The Godless Boys 121
Goethe, Johann Wolfgang von 2, 136–137
Goering, Hermann 7, 64, 68
Golden Gate Bridge 140
Golden Globe 193
A Good Day to Die (film) 65
Goodbye to All That 49
Goodfellas 63
Goodreads.com 84, 110
Goofy 147
Gordon, Joan 141
Gordon's gin 224
Gorev, Vladimir 92
Gotham Group 146

Gounod, Charles 137
Grahame-Smith, Seth 147
Granger, Bill 160
The Grapes of Wrath 14
Graves, Robert 49
The Great American Novel (Roth) 79
The Great American Novel (Williams) 50
Great Depression 24, 39, 77, 85, 88
The Great Gatsby 14, 49
The Great War *see* World War I
Greek tragedy 126
Greeks 126, 196
Green, Layton 143–144
Green Hills of Africa 10, 39, 77, 80, 88, 145, 166
Greene, Graham 82, 133
Greenwich Village 108
Griffin, Peter 47, 200
Grosse Pointe, Michigan 135
The Guardian 121
Guernica 96, 175
Guest, Winston 111
Guevara, Che 116, 118
Gulf of Mexico 224
Gulf Stream 22, 162
Gungha Din 161
Guyana 214

Hadley: The First Mrs. Hemingway 56
Hadrian 72
Haglund, David 187
Haldeman, Joe 11, 62, 140–142, 146, 150, 152, 154, 229, 230
Hale, Mike 193–194
Hamlin, Elizabeth (Dos Passos) 50
Hammett, Dashiell 69, 72, 158
Hampton, Wilborn 183
Hancock, Michigan 164
Hardin, Nils 44
Hari, Mata 65
Harlequin romance 60, 86
Harris, Julie 168
Harris, MacDonald 59, 62, 150–153, 154, 160, 230
The Harvard Crimson 169
Harvard University 31, 34, 148, 169
Hasleberger, Manuela 156
Hassan, Ihab 134–135
Havana: Autobiography of a City 82
Havana, Cuba 10, 29, 40, 78, 80–82, 88, 104–121, 123, 140, 181, 209, 215
Hayes, Helen 22, 77, 187
Hays, Peter L. 171
Hays, Tony 55, 67–68, 69
HBO 193
Head Games 71
Hebrew 15, 56, 170
Heiney, Donald *see* Harris, MacDonald
Hellekson, Karen 27–28
Heller, Nathan 7, 22
Hellman, Lillian 158, 173, 175

Index

The Heming Way 146, 223, 230, 238n
Hemingsteen 3, 11–12, 32–27, 38, 44, 80, 230
Hemingway (Christopher Cook Gilmore) 11–12, 25, 27, 33, 55, 62, 74, 79–80, 87, 93–94, 125
Hemingway (Kenneth S. Lynn) 9, 33, 51–52, 61, 93, 124, 126, 128, 129, 155, 158
"Hemingway" (MacLeish) 210
Hemingway (TV miniseries) 22, 55, 80, 191–192
Hemingway, Anson 37
Hemingway, Carol 34
Hemingway, Clarence (father) 25, 30, 33–34, 37, 41, 45, 53, 74, 76, 86, 87, 124–125, 169, 178–179, 206, 208, 211, 219, 234n
Hemingway, Grace Hall (mother) 30, 32, 33–34, 48, 50–53, 76, 85, 124, 178, 189, 208, 216
Hemingway, Gregory 74, 76, 78, 113, 115–116, 122, 134, 163–164, 207, 237n
Hemingway, Hadley Richardson 3, 15, 18, 24, 25, 38–39, 41, 43, 49–53, 56–67, 73–75, 76, 87, 90–91, 100, 102–103, 104, 121–122, 131, 150, 153, 178–179, 182, 190, 191–192, 216, 229
Hemingway, Hilary 152, 162–164, 170–171
Hemingway, John Hadley (Jack, "Bumby") 18, 40, 95, 122, 143–144, 174, 148
Hemingway, Leicester 36, 143, 162–163, 170
Hemingway, Lorian 163–164
Hemingway, Madelaine ("Sunny") 9, 34, 52, 216
Hemingway, Marcelline ("Marsh," "Ivory") 9, 30–32, 34, 37, 41, 44–45, 195
Hemingway, Mariel 22, 148, 231, 235n
Hemingway, Martha Gellhorn 20, 21, 78–80, 88–89, 91, 92–93, 94, 97–98, 102–103, 104, 111, 122–123, 158, 171, 172, 174, 181, 193–195, 217
Hemingway, Mary Welsh 9, 19, 21, 40, 69, 100, 103, 104, 105, 115–116, 120–124, 126, 133–136, 161, 176–178, 181, 187, 192, 198, 199, 210, 217–218
Hemingway, Patrick 74, 76, 78, 115–116
Hemingway, Pauline Pfeiffer 38, 39, 45, 50, 55, 60, 73–74, 76–78, 80, 85–88, 91, 95, 97, 99, 102–103, 104, 115, 121–122, 158, 169, 174–175, 181, 193, 205–206, 207, 216, 237n
Hemingway, Ursula 34, 52, 216, 223
Hemingway, Valerie 134
Hemingway: A Desperate Life 216–219
Hemingway: A Life in Pictures 22
Hemingway: A Life Without Consequences 223
Hemingway and Film 187
Hemingway and Fuentes 171
Hemingway and His Conspirators 170, 187–188
Hemingway and His World 21, 22
Hemingway and the Mechanism of Fame 166–167
Hemingway and the Movies 187
Hemingway at Oak Park High 31

The Hemingway Book Club of Kosovo 162
Hemingway Code 208
Hemingway Colloquium: The Poet Goes to Cuba 204–205
The Hemingway Cookbook 9
Hemingway Cutthroat 26, 80, 95–96, 115
Hemingway Days (Key West) 166, 170, 180
Hemingway Deadlights 26, 95, 107, 115–116
"Hemingway Dines on Boiled Shrimp and Beer" (McGrath) 213
"The Hemingway-Dos Passos Relationship" (Pizer) 100–101
The Hemingway/Dos Passos Wars 97, 168, 173–176
Hemingway: Eight Decades of Criticism 11
Hemingway Festival (Moscow, Idaho) 10
The Hemingway Hoax 62, 140–142, 150, 152, 229, 230
"The Hemingway House in Key West" (Schultz) 206
"Hemingway in Africa: The Untold Story" (McFarland) 224–225
Hemingway in Cuba (Carlene Brennen) 163
(Norberto Fuentes) 209, 218
Hemingway in Love and War: The Lost Diary of Agnes Von Kurowsky 51
Hemingway in Spain: Words and Images 219–222, 231
Hemingway in the Autumn 20–21
"The Hemingway Look-alike Society Meets Bimini Bay Developers" (Brewer) 214
"Hemingway Meets Evangeline" (McFarland) 225
Hemingway Notes 211
Hemingway on Stage 168, 180–181
Hemingway on the Edge 180
The Hemingway Papers 1, 55, 62–64, 68, 73, 82, 146, 154, 230
Hemingway-Pfeiffer Museum 88
The Hemingway Play 169, 184, 185, 187, 230
The Hemingway Poems 222–225
"The Hemingway Project" (blog) 141, 181
Hemingway Reminisces 168, 180
Hemingway Review 1, 2, 56, 57, 62, 81, 85, 134, 140, 156–157, 162, 163, 171–172, 176, 199, 223, 232
The Hemingway Sabbatical 149, 150, 158–160
Hemingway Society 120
"The Hemingway Syndrome" (Louis) 204
Hemingway: The Final Years 106, 109, 113, 126, 129, 162, 196
Hemingway: The Homecoming 75
Hemingway: The 1930s 88, 93, 224
Hemingway: The Paris Years 61, 66
The Hemingway Women 40, 56, 121
Hemingway: Wrestling with Life 22, 188
Hemingway's Boat 5, 9, 36, 78, 87, 164, 207, 213
"Hemingway's Bullfighter Poems" (Junkins) 199
Hemingway's Chair 3, 25, 150, 156–158, 230

"Hemingway's Contribution to American Poetry" (Junkins) 199
"Hemingway's Garden" (Ray) 218–219
Hemingway's Garden of Eden 22
Hemingway's Genders 208
Hemingway's Ghost 143–144
Hemingway's Girl 27, 80, 82–88, 94, 110, 121
"Hemingway's Hat" (Feaver) 207–208
Hemingway's HOT Havana 181
Hemingway's Key West 10, 206
Hemingway's Notebook 160
Hemingway's Quarrel with Androgyny 208
"Hemingway's Shadow" (Bukowski) 213–214
Hemingway's Suitcase 59, 62, 150–152, 230
Henderson, William McCranor 11, 129–132, 134, 146, 154, 157, 229, 230
Hendrickson, Paul 5, 9, 36–37, 78, 87, 163, 174, 207, 213, 234n
Henry, O. (William S. Porter) 31
Henry McGee Is Not Dead 160
Herbst, Josephine "Josie") 93, 96, 98
Hermann, Thomas 156–157
Heston, Charlton 188
Hicks, Granville 88
"Hills Like White Elephants" 76, 170
Historic Photos of Ernest Hemingway 22
A Historical Guide to Ernest Hemingway 15
Hitler, Adolf 7, 64, 102, 147, 173, 219
Hofler, Robert 186
Holbrook, Hal 168
Holiday (magazine) 217
Hollinger, Michael 168, 184–187, 230–231
Hollywood 23, 77, 88, 169, 182, 187, 188, 190, 191, 195, 221
Hollywood Court Theatre 173–174, 176
Hollywood Television Theater 169
Homage to Catalonia 172
Hong Kong 24, 155
Honkytonk Man 64
Hoover, J. Edgar 109, 111, 112, 133, 135, 179
Hopkins, Anthony 171
Horace 82, 106
Horne, William D., Jr. 189
Horton Bay, Michigan 37, 53, 155, 164
Hotchner, A.E. 21–22, 153, 156, 170, 213, 223
Houdini, Harry 72
How It Was 9, 103, 133, 181, 187, 199
Huckleberry Finn 14, 79
Hudson Guild Theatre 169
Hugo, Richard 226
Hugo Award 109, 140
Hunt, George P. 127
Hunter, Frederic 169, 184–185, 197, 230
Hunting for Hemingway 62, 150, 152–153
Hunting Hemingway's Trout 150, 164–166
"Hunting Hemingway's Trout" (Anderson) 164–165
Hunting with Hemingway 152, 162–164
Huntley, Paula 162
Huston, John 232

Hutt, John 184
Hyperion 109

"I Bought Hemingway's Ghost a Drink" (White) 215
I Elvis: Confessions of a Counterfeit King 130
I Killed Hemingway 11, 129–132, 133, 229, 230
I Sing the Body Electric 128
Idaho 10, 20, 23, 24, 25, 69, 99, 104, 106, 123, 128, 133, 154, 176, 177, 182, 191, 212, 221
Illinois 9, 17, 37, 127
"I'm Gonna Sit Right Down and Write Myself a Letter" 178
Immortality 2, 136–137, 230
The Importance of Being Earnest 184
The Importance of Being Ernest Hemingway 184
"In Another Country" 200
In Love and War 23, 188–192, 193, 195
"In Normandy" (Ray) 217
in our time 89
In Our Time 18, 25, 38, 44, 49, 50, 70, 71, 90, 133, 151, 169, 190, 217
"In the Barrio de la Judería" (Reiter) 221
In Watermelon Sugar 138
Inconsolable Memories see *Memories of Underdevelopment*
India 162
Indian 139
"Indian Camp" 44–45, 71, 154
"An Industrial Accident" (Ray) 216
Inland (magazine) 36
Interactive Press 219
International Brigade 88, 93
Iowa 117, 138, 139, 140, 206
Ipsos survey 84–85
Iraqi 210
Ireland, Irish 180, 200, 204
Isaac Asimov's Science Fiction Magazine 140
Islamic 159
Islands in the Stream 44, 62, 107, 120, 134–135, 138
Italian front 16, 32, 52
Italian Tirol 155
Italy 15, 16–17, 24, 25, 38, 65, 69, 89, 90, 93, 95, 105, 108, 140, 155, 182, 195, 199, 227
Ivancich, Adriana 105, 193
Ivens, Joris 92, 97, 98

Jack the Ripper 73, 117
Jackson, Thomas J. ("Stonewall") 105
JAG (Judge Advocate General) officer 136
James, Henry 13, 24, 54, 123, 174
Jameson, Frederic 151–152, 219
Japanese 139, 140
Jason [John Arne Sæterøy] 147
Jazz Age 24
Jeep 166
Jeffers, Robinson 214
Jenson, Joli 11, 46
Jesus Christ 7, 52, 90, 118, 147, 170

Jesus Christ: In the Name of the Gun, "Volume One: A Hollow Cost" 147
Johns Hopkins University 93
Johnson, L.E. (Erv) 147, 176–178
Johnson, Robert 207
Joplin, Scott 178
Joseph Andrews 157
Journal of Modern Literature 100
Journal of Popular Culture 1, 163
Joyce, James 14, 25, 48, 49, 65, 68, 69, 147, 203
Junkins, Donald 199
"Just Out of High School" (Ray) 216

Kale, Verna 173, 199
Kansas City, Missouri 3, 9, 15–16, 32, 36, 37, 45, 50, 76, 88, 195, 216
Kansas City Star 3, 15, 16, 37, 45, 50
Kaplan, Deborah 27–28
Karsh, Yousuf 19–20, 231
Kaufman, Philip 194, 195
Kazin, Alfred 40
Keach, Stacy 22, 55, 80, 191–192
Keats, John 109, 140
Keene, Jarret 217, 223
Kempley, Rita 192–193
Kendrick, Patrick 26, 80, 102–103, 112
Kennedy, J. Gerald 61
Kennedy, John F. 111, 165
Kennedy, William 19, 114–115
Kennedy Library [John F. Kennedy Library, Boston] 5, 56, 84, 156
Kenya 24, 88, 104, 106, 155, 191
Kenyon College 83
Kenyon Review 124
Kert, Bernice 40, 56, 121, 123
Ketchum, Idaho 3, 23, 24, 26, 29, 69, 99, 104, 123, 124–125, 128–129, 133, 135, 144, 154, 155, 177, 182, 185, 192, 206, 212, 213, 221
"Key West" (Eberhart) 206
Key West Art and Historical Society 180
Key West, Florida 5, 10, 24, 26–27, 29, 38, 39, 45, 50, 55, 74, 76, 77–80, 91, 94–96, 101–103, 104, 107, 115, 121, 122, 130, 135, 140–145, 148, 153, 155, 158, 166, 170, 173, 176, 180–182, 187, 191, 205–208, 213, 216–217
Key West Hemingway: A Reassessment 10
Key West Story 144–145
Key West Writers Lab, Inc. 145
Kidman, Nicole 23, 78, 193–194
"The Kilimanjaro Device" (Bradbury) 127–129
"The Killers" 22, 32–33, 76, 79, 170
King, Stephen 14, 109
Kingsolver, Barbara 14
Kirkpatrick, Robert J. 176
Kirkus 156
Klems, Brian A. 59
Knights, L.C. 14
Koch, Kenneth 201
Koch, Stephen 35, 92–97, 172
Koethe, John 212–213, 215

Koltzov, Mikhail 93, 94
Köpf, Gerhard 24, 25, 62, 150, 154–156, 157, 159, 160, 230
Korean 15
Kundera, Milan 2, 19, 136–138, 230
Kyoto, Japan 139

Labor Day hurricane of 1935 80, 85, 94
Lady Chatterley's Lover 49
Lake Forest, Illinois 34
Lamb, Robert Paul 9
Lambert, Marion 34
Lamont Prize for Poetry 206
Lancaster, Burt 22
Lanham, Charles ("Buck") 105, 113
Lansky, Meyer 116
Lanza, Mario 135
Lardner, Ring 31
The Lark (magazine) 83
"The Last Good Country" 106
Latin 82, 125
Latin Quarter 55, 67–68
Latino 81, 206
Laurence, Frank M. 187–188, 191
Lausanne, Switzerland 51, 62, 66
"The Law of the Jungle" (White) 201
laweekly.com 193
Lawrence, D.H. 49, 65, 69, 72
Lawrence, Louise 65
Lear, James Mitchell 168, 180
Leavis, F.R. 14
Leavitt, Caroline 83
Leff, Leonard J. 170, 187–188
The Left Bank Gang 147
Lehman, David 133
Lehman-Haupt, Christopher 65–66
Leopold and Loeb murder 73
The Letters of Ernest Hemingway (Spanier) 10, 16, 17, 30, 32, 37, 53, 90, 103, 133, 189, 195
Lewis, C.S. 189
Lewis, Lisa A. 53
Lewis, Robert W. 17–18
Lewis, Sinclair 40
Lewis, Wyndham 131, 185, 201
Library Journal 110
Library of Congress 148, 163
Life (magazine) 118, 127, 128, 179, 209
Like Family: Growing Up in Other People's Houses 56
Lincoln Park (Chicago) 190
Lindbergh, Charles "Lucky Lindy" 12
Lindsay, Jeffry P. 153, 162–163, 170
"A Literary Friendship" (Ray) 216
Literary Topics: Ernest Hemingway and the Expatriate Modernist Movement 1
Little, Malcolm 97
"Little Gidding" (Eliot) 209
The Little Review 49
Lloyd, Robert 194–195
Locklin, Gerald 204–205

Loeb, Harold 73–74
Loeb Dramatic Center 169
Logan, John 207, 209, 231
London, England 37, 123, 158
Long After Midnight 129
"The Long Hot Summer" (Ray) 217
Long Island University/C.W. Post 95, 115
Look (magazine) 106
"Looking for Hemingway's Ghost at the Crillon" (Barnes) 208–209
Lorca, Federico García 210
Los Angeles 57, 58, 127, 150, 173, 176, 177, 178, 186
Los Angeles Times 57, 58, 176, 178, 186
Lost Generation 24, 134, 181, 191, 192
The Lost Generation 181
Louis, Adrian C. 204
Lovelock, Nevada 204
Lower Matecumbe Key, Florida 85
Loyalist/s 89, 92, 109, 171–172, 175, 194
LSD 139
Ludington, Townsend 38, 98, 99, 100
Lynn, Kenneth 9, 33, 51, 52, 61, 93, 124, 126, 128, 129, 155, 158

Macbeth 127
Machado, Gerardo 80–81
Machlin, Milt 9
MacLeish, Archibald 19, 199, 201, 202–204, 210, 231
The Macomber Affair (film) 201
Madrid, Spain 39, 40, 77, 80, 91–98, 122, 169, 170, 173, 174–175, 185, 210, 220
Madsen, Diane Gilbert 62, 150, 152–154
Maglie, Sal "The Barber" 113
Maigret mysteries 71
Mailer, Norman 179
Majestic Hotel 89
The Making of the Americans 139
Málaga, Spain 222
The Man-Eaters 181
"The Man Who Beat Hemingway" (Espada) 206–207
The Man Who Shot Liberty Valence (film) 134
"The Man with the Blue Guitar" (Stevens) 175
Manca, John 63
Manhattan Transfer 39, 44, 49, 90, 97
Manifest Destiny 215
Mann, Thomas 14
Manus, Willard 216
Many Marriages 133
Mariani, Paul 215
"Marks on a Wall" (Ray) 217
Marsh, Mae 9, 195
Marshall, Thomas A. 150
Martin, Adrienne 110
Marx, Groucho 194, 232
Marxism 87, 88
Mary Magdalene 170
Masai 129

Maslin, Janet 57–58
Mason, Jane 81, 86–87, 175, 181
Mason & Dixon 11
Masquerade 55, 71–72
Massachusetts Institute of Technology (MIT) 83
McAlmon, Robert 63, 66, 72, 90, 99
McCarthy, Cormac 12
McClellan, George B. 16
McDonald, Craig 7, 25, 55, 67, 68–72, 94–95, 102, 125, 129, 132–135, 141, 145, 230
McDowell, Malcolm 117
McFarland, Ron 222–225
McGrath, Campbell 213, 215, 219, 231
McIver, Stuart B. 10, 79, 103, 206
McLain, Paula 3, 11, 15, 27, 39, 55, 56–60, 63, 66, 85, 91, 102, 109, 121, 125, 229
McMorris, Kristina 83
McNulty, Charles 186
Meagher, L.D. 156
"Meditation on a News Item" (Updike) 209
Mediterranean 151, 222
"A Meeting in Copenhagen" (Yevtushenko) 202–203, 214
Mellow, James R. 91, 100, 126, 223
Melville, Herman 13, 88
Memories of Underdevelopment (*Memorias del subdesarollo*) 160–162
Men Without Women 50, 70, 76, 77, 131, 151, 169, 170
Merchant Marine Academy 151
Merton, Thomas 210–211
Metzger, Ed 180
Metzner, Marla 166
Mexican League 113
Mexican War 16
Meyer, Adam 215
Meyers, Jeffrey 101, 105, 118, 167, 223
Miami, Florida 81, 111, 145, 178–179
Miami Herald 114
Michael Palin's Hemingway Adventure 24, 150, 156
Michelangelo 13, 54
Michigan 9, 18, 24, 30, 36, 37, 41, 53, 56, 68, 90, 106, 107, 135, 142, 150, 155, 164, 190, 195
Middle Tennessee State University 214
Midnight in Paris 23, 57, 188, 193
Milan, Italy 16, 20, 90, 179, 200
Millay, Edna St. Vincent 199Fpoem
Miller, Henry 133
Miller, Madelaine "Sunny" Hemingway 9, 34, 52, 216
Mink, George 96
Mint Theater 171
Miró, Joan 45
Missoula, Montana 94
Missouri 208
Missouri Home Guard 37
"Mr. and Mrs. Elliot" 23, 200–201
Mitgang, Hebert 135

"Mitraillitrice" 199
Mizener, Arthur 44
Möbius strip 141
Moby Dick 79
Moddelmog, Debra A. 8, 85
Modern Language Association 10, 148
modernism 1, 14, 65, 69, 71, 130, 134, 192, 197
The Moderns 23, 188, 192–193
Mogen, David 129
Monroe, Harriet 198
Monroe, Marilyn 130
Montana 42–43, 94, 104, 106, 226
Montblanc pens 166
Montreal, Canada 188
Monty Python's Flying Circus 150, 219
Moore, Burness E. 46, 47
Moore, John 185, 186
Moore, Lynn 168, 182
Moore, Marianne 199
"The Moose and the VW Bug" (Anderson) 165
Morgan, Henry 107–109, 125, 154, 230
Morrison, Jim 130
Morrison, Toni 13, 14
Morse, Donald E. 141, 142
Mount Kilimanjaro 129
A Moveable Feast 1, 23–24, 26, 28, 32, 50, 55, 56, 60, 63, 68, 69, 70–72, 75, 100, 102, 106, 118, 120, 131, 145, 151, 169, 182, 183, 184, 193, 196, 200, 201, 216, 220
Mowrer, Hadley *see* Hemingway, Hadley Richardson
Mowrer, Paul 102
Mozart, Wolfgang Amadeus 178
Mrs. Hemingway 12, 121–123
Muhammad XII 221
Mullholland, John 188
Munich Technical University 154
Munro, Alice 2
Murder in Montparnasse 55, 72–73, 236n
Murder in the Latin Quarter 55, 67–68
Murphy, Gerald 90, 122
Murphy, Michael 32–36, 37, 38, 42, 44, 45, 80, 230, 234n
Murphy, Sara 90, 122
Muslim 221
Mussolini, Benito 108, 147, 173
My Brother Ernest Hemingway 162

Nabokov, Vladimir 133
Nagel, James 188, 190
Nairobi, Kenya 129
narcissism 46–48, 121
Narcissus 48, 235n
Naropa University 138
Nash, Ogden 201
Nation (magazine) 85
National Prize for Literature (Cuba) 119
National Public Radio 84–85
National Socialists 68

"A Natural History of the Dead" 16
Nazis 64, 102, 107–110, 173
Nebula Award 140
Neil M footwear 166
"Neothomist Poem" 199
New Masses (magazine) 87–88, 244n
New Millennium Writings 218
New Republic (magazine) 50
New York City 37, 88, 97, 171, 176, 184, 206
New York Daily News 63
New York Giants 113
New York Herald Tribune 201
New York International Independent Film Festival 182
New York Review of Books 152
New York Review of Science Fiction 141
New York Sun 16
New York Times 44, 49, 55, 57, 58, 65, 105, 123, 130, 147, 156, 188, 192, 193,
New York Times Book Review 44, 57, 193
New Yorker 48, 77, 105, 148, 202, 207, 209
Newman, Paul 21
Newsweek 40
NFL 128
The Nick Adams Stories 39, 106
Nicolle, Ethan 147
Nietzsche, Friedrich 133
"No Possum, No Sop, No Taters" (Stevens) 224
"No Writers in the Prado" (Reiter) 221
Nobel Prize 14, 25, 35, 106, 113, 118, 159, 203, 217
None So Blind 140
Normandy, France 25, 217
North American Newspaper Alliance (NANA) 40, 92
North Carolina 130, 182
North Carolina State University 130
North Dakota Quarterly 171, 224
Northwestern University 153
Norway 173
Norwegian 147
Notes from the Underground 161
November Man 160

O. Henry (William S. Porter) 31
Oak Park, Illinois 5, 9, 17, 24, 31–34, 51, 81, 153, 155, 189, 196, 216
Oates, Joyce Carol 19, 123–125
Oberlin College 130, 184
O'Brien, Edward 61
O'Connor, Flannery 2
O'Connor, John 55
O'Connor, Kevin J. 23, 192, 193
O'Donnell, Chris 23, 189–191, 192
Odysseus 48
Ohio 44, 68, 132, 210, 228
Ohio State University 68
Oklahoma 18
Oklahoma Territory 64
Old Dominion University 145

"Old Hem Was a Sport" (Dos Passos) 101
The Old Man and the Sea 13, 25, 48, 80, 104, 105, 106, 108, 120, 127, 156, 157, 158, 162, 171, 177, 203, 204, 211, 228, 231
"Old Man at the Bridge" 77
Oliver, Charles M. 140, 171
Olsen, Mark 193
Omaha Beach 25
One True Sentence 55, 67–72, 133
"The Open Boat" (Stephen Crane) 77
Oprah's Book Club 231
Opus 184
Order of Canada 73
Ordóñez-Dominguín bullfights 217
Ordway, Holly E. 191
Orpet, William 34
Orwell, George 172
Oswald, Lee Harvey 166
The Other Side of the Wind 232
Ottawa Indians 45
Ouija board 143
"Out of Season" 67, 132
Ovation Award 168, 176
Owen, Clive 23, 78, 193–194
Oxford University 156

Pacific 151
Padua, Italy 190
Palin, Michael 3, 24, 25, 150, 156–159, 160, 230
Pamplona, Spain 24, 38, 135, 140, 155, 159, 181, 212
Pan American Airlines 167
Papa 103
Papa and Fidel 25, 107, 117–119, 229
Papa Hemingway 21, 153, 156, 213, 223
Papa: The Man, the Myth, the Legend 181–182
Papa: The One-Man Play 168, 176–177
"Papa's House, Son's Room" (Logan) 207
Papa's Problem 26, 80, 102–103
Papa's Suitcase 25, 62, 150, 154–156, 230
Paramount Studies 111
Paris 1, 18, 19, 20, 24, 29, 38, 49, 50, 55–75, 76, 77, 81, 90, 93, 94, 95, 98, 99, 104, 106, 121, 122, 123, 130, 132, 133, 134, 135, 138, 140, 142, 147, 150, 153, 155, 169, 170, 175, 177, 178, 182, 184, 185, 191, 192, 193, 198, 200, 201, 203, 215, 216, 229
Paris 208
Paris (Jim Barnes) 208–209
The Paris Pilgrims 11, 55, 59, 62, 63, 64–67, 74, 90, 99, 146, 229
Paris Review 162, 213
The Paris Wife: The True Story of Hemingway's First Wife 3, 11, 15, 27, 39, 55–60, 62, 66, 70, 91, 109, 121, 229
Paris Without End 56
Parker, Dorothy 76
Parker pens 167
Parkinson, Michael 232

"The Parrot Who Met Papa" (Bradbury) 129
Parts of a World: Wallace Stevens Remembered 223
Pathé 9
Patton, Georghe S. 228
Paul, Steve 81
Payne, Basil 204
PBS 22, 150, 188
Pears, Iain 110
Pecan Grove Press 222
Peck, Gregory 201
Peirce, Waldo 22
PEN/Hemingway Award 166
Penrod 228
Peppard, George 176, 179
Percival, Philip 80
Perkins, Maxwell 9, 22, 87
Peru 104, 158
Peterson, Eric 147
Petoskey, Michigan 30, 150, 164
Pfeiffer, Gus 55, 77
Pfeiffer, Virginia (Jinny) 86
Philadelphia, Pennsylvania 186
Philip II of Spain 222
Phillips, Gene D. 187
Phillips, Jeanne 231
Picasso, Pablo 72, 90, 175, 207
"Picking on Papa" (Keene) 217
Picturing Hemingway: A Writer in His Time 20, 22, 23
Piggott, Arkansas 88, 122
Pilar 78, 84, 87, 102, 107–113, 145, 171, 213, 218
Pinkerton agent 71
Piranesi's Dream 154
Pittsburg State University (Kansas) 215
Pizer, Donald 91, 100–101
Plath, James 22
Plath, Sylvia 133
Plato 232
Plaza Hotel (Paris) 175
Pleasants, Ben 97, 168, 173–176, 224
Plei Me 208
Plimpton, George 134, 162
Poe, Edgar Allan 31
Poem-a-Day 212
"Poem for Hemingway & W.C. Williams" (Carver) 215
"Poem to Mary (Second Poem)" 198
Poems and Plays (magazine) 214
Poems, 1924–1933 (MacLeish) 210
"Poet" (MacLeish) 203
Poetry (magazine) 198, 199
Poitier, Sidney 65
Poland 102, 147, 173
Polish 15, 80
Popular Front 94, 172
Portland, Oregon 83
Portuguese 15, 94
Posada, Juan 96, 98
postmodernism 71, 131, 134, 151

Postmodernism: Or, The Cultural Logic of Late Capitalism 151–152
Pound, Ezra 24, 25, 61, 63, 66, 69, 108, 130, 147, 198, 199, 200, 201, 224
Powell, Arthur G. 224
The Power and the Glory 82
Prados-Terreira, Teresa 119
Pravda 93, 94
Presley, Elvis 71, 130, 204
Pride and Prejudice and Zombies 147
The Pride of the Yankees 111
Princeton University 5, 223
Print the Legend 69, 129, 132–134, 141
Private Demons 151
The Private Hell of Hemingway 9
Prohibition 43
Prosser, William 183
Proust, Marcel 14
The Psi Delegation 159
Psychology Today 148
Publishers Weekly 110, 155, 163
Pulitzer Prize 25, 102, 106, 176, 203, 231
Pulpcon 44
"The Purple Cow" (Burgess) 83
Pynchon, Thomas 11

Quad Cinema (New York City) 188
Queens University 215
Quick, Elliott 184
Quinlan, Grace 52–53
Quintanilla, Luis 98
Quintanilla (Quintinilla), Pepe 93, 96, 98
Quisling, Vidkun 173

Raeburn, John 8–9, 12, 171–172, 203–204
RAF (Royal Air Force) 37
Ragged Dick 31
Rahv, Philip 48
Ramp Theatre (Los Angeles)
Ramsey, Paul 211–212
Random House 59
Ray, David 216–219, 222, 223, 231
Ray, Man 22, 70
"Reading as a Writer" (Oates) 125
Reading Desire: In Pursuit of Ernest Hemingway 7–8, 85
Red Cross 17, 38
Red Harvest 69
Reiter, David 219–222, 231
Remarque, Erich Maria 15
Renaissance art 103
"Reports of Hemingway's Failure Greatly Exaggerated" (Ray) 218
Republican forces (Spain) 92, 93, 96, 99, 172
Requiem for a Nun (197)
"The Resurrection of Elvis Presley" (Ai) 204
Reynolds, David S. 124
Reynolds, Michael 9, 12, 15, 16, 17, 20, 23, 24, 25, 32, 61, 66, 75, 88, 93, 105–106, 109, 113, 126, 129, 131, 134, 162, 196–197, 224

Reynolds, Susan Salter 57
Rhino Ritz 26, 138–140, 230
Rhodes, Jordan 168, 181–182
Richard Brautigan 138
Rifkind, Donna 58
"Riparto d'Assalto" 199
Rise of the Zombies (film) 148
Rizzoli and Isles 115
Roaring Twenties 24
Robles Passos, José ("Pepe") 92–98, 120, 174–175, 194
Robles Passos, Márgara 96
Robuck, Erika 27, 80, 82, 83, 84–88, 94, 102, 110, 111, 121, 125
Rogers, Michael 110
"Roll On, Thou Deep and Dark Blue Copy Writer—Roll!" (Nash) 201
Rolo, Charles J. 44
Roman Catholic, Catholicism 144, 181
Roosevelt, Franklin Delano 81
Roosevelt, Theodore 8, 23, 222
Roosevelt University 152
Rosene, M.R. 77
Rosenfeld, Paul 50
Ross, Crystal 38, 90
Ross, Lilian 105, 125
Roth, Philip 2, 19, 79
Rough and Ready 31
Royal-George Theatre (Chicago) 176
The Rubaiyat of Omar Khayyam 200
Rudolph, Alan 192, 193
Running with Nature 231
Running with the Bulls: My Years with the Hemingways 134
Russell, Joe 81
Russian 15, 64, 96, 147, 161, 202
Russians 92, 93, 159, 161
Russo-Finnish War 173
Ruth, George Herman "Babe" 12, 113
Rutherford, James 184

Le Sacre du Printemps 50
St. Bernard (canine) 139
St. John's College (Maryland) 207
St. Louis, Missouri 21, 32, 91, 109, 145
Samuelson, Arnold Morse 54
San Fermin 38
San Francisco 138–140
San Francisco de Paula, Cuba 104
San Francisco State University 117
Sandburg, Carl 29, 200, 213
Sandweiss, Martha A. 134
Sanford, Marcelline *see* Hemingway, Marcelline
Sartre, Jean-Paul 147
Satterthwait, Walter 55, 71–72
Save Me the Waltz 182
Scapa Flow 173
The Scarlet Letter 14, 79
Schaller, Al 161

Schlozman, Steven 148
Scholes, Robert 208
Schruns, Austria 24, 74, 135, 140, 155, 191
Schultz, Philip 206, 207, 209
Science (magazine) 85
Scorsese, Martin 63
Scotland Yard 102
Scotsman 102
Scott, Ginger 171
Scott, Helen 44, 45
Scott, Sir Walter 31
Scribner 9, 13, 21, 87
Scribner, Charles 12, 22, 54
Scribner's (magazine) 77
"The Sea Change" 183
Seals, Marc 163
Selznick, David O. 188
Seney, Michigan 155, 164
Serbian 15, 56
Seville, Spain 135
sfsite.com 110
Shadowlands 189
Shakespeare, William 5, 12, 31, 82, 112, 127, 139, 208, 209
Shakespeare and Company Bookstore 65, 147
Shakespeare: The Invention of the Human 5
Shelley, Percy Bysshe 225
Shipman, Evan 200
"The Short, Happy Life of Francis Macomber" 77, 80, 160, 165, 201, 223, 225
"A Short Unhappy Life" (Anderson) 164, 165–166
Sidney, Sir Philip 82
Sierra Maestras, Cuba 116, 117
Sig Sauer 125
Sigman, Joseph 198–199
Silver Medal for Valor 16, 17
Simenon, Georges 71
Simmons, Dan 3, 11, 25, 107, 108–112, 115, 116, 117, 125, 135, 146, 154, 229, 230
Simon, John 183
"A Simple Enquiry" 183
Sinclair, Brian Gordon 168, 180–181, 187, 231
Sinclair, Gail D. 10, 57–59
Sinkel, Bernhard 55, 192–193
"A Situation Report" 106
Skwiot, Rick 144–145
slate.com 22, 187
Sloppy Joe's Bars (Havana, Key West) 10, 78, 80, 104, 122, 207, 213
Smith, Agnes W. 77
Smith, Bill 42
Smith, Chard Powers 200
Smith, Genevieve ("Doodles") 43
Smith, Katherine (Kate, Katie, Katy) 31, 38–39, 41, 45–46, 90–91, 97–98, 174–175
Smith, Paul 18, 166
Smith, Y.K. (Kenley) 39, 41, 43
"The Snows of Kilimanjaro" 36, 51, 77, 80, 129, 170, 177, 179

Sokoloff, Alice Hunt 56
"Soldier's Home" 18, 43, 51, 126, 170
Something Wicked This Way Comes 127
Sondheim, Stephen 213
Sons and Lovers 65
South America 214–215
Soviet 92
Spain 19, 24, 26, 35, 40, 46, 62, 66, 77–80, 88, 89, 92–99, 101, 104, 106, 120, 169, 172–173, 175, 182, 194, 207, 210, 214, 217, 219–222, 227
Spaniards 109
Spanier, Sandra 10, 30, 85
Spanish 15, 69, 80, 92, 93, 98, 140, 160, 171, 178, 194
Spanish Civil War 9, 19, 25, 26, 35, 40, 45, 46, 62–77, 80, 88, 92–99, 101, 170, 171–173, 176, 181, 182, 193, 210, 217, 221–222
The Spanish Earth 9, 75, 88, 92, 94, 98–99, 172, 175, 181, 194
Sparks, Adrian 168, 176, 179
Spartan 116
Spilka, Mark 208
Spillane, Mickey 72
Spokane-Coeur d'Alene 219
Sports Illustrated (magazine) 101
SS 179
Stafford, William 200, 226
Stalin, Josef 93, 96, 173, 219
Stalinist 93, 172, 175
Stallings, Leonard 170
Stanford University 83
Star Trek 27
Stark Raving Elvis 130
State University of New York (SUNY) at Buffalo 207
Steele, Danielle 14
Steenburgen, Mary 117
Steffens, Lincoln 66
Stein, Gertrude 10, 25, 36, 63, 65, 68–69, 70, 71, 73, 101, 114, 138, 139, 147, 148, 191, 192
Steinbeck, John 2, 82
Stendhal 54
Stevens, Elsie 224
Stevens, Wallace 4, 174, 175, 216, 223–224
Stevenson, Robert Louis 31
Stewart, James 134
Stockholm, Sweden 35
Stoll, Corey 23, 57, 193–194
Stone, Irving 11
"The Strange Country" 62
The Stranger 161
Strater, Henry (Mike) 22, 61, 63, 72
Stroh's beer 164
Stuart Little 201
Styron, William 11
Summer Nights 109
"Summer People" 39, 42, 50
Summit, Illinois 33
The Summoner 143

The Sun Also Rises 14, 23, 25, 27, 38, 50, 68–71, 73, 85, 104, 122, 148, 151, 153, 169, 184, 185, 191, 210, 220
Sun Valley, Idaho 20, 23, 133, 136, 140, 177, 212, 216
Sunrise at Ketchum 26, 135–136
Sunrise: The Early Years 180–181
surrealism 70, 71, 94, 145, 154
Swiss 31, 34
Switzerland 24, 51
Sylvester, Harry 54–55
Syria 210

Tarkington, Booth 228
Telegraph Avenue 231
"Ten Indians" 150
Tennessee 67
Tennessee Technological University 67
Texas 215
Texas A&M at Commerce 67
Thackery, William Makepeace 31
There Is No Borges 154
"They All Made Peace—What Is Peace" 199
Third Reich 108
Thomas, Dylan 226
Thomasville furniture 166
Thompson, Charles 78, 81
Thompson, Lorine 78, 103
Thompson submachine gun 120
Three Soldiers 39, 90
Three Stories and Ten Poems 8, 66, 190, 198, 199
Thurber, James 148
A Ticket to Ride 56
"A Ticket to Ride" (Beatles song) 222
Time (magazine) 44, 91
Time After Time 117
Tin for Sale: A Crooked Cop's Journey from the NYPD to the Mob 63
"To Ernest Hemingway" (Al-Bayati) 210
To Have and Have Not 13, 38, 40, 54–55, 77, 81, 88, 91–92, 96, 100, 107, 160, 175, 211
"Today Is Friday" 170
Toklas, Alice B. 63, 139
Tolstoy, Leo 2, 13, 65, 112, 147
Tone, Franchot 77, 171
Toro 107–108, 230
Toronto, Canada 24, 37, 38, 73, 155, 182
Toronto Star 18, 51
Toros and Torsos 69, 70, 80, 94–95, 134, 230
Torrents of Spring 45, 50, 139, 157, 187–188, 223
Tracy, Spencer 204
"Tradition and the Individual Talent" (Eliot) 197
Trail Creek (Idaho) 212
The Tramp (film) 9
Trapese 31
Trappist 211
Travels with Myself and Another 103, 123
Trenning, Lynn 181–182

Treu, Wolfgang 55
Trogdon, Robert W. 10
Trout Fishing in America 138
Trudeau, Gary 187
True at First Light 10, 24, 56, 107, 193
The True Gen 23, 46, 56, 61, 76, 100
Truman State University 208
The Truth 156
Tucson Weekly 217
Tunney, Gene 113
Turgenev (Turgenieff), Ivan 13, 54, 65, 112
Turner, Nat 13
Turner, Rodger 110
Twain, Mark 11, 14, 109, 123, 168
The Twilight Zone 127
Two Hearted River (Michigan) 165
Twysden, Lady Duff 73–74
Tyler, Lisa 134–135

"Ultimately" 199
Ulysses 176
Ulysses 49, 65
The Unbearable Lightness of Being 136
"The Undefeated" 76, 77
Under Kilimanjaro 10, 24, 107
Unitarian 31
United States, U.S. 2, 8, 9, 11, 37, 44, 48, 78, 84, 88, 104, 108, 117, 127, 140, 151, 159, 187
University of California at Berkeley 83
University of California at Irvine 151
University of California at Los Angeles (UCLA) 83
University of Denver 180, 219
University of East Anglia 121
University of Idaho 10
University of Illinois 37
University of Iowa 117, 138, 139, 140
University of Maryland 140
University of Massachusetts 207
University of Michigan 56
University of Missouri at Columbia 145
University of Missouri at Kansas City 216
University of Missouri at St. Louis 145
University of Munich 154
University of North Carolina 130
University of Redlands 151
University of Southern California 151
University of Tennessee at Chattanooga 211
University of Utah 151
University of Wisconsin 34
University of Wisconsin at Milwaukee 212
"Up in Michigan" 36, 68, 90, 142, 150
Updike, John 1, 209
Upper Peninsula (Michigan) 164
USA Trilogy 39, 91

"Valentine" 199
Valis, Noël 172
Valley of the Fallen (Spain) 222
Van Guilder, Gene 212

Vanity Fair (magazine) 194
Vanity Fair (Thackery) 31
Variety (magazine) 146, 186
Vassar College 79, 171
Vejdovsky, Boris 22
Venice, Italy 24, 29, 38, 104, 105, 135, 136, 155, 188, 205
The Veracruz Blues 113–114
"A Very Short Story" 45, 185, 190
Vietnam 117, 140, 141, 208
Villanova University 185
Villard, Henry S. 58, 188, 190
Villarreal, René 161
"Virtual Hemingway" (McFarland) 225
"A Visit from Saint Nicholas in the Ernest Hemingway Manner" (Thurber) 148
Vista (magazine) 81
Vittorio Veneto 188
Von Kurowsky, Agnes 45, 51, 90, 144, 169, 178, 188–190, 195, 216
Vonnegut, Kurt, Jr. 176
Vose, Ken 168, 181–182
Voss, Frederick 19–20, 22
Vox Humana Theatre (Los Angeles) 179
"Voyage" (MacLeish) 210

Wabash College 109
Wagner-Martin, Linda 11, 15, 85
Wagoner, David 212
Wakoski, Diane 219
Walcott, Derek 201
Walk on Water 163–164
Walks in Hemingway's Paris 10
Wall Street Journal 166
Waller, Fats 178
Walloon Lake, Michigan 30, 37, 38, 51, 53, 90
"The Walls of Toledo" (Reiter) 221
Walsh, Ernest 200
Walt Disney 147
War and Peace 65, 147, 152
Warren, Robert Penn 201
Washington (state) 212, 231
Washington, George 219
Washington, DC 88
Washington Post 58, 192
Washington Times 58
Washington University (St. Louis) 21, 109
Waterston, Sam 188
Weber, Bruce 156, 157
Welcome to Havana, Señor Hemingway 80–82
Welles, Orson 232
Welles, Sumner 81
Wells, H.G. 117
West, Jessamyn 133
West Palm Beach, Florida 102
West Point 16
Western Front 15, 16, 43, 89
Western Washington University 138

White, E.B. 48, 105, 133, 201–202
White, Lowell Mick 215
White, William 62
White Horse Theater Company 169
White House 88, 99
Whitman, Walt 128
"Who Killed Poetry?" (Epstein) 225
"Who Murdered the Vets?" 87–88, 244n
Wikipedia 232
Wild Nights! 123–125
Wilde, Oscar 66, 72, 184
William Morrow (publisher) 141–142
Williams, Bobby 231
Williams, Tennessee 19, 168, 182–183
Williams, William Carlos 50, 214, 215–216
Wilmington, Michael 191
Wilson, Edmund 76–77, 198
Windemere 52–53
"Windfall or Wife" (Ray) 217
Wineapple, Brenda 57, 123–124
Winegardner, Mark 113–114
Winger, Debra 189
Winner Take Nothing 77
Winton, Tom 143–144, 146
Wolcott, James 194
Wolff, Milton 19, 88–89
Wood, Naomi 12, 27, 121–123
Woolf, Virginia 76
World War I (First World War) 9, 15, 24, 32, 38, 42, 46, 51, 64, 68, 105, 169, 178, 201
World War II (Second World War) 3, 21, 24, 40, 78, 104, 173, 179, 181, 182, 193, 208, 217, 227, 228, 230
Wormwood Review 214
Wright, Charles 201
Wright, James 201
Wright, Tom 169
Writers Digest 59
Writers Studio (New York) 206
"Written of and to Write" (Ray) 217
Wyoming 24, 88, 104, 106, 181

X-Files 27

"Years of the Dog" 203
Yeats, William Butler 199
Yellowstone River 215
Yevtushenko, Yevgeny 19, 202, 214, 219, 231
Young, Philip 39, 106, 171
The Young Hemingway 16, 17
YouTube 93, 168, 180, 198, 232

Zanuck, Darryl F. 188, 191
Ziegfeld girl 213
Zink, Jack 178, 179
Zombie Autopsies: Secret Notebooks from the Apocalypse 148